BUSINESS
COMMUNICATIONS

BUSINESS COMMUNICATIONS

A GUIDE TO EFFECTIVE WRITING, SPEAKING, AND LISTENING

William C. Himstreet

Professor of Business Communications
University of Southern California
Los Angeles, California

Gerald W. Maxwell

Professor of Business
San Jose State University
San Jose, California

Mary Jean Onorato

Business Education Instructor
Woodside High School
Woodside, California

Pitman Business Education, a division of **PITMAN LEARNING, INC.** Belmont, California

Supplementary Materials

Activities Book
Teacher's Guide and Keys

Development editor: *Mary S. Lorenz*
Production editor: *Mary McClellan*
Cover designer: *Ruth Scott*
Text designer: *Kristina M. Gough*
Illustrator: *Mario Risso*

Library of Congress Cataloging in Publication Data

Himstreet, William C.
    Business communications.

    Previous eds. published under title: Business English in communications.

    Includes indexes.
    Summary: A textbook for business students examining the funda-
mentals of English grammar and usage and including exercises in written
and oral communication.
        1. Commercial correspondence. 2. English language—Business
English. 3. Communication in management. [1. English language—
Grammar. 2. English language—Business English. 3. Commercial
correspondence. 4. Communication in management.] I. Maxwell,
Gerald W., 1924–   joint author. II. Onorato, Mary Jean, 1939–
joint author. III. Title.
HF5721.H52 1982   651.7   81-81393
ISBN 0-8224-1180-6   AACR2

1.9 8 7 6 5 4 3 2

ABOUT THIS BOOK

Business Communications: A Guide to Effective Writing, Speaking, and Listening, is the fourth edition of *Business English in Communications* (originally published by Prentice-Hall, and later published by Pitman Learning). This new edition contains the same logical organization and the same special learning features that made previous editions popular.

However, some significant changes have been made in this edition to keep pace with trends in business writing and, indeed, to maintain the content at the forefront of the study of business English. First, a new section on eliminating sex-stereotyped language has been added. Students can now learn how to avoid needless, and often controversial and ambiguous, sex stereotyping. Second, the end-of-chapter exercises have been adapted to the needs of those who might become engaged in careers in word processing. Despite the advances made by word processing in the last few years, the output of such systems cannot be better than the input of people. We've attempted to strengthen this input.

That the lack of satisfactory communications skills is a major weakness of beginning business workers should almost go without saying. Although we often hear that emphasis on such study is fruitless, employment tests and job performance evaluations seek constantly to assess a person's communications skills and related applications. The inescapable fact is that we will all continue to be evaluated in terms of our writing and speaking skills—the "signature" of an educated person. Consequently, the emphasis on developing an understanding of grammar and English usage has been increased in this edition.

The textbook is divided into three broad areas. Area One is a comprehensive coverage of the fundamentals of English usage, including many answers to actual questions arising on the job—questions that most other books do not answer. Area Two provides abundant practice with written communications, with emphasis on the most important kinds of business letters. Although we have reviewed literally thousands of letters, we do not think the aim of instruction in writing various types of business letters should be to develop experts in credit letters, claim letters, sales letters, and so forth. Rather, we believe that practice in writing those letters provides not only the most effective means of applying English skills, but also a realistic awareness of the environment—both internal and external—within which business functions. Area Three develops an aspect of business communication too often neglected—speaking and listening skills.

In using the book, emphasize that communication occurs only in the mind of the receiver of a message! This concept should guide students in their efforts to use words effectively and to develop appropriate composition skills. The prettiest, neatest message can be communicative only when the receiver of the message interprets it in the way the sender intended. This concept is at the heart of communications study.

To that end, both the textbook and the *Activities Book* provide learning experiences in locating errors, analyzing written material, and correcting or rewriting sentences, paragraphs, and other messages. Students cannot become experts unless they first become critics.

The text has several carefully organized features for accelerating learning and for measuring progress. The techniques employed in the text are in line with the critical analysis approach to developing and improving skills. After new information has been presented, the student is given practice in its application. Throughout the text, progress quizzes reinforce and measure the student's learning. Other end-of-section features, such as "Build Your Word Power," "Skill Builders," "Business Speech," "Spelling," and "Be an Expert Writer," help provide a complete, well-motivated course.

The *Activities Book* contains a substantial amount of skill-oriented enrichment materials, including a variety of projects and quizzes and a series of objective tests correlated to the various sections of the textbook. The *Teacher's Guide and Keys* contains the following materials: specific suggestions for course planning and for teaching and testing each section; tests to be duplicated, including a Survey Test of Fundamentals, a midyear and a final examination, a sample Job Entrance Test, and a sample Civil Service Test; and the answers to all material in the text, the *Activities Book*, and the tests.

All in all, *Business Communications: A Guide to Effective Writing, Speaking, and Listening* represents the best of some 20 years of experience and learning we have accumulated since we began work on the first edition of *Business English in Communications*. The student who has the opportunity to work with this teaching-learning package should be able to enter an office job with a high degree of confidence based on a solid foundation of communications skills.

The Authors

OUR THANKS ——————————————————————————————————————
The authors are grateful to the many teachers who have provided helpful comments about the first three editions of this book and suggestions for this new edition. The authors were also assisted by hundreds of companies, associations, and persons who provided ideas or materials. The following deserve special recognition.

AMERICAN BUSINESSES AND INSTITUTIONS. The following companies and institutions gave permission to study their communications systems or provided materials especially for this book:

Administrative Management Society; Aero Mayflower Transit Co., Inc.; Aetna Life & Casualty Company; American Heritage Publishing Co., Inc.; *The American Home*; American Medical Association; The American Museum of Natural History; American Mutual Insurance Alliance; American Telephone & Telegraph Company; Bankers Trust Company, New York, New York; Beneficial Management Corporation; Caldwell, Larkin & Sidener-Van Riper, Inc., Advertising; *Changing Times;* Columbia Broadcasting System; Connecticut General Life Insurance Company; Crocker-Anglo National Bank; Curtis Circulation Company; Encyclopaedia Britannica, Inc., Eureka Western Printing Co.; First National Bank, San Jose, California; Ford Motor Company; The Franklin Life Insurance Company; Friden, Inc.; General Foods Corporation; *Good Housekeeping;* Great Books of the Western World; Hansen-Argall Insurance Company; Hughes Aircraft Company; International Business Machines Corporation; Levi Strauss & Co.; Lindy Pen Co.; Litton Industries; *McCall's Magazine*; Mutual of Omaha; National Radio & TV; New York Life Insurance Company; New York Stock Exchange; New York Telephone Company; Pacific Gas and Electric Company; PepsiCo, Inc.; Pioneer Investors Savings and Loan Association; Port of New York Authority; The Prudential Insurance Company of America; Remington Rand Division of Sperry Rand; Atlantic-Richfield Company; Roos-Atkins; San Jose Medical Clinic; San Jose State University; Shell Oil Company; Simon & Schuster, Inc.; Southern Counties Gas Company; *Sports Illustrated;* Texaco, Inc.; *Time;* United Air Lines; United States Postal Service; University of Southern California; *The Wall Street Journal*; Western Life Insurance Company; and Western Union.

BUSINESS EDUCATORS. The following educators have assisted us throughout the long development of this book by providing materials, making valuable suggestions, and reviewing manuscripts:

Dr. Ruth I. Anderson, North Texas State University; Dr. Wayne Murlin Baty, Arizona State University; Martha L. Miller, Herbert Hoover High School, San Diego, California; Mrs. Grace C. Rust, Lake Shore Central School, Angola, New York; Dr. William Selden, Pennsylvania Department of Education; Lura Lynn Straub, San Diego State University; Donald Teani, Carlmont High School, Belmont, California; and Dr. Louis C. Nanassy, Emeritus Professor, Montclair State College, Upper Montclair, New Jersey.

In particular, we are extremely grateful to our former colleague and coauthor, Leonard J. Porter, former Business Education Editor, Educational Book Division, Prentice-Hall, Inc. Mr. Porter spent countless hours supervising and coordinating our work on the first three editions. Many of his contributions remain in this edition, and his warmth, understanding, and creativity will long be remembered.

Contents

AREA
ONE

THE ENGLISH
OF BUSINESS
COMMUNICATIONS

Communication in the business office is literally in the middle of a revolution. In today's society, tremendous amounts of information need to be handled and processed quickly and efficiently. Business has become increasingly more complex, and the government requires more accountability. The United States Postal Service processes billions of pieces of mail each year. Many authorities say we are in the "Information Age."

In such a world, it is essential that you develop business communication skills. In a California study, 59 office authorities were asked, "What can schools do to meet future office needs?" The response given most frequently was "Teach business English [grammar, spelling, punctuation, and editing]."

The ability to edit is the most important communications skill needed in business. Editing checks the construction and effectiveness of sentences and paragraphs. It also involves rewriting where necessary.

Since many modern offices use word processing, in which procedures and electronic equipment transform words originated by someone into a form of communication, typists, word processing operators, and data entry personnel need to be especially proficient in punctuation, spelling, capitalization, and paragraphing.

We all need a working understanding of how word processing messages are created, forwarded, stored, and retrieved. Our lives are all affected by this type of communication. People who have good communications skills are better able to analyze the countless messages sent via automated media forms—home computers, television, radio, and so forth. By acquiring the proper skills, we can write and speak more effectively, thereby enhancing our own business and personal lives.

Skill in applying English to everyday business communications is only the beginning. Business English can be a key—your key—to a successful and rewarding life.

Unit
One

PREPARING TO BUILD SKILL
IN BUSINESS COMMUNICATIONS

THE POWER OF SPEAKING AND WRITING

To be effective, ideas must be put into action. Such action is achieved by the use of words, either spoken or written. The act of expressing ideas to other persons is called *communication*. Today's offices use word processing to speed the preparation of business messages. This operation of electronic equipment by skilled personnel has contributed greatly to progress in the business world.

Forceful English Gives You Power. Words that express ideas logically are the foundation of good communication. By increasing your word power, you increase your earning power. American business spends billions of dollars on communications each year. Business recognizes as a valuable employee any worker who, by handling communications efficiently and by being aware of word processing procedures, helps increase profits.

Employers say that superior English skills are a prime requisite for obtaining and holding a good job, as well as for advancing to a better job. Thus, time invested in studying business communications will pay big dividends in the years ahead.

Communications in Your Life. Without communications of many types, the activities of business, government, the professions, and social life could not exist. Even your recreation and entertainment depend on communications. When you read a book, watch a play, or listen to music, many people are communicating their ideas and feelings to you. Such communications are often *indirect*. Business communications, however, are mainly *direct*, since some type of action is usually expected.

Many of the communication activities of business are simply adaptations of those you already use—writing letters, using the telephone, and so forth.

Business Requires Precision Tools. A skilled worker requires the best tools. The tools of communication include grammar, spelling, punctuation. word usage, and the principles of composition. To communicate effectively, business workers must use the best tools. If they are not certain of a point, they search for the answer by using a dictionary, a thesaurus,* or some other reference book.

Many forms of business communications may be composed, edited, stored, and retrieved with the help of electronic devices. Material stored on tape, for example, can be displayed on a cathode ray tube (CRT) screen so that it may be read and edited. It is also possible to transmit written messages electronically by means of equipment that can display the message on a screen thousands of miles away.

Types of Business Communications. Some large companies handle hundreds of thousands of pieces of mail a week. But for any size office, workers must engage in various activities related to business communications. The most common activities are shown in the following list.

Some Business Communications Activities

ORAL

1. Listening to instructions
2. Giving instructions
3. Using the telephone
4. Dealing with visitors
5. Requesting information
6. Listening while taking dictation
7. Listening to a transcribing machine
8. Proofreading (one person reads, the other checks copy)
9. Dictating to a machine
10. Explaining about a product or service
11. Introducing new workers
12. Interviewing job applicants
13. Speaking at meetings
14. Participating in conventions, conferences, and so on

WRITTEN

1. Writing letters
2. Writing memorandums
3. Writing telegrams
4. Writing reports
5. Writing orders
6. Making notes of telephone calls, interviews, and so forth
7. Transcribing shorthand notes
8. Transcribing machine dictation
9. Filling in printed forms
10. Writing postal cards
11. Abstracting minutes of meetings and conferences
12. Writing copy for advertising, news releases, and so forth
13. Writing data for office manuals, sales manuals, and so forth
14. Drawing up outlines
15. Composing and editing on word processing equipment

Thesaurus, a Greek word meaning *treasure house,* refers to a book containing information more specific than that usually found in a dictionary. It includes synonyms as well as specific words for expressing whole ideas.

How to Make Friends. "Think of the other fellow first." "Be a good listener, and you will be a good conversationalist." The preceding statements are but two of many that apply to communications. In speaking or writing, always think of the other person first. If you consider yourself first, you may end up last!

The person who engages in interesting conversation makes friends quickly. The one who is a poor listener often monopolizes the conversation and is considered a bore. (A *bore* is sometimes humorously defined as a person who talks about his or her operation when you want to talk about yours.)

The person who writes interesting letters keeps those friends who are no longer close at hand. If you can write good business letters, you will make and keep friends for your employer, too.

The "You" Attitude. In speaking or writing, you take the first step toward good communications by adopting the "you" attitude—considering other people first, making them feel important, trying to take their points of view, and treating them as you like to be treated.

The Master Key to Success. A young man wondered why, after three years, he had not been promoted. His supervisor told him, "The job you seek requires outstanding English skills. If you improve yours, you may be eligible for promotion." The young man enrolled in an evening course in business communications; and at the end of a year, he received the promotion he wanted.

Evening classes throughout the nation are attended by persons who feel the need to develop further English skills. You have the opportunity *now* to acquire the English skills that may bring opportunities for both personal satisfaction and job advancement.

Good English can be your master key to open the door to success in life and work.

Build Your Word Power

Antonyms and Synonyms. An *antonym* is a word meaning the opposite of another word. Examples: *right—wrong; dark—light.*

A *synonym* is a word meaning the same or nearly the same as another word. Examples: *attraction—magnetism; dynamic—powerful.*

Oral, Verbal. The word *verbal* means *in words;* the words, however, may be either oral or written. Although many persons associate *verbal* with that which is spoken, other persons realize that the word is not limited to that which is spoken. "He attacked me verbally" can mean that the attack was spoken or written. To be on the safe side, therefore, use *oral* in referring to that which is spoken.

Fact. A fact is an existing truth. The expression "deny the fact," therefore, should be avoided.

> Wrong: He denied the fact that she had been ill.
> Right: He denied that she had been ill.

Cope with. *Cope with* always should be expressed in full; also, it always should be followed by an object. "I cannot cope with this problem."

Whatever, What ever. Note the difference between these two words:

> Wrong: Whatever happened to her?
> Right: What ever happened to her?
> Right: Do whatever you wish.

Without. The word *without* is a preposition. Notice the illiterate use of the word in this sentence: "He can't be present without he receives an invitation." If you change *without* to *unless,* the sentence is correct.

Check Your Knowledge

1. List five communication activities in which a secretary might engage.
2. Why does a good listener make a good conversationalist?
3. Since machines are speeding up and changing office routines, are business communications decreasing in importance? Explain.
4. Explain this statement: On the job, English must be used as a skill.
5. Which communication skills are used by a clerk who places and answers many telephone calls?

Business Speech

The careful speaker pronounces each word correctly. Note the proper pronunciation of the following words. Pronounce each word aloud several times. If you do not know the definition of a word, consult a reliable dictionary.

SAY

1. comparable   KOM-pa-ra-bl
2. genuine   JEN-yoo-in
3. grievous   GRE-vus
4. mischievous   MIS-chi-vus
5. radiator   RAY-de-ay-ter
6. reputable   REP-ut-able

Spelling

Beginning on page 407 are forty-two spelling lists numbered to correspond to the Section numbers of the text. At this point study List 1. Before you study this and all future lists, however, be sure you understand each "Guide" that is presented.

Guide: A word beginning with *over* or *under* is written as one solid word. The expression *under way* is always two words. A word ending with *like* or containing *proof* is written as one solid word. If *like* is added to a word ending with two *l*'s or to a capitalized word, however, it is preceded by a hyphen.

Study Help: You can become a better speller faster if you consider the following: (1) Learn the rule or rules that govern a word or a group of words. (2) Type each word ten times (in a column). (3) Each time you misspell a word on any school paper, type it ten times. If a typewriter is not available, write in longhand. Such practices are recommended by expert spellers.

Section

2

THE QUALITIES OF BUSINESS COMMUNICATIONS

Today computers and other automated devices that store and feed back information are called "giant brains." Such machines, however, cannot think; they are only as effective as the persons who use them. Only human beings can initiate and develop productive ideas, which are put into action through communication.

Each communication has a specific purpose. To achieve its purpose, a business communication must have five qualities—*courtesy, clearness, completeness, conciseness,* and *correctness.* Consider each of these qualities a target. If you aim properly, you will score a bull's-eye on each one!

Courtesy. Courtesy is more than saying "Thank you" and "Please." It is found not only in what you say but also in the manner in which you say it. In conversing with a person, you may sound polite; but just a lift of the eyebrow or a turn of the lip can add sarcasm to your words, even though your voice sounds courteous. A letter may seem courteous, too; but if you have misused a comma, the reader may become confused. Courtesy pleases, never confuses. It gives the receiver a feeling of importance and satisfaction. Business people realize that courtesy pays big dividends. The companies that have grown fastest usually attribute much of their success to the goodwill they have established with their customers and clients.

The successful business person is always courteous, knowing there is never an excuse for being otherwise. "Count to ten before losing your temper" is good advice. By the time you have counted to ten, your anger has subsided, and you can act in a rational manner. If you receive a letter that displeases you, don't hastily sit down and write a blasting reply. Write your answer the next day, when you are calmer and may see the matter in a different light. Some people who feel they must "blow off steam" write their replies immediately but never mail them.

How to Hit Target 1—Courtesy: (1) Be prompt in answering the telephone, replying to letters, and so on. (2) Keep the "you" attitude. The first step in this direction is accomplished by reducing the number of times that you use the words *I, my, we,* and *our.* Use *you* and *your* more often. The following pointers also help. (3) Mentally put yourself in the other person's place. (4) Abide by the Golden Rule: Treat the other person as you wish to be treated. If you show unusual consideration, treating a person even better than expected, you may make a new friend or gain a new customer. (5) Courtesy is also shown when you hit the following four targets.

Clearness. What you say or write should be perfectly clear. If a person must reread your letter to grasp its meaning, your message is not clear. If you write clearly, the reader speeds along a straight mental highway and reaches the end quickly. Prompt action, therefore, is the result. If you do not write clearly, the reader is in a blind alley or, at best, on a road with many detours.

Clear writing is coherent. To *cohere* means to *stick together.* If your message is well planned, one idea leads logically to another; your whole message is clear.

To express ideas clearly and vividly, you should use *concrete* expressions. Concreteness gives the exact meaning immediately. The following examples show the advantage of changing general words to specific, concrete words:

GENERAL	CONCRETE
The plane took off and rose to a high altitude.	The 747 jet zoomed to an altitude of 25,000 feet.
Our soap assures you of a quick wash of which you will surely be proud.	In only 15 minutes, SNOW DROPS give you fresher, whiter linens.
This especially fine stone is inexpensive.	This perfect blue-white diamond costs only $1,000.

Always use language that can be quickly understood by those to whom your message is addressed. In writing to a scientist, you should use a vocabulary different from that used in writing to a teenager. When your language is suited to your listener or reader, your message is more likely to be courteous and clear.

How to Hit Target 2—Clearness: (1) Know exactly what you wish to say. By organizing your thoughts before you begin to speak or write, you save time and have greater assurance of clearness. (2) Use simple language. Short words are more effective than long ones. This does not mean, however, that you should always limit your vocabulary to one-syllable words. (3) Be specific. Don't beat around the bush. Make each fact or request stand out sharply. The use of concrete words helps produce clearness. (4) When you have written something, read it aloud to see how it sounds. Until you are certain that you are a clear writer, it may be a good idea to ask someone to read your message; or you might read it to that person to find out whether the meaning is immediately clear. (5) Use proper punctuation, for it is one of the most important aids to clearness.

Completeness. Company expenses increase when letter writers fail to send complete messages. Assume that you write a letter to Jones Company but do not say everything you should. Jones Company must write you for more information—information you should have supplied in the first place. Then you must write a second letter—one that would not have been necessary if your first letter had been complete. When it is not complete, your letter is neither courteous nor clear. You inconvenience the reader and probably create a bad image of your company. Also, you create more work for yourself.

Although a letter itself may be complete, the entire business message may not be complete. For example, if your letter states that you are enclosing some materials, the message is not complete if you forget to enclose all the items mentioned in the letter.

People ordering by mail commonly forget to include all the facts necessary—size, color, catalog number, quantity, and so on. Mail-order houses, such as Sears Roebuck and Co., cannot fill orders until they obtain complete information from the customer.

> *How to Hit Target 3—Completeness:* (1) Be fully prepared; have all the facts. (2) In step-by-step order, outline what you are going to say. (3) Say exactly what you have planned to say. (4) Check your finished writing to see that it is complete in every way.

Conciseness. You no doubt remember your reaction to hearing a long-winded speaker. Don't be carried away by the sound of your voice or the flow of your written words. In speaking or writing, say everything you have to say—then stop. Many an otherwise good message is ruined because it is too wordy; its main thoughts are lost in a maze of irrelevant words or details.

Concise writers are not miserly with words. They do not squander them, either. Rather, they treasure words, making those words work for them.

Remember that there is a difference between being brief and being concise. Sometimes a two-page letter is necessary; and by trying to crowd all your thoughts on one page, you may defeat your purpose. Your letter may be brief but not complete.

Several years ago many business letters were so brief that they were curt. Connecting words were often omitted, and sentences sounded like those in a telegram; for example, "Yours received and contents noted." This style of writing is called *telegraphic;* it should be avoided in all writing except telegrams.

Concise writing or speaking gets to the heart of the matter, sticks to essentials, and stops when the job is done. A person who writes concisely is said to have a *tight style.*

How to Hit Target 4—Conciseness: (1) Carefully organize your facts. (2) Get to the point and don't stray from it. (3) If one word can do the work of two or more, use that word. (4) Avoid words and expressions that add nothing to your message. Some people tend to overwork certain words to the point that they have little meaning. Editors say that authors are fond of the word *very;* it is one of the words most commonly deleted from manuscripts. You may have some pet words, too; if so, be on guard against overworking them. Avoid redundant words and expressions—those that merely repeat what has already been said. Concise language is forceful language.

Making Wordy Sentences Concise

The figures in parentheses indicate the number of words in each sentence.

WORDY	CONCISE
1. He repeated it again. (*4*)	1. He repeated it. (*3*)
2. She likes the exchanging of ideas. (*6*)	2. She likes exchanging ideas. (*4*)
3. I should like for you to go to see her a week from next Monday. (*15*)	3. I should like you to see her on June 10. (*10*)
4. Please rest assured that we shall do everything in our power to bring this case to a very successful conclusion. (*20*)	4. We will do everything possible to end this case successfully. (*10*)
5. If it will not be too much trouble, will you be kind enough to let us hear from you on or before the first of next month. (*27*)	5. Please write us by June 1. (*6*)
6. Knowing that most workers today are eager for advancement on whatever kind of job they may take, I should like to inform you that in our company we promote all employees—even those who have not been with us for a very long period of time—just as soon as they have proved themselves capable of doing a good job. (*60*)	6. Knowing that most workers desire advancement, we promote employees as soon as they prove capable. (*15*)

Correctness. If something is correct, it is perfect. If a speaker distorts the truth and falsifies statements, people soon become skeptical. The message of a business letter, also, must contain true statements.

A speaker or writer must use correct grammar and select words to fit the occasion. A writer must know how to spell and punctuate. A typist or secretary must set up a letter so that it is attractive and arranged in acceptable form. No matter how much people know, they must constantly check themselves to be certain that what they say or write is correct. When a letter or any other material is typed, it should be checked immediately to be certain that it is correct in every way.

> *How to Hit Target 5—Correctness:* (1) Know exactly what you are supposed to do and how to do it. (2) If you are not sure of your information, check a reference book, such as a dictionary, a thesaurus, or an encyclopedia. (3) If a letter involves any legal matter, always consult your company's legal department before

writing. (4) In writing, constantly ask yourself, "Am I doing it correctly?" (5) When you have finished writing, carefully proof-read what you have done and correct all errors.

Build Your Word Power

English is *formal* or *informal*, depending on its purpose. Formal English is used in most academic or literary prose. Informal English is used in conversations, personal letters, and everyday speaking and writing. Both formal and informal English are correct. *Substandard* English is never correct. Since it is often used by uneducated persons, substandard English is sometimes called *illiterate* language. Avoid its use.

Business letters usually have a conversational tone, which makes them informal in style. You should, however, avoid many of the common, informal expressions found in everyday speech.

In all business communications, you should avoid "second choices." When there are two ways of spelling or pronouncing a word, use the "first choice." For example, your dictionary may show *traveled* and *travelled*. Your spelling should be *traveled*—the first choice.

Throughout your course in business communications, you will be expected to improve your grammar and to develop a broader working vocabulary. The following terms are sometimes used in this text; therefore, you should become acquainted with them.

Idioms. Idioms are expressions that are peculiar to a language. Often they are not governed by grammar, and at times they may even seem illogical. Users of a language, however, learn the most common idioms early in life and do not have many problems using them. Examples: *catch a cold, look up someone, have a try at.*

Colloquialisms. Colloquialisms are expressions commonly used in informal conversation but usually avoided in formal writing. Examples: *aren't I? so* instead of *so that, put across* instead of *was successful.*

Localisms. Localisms are expressions peculiar to a certain section of the nation. Example: *tote* instead of *carry.* Localisms, also called *provincialisms*, are substandard English. Avoid their use.

Vulgarisms. Vulgarisms are illiteracies; therefore, they are substandard English. Examples: *ain't, could of, he done, he don't, we was, you was.* These should also be avoided.

Slang. Slang consists of expressions in current use that have a humorous, forced, fantastic, or grotesque meaning. Many slang expressions wear themselves out in a short time; others, such as *rascal,* eventually become accepted as good usage. Slang, particularly individual words, appeals to people who lack imagination and energy enough to select the precise expression to convey their meaning. Examples of slang: *lousy, swell, blockhead, rap (to talk).*

Not all slang is vulgar. Good speakers sometimes use a slang expression, realizing that their listeners recognize the expression as slang. Only the best speakers, though, know how to use slang effectively.

Clipped Words. Clipped words are those that are usually expressed by one or two syllables of the original word, all other syllables being cut off. Examples: *ad, auto, gym, photo, phone.* Clipped words are seldom acceptable in business letters but are commonly used for informal purposes, especially in conversation.

Progress Quiz 2-A. Make the following expressions concrete by using specific words.

1. A fast trip.
2. A letter containing too many words.
3. A raincoat that sheds water and can be turned inside out and worn at any time of year.
4. Fabric that will not fade.
5. A flower that blooms every year until cold weather comes.

Progress Quiz 2-B. Tell whether each statement is true or false.

1. Courtesy helps in achieving the "you" attitude.
2. A coherent sentence is necessarily a courteous sentence.
3. Punctuation is an important aid to clearness.
4. Speakers and writers find a *thesaurus* useful.
5. Idioms should be avoided in formal speech and writing.

Check Your Knowledge

1. What are the five characteristics of a good business letter?

2. How is the "you" attitude achieved in a business letter?

3. In what ways can a letter be incorrect?

4. Are business letters friendly in style? conversational? formal?

5. Why should concrete expressions be used in a business letter?

6. Tell why a speaker or writer should or should not avoid the following: redundant expressions, telegraphic style, first choices.

7. Why is business writing called *power* writing?

8. Why does an incomplete letter often increase a company's expenses?

9. Defend this statement: When you speak or write, use the language of your audience or readers.

10. How does a colloquialism differ from a localism?

Skill Builders

Rewrite the following sentences so that they will be concise.

1. If you would like to take immediate advantage of this very special offer, sign the little card enclosed with this letter and return it to us without delay. 2. If you can stop in to talk with us a week from today, we can sit down and decide what to do about this matter, which has perplexed all of us for so long a time. 3. Your savings account at our bank will pay you 6 percent interest on your principal; this interest is compound interest and is credited to your bank account every three months during the year. 4. If you will be good enough to tell Mr. Smith about these changes, we shall appreciate your doing so. 5. The meeting will be held at our company's main office, which is located in your city—right in the heart of the city—at 300 Main Street.

Business Speech

Careful speakers always accent the proper syllable of a word. Learn the correct pronunciation of the following words. The accented syllables are capitalized.

	SAY		SAY
1. admirable	AD-mirable	3. incomparable	in-COM-parable
2. applicable	AP-plicable	4. preferable	PREF-erable

Spelling

Guide: In adding *able* to words ending with *ce* or *ge,* keep the full word. On most other words ending with silent *e*, drop the *e* before adding *able*.

Examples: *service—serviceable; sale—salable.*

Study List 2 on page 407.

Unit Two

USING THE LANGUAGE
OF BUSINESS COMMUNICATIONS

Section

3

NOUNS—WORDS THAT NAME PERSONS, PLACES, AND THINGS

Every English word can be classified as at least one of eight different *parts of speech*—noun, pronoun, verb, adjective, adverb, preposition, conjunction, and interjection. The parts of speech, therefore, are the basic raw materials of communication.

Kinds of Nouns

Nouns are the names of the persons, places, and things about which we speak or write. If there were no nouns, our language would be vague; we should have difficulty in expressing exact meanings. Nouns are related to the actions we express; they are the doers or the receivers of such actions.

Common Nouns and Proper Nouns. *Common noun* is the name applied to each of the members of a group of persons, places, or things. A *proper noun* is the specific name of a particular person, place, or thing. Proper nouns are always capitalized.

COMMON NOUNS	PROPER NOUNS
man	Robert Jones
woman	Alice Johnson
nation	United States
company	Star Paper Company
school	West High School
river	Mississippi River

Concrete Nouns and Abstract Nouns. *Concrete noun* is the name of something that can be identified by any one of the five senses. An *abstract noun* is the name of an idea, a quality, or an emotion. Abstract nouns represent things that you can think about or feel emotionally.

Concrete Nouns: typewriter, odor, music, flavor, photograph
Abstract Nouns: initiative, friendliness, fear, kindness

Collective Nouns. *Collective noun* is the name applied to a whole group. Collective nouns are usually singular in meaning, even though they embody the idea of more than one person or thing.

> *Collective Nouns:* group, crowd, committee, army, flock

Gerund Nouns. *Gerund noun* is the name of an action; it is derived from a verb and always ends with *ing*. A gerund noun is also called a *verbal noun*.

> *Reading* and *writing* are communication skills.
> She likes *transcribing* Mrs. Smith's letters.

Capitalizing Nouns and Other Words

1. Capitalize the names of particular persons, places, and things.

Thomas E. Davis	the First Methodist Church
Queen Elizabeth	the Second National Bank
South Dakota	the Mercantile Building
Rocky Mountains	the Carnegie Library
Lake Superior	Harvard University

Note: (a) Capitalize the word *the* when it is a part of an official title— *The Ohio State University.* (b) Do not capitalize any words that are not a part of a specific title. (c) Do not capitalize plurals.

the river Clyde	the Atlantic and Pacific oceans
Yale and Harvard universities	BUT the Atlantic Ocean and
the Coral Room	the Pacific Ocean
Room 302	

2. Capitalize the names of particular localities but do not capitalize words indicating directions.

CAPITALIZE	DO NOT CAPITALIZE
West Virginia	western Virginia
the South	south of Boston
North America	northern products
the Far East	going east two miles

3. Capitalize the names of the days of the week and the months of the year. Do not capitalize the names of the seasons unless they are part of a title, such as *Summer Sale.*

> The meeting will be held on Monday, April 15.
> Our spring and summer fashions are now on display.

4. Capitalize important words in the names of companies, organizations, and publications. (Note how newspaper titles are indicated.) When you type, indicate italicized words by underscoring them.

> the University Club   Department of Labor
> *Reader's Digest*   *Gone with the Wind*
> the Sacramento *Tribune* *   The Civic Leaders Group

5. Capitalize the names of divisions of knowledge and learning when the names are used as course titles, such as those found in a college catalog. Otherwise, do not capitalize such names unless they are derived from proper nouns.

> Bookkeeping I and Stenography II will be offered this year.
> He is studying biology, French, and advanced typing.

6. Capitalize trade names but do not capitalize names that are not trade names.

> *Trade names:* Dacron, Orlon, Royal typewriter, Polaroid camera
> *Not trade names:* vinyl, nylon, rayon, diesel

7. Capitalize the main words in headings and titles of articles.

> This fact is presented in Chapter X, page 99, of *Science for the Masses.*
> His article, "Travel on a Low Budget," appears in the *Monthly Review.*

8. Capitalize honorary or business titles when they immediately precede or follow a proper name. Such titles *may* be capitalized when they refer to a specific person without including the personal name.

> Mr. Edward Day, Sales Manager, will call on you next week.
> He is the sales manager (*or* Sales Manager) of this company.

9. Capitalize the first word, all titles, and all nouns in the salutation of a letter.

> My dear Sir: Dear Friends of the Library:
> My dear Mrs. Clark: Dear Madam:

---

* Some newspapers, such as *The New York Times,* require that the full title be italicized.

10. Capitalize only the first word in the complimentary close of a letter.

> Very truly yours,   Cordially yours,
> Yours very sincerely,   Yours respectfully,

11. Capitalize the first word of a direct quotation that is a sentence.

> He said, "This report should be circulated at once."

12. Capitalize any noun or pronoun referring to the Deity.

> God in His wisdom has permitted this to happen.

13. Capitalize the names of all specific parts of a work except *page*.

> Underline the first topic in Volume II, Unit V, page 17.
> Today we shall read Act II, Scene i, of *Macbeth*.

14. Capitalize periods of history and the names of special events.

> Dark Ages   World War II
> the Renaissance   Olympic Games

15. Capitalize the words *I* and *O*. The word *oh* is capitalized only when it is the first word in a sentence or quotation. The word *O* immediately precedes a personal name. It is not followed by a comma. Since *O* is used in entreating, it is commonly found in prayers.

> It is I, O Lord.
> Why, oh why, did you go?

16. Capitalize words that are personified, as in poetry.

> Then Nature greets the silver dawn of Winter.
> The mighty Ocean swelled and heaved its waves upon the shore.
> Like Milton, he bade Melancholy begone.

Progress Quiz 3-A. Indicate necessary capitals in the following.

1. i visited the famous first united methodist church in western ohio.
2. my sister is studying english history, spanish, shorthand, and type-writing.
3. learning was revived in european countries during the renaissance, which followed the dark ages.

Section 3 - Nouns—Words That Name Persons, Places, and Things   **21**

4. you can buy nylon and orlon articles at the textiles building, which is located at 200 west broadway.
5. last spring I traveled west until I reached the grand canyon.
6. is houston the largest city in the south?
7. franklin and washington high schools are the two largest high schools in the state.
8. i am reading *the house of the seven gables* for my book report.
9. professor jones is one of the professors who will attend the convention of the national education association at the statler hotel.
10. davis & co., inc., is mentioned in chapter iii, section ii, page 14.

Making the Plurals of Nouns

A *singular* noun denotes one person, place, or thing. A *plural* noun denotes more than one. Most nouns form the plural by simply adding *s* to the singular. To form other plurals, follow these rules:

1. Add *es* to words ending with *ch, s, sh, x,* or *z*.

> *churches, brushes, boxes, topazes, Collinses, Joneses.*

2. If a word ends with *y* preceded by a consonant, change the *y* to *ies*. Merely add *s* to capitalized nouns ending with *y*.

> *party—parties; city—cities;* but *Mary—Marys.*

3. If a word ends with *y* preceded by a vowel, add *s*.

> *valley—valleys; attorney—attorneys; journey—journeys.*

4. Some words ending with *f* or *fe* change to *ves*.

> *knife—knives; wife—wives; scarf—scarves; loaf—loaves.*

5. Words ending with *o*: (a) If a vowel precedes the *o*, add *s*. (b) If a consonant precedes the *o*, usually add *es*, but some words of this type require only *s*. (c) If the word is related to music, add *s*.

(a)	(b)	(c)
cameos	cargoes	radios
folios	heroes	sopranos
ratios	tacos	solos

6. Compound words, abbreviations, and symbols: (a) The most important part of a compound word is pluralized. (b) Add *s* to pluralize common abbreviated words.* (c) Add *'s* to pluralize letters or symbols.

    (a) men-of-war, runners-up, passersby, by-products, attorneys at law.
    (b) Dr.—Drs.; asst.—assts.
    (c) ABC's, *x*'s, #'s, 5's. (*Note:* 1970's *or* 1970s)

7. Some English words borrowed from foreign languages keep the foreign plural; others have two plural forms.

SINGULAR	PLURAL
alumnus (*masc.*)	alumni (Pronounced with long *i.*)
alumna (*fem.*)	alumnae (Final syllable rhymes with *me.*)
datum	data
basis	bases
crisis	crises
criterion	criteria *or* criterions
phenomenon	phenomena
tableau	tableaux *or* tableaus

8. Note how the plurals of titles and surnames are made. The titles used in the following examples are those commonly used in addresses.

SINGULAR	PLURAL
Mr. (Mister)	Messrs. (Pronounced MES-sers.)
Madam	Mesdames (Pronounced may-DAHM.)
Miss Smith †	the Misses Smith
Mrs. Smith	Mesdames Smith
Collins	the Collinses *or* the Collins family ‡

---

*Some authorities say that *s* should not be added to form the plural of a foreign abbreviation; for example, *m* can mean *meter* or *meters*. Regular American abbreviations of measurement and weight may or may not be pluralized.

†*Ms.* should be used before a woman's name if (a) her title or marital status cannot be determined or (b) it is known that she prefers this title regardless of her marital status. *Ms.* is the feminine counterpart to *Mr.,* and misusing *Miss* or *Mrs.* could be offensive. *Ms.,* however, should not be used if it is known that a woman prefers *Miss* or *Mrs.*

‡ In an address each word would be capitalized: The Collins Family.

Progress Quiz 3-B. Give the plural of each of these nouns:

1. alto	3. chimney	5. nucleus	7. sister-in-law	9. tomato
2. axis	4. dictum	6. pantry	8. tax	10. Tommy

Making the Possessive of Nouns

Possessive Singular. To make the possessive singular, add *'s*.

> *Note:* In names of more than one syllable, use only the apostrophe if the word ends with *s:* Mrs. Collins' car.

Possessive Plural. To make the possessive plural of nouns, add the apostrophe after the plural form if it ends with *s*; if it does not end with *s,* add *'s*.

POSSESSIVE SINGULAR	POSSESSIVE PLURAL
company's	companies'
attorney's	attorneys'
man's	men's
child's	children's
sister-in-law's	sisters-in-law's

Expressions of Time and Value. Although such expressions as *two days' work* do not denote ownership, the possessive is used if a noun follows the word ending with an *s*. If a noun does not follow, do not use the apostrophe.

USE APOSTROPHE	DO NOT USE APOSTROPHE
one hour's time	two hours longer
a year's experience	two years ago
three months' pay *	three months previously
ten dollars' worth	ten dollars in payment

Titles of Companies and Organizations. If a company uses the apostrophe in its title, the writer should do so. Some institutions, such as

---

*The hyphen is used in such expressions as *a three-month trip*.

teachers colleges, never use the apostrophe. To make a company title possessive, make the last word possessive.

> Johnson's, Inc.; Manufacturers, Ltd.; State Teachers College
> Smith Company's sale; Jones & Clarke's report

The Possessive in of Phrases. An *of* phrase may be used to show possession. (a) When the possessed item or items are a specific number or group, use *'s*. (b) When the possessed item or items are not a specific number or group, do not use *'s*.

> (a) The three stocks of his father's are paying dividends.
> (b) The stocks of his father may pay dividends this year.

Progress Quiz 3-C. Insert all necessary apostrophes.

1. There will be a stockholders meeting soon.
2. Two days ago she paid me three months wages.
3. A years experience is not much for that companys job.
4. The two families gardens are in full bloom.
5. His brothers-in-laws homes are all located in different states.
6. The sales meeting will be held at the teachers college.
7. Three months before her wedding, her father gave her a certificate for a hundred dollars worth of furniture.

8. Each taxpayers blank must be returned within five days.

9. Weber and Schultz devised the plan, and these Germans inventions are always successful.

10. These womens dresses should be sold before the end of next weeks event.

The Gender of Nouns. Nouns may be in one of four genders: (1) *masculine,* which pertains to the male; (2) *feminine,* which pertains to the female; (3) *common,* which pertains to mixed genders, such as *people, persons, teachers;* (4) *neuter,* which pertains to inanimate objects, such as *book* and *desk*.

Italicizing Nouns and Other Words

Italics consist of slanted printing that looks somewhat like disjoined handwriting. When you type or write, indicate italics by underscoring all words to be italicized. Italics are used to indicate the following:

1. The title of a book, magazine, or other published work. Italicize only the important word or words in most newspaper titles. The title of a short story usually is not italicized; it is preceded and followed by quotation marks.

2. The title of ships, aircraft, works of art, plays, and motion pictures.

> the *Titanic,* the *Mona Lisa, The Empire Strikes Back*.

3. Letters, words, and figures used as words.

> Your *5*'s and your *S*'s look alike.
> Delete the word *never* each time it occurs.

4. Foreign words and phrases not yet accepted in common English usage.*

> His action was indeed a *coup d'état*.

5. To add emphasis. (Use this device sparingly.)

> I have never before seen such a *perfect* specimen.

---

*Consult your dictionary to determine whether a foreign expression is in English usage.

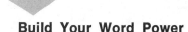

Build Your Word Power

Omitting a and of. Do not use *a* after *kind of, sort of, style of,* and *type of.* With such expressions do not omit *of* before a noun: "I like this type *of* dress."

Use *all of* before a pronoun, but use *all the* before a noun.

> All of them will attend the meeting.
> All the letters have been typed.

Can, Could. Note the uses of *can* and of *could,* which is the past tense of *can.*

> I do, am doing, have done, shall do WHAT I CAN.
> I did, was doing, had done WHAT I COULD.
> I would have done WHAT I COULD.

Et cetera, Etc. Avoid *et cetera* and its abbreviation *etc.* in business writing. Instead use *and so forth, and so on,* or *and the like.* If the boss insists that you use *et cetera,* never place *and* before it.

Check Your Knowledge

1. How do abstract nouns differ from concrete nouns?
2. How is the possessive singular of nouns made?
3. How do you form the plurals of nouns ending with *y*?
4. Name five kinds of titles that should be italicized.
5. Give the gender of *children, tree, desk, executrix, alumnae.*

Skill Builders

3-A. Rewrite the following letter, making all necessary corrections.

My Dear Mr. Jones:

When I saw you in Northern Michigan last month, I knew that soon I would be making use of your twenty years experience. However, when I read the new york times today, I realized that you are exactly the person to right a book about The Revolutionary war. Although I have been considering Professors at Princeton and Boston Universities for this writing job, it's my opinion that you will be a better author.

The enclosed sheet contains the points we think desirable to include in our book, as well as data about royalties. If you are interested, Mr. Jones, please let me here from you at once, for my companys plans must be made by April 5.

Very Cordially Yours,

3-B. Mrs. E. Iwasa, a customer of Eagle Co., wrote inquiring about the price increases of three products. She also stated that she would place an order as soon as she received this information. Mrs. Iwasa ended her letter by saying that she had not yet met the new salesperson in her city and hoped that she would be called on soon. Following is the answer she received from a new correspondent. Analyze the letter, stating whether the correspondent hit the five necessary targets—courtesy, completeness, conciseness, clearness, and correctness.

My Dear Mrs. Iwasa:

I want to inform you that the prices mentioned in your recent letter will be effective on June 15. This ought to answer your question.

I can't understand what you are getting at when you say that you wish to order some goods. In fact, your statement really has me puzzled. You did not include any order.

Mr. Unger is the new sales representative in your city.

Very Truely Your's,

3-C. Rewrite the following sentences, making all necessary corrections.

1. His article Jogging appeared in Running Along last month. 2. Ten years growth can be seen in the city's near the Pacific ocean. 3. She was headed East with the companys products. 4. Ms Jones's experience happened over four years' ago. 5. Joan Spence, president of Orlandos, inc., gave us two hours time. 6. The datum have shown there were four Mary's among the ten attorneys' listed in the Roster. 7. Three churchs are located within two blocks of the Community bank. 8. the honorable Samuel Smith [*part of a salutation*].

Business Speech

Be sure to accent the proper syllable in these words. Remember to look up the definitions of unfamiliar words.

1. amicable   (AM-icable)   3. dirigible   (DIR-igible)
2. lamentable   (LAM-entable)   4. disputable   (dis-PYOOT-able)

Dictionaries indicate pronunciation by using *diacritical marks* over vowels and by writing vowels in various kinds of type. The most common diacritical marks follow:

‾ is placed over a *long* vowel: fāte, Pēte, kīte, vōte, cūe.
˘ is placed over a *short* vowel: făt, pĕt, kĭt, lŏt, cŭt.
¨ is placed over *a* to indicate that it has the broad sound of *a,* as in *fäther.*

Note: one dot over an *a* indicates that the sound is between short *a* and broad *a:* ȧsk.

The *oo* may have a long or short sound; o͞o sounds like the *oo* in *boot,* and o͝o sounds like the *oo* in *foot.* The words *hoof, roof, room,* and *root* have the long sound.
Certain dictionaries use the *schwa* (ə) to indicate the common sound of various vowels, such as the *a* in *sofa.* This symbol is sometimes used to indicate such sounds as the *u* in *but* and the *e* in *her.*
Since dictionaries differ in their use of diacritical marks and vowel indications, this textbook rarely uses them. Occasional reference is made, however, to long vowels and short vowels.

Spelling

Words ending with *able* and *ible.*

Guide: If a noun ends with *ation,* change the ending to *able;* if it ends with *sion* or *tion,* change the ending to *ible.* The ending *able* is usually added to a full word.

Examples: *dispensation—dispensable; collection—collectible; profit—profitable.*

Study List 3 on page 407.

PRONOUNS—WORDS THAT TAKE THE PLACE OF NOUNS

Pronouns are substitutes for nouns. They relieve the monotony of repetition and add variety to our language. Pronouns do all the things that nouns can do and often do such things better.

Variety Is the Spice of Language. No one likes monotony. Monotonous language is repetitious and unpleasant to both ear and eye. Pronouns save language from the many repetitions that would be necessary if we used only nouns for the names of persons, places, and things.

Without pronouns   Mrs. Clay and **Mrs.** Clay's daughter were excited about Mrs. Clay's and **Mrs.** Clay's daughter's proposed trip. Mrs. Clay and Mrs. Clay's daughter knew that Mrs. Clay and Mrs. Clay's daughter would spend too much money, though.

With pronouns   Mrs. Clay and *her* daughter were excited about *their* proposed trip. *They* knew that *they* would spend too much money, though.

Kinds of Pronouns

Personal pronouns take the place of the names of persons, places, and things. Some personal pronouns are *I, you, he, she, we, they.*

> *I* gave the watch to *you*; both *he* and *she* saw me do it.

Interrogative pronouns are used in questions. The interrogative pronouns are *who, whose, whom, which,* and *what.*

> *Who* wrote this letter? *Which* parcel was dropped?

Relative pronouns introduce adjective clauses or noun clauses. The relative pronouns are *who, whose, whom, which, that,* and *what* (when it means *that which*). Relative pronouns may be called *clause relators.*

> The woman to *whom* you spoke is the manager.
> This is the package *that* arrived three days late.

Note: Who, whose, and *whom* refer only to persons. *Which* refers only to things. *That* usually refers to things but can refer to persons when introducing a restrictive clause—a clause needed for sense.

Indefinite pronouns refer to an uncertain person or an indefinite number of persons or things. A few indefinite pronouns are *one, anyone, someone, somebody, everybody, everyone.* (These words all take a singular verb.) Other examples are *few, several, many, some.* (These require plural verbs.)

Demonstrative pronouns point out. The demonstrative pronouns are *this, that, these,* and *those.*

The Person and Gender of Pronouns

Pronouns are in one of three persons. The *first person* denotes the speaker, the *second person* denotes the person spoken to, and the *third person* denotes the person or thing spoken about.

The genders of pronouns are the same as those of nouns.

The Cases of Nouns and Pronouns

Nouns and pronouns may be in one of three cases—*nominative, possessive,* or *objective.*

Nominative Case. A noun or a pronoun is in the nominative case when it is (1) the *subject* of a finite verb (the predicate); (2) a *predicate nominative* after the verb *to be* or other linking verbs; (3) *in apposition* with a noun already in the nominative case.

> *John* and *you* should be more careful of details. (*subject*) *
> It could not have been *he.* (*predicate nominative*)
> Jane Adams, our *salesperson,* is in Houston today. (*in apposition*)

Possessive Case. The apostrophe is never used to show possession of personal, interrogative, or relative pronouns—*hers, yours, its,*† *whose,*

---

*This sentence has a *compound* subject—two subjects of equal value joined by *and.*

† *It's* is a contraction of *it is.*

and so on. The apostrophe is used to make the possessive of indefinite pronouns—*everyone's, somebody's, anyone's,* and so on.

Objective Case. A noun or a pronoun is in the objective case when it is (1) the *direct object* of a verb, (2) the *indirect object* of a verb, (3) the *object* of a preposition, (4) *in apposition* with a noun already in the objective case, (5) the *complement* of the infinitives *to be* and *to have been.**

(1) Every one of the girls saw *him* at the show. (direct object of verb *saw*)
(2) Write *me* a letter. (indirect object of verb *write*)
(3) Please let me do this job for *them*. (object of preposition *for*)
(4) Be sure to include us *girls*. (in apposition with *us*, which is objective)
(5) I thought you to be *him*. (complement of the infinitive *to be*)

Personal Pronouns

(The figures *1, 2, 3*, indicate the first, second, and third persons.)

NOMINATIVE		POSSESSIVE		OBJECTIVE	
Singular	*Plural*	*Singular*	*Plural*	*Singular*	*Plural*
1. I	we	1. my, mine	our, ours	1. me	us
2. you	you	2. your, yours	your, yours	2. you	you
3. he, she, it	they	3. his; her, hers; its	their, theirs	3. him, her, it	them

Other Pronouns: All the relative and interrogative pronouns have the same forms for the nominative and objective cases except *who*. Nominative —*who;* possessive—*whose;* objective—*whom*.

The Uses of Nouns and Pronouns

Subject. The subject is always a noun, a pronoun, or a group of words used as a noun. The subject performs or receives the action of the predicate. The predicate is always a verb.

He talked too long. (*He* is the subject; *talked* is the predicate.)

Some conjunctions are followed by the nominative case, even though the predicate is not expressed. *As well as, such as,* and *than* are

---

* These two infinitives require a complement when a subject precedes them. In such cases the direct object of the verb becomes the subject of the infinitive; therefore, the subject of the infinitive is in the objective case. The complement following the infinitive must be in the objective case, too. *Example:* She thought him to be *me*.

examples of conjunctions that are often followed by a subject having a predicate that is not expressed.

> You know the answer as well as *I* (do).
> We need a clerk such as *he* (is).
> He is taller than *she* (is).

Direct Object. The direct object is the noun or pronoun that receives the action of the verb.

> She mailed the letter yesterday. (*Letter* is the direct object of *mailed.*)

Indirect Object. The indirect object is a noun or pronoun that names the person who indirectly receives the action of the verb. When there is an indirect object in a sentence, there is often a direct object, too. The words *to* or *for* usually are "understood" before an indirect object; that is, these words are not expressed, but one of them is present in meaning.

> We gave (to) *him* the money to deposit. (*Him* is the indirect object of the verb *gave; money* is the direct object.)

Object of a Preposition. A noun or pronoun following a preposition is the object of that preposition. Some common prepositions are *among, at, between, by, for, from, in, into, of, on, to, with.*

> The box of *stationery* is lying on the *table.* (*Stationery* is the object of *of; table* is the object of *on.*)

Apposition. A noun or pronoun is *in apposition* with another noun or pronoun when it has the same meaning as or explains the word with which it is in apposition. A word in apposition is called an *appositive.*

> Ms. Green, our new *manager,* will speak at the meeting. (*Manager* is in apposition with *Ms. Green.* Observe that the entire appositive expression is set off with commas.)

Predicate Nominative. A noun or pronoun following any form of the verb *to be* or a *linking verb* is in the nominative case and is known as a *predicate nominative.* These are the forms of the verb *to be: be, being, been, is, am, was, are, were.* Some linking verbs are *to appear, to become, to seem.*

> If I were *she,* I would take the plane. (*She* is in the nominative case following *were,* a form of the verb *to be.*)

Progress Quiz 4-A. Select all the nouns and pronouns. Tell the case and use of each.

Frank Devlin, our new manager, will be in your city soon. If you would like to meet him, please write me. He is a person whom you would enjoy meeting. Frank knows the important people in your field, and you and he should have a number of mutual interests.

Progress Quiz 4-B. Select the correct word.

1. Could it have been (*he, him*)?
2. Everyone (*is, are*) requested to be prompt.
3. It is a secret between you and (*I, me*).
4. Do you know where John and (*she, her*) went?
5. (*We, Us*) workers will attend the convention.
6. Please send a copy to (*we, us*) secretaries.
7. Suzanne and (*they, them*) will be the new delegates.
8. The dog wagged (*its, it's*) tail.
9. He told me that this book is (*theirs, their's, theirs'*).
10. I saw Alice and (*he, him*) enter the office.
11. Captain Brown, (*who, which*) addressed our group, lives in Dallas.
12. The company (*who, that*) published this book has made a big profit on it.
13. Is this pen (*hers, her's, hers'*)?
14. Paul and (*we, us*) will be the only ones there.
15. He showed the blueprint to Miss Blake and (*I, me*).

Using Interrogative Pronouns

Interrogative pronouns are always used in questions. The following forms are among the ones most commonly misused:

NOMINATIVE	POSSESSIVE	OBJECTIVE
who	whose	whom

Cautions: (1) *Who's* means *who is* and should not be confused with *whose.* (2) To decide whether *who* or *whom* should be used in a question, make the question a statement.

Progress Quiz 4-C. Select the correct word.

1. (*Whose, Who's*) book is lying on the table?
2. (*Who, Whom*) did he mention?

3. (*What, Which*) of these three letters is the best?
4. (*Who, Whom*) do you think should go?
5. (*Who, Whom*) did you believe her to be?
6. (*Who, Whom*) would he like to be?
7. (*Who, Whom*) is responsible for this error?
8. (*Whose, Who's*) boss is in Europe this month?
9. (*Whom, Who*) do you wish to see?
10. About (*who, whom*) is he inquiring?

Using Demonstrative Pronouns

There are only four demonstrative pronouns—*this, that, these,* and *those*. They may take the place of a noun or modify an expressed noun. (In the latter case they have the function of demonstrative adjectives.)

> *These* are not as good as *those*.
> *This* book belongs to *that* student.

Cautions: (1) Never say "this here" or "that there" directly before a noun. *Correct:* Use this desk, NOT Use this here desk.

(2) *This* and *that* are singular; *these* and *those* are plural. Keep these facts in mind in speaking and writing. *Correct:* I like *that kind* of book OR I like *those kinds* of books. *Incorrect:* I like those kind of books.

(3) *This* and *these* refer to things that are near in distance or time. *That* and *those* refer to things that are farther away in distance or time.

(4) Never use *them* instead of *those* before a noun. *Correct:* He will not use *those* books, NOT He will not use *them* books.

Build Your Word Power

The nominative pronoun follows all finite forms of the verb *to be*. In conversation, however, it is permissible to say, "It's me," although to be grammatically correct, you should say, "It's I." In all other similar cases, the nominative form must be used—*It's he, It's she, It's we, It's they*.

Reflexive Pronouns. *Myself, ourselves, yourself, yourselves, himself, herself, itself, oneself,* and *themselves* are called *reflexive pronouns*.

They are used for emphasis and clearness. Do not place such pronouns immediately after the subject except to avoid confusion.

Right: You must do this work yourself. (emphasis)
Right: She injured herself when she fell. (*Her* alone is not clear.)
Wrong: I myself must do it. (This is considered conceited!)
Right: I must do it myself.
Wrong: He cannot sew himself. (confusing)
Right: He himself cannot sew.

Caution: Never use *hisself, ourself, theirself, theirselves, themself.*

Contractions. The apostrophe is used to show that two words have been combined and shortened to form one word. Such words are called *contractions.* Examples: *cannot—can't; will not—won't; does not—doesn't; do not—don't; is not—isn't.*

Cautions: (1) Contractions should be avoided in formal writing. They are acceptable in both formal and informal speech. Formal speakers, however, tend to avoid such contractions as *we're* (we are), *I'll* (I shall), *they're* (they are). In informal conversation the expression "aren't I?" is acceptable, but in formal speech and in all writing, it should be avoided. Instead say, "Am I not?"

(2) *Doesn't* is the correct form to use after a singular subject; *don't* is used after a plural subject only.

(3) In conversing, we tend to say *there's* instead of *there is.* This contraction is permissible in speaking; however, be sure that the noun following it is singular. If you mean *there are,* you cannot say "there's." *Example:* There *are* a number of people without shelter (not *There's*).

Like, Such as. (a) *Like* is a preposition meaning *similar to;* it is followed by the objective case. (b) *Like* should not be used as a conjunction. (c) To mean *for example,* use *such as,* not *like.*

(a) Right: She looks like him.
(b) Wrong: He acts like he is tired.
    Right: He acts as if he were tired.
(c) Wrong: Use a warm color like red.
    Right: Use a warm color, such as red.

Note: Omit *like* in such expressions as "Come at like five o'clock."

Check Your Knowledge

1. For what three purposes is the apostrophe used?
2. Which kind of pronoun is most commonly used? Why?
3. List the possessive forms of the pronouns *I, it, them.*
4. Tell whether a singular or plural verb follows each of these: *someone, everybody, these.*
5. Tell whether a singular or plural subject is used with each of these: *don't, there's, has, isn't.*

Skill Builders

Rewrite the following, making all the necessary corrections.

1. I told the clerks that they had to do the job theirself. 2. This here book looks like a good one. 3. Our workers opinions can be trusted when there's several important matters to be decided. 4. Is it permissable to tell his company that it's orders are not clear? 5. If this persons' work is useable, tell him to show it to Mrs. Charles and I. 6. I saw them there gloves advertised in this mornings paper. 7. The parents committee wrote Mr. Dale and he that we shall do the work ourself. 8. Whom could it of been that he mentioned? 9. Everybody in the branch offices are always being asked to contribute for somebodies gift. 10. Us secretarys spoke to her about this situation, but she don't seem to understand it.

Business Speech

Be sure to accent these words on the proper syllables. Do you know the meaning of each word?

		SAY
1.	acumen	a-KU-men
2.	affluence	AF-fluence
3.	condolence	con-DOE-lence
4.	formidable	FOR-midable
5.	charisma	ka-RIZ-ma
6.	viable	VI-able

Spelling

There is no guide to help you with the spelling of some words ending with *able* and *ible*. The words in List 4, page 407, are of this type.

Section 5

VERBS—WORDS THAT SHOW ACTION

Verbs give action to our ideas. Most verbs express the action performed by the subject, but some verbs express the action received by the subject. Certain verbs, such as *be* and *have,* express condition. The effective use of verbs helps produce powerful speaking and writing.

You Can't Get Along Without Them. It is possible to have a sentence consisting of only one word; that word must be a verb. The following are complete sentences, the subject *You* being understood: "Hurry." "Begin." "Relax."

Since most business letters attempt to obtain some kind of action, the right choice and use of verbs are important. Nouns and pronouns, no matter how specific and vivid they may be, express ideas that resemble photographs or filmstrips. When verbs are added, however, ideas become mental motion pictures.

Verbs are the most powerful words in the language. Since there is more to know about them than about the other parts of speech, many speakers and writers tend to misuse verbs.

Verbs indicate the kind of action, the time of action, and the method of action. They also help to show the relationship of all persons and things involved in the action. If you can master the use of verbs, they will serve you faithfully.

Kinds of Verbs

Verbs are classified according to use—*transitive* or *intransitive*—and according to spelling—*regular* or *irregular*. To form a complete verb phrase, it is often necessary to use more than one verb. Verbs are further classified, therefore, according to their relation to other verbs. For example, *auxiliary verbs* help other verbs. The following are commonly used as auxiliary verbs: *shall, will, can, may, could, would, should*. All forms of the verbs *to be* and *to have* are often used as auxiliary verbs.

Transitive Verbs. A transitive verb *always* takes a direct object to complete its meaning. (*Remember:* The word *transitive* and the word *takes* begin with *t.*) "Peter typed a letter." The verb (predicate) is *typed*; it is a transitive verb because the object *letter* receives the action.

Caution: In the following sentence *mile* is not a direct object; rather it is the object of the understood preposition *for*: "He traveled (for) a mile."*

Intransitive Verbs. An intransitive verb does not take a direct object to complete its meaning. "Mary typed rapidly." *Typed* is intransitive because it does not require an object; you are not told what Mary typed.

Some verbs may be either transitive or intransitive, depending on their use in a sentence. Other verbs are always transitive, such as *put, raise,* and *set*. Still other verbs are always intransitive, such as *go, come,* and all forms of the verb *to be* and other linking verbs. Some intransitive

---

*A noun used in this way is called an *adverbial objective*.

verbs can be followed by a predicate nominative, although they cannot be followed by a direct object.

Most verbs indicating motion are intransitive, such as *come, go, jump, travel*.

Regular Verbs. A regular verb forms its past and past participle by adding *d* or *ed* to the present. Most verbs are regular.

Irregular Verbs. An irregular verb changes its spelling to form the past and past participle, such as *go,* which is *went* for the past and *gone* for the past participle; or an irregular verb, such as *put,* may keep the same spelling for all forms.

Progress Quiz 5-A. Select each verb and tell whether it is transitive or intransitive, regular or irregular.

1. She read the book.
2. They walked a mile.
3. Tell him the story quickly.
4. He is the new treasurer.
5. Was she there today?
6. Find the errors on this page.
7. We have a new teacher.
8. Run!
9. Get me a pen.
10. He places business before pleasure.

The Principal Parts of Verbs

Most verbs have four principal parts from which all other forms of the verb are made. The principal parts are *present, past, present participle,* and *past participle*.

	Present	*Past*	*Pres. Part.**	*Past Part.†*
REGULAR	talk	talked	talking	talked
IRREGULAR	go	went	going	gone

* The present participle always ends with *ing*.

† The past participle is used with some form of the verb *to be* or *to have*.

The Voice of Verbs

The *voice* of a verb indicates the doer of the action. If the subject performs the action, the verb is in the *active voice*. If the subject receives the action, the verb is in the *passive voice*.

Active: He mailed the letters.

Passive: The letters were mailed by him.

Active verbs are more direct and thus more forceful. Good writers try to use active verbs whenever possible. The passive serves a good purpose, however, in expressing an idea such as this: "Hogs are raised in Iowa." If you say, "They raise hogs in Iowa," the word *they* is indefinite and should be avoided.

Only transitive verbs can be made passive, since they are the only verbs that take direct objects.

Progress Quiz 5-B. Recast the following sentences. If a verb is passive and can be made active acceptably, make the desired change. If a verb is active and should be made passive, make that change, too.

1. The letter was written by the new clerk.
2. Miss Davis has been appointed treasurer by our president.
3. He was seen entering the building.
4. They catch tuna in the warm waters of this harbor.
5. He was paid $5 by Paul on April 10.
6. While skin diving, she was frightened by a shark.
7. She was given an award by Mr. Fiske.
8. A wild story, which he did not believe, was told him by the child.
9. In that restaurant they serve excellent meals.
10. While a song was sung by Jean, the piano was played by Tom.

The Mood of Verbs

The mood indicates the manner in which the action of a verb is developed. The three moods are *indicative, imperative,* and *subjunctive.*

The verbs in statements and questions are in the *indicative* mood.

The indicative mood is that which is most commonly used.

The *imperative* mood is used in commands or requests.

> *Indicative:* An office worker *must be* accurate. (statement)
> *Indicative: Is* he an outstanding speaker? (question)
> *Imperative: Stop* wasting time on useless details. (command)
> *Imperative: Will* you please *send* your check by May 1. (request)

The last sentence, called a *request*, is sometimes referred to as a "polite command" or a "courteous request." It may appear that the period should be replaced with a question mark. When a person asks a question, however, an answer is expected. In this case no answer is expected. Also, the statement indicates that the writer expects a check by May 1; therefore, it is a "polite command."

The Subjunctive Mood. Many foreign languages contain complex uses of the subjunctive. In English, however, the subjunctive is seldom necessary. Remember, though, that the subjunctive *must* be used in the following cases:

The *subjunctive* mood expresses an idea that is (a) a statement contrary to fact or (b) a wish, request, requirement, or doubt.

> If wishes *were* horses, beggars would ride.   (contrary to fact)
> I wish that I *were* a faster typist.   (wish)
> She requests that you *be* here.   (request)
> We resolved that he *pay* at once.   (requirement)
> If this *be* treason, make the most of it.   (doubt)

The most common subjunctive form of the verb *to be* is *were,* which is used for both singular and plural. Subjunctive verbs in a *that* clause have the same form as the imperative of the verb.

> I request that she *be* excused from this task.
> He resolved that John *investigate* the matter.
> We moved that the meeting *be* adjourned.

The Tense of Verbs

The *tense* of a verb indicates the time of the action. An explanation of the various English tenses and their forms follows.

Present Tense. The *present tense* indicates (1) a current action, (2) an action that is habitual, (3) an action related to a future action, or (4) a statement of universal truth.

> I *see* him standing by the entrance. (current action)
> She *visits* Los Angeles every month. (habitual action)
> When I *write* him, I shall mention you. (related to future action)
> Columbus believed that the earth *is* round. (universal truth)

Past Tense. The *past tense* indicates one or more specific completed actions.

> I *went* to the meeting last week. (completed past action)
> They *visited* me many times last winter. (repeated past action)

Future Tense. The *future tense* indicates an action that will take place at a later time. (*Shall* or *will* is the sign of the future tense.)

> She *will visit* her father next Monday.

Present Perfect Tense. The *present perfect tense* indicates (1) an action that has just been completed or (2) a repeated past action not related to any other action. (*Have* or *has* is the sign of the present perfect tense.)

> They *have announced* the winner. (action recently completed)
> I *have visited* New York City many times. (repeated past action)

Past Perfect Tense. The *past perfect tense* indicates a past action completed before the beginning of a different past action. (*Had* is the sign of the past perfect tense.)

> They *had eaten* dinner before I arrived.

Future Perfect Tense. The *future perfect tense* indicates an action begun in the past but to be completed in the future. (*Shall have* or *will have* is the sign of the future perfect tense.)

> Next month I *shall have lived* here ten years.

The Progressive Forms of Tenses. The *progressive* form indicates (1) a continuing action in relation to another action or (2) an action taking place at the moment of speaking or writing. The progressive form of a verb is made by using some form of the verb *to be*, plus a present participle.

Pres. Prog.:	I *am making* a note of your address.
Past Prog.:	We *were painting* when she called me.
Future Prog.:	When we arrive, she *will be leaving.**

Pres. Perf. Prog.:	He *has been speaking* too long.
Past Perf. Prog.:	I *had been typing* an hour when he entered.
Fut. Perf. Prog.:	When we meet, you *will have been working* a year.

The Emphatic Forms of Tenses. The emphatic form is used for (1) emphasis, (2) questions, and (3) negative statements. There are only two emphatic forms—the *present emphatic* and *past emphatic.*

Pres. Emph.:	I *do mean* you. (emphasis)
	Does she *wish* to go? (question)
	Joan *doesn't intend* to stay long. (negative statement)

Past Emph.:	I *did try* to see him. (emphasis)
	Did he *go* to France last summer? (question)
	You *did* not *believe* me. (negative statement)

The verb *did* is in the past tense. *Did* should not be used to indicate a present action or condition or an action not yet performed.

Right: Did you work on Monday?	Wrong: Did you see her new car yet?
Wrong: Did you know he is here?	Right: Have you seen her new car yet?
Right: Do you know he is here?	

Some Auxiliary Verbs Requiring Attention

Shall, Will; Should, Would. To indicate simple future, use *shall* in the first person and *will* in the second and third persons. To indicate determination or a promise, use *will* in the first person and *shall* in the second and third.† In questions always use *shall* in the first person and usually use *will* in the second and third. Formal speakers and writers always follow the preceding rules; however, for informal purposes *will* is becoming much more popular than *shall.*

---

*A future action may be expressed in various ways: (1) I shall leave at three. (2) I am going to leave at three. (3) I shall be leaving at three. (4) I am leaving at three. (5) I am to leave at three.

† In constitutions, bylaws, and certain regulations, *shall* is always used in the third person. "All dues shall be paid to the treasurer before the first Monday in December."

SIMPLE FUTURE	PROMISE, DETERMINATION	QUESTIONS
Singular	*Singular*	*Singular*
1. I shall work	1. I will work	1. Shall I work?
2. you will work	2. you shall work	2. Will you work?
3. he, she, it will work	3. he, she, it shall work	3. Will he, she, it work?
Plural	*Plural*	*Plural*
1. we shall work	1. we will work	1. Shall we work?
2. you will work	2. you shall work	2. Will you work?
3. they will work	3. they shall work	3. Will they work?

Should and *would* follow the same rules as *shall* and *will*. *Should* and *would* indicate a conditional action, which is dependent on another action; however, the other action is not always expressed. *Example:* I should be happy to help you (if you need my help). *Should* also indicates necessity in all persons, both singular and plural. *Example:* You should be on time. (It is necessary that you be on time.)

Can, May; Could, Might. *Can* (present) and *could* (past) denote ability. *May* (present) and *might* (past) indicate permission or probability. Some users of informal English use *might* instead of *may*.

> Can he do this kind of work? Could he have done it last year?
> May I leave early? It may rain. You might have done better work.

Using Irregular Verbs. At this point turn to Reference Section B and study the list of irregular verbs. If you do not know all the principal parts of certain verbs, be sure to learn them.

Using Some Verbs Correctly

Leave, Let. The word *leave* should not be used instead of *let* in expressing ideas similar to the following. *Let* means *to permit*.

> Wrong: Leave me go.   Wrong: Leave us do it.
> Right: Let me go.   Right: Let us (Let's) do it.

Lie, Lay. Since the present of *lay* has the same spelling as the past of *lie*, many persons confuse these verbs. If you know the meanings and the principal parts, you should use *lie* and *lay* correctly. Remember that all forms of *lie* are intransitive, and all forms of *lay* are transitive.

Note: The verb *to lie,* meaning *to tell a falsehood,* is regular except for the present participle, which is *lying.*

I told the dog to *lie* down. (*recline*—intransitive)
Please *lay* the bills on my desk. (*put*—transitive)
The book is *lying* in the corner. (*reclining*—intransitive)
Yesterday he *lay* in the sun. (*reclined*—intransitive)
They *laid* down their knives. (*put*—transitive)
The foundation has been *laid.* (*set down*—transitive)

Raise, Rise. *Raise* is transitive; *rise* is intransitive. *Rise* may also be used as a noun. Informally *raise* is used in speaking of an increase in salary; formal use, however, requires *increase* or *increment.*

Pat *raised* the window. (transitive)
The dough *has risen.* (intransitive)
The *rise* in prices is steep. (noun)

Set, Sit. *Set* is transitive; *sit* is intransitive. However, we say that the sun *sets.*

The box *is sitting* near my chair. (intransitive)
Please *set* the machine here. (transitive)

Cautions: (1) The verb *dive* is regular; therefore, the preferred past and past participle are *dived.* (2) The regular verb *learn* should not be confused with *teach.* A person learns as a result of what is taught. (3) *Busted* is slang; the correct word is *burst.* (4) *Bring* is related to *come; take* is related to *go. Bring* indicates an *action* toward you; *take* indicates an action *away* from you.

Progress Quiz 5-C. Complete each of the following sentences by selecting the correct verb.

1. (*Can, May*) I leave early today?
2. The murderer will be (*hung, hanged*) next week.
3. The report is (*laying, lying*) on my desk.
4. Ask him to (*set, sit*) the typewriter on this table.
5. If you had tried, you (*might, could*) have done it.
6. Has she (*paid, payed*) the bill yet?
7. It is difficult to (*learn, teach*) him anything.
8. The horse has (*drank, drunk*) too much water.
9. You should have (*wrote, written*) her sooner.
10. I vow that he (*shall, will*) not do it.

11. Our bylaws require that members (*shall, will*) attend at least five meetings.
12. (*Bring, Take*) this memo to Mrs. Lalor on the third floor.
13. Before he telephoned me, I (*received, had received*) his telegram.
14. The paper was (*lying, laying*) exactly where I (*put, had put*) it.
15. On May 5 he (*has worked, will work, will have worked*) in this company ten years.
16. (*Sit, Set*) those books on the desk where my coat is (*laying, lying*).
17. She (*had been speaking, was speaking*) ten minutes when I entered.
18. If he (*don't, doesn't*) know how to work, I shall (*teach, learn*) him.
19. Please (*rise, raise*) the curtain so that I can see whether the dog is (*laying, lying*) in the yard.
20. She (*practiced, was practicing, had practiced, had been practicing*) an hour when I (*burst, busted*) into the room.

Progress Quiz 5-D. In each of the following, use the correct tense and form of the verb given in parentheses.

1. Yesterday he (*lie*) in the sun for an hour.
2. By next Tuesday the foundation of the building (*complete*).
3. The untruthful little boy was (*lie*) to his teacher.
4. After Mary (*receive*) his letter, she telephoned my brother.
5. The program will be (*broadcast*) at two o'clock.
6. How many letters has he (*type*)?
7. At this moment she (*write*) a letter.
8. Ruth has (*sit*) there too long.
9. Frank (*do—negative*) know how to speak correctly.
10. The invoices have (*lie*) on the file cabinet an hour.

The Spelling of Some Regular Verbs

If a one-syllable word ends with a consonant preceded by a vowel, double the consonant before adding another syllable. If the accent falls on the second syllable of a two-syllable word, double the final consonant before adding another syllable. If the accent falls on the first syllable of such words, do not double the final consonant before adding another syllable.* The following lists include some common verbs to which these rules apply.

---

*In British usage, final consonants are always doubled. American usage, however, requires that the consonant be doubled only when the accent falls on the second syllable. Dictionaries give the British spellings as second choices.

Some One-Syllable Verbs That Double Final Consonant

PRESENT	PAST & PAST PART.	PRES. PARTICIPLE
fit	fitted	fitting
plan	planned	planning
ship	shipped	shipping
quiz	quizzed	quizzing

Some Two-Syllable Verbs That Double Final Consonant

(Accent on Second Syllable)

PRESENT	PAST & PAST PART.	PRES. PARTICIPLE
acquit	acquitted	acquitting
annul	annulled	annulling
compel	compelled	compelling
confer	conferred	conferring
control	controlled	controlling
defer	deferred	deferring
impel	impelled	impelling
omit	omitted	omitting
prefer	preferred	preferring
propel	propelled	propelling
refer	referred	referring
remit	remitted	remitting
transfer	transferred	transferring

Some Two-Syllable Verbs That Do Not Double Final Consonant

(Accent on First Syllable)

PRESENT	PAST & PAST PART.	PRES. PARTICIPLE
cancel	canceled	canceling
counsel	counseled	counseling
equal	equaled	equaling
label	labeled	labeling
profit	profited	profiting
travel	traveled	traveling
benefit*	benefited	benefiting

---

* Benefit contains three syllables.

Progress Quiz 5-E. Spell the correct form of each word in parentheses.

1. He is (*refer*) to three (*cancel*) checks.
2. Yesterday we (*ship*) him all the items that we had been (*label*).
3. Our company's sales have not (*equal*) those of your company, but we have (*profit*) on our merchandise.
4. She kept (*quiz*) me about the stock that had been (*transfer*).
5. Two years ago he (*excel*) in French, but today he feels (*compel*) to say that he does not speak it well.
6. She is (*plan*) to go to Europe this summer, since she has never (*travel*) there.
7. Do you think that she has (*benefit*) by (*control*) her temper?
8. I saw him when he (*lay*) the book on the table, but I (*prefer*) not to mention it last night.
9. Will you be (*write*) about the bill for which he has not yet (*remit*)?
10. The court is (*control*) the records of this (*acquit*) woman.

Verbals—Verb Forms Used as Other Parts of Speech

There are three types of verbals—*infinitives, participles,* and *gerunds.*

Infinitives. An *infinitive* is the form of the verb from which all other forms are derived, such as *to walk.* It is made by placing *to* before the present. An infinitive is never a finite predicate; rather, it is usually used as a noun, adjective, or adverb. Sometimes an infinitive may be a verb following an objective subject. There are three types of infinitives—*present,* such as *to see; perfect,* such as *to have seen;* and *passive,* such as *to have been seen.*

> *To eat* is *to live.* (noun as subject; noun as predicate nominative)
> I showed him the road *to be paved.* (adjective)
> She went *to see* the new office. (adverb)
> I thought him *to be* you. (verb after objective subject)

Users of formal English often try to avoid a split infinitive—that is, an infinitive with an adverb between *to* and the verb. (If trying to avoid a split infinitive causes an awkward expression, it is better not to avoid it.)

> Split: I wanted to quickly tell him.
> Correct: I wanted to tell him quickly.

The words *try* and *come* are followed by an infinitive rather than *and*. For example, say, "Try to come to see me" instead of "Try and come and see me."

A past verb is followed by a *present* infinitive: "I wanted to go" *not* "I wanted to have gone."

Participles. A *participle* is a word derived from a verb and used either as part of a verb phrase or as an adjective. As an adjective a participle can be used alone or used to introduce a participial phrase.

There are three kinds of participles—*present,* such as *speaking; past,* such as *spoken;* and *perfect,* such as *having spoken.* The present participle always ends with *ing.*

> The *setting* sun is red. (adjective modifying *sun*)
> *Running* to meet me, she fell. (adjective introducing participial phrase)
> He is *eating.* (part of a verb phrase)

Gerunds. A *gerund* is a noun derived from a verb; it always ends with *ing.* Gerunds are often called *verbal nouns.* Although a gerund is a noun, it retains some of the power of a verb. Consequently, if it is made from a transitive verb, a gerund can take a direct object. The underscored items are either single gerunds or gerund phrases.

> <u>Eating the big meal</u> took two hours. (subject)
> He enjoys <u>typing long manuscripts.</u> (direct object)
> After <u>bathing,</u> she dressed hurriedly. (object of preposition) *

---

*Gerunds have only one form; a gerund, therefore, cannot be preceded by *having.* Say, "After eating, we left"—*not* "After having eaten, we left."

The Possessive Case Before Gerunds. Formal speakers and writers use the possessive case before gerunds except when doing so would change the meaning of a sentence.

> *Your* inviting him was considerate. (Possessive *must* be used.)
> Can you imagine *my* doing it? (*My* is preferable to *me*.)
> Think of *Kim's* winning. (Possessive *must* be used.)

Participial Expressions to Be Avoided

Certain participial expressions are either incorrect or weak. Although participles are usually strong action words, good usage demands that they be avoided in the following cases:

1. *Being that.* Never use *being that,* which is often used by speakers who have a poor command of English.

> Wrong: Being that I was ill, I went home.
> Right: Since I was ill, I went home.

2. *First and last sentences in business letters.* Avoid participial expressions in the first and last sentences of business letters.

> Poor: Having received your letter . . .
> Good: Thank you for your letter . . .
> Poor: Hoping to hear from you soon, we remain . . .
> Good: We look forward to your prompt reply.

Progress Quiz 5-F. Rewrite the following sentences, correcting all types of errors. Your writing is to be *formal* in all cases.

1. Come and see me tomorrow, and we shall try and make final plans for us travelling together this summer.
2. He wanted me to have seen his new sports car.
3. Mr. Tawker finished speaking before I had arrived.
4. After having eaten the big meal, I felt sleepy.
5. She asked me to rapidly type the letter about the canceled check.
6. He don't know very much about his fathers refusing to pay the bill.
7. Our school has benefitted by that womans gift.
8. Mary looked up and said, "I just finished the first letter, but there's still three more."
9. It was not permissable for her to have drunk so much soda.
10. His uncontrolible temper impelled him to swiftly strike his opponent.

Progress Quiz 5-G. Select the correct verb form.

1. I should have (*went, gone*).
2. He (*saw, seen*) me.
3. Could he have (*went, gone*)?
4. I (*did, done*) it correctly.
5. Maybe they (*did, done*) it.
6. Yesterday I (*saw, seen*) her.
7. He (*brung, brang, brought*) the water.
8. We (*saw, seen*) the two boys.
9. She said she (*did, done*) it.
10. You know I (*saw, seen*) it.

Build Your Word Power

Lend, Loan. Many authorities recommend using *loan* as a noun, not a verb. "When your *loan* is paid, we can *lend* you more money."

So. When no comparison is being made, use *so* instead of *as*:

So long as you remain here, you must abide by the rules.

Hope. (a) After *no* always use the singular form. (b) In the passive voice the verb *hoped* must be preceded by *it is*.

(a) Wrong: He has no hopes of winning.
     Right: He has no hope of winning.

(b) Wrong: He has learned what is hoped is a good lesson.
     Right: He has learned what, it is hoped, is a good lesson.

Kind of. When *kind of* is followed by a singular noun, the entire idea must be kept singular.

Wrong: The kind of hat I prefer are those without feathers.
Better: The kind of hats I prefer are those without feathers.
Or: The kind of hat I prefer is one without feathers.
Best: I prefer a hat without feathers.

Provided. Many authorities insist that, when *provided* means *provided that*, the word *providing* should not be used instead.

I shall go, provided he asks me.

Way. Do not use *ways* instead of *way*.

Wrong: She is a long ways ahead of me.
Better: She is a long way ahead of me.
Best: She is considerably ahead of me.

Certainly, Surely. Do not use *most* before these two words.

> Wrong: I shall most certainly be glad to help.
> Right: I shall certainly be glad to help.

Biannual, Biennial. *Biannual* means *occurring twice a year.* (*Semi-annual* has the same meaning.) *Biennial* means *occurring once in two years.* If these and similar words are misused, problems, including legal complications, may arise. In taking dictation, secretaries should be certain to write the correct shorthand outlines for such words.

> The *biannual* report is published in June and December.
> Our *biennial* meeting is held in even-numbered years.

Check Your Knowledge

1. List the forms of the verb *to be.* Which case follows these verbs?
2. What is the sign of each of the following? (a) future tense, (b) present perfect, (c) progressive, (d) emphatic.
3. In what ways are gerunds and present participles similar? dissimilar?

4. When should participial expressions be avoided in business letters?

5. Explain the times that the subjunctive mood must be used.

Skill Builders

5-A. Analyze the following letter. If the writer did not hit the five targets (each of which begins with *c*), tell why they were missed.

Dear Mr. Jackson:

Having investigated the matter you brought to our attention, I am writing to let you know that you are wrong. We cannot find any error in our new pamphlet. It is true that the print is blurred on two of the pages, but these pages don't have any information in which you are interested.

If you would like a new price list, we shall send you one. Hoping that this will take care of your needs, we are,

Sincerely yours,

5-B. Mrs. Lucy Bay wrote the Eagle Company inquiring about the following:

(a) available colors in women's dresses, size 9; (b) discounts permitted on quantity orders; (c) the length of time it will take to fill her order; (d) the date on which she can expect delivery. Mrs. Bay stated that she had written about these matters once before but had not received an answer. She received the following letter in reply. Analyze the letter.

Dear Mrs. Bay:

Thank you for your letter of June 4 in which you inquire about our new ladies' dresses. These items are available in all sizes, including size 9.

As soon as we receive your order, it will be filled and go out to you. It should reach you soon thereafter. During this busy season we know how important it is to fill orders promptly.

If you would like further facts about the articles we advertised in last evening's newspaper, just write us.

Yours sincerely,

Business Speech

Some poor speakers add unnecessary syllables to certain words. Observe the following:

1. drowned   (one syllable)
2. elm   (one syllable)
3. film   (one syllable)
4. athlete   (two syllables)
5. attacked   (two syllables)

Spelling

Guide: In this Section you have learned when and when not to double the final consonant in adding a syllable to verbs. The same rules apply to related words that are other parts of speech. List 5 (page 407) includes such words. Note that, when an accent shifts back to the first syllable, the consonant is not doubled—*preference, reference.*

Section

6

AGREEMENT OF NOUNS, PRONOUNS, AND VERBS

Logical language is correct language. If language is to be logical, certain parts of speech must agree with other parts of speech in a sentence. Forceful writing is crystal clear; it contains no indefinite words or expressions that might confuse the reader or the listener.

Agreement of Subject and Predicate

A noun or pronoun that is the subject of a sentence or a clause governs the person and number of the verb that is its predicate. The predicate, therefore, must always agree with the subject. That is, if the subject is singular, the predicate must be singular; if the subject is plural, the predicate must be plural.*

Many writers, speakers, and persons who dictate letters overlook the agreement of subject and predicate, especially when the predicate is far removed from the subject. Always check your written work carefully to be certain that subjects and predicates agree.

"Things are not always what they seem." This expression can be applied to agreement, for sometimes a word that seems to be singular requires a plural verb and vice versa.

Agreement Requiring Special Attention

Compound Subjects. A compound subject consists of two or more nouns or pronouns, usually joined by *and*. Such a compound subject requires a plural predicate.

> My mother and father were in Dallas today.

When two singular subjects are joined by *or* or *nor,* the predicate is singular. When one subject is singular and the other is plural, the predicate agrees with the nearer subject.

Neither Joe nor Emily *was* in the yard.	(both subjects singular)
Either John or Paul *is* expected to drive.	(both subjects singular)
Neither he nor his friends *are* correct.	(subjects vary in number)
Neither his friends nor he *is* correct.	(subjects vary in number)
Either they or he *is* the culprit.	(subjects vary in number)

Caution: Sometimes a person's title contains *and*. In such cases the predicate should be singular. In the second sentence the use of a second *the* makes it clear that two persons are involved.

> The secretary and treasurer *is* Ms. Karney. (one person)
> The secretary and *the* treasurer *are* out of town. (two persons)

Either, Neither. When *either* or *neither* is the subject, the predicate is always singular.

> Either of these typists *is* excellent.
> Neither of the men *has* had much experience.

---

*The predicate *always* agrees with the subject, regardless of the predicate nominative: "The most interesting part of the program *was* the piano solos," or "The piano solos *were* the most interesting part of the program."

A Number, The Number. (1) *A number* requires a plural predicate. (2) *The number* requires a singular predicate. (3) The word *variety* follows the same rules as those for *number*.

(1) A large number of people *are* attending.
(2) The number of people attending *was* small.
(3) A variety *are* available. The variety *is* limited.

Fractions. When the subject is a fraction, the predicate agrees with the noun immediately preceding it. The word *most* also follows this rule.

Two-thirds of the letter *is* typed.   Most of the cake *is* eaten.
Three-quarters of the letters *are* typed.   Most of the cakes *are* eaten.

Collective Nouns. Use a singular verb with a collective noun when the group is considered as one unit. Use a plural verb when the individual members of the group are acting separately.

The committee *is* meeting this afternoon. (acting as a unit)
The committee *are* unable to agree.*   (acting individually)

Depending on their meanings, some collective nouns may take either a singular or a plural predicate.

Statistics *is* an interesting subject.
Your statistics *are* not correct.

Everyone, Everybody, Every one. The words *everyone, everybody, every one,* and similar words require a singular predicate.

Everyone *is* expected to report on time.
Every one of the women *needs* a notebook.

Many a, More than one. Formal English requires that *many a* and *more than one* be followed by singular predicates.

Many a boy and girl *was* absent yesterday.
More than one of the clerks *was* absent.

Majority. Majority is a collective noun that is used in referring to elections or voting. Note the following examples:

Wrong: The majority of his time was wasted.
Right: Most of his time was wasted.
Right: *The* majority *is* against the proposal.
Right: A majority *are* against the proposal.

---

*Some people prefer saying "committee members" or "members of the committee." Such expressions take a plural verb to agree with *members.*

None. When *none* means *no one* or *not any,* its predicate agrees with the word immediately before the verb: "None but a fool wastes money"; "None but fools waste money." When *none* means *not one,* most formal users of English recommend a singular verb: "None of the men has been asked."

Expletives. The words *it* and *there* sometimes come before the predicate, the logical subject following the predicate. In such cases remember that *it* and *there* are not the subjects but are used as *expletives.*

> It *is* a beautiful day. (Subject is *day.*)
> There *are* the books you need. (Subject is *books.*)

Separated Subjects. A subject is sometimes separated from its predicate when a word or a group of words is placed between the subject and the predicate. Such expressions, although they may interrupt the basic thought of the sentence, do not have any effect on the agreement.

> Mr. Reiff, as well as his family, *is* going to Maine.
> John, the captain of three teams, *was* elected president.
> The writer of powerful business letters *is* always in demand.
> Ms. Friedman, together with all the others, *is* resigning.
> Ruth, along with her two companions, *has* been gone a week.
> This book of successful Broadway plays *was* recommended.
> The women who edited my book *were* in town today.

Transposed Subjects. Agreement must be maintained even though the predicate precedes the subject.

> Behind the desk *are* the file *cabinets.*
> Under the papers *was* the missing *pen.*

The Agreement with <u>What.</u> When *what* is a relative pronoun, it may be either singular or plural. When it is the first word in a sentence, however, *what* is always singular.

> Here is a list of what *is* needed.
> We sell what *are* considered prime meats.
> What *is* needed *is* a few new ideas.

Progress Quiz 6-A. Select the verb that correctly completes each of the following sentences.

1. Neither you nor Anne (*is, are*) invited.
2. Mr. Parks, as well as his three sons, (*attend, attends*) this game each year.

3. None but the most miserly person (*hoard, hoards*) money.
4. Every one of the women (*is, are*) to wear a costume.
5. A number of the invitations (*has, have*) been written.
6. One-half of the desks (*is, are*) made of oak.
7. The best part of the program (*is, are*) the violin solos.
8. The first six chapters of this novel (*is, are*) exciting.
9. The size of her shoes (*amaze, amazes*) us.
10. Both the conductor and the musicians (*was, were*) in high spirits.
11. Everyone in our branch offices (*is, are*) expected to abide by this rule.
12. The secretary and treasurer (*is, are*) Miss Clay.
13. There (*is, are*) only a book and a vase on the table.
14. This collection of long poems (*seem, seems*) interesting.
15. The small number of people present (*cause, causes*) me some concern.
16. Five-eighths of the profits (*accrue, accrues*) to me.
17. The jury (*is, are*) unable to agree.
18. The executive, with his private secretary, (*has, have*) gone to the meeting.
19. Nobody in these offices (*is, are*) to have a vacation.
20. Neither Tom nor they (*is, are*) present today.

Agreement of Pronouns and Their Antecedents

The word to which a pronoun refers is called the *antecedent*. All pronouns must agree with their antecedents.

Every worker must do *his* or *her* best.	(antecedent—*worker*)
Everyone is required to bring *his* or *her* report.	(antecedent—*everyone*)
The company is sending us *its* new price list.	(antecedent—*company*)
She asked each of us to bring *his or her* own lunch.	(antecedent—*each*)
Neither Bob nor Tom was ready for *his* dinner.	(antecedent—*neither*)

Agreement of Relative Pronouns. When a relative pronoun is the subject of a dependent clause, the predicate of that clause agrees with the relative pronoun, which, in turn, agrees with its antecedent. (In the following the relative pronouns are in capitals; their antecedents and predicates are in italics.)

It is *I* WHO *am* wrong.
He is the only *one* of our men WHO *is* going.
He is one of the *men* WHO *are* going.
It is *you* WHO *are* too noisy.

Definite Reference of Pronouns. A pronoun must always refer to a *definite* antecedent. Careless writers sometimes tend to use *it, which,* and some other pronouns indefinitely so that they do not refer to specific antecedents.

Indefinite: If the water is too cold for the baby, throw it out.
Definite: Throw out the water if it is too cold for the baby.
Indefinite: I saw the snow begin to fall, which made me happy.
Definite: I was happy when I saw the snow begin to fall.
Indefinite: Paul told Frank that he was wrong.
Definite: Paul said to Frank, "You are wrong." OR
            Paul said to Frank, "I am wrong."
Indefinite: While Mary scolded her daughter, she began to cry.
Definite: While scolding her daughter, Mary began to cry. OR
            Mary began to cry while scolding her daughter.
            While Mary scolded her daughter, the latter began to cry.

Remote Antecedents. Avoid references to remote antecedents—those that are not near the pronouns to which they refer.

Remote: The letters contained many errors, erasures, smudge marks, and a number of grammatical errors. They were the worst I had ever seen.
Clear: The letters, which were the worst I had ever seen, contained many errors, erasures, smudge marks, and a number of grammatical errors.

The Logical Antecedent. The antecedent of a pronoun must always be a specific noun or pronoun. By remembering this fact, you will avoid vague references.

Vague: We set the bear traps and caught two of them.
Clear: We set the traps and caught two bears.
Vague: She is a lawyer; her son is choosing this profession, too.
Clear: She is a lawyer; her son is choosing law as a profession, too.
Vague: At our school they require you to study French.
Clear: At our school the rules require all students to study French.
       At our school all students are required to study French.

Using It in Idioms. The indefinite use of *it* is perfectly correct in such idioms as *it is cloudy, it is snowing, it seems, it is late.*

Progress Quiz 6-B. Select the correct word.

1. Do you think it is (*I, me*) who (*is, are, am*) to go?
2. Everyone (*is, are*) asked to place (*his or her, their*) card in this box.
3. Was it (*they, them*) who (*was, were*) supposed (*to go, to have gone*)?

4. He is the only one of the boys who (*was, were*) on the pier.

5. She is one of those teachers who (*know, knows*) how to praise good work.

6. Neither David nor Joe (*has, have*) heard the news.

7. You, as well as I, (*am, are*) to report to the class.

8. I am sure it was (*us, we*) whom she discussed when she saw all (*them, those*) new girls.

9. Was it (*he, him*), (*she, her*) or (*I, me*) to whom she referred?

10. She started to laugh, making John and (*I, me*) happy.

Progress Quiz 6-C. Rewrite the following letter, making all necessary corrections.

Dear Miss Fleming:

When the committee were meeting yesterday, I had a chance to look at your report. At your company they certainly know how to write a detailed report, for I found all the figures I needed. The statistics makes a good addition to my own report, which will have been finished by next Wednesday. As you probably know, in my company they tell you to have all reports ready for release on Wednesday.

Thanking you for your help, I am,

Sincerely yours,

Build Your Word Power

Say What You Mean and Mean What You Say. When we use logical English, we clearly say what we mean. Sometimes we tend to accept as logical and correct certain expressions that actually should be avoided. For example, avoid *Thanks* in place of *Thank you* at the beginning of a sentence. *Thank you* means *I thank you.* You can see, therefore, that it is illogical to say "Thanks," meaning *I thanks you.*

Amount, Number. *Amount* indicates a sum or a total mass. *Number* refers to a group of individual parts that can be counted.

A large amount of mail was processed.
A large number of letters were processed.

The Indefinite Pronoun One. Colloquially the pronoun *you* is often used instead of the pronoun *one*. *One* is correctly used when not referring to a specific person but to everyone generally.

Colloquial: You should not judge a book by its cover.
Formal: One should not judge a book by its cover.

Caution: *One* is always singular; therefore, it requires a singular predicate. Any pronoun of which *one* is the antecedent must also be singular.

Incorrect: One should always do their best work.
Right: One should always do his or her best work.

Check Your Knowledge

Tell whether each of the following statements is true or false. If a statement is false, tell why it is not true.

1. A predicate must agree with its subject.
2. A pronoun must agree with the subject of the sentence.
3. The word *it* is correctly used in such idioms as *it is raining*.
4. Plural verbs end with *s*.
5. The indefinite reference of a pronoun is permitted so long as the idea being expressed is clear.

Skill Builders

Turn to Skill Builder 5-A, page 55, and rewrite the letter so that it will be acceptable.

Business Speech

Careful speakers never omit the sounds of certain letters in words. Practice pronouncing the following words, strongly emphasizing the capitalized letters in each word.

1. aCcept
2. aCcessory (ak-sessory)
3. Eleven
4. FebRuary
5. gEOGraphy

6. goverNment
7. leNGth
8. libRary
9. streNGth
10. wiDth

Spelling

Guide: Only one word ends with *sede—supersede.* Only three words end with *ceed—succeed, exceed, proceed.* All other words having this sound end with *cede.*

Study Spelling List 6. (See page 407.)

Section

7

ADJECTIVES AND ADVERBS—WORDS THAT DESCRIBE

Adjectives and adverbs are picture-makers. When adjectives are used in a sentence, an idea gains dimension and seems to come to life, as a drawing does when color and shading are added. Certain adjectives are sometimes called *noun markers.* Adverbs help to make the meanings of verbs, adjectives, and other adverbs more specific.

Adjectives

Adjective Power. The choice of proper accessories completes a costume and adds to the general eye appeal of an ensemble. Beautiful pictures and attractive colors may cause you to select a certain book.

In the preceding cases, the right use of "something extra" helps create a good impression—the right impression for a certain occasion.

Adjectives assist you to make a good impression in using English, for they help to create picture ideas by (1) giving definite descriptions, (2) telling the exact number, and (3) separating the definite from the indefinite.

NOUN ALONE	NOUN WITH ADJECTIVES
book	heavy book
	old red book
men	young men
	six young men

The Use of Adjectives. Adjectives have two important functions: they (1) modify nouns and pronouns and (2) complete the meaning of linking verbs.*

Comparison of Adjectives. Most adjectives may be expressed in one of three degrees—*positive, comparative,* and *superlative.*

The comparative is used in comparing two persons or things. The superlative is used in comparing more than two persons or things; it indicates the highest or the lowest degree.

POSITIVE	COMPARATIVE	SUPERLATIVE
tall	taller	tallest
sweet	sweeter	sweetest
low	lower	lowest
contrary	more contrary	most contrary †
able	less able	least able

Irregular Comparison. Some adjectives change their spelling in the comparative and the superlative.

POSITIVE	COMPARATIVE	SUPERLATIVE
good	better	best
bad	worse	worst
much	more	most
far	farther	farthest
little (amount)	less	least

---

* *To modify* means *to cause a change* in a word by describing or limiting it.

† Many adjectives of two syllables can be compared by adding *er* or *est* or using *more* or *most.* Adjectives of more than two syllables require *more* or *most* for comparison. Never use *more* or *most* with words already ending with *er* or *est.*

Section 7 - Adjectives and Adverbs—Words That Describe   **65**

The Articles—A, An, The. The adjectives *a, an,* and *the* are commonly called *articles.* *A* and *an* are the indefinite articles, and *the* is the definite article. Articles are often called *noun markers.*

Pronunciation and Use of Articles. The article *a* is always pronounced *uh*—that is, like the sound of *a* in *about.*

Before a consonant, *e* in the article *the* is pronounced like the *a* in *about;* before a vowel sound it is pronounced like the *e* in *be.*

The article *a* is used before a word beginning with a consonant. The article *an* is used before a word beginning with any vowel sound except long *u,* as in the word *uniform.**

Absolute Adjectives. Adjectives that cannot be compared are called *absolute* adjectives. Therefore, the ending *er* and *est* and the words *more* and *most* cannot be used with absolute adjectives. *More nearly* may be used before such adjectives. A partial list of absolute adjectives follows:

circular	empty	full †	square
complete	entire	impossible	straight
correct	eternal	perfect	unique
dead	fatal	right	whole
direct	final	round	wrong

Adjectives of color are absolute adjectives. For example, one thing cannot be "redder" than another. The logical manner of expressing such an idea is to say, "a brighter red" or "a brighter shade of red."

Adjectives Requiring Special Attention

First, Last; Former, Latter. *First* and *last* are used to refer to one of a group consisting of more than two. *Former* refers to the first of two; *latter* refers to the second of two.

> Of the three acts in the play, I prefer the *last.*
> I like red and blue but prefer the *former,* not the *latter.*

Only one person or thing can be last; therefore, do not say "the two last years"; rather, say, "the last two years." Some authorities recommend "the past two years" when that is the meaning intended.

---

* British usage sanctions the use of *an* before a word beginning with sounded *h.*

† Merchandisers say that one garment is "fuller" than another.

Fewer, Less. *Fewer* refers to a number of persons or things; *less* refers to degree or quantity. *Memory aid:* If the word being described can actually be counted, use *fewer;* if it cannot be counted, use *less.*

> *Fewer* persons attended this month's meetings.*
> I am having *less* trouble than you.

Progress Quiz 7-A. Correct all errors in the following sentences.

1. He is the most competent of the two men.
2. I wish that there was less westerns on TV.
3. Your desk drawer is fuller than mine.
4. Of the two errors, yours' is indeed the worst.
5. This typewriter is more better than his.
6. This is the contentest cow in the pasture.
7. This cloth is whiter.
8. New York is the most large city in the United States.
9. The closet contains a coat, umbrella, an uniform, an hat, and a overcoat.
10. This is the least common of the two.
11. On this paper there are less errors.
12. The worse of the fight had been over by the time I had arrived.

Adverbs

Adverb Power. Adverbs modify verbs, adjectives, and other adverbs. They are powerful words, therefore, because they can change the meaning of three parts of speech, thus helping your language to be clear and forceful.

Recognizing Adverbs. An adverb answers one of these questions: "When?" "Where?" "How?" or "How much?" An infinitive used as an adverb sometimes answers the question "Why?"

> I shall talk with you *soon*. (*when*—adverb of time)
> Please put the carbon paper *there*. (*where*—adverb of place)
> She transcribes her notes *rapidly*. (*how*—adverb of manner)
> He was *partially* prepared. (*how much*—adverb of degree)
> I came *to talk* with you. (*why*—infinitive as adverb)

---

* If you say "less people," the expression is the comparative of *little people*, which means something entirely different! (Use *persons* rather than *people* if the number of them can be counted.)

Note that an adverb can modify a verb, an adjective, or another adverb.

Mary types *accurately*. (modifies the verb *types*)
This is a *really* good book. (modifies the adjective *good*)
He speaks *too* slowly. (modifies the adverb *slowly*)

Comparison of Adverbs. Many adverbs can be compared in the same manner as adjectives. Adverbs of two or more syllables are compared by using *more* or *most*.

POSITIVE	COMPARATIVE	SUPERLATIVE
soon	sooner	soonest
quickly	more quickly	most quickly

Formation of Adverbs. Many adverbs are made by adding *ly* to adjectives.* Other adverbs made from adjectives change their spelling.

ADJECTIVE	ADVERB
soft	softly
slow	slowly †
satisfactory	satisfactorily
good	well
real	really
whole	wholly

Nouns Cannot Be True Adverbs. At first sight many words that are actually nouns appear to be adverbs—for example, *home, hour, mile, yesterday.*

I think that she went (to) home.
He will work (for) an hour longer.
Has he driven (for) a mile yet?
She talked with me (on) yesterday.

Observe that the preposition is understood before each noun in the preceding sentences. Such nouns are called *adverbial objectives*, for they have the meanings of adverbs but actually are objects of prepositions that are understood.

---

*When *ly* is added to a noun, the noun becomes an adjective—*world—worldly.*

† *Slow* may be used as an adverb and compared like the adjective—*slow, slower, slowest.*

Caution: Do not use *home* when you mean *at home*.

> Wrong: Gene was home all day today.
> Right: Gene was at home all day today.

Using Adjectives and Adverbs Correctly

Adjectives and adverbs have specific uses. Careful speakers and writers do not confuse adjectives and adverbs but properly apply the rules for their uses.

Farther, Further (either adjectives or adverbs). *Farther* refers to space; *further* refers to time or degree.

> This time he has reached a *farther* point. (adjective)
> John drove *farther* than the other men. (adverb)
> She made *further* efforts to succeed. (adjective)
> To excel, you must study *further*. (adverb)

Caution: The expressions "all the farther" and "all the faster" are incorrect. Instead use *as far as* and *as fast as*.

Only, Merely, Nearly. *Only* may be used as an adjective or an adverb. In using *only,* check the sense of your sentence carefully, for by placing *only* in the wrong location, you may confuse your meaning.*

> *Only* you can do that work. (Meaning: *You alone*)
> You can do *only* that work. (Meaning: *That work and no other*)
> I could get him to come at five *only*. (Meaning: *At five—no other time*)

The adverbs *merely* and *nearly* should be placed in their proper locations.

> Wrong: You will not succeed merely by wishing to succeed.
> Wrong: You will not merely succeed by wishing to succeed.
> Right: You will not succeed by merely wishing to succeed.
> I have nearly finished everything. (Nothing is completely finished.)
> I have finished nearly everything. (Most things are finished; a few are not.)

What Is Being Described? In trying to determine whether to use an adjective or an adverb, ask yourself, "What is being described?" If a

---

*The words *alone* and *simply* require the same careful placement.

noun is being described, use an adjective. If a verb, an adjective, or an adverb is being described, use an adverb.

> His *eager* attitude was noticeable. (adjective describing noun)
> This chocolate is not *sweet*. (adjective describing noun)
> They *eagerly* await your answer. (adverb describing verb)
> She responded *eagerly*. (adverb describing verb)
> This is a *really* good book. (adverb describing adjective)
> Paul talked *too* rapidly. (adverb describing adverb)
> I am *surely* glad that you are here. (adverb describing adjective)

Using Adjectives with Linking Verbs. When the subject is being described, all forms of the linking verbs *be, appear, become, look, seem, smell, feel,* and *taste* are followed by adjectives, not adverbs. An adjective following a linking verb is called a *predicate adjective*. If the verb is being described, use an adverb.

> The fresh bread smells *good*. (subject being described)
> Yesterday she looked *sick*. (subject being described)
> She looked *quickly* in our direction. (verb being described)
> This cloth feels *smooth*. (subject being described)
> I *hastily* felt the cloth. (verb being described)

Real, Really, Very. *Real* is an adjective; its adverbial form is *really*. *Very* is an adverb that modifies an adjective or another adverb. When *very* comes before a past participle used as an adjective, users of formal English always say *very much*.

> His remark was a *real* challenge to me. (adjective modifying noun *challenge*)
> This is a *really* fine shoe. (adverb modifying adjective *fine*)
> The dog is *very* smart. (adverb modifying adjective *smart*)
> I prepared *very* quickly. (adverb modifying adverb *quickly*)
> I am *very* much interested in your offer. (adverb modifying adverb *much*)

Good, Well. *Good* is an adjective. *Well* is usually an adverb; however, when pertaining to *being in good health, well* is an adjective.

> This little boy is *good*. (free from evil)
> This little boy is *well*. (in good health)
> Miss Clark works *well*.
> Miss Clark does *good* work.

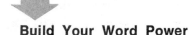

Build Your Word Power

As . . . as; So . . . as. When a comparative expression follows a negative, use *so* instead of *as.* (Users of informal English do not always abide by this rule, but users of formal English insist on it.)

> Formal: He is not *so* tall as his sister.
> Informal: He is not *as* tall as his sister.

Some, That, This. The words *some, that,* and *this* should never be used as adverbs.

> Wrong: She feels some better this morning.
> Right: She feels somewhat better this morning.
> Wrong: I did not think I would be that lucky.
> Right: I did not think I would be so lucky.
> Wrong: Don't act this slowly.
> Right: Don't act so slowly.

Any other; Never before. In comparing one person or thing with all the others in a group, use *any other.* In mentioning an action or a condition existing while you are speaking, use *never before.*

> Wrong: He is taller than any boy in the class.
> Right: He is taller than any other boy in the class.
> Wrong: Never have I been so happy!
> Right: Never before have I been so happy!

Sometime, Some time. *Sometime* (one word) is an adverb meaning *at an indefinite future time. Some time* (two words) is the noun *time,* modified by *some,* meaning *an indefinite amount of time. Sometimes,* an adverb meaning *occasionally,* is always one word.

> She will call on you *sometime* next week. (future time)
> It will take *some time* to answer these letters. (amount of time)
> *Sometimes* I am very busy. (occasionally)

Progress Quiz 7-B. Choose the correct words to complete each sentence.

1. He (*sure, surely*) transcribes his letters (*well, good*).
2. This shoe goes on (*easy, easily*); therefore, it is (*satisfactory, satisfactorily*).
3. (*Less, Fewer*) children pranced about (*happy, happily*) today.

Section 7 - Adjectives and Adverbs—Words That Describe   71

4. New York is larger than (*any, any other*) city in the (*East, east*).

5. If you do the job (*satisfactory, satisfactorily*), I shall notify you (*quick, quickly*).

6. This cloth feels (*soft, softly*), but it is not (*so, as*) pretty as yours.

7. This is a (*real, really*) good opportunity for (*we, us*) girls.

8. She drove two miles (*farther, further*) before finding a (*real, really*) good inn.

9. It will take me (*sometime, some time*) to finish this work, especially if you want it done (*more correctly, more better, better*).

10. Since he feels (*some, somewhat*) better, we shall visit him (*sometime, some time*) next week.

Check Your Knowledge

1. The word *fast* can be used as a noun, a verb, an adjective, and an adverb. Give a sentence to show each use.

2. List the linking verbs. When are they followed by predicate adjectives? When are they followed by adverbs?

3. How do adjectives and adverbs add power to your language?

4. Why must the word *only* receive careful attention in a sentence?

5. In what ways do adjectives and adverbs differ?

Skill Builders

7-A. Write the body (message) of a letter in which you inquire about the rates and accommodations at a certain hotel. Be sure to inquire about all the features in which you are interested. You will be staying at the hotel one week in August.

7-B. On the letter completed in Skill Builder 7-A, underscore each adjective once and each adverb twice.

Business Speech

Strongly pronounce the capital letters in each of these words:

1. aCcelerate (ak-SEL)
2. asKed
3. accUrate
4. figUre
5. kepT

6. particUlar
7. probaBly (three syllables)
8. recoGnize
9. regUlar
10. SuCcinct (suk-SINKT)

Spelling

Guide: Some adjectives ending with *y* are formed from nouns, as *ice—icy*. In such cases drop the silent *e* at the end of the noun before adding *y*. Exception: *fire—fiery*.

Study Spelling List 7.   (See page 408.)

REMINDER: Are you practicing the correct spelling of each word you misspell?

Section

8

PREPOSITIONS AND CONJUNCTIONS— WORDS THAT CONNECT

Prepositions and conjunctions are parts of speech that connect the related parts of sentences. In other words, they show the relationships among the aspects of the thought contained in a sentence. Without prepositions and conjunctions our language would be awkward and would lack the smoothness necessary for clearness.

Prepositions

The Use of Prepositions. Prepositions introduce *prepositional phrases,* which modify nouns, pronouns, or verbs. Prepositional phrases are of two types—the *adjective phrase,* which modifies a noun or pronoun; and the *adverbial phrase,* which modifies a verb.*

> The box *of stationery* is on your desk. (adjective phrase)
> The box of stationery is *on your desk.* (adverbial phrase)

Some common prepositions are *about, after, among, at, between, by, during, except, for, from, in, into, of, on, with, without, to.*

There are a few idiomatic prepositions, such as *because of, instead of,* and *owing to.* Except for such idiomatic prepositions, single prepositions should be used.

> Wrong: Please keep *off of* the grass.
> Right: Please keep *off* the grass.
> Wrong: Did John look *out of* the window?
> Right: Did John look *out* the window?

Some words may be used as adverbs or as prepositions.

> The elevator is going *up.* (adverb)
> We went *up* the hill. (preposition)

Using Prepositions After Certain Words

If you have studied a foreign language, you often probably had to think about which preposition to use, especially after verbs. Foreigners who study English have the same problem. Because the use of most prepositions is "second nature" to you, however, you do not have many problems. There are some prepositions, though, that need careful attention.

abbreviation of (*not* for)	What is the abbreviation of *number?*
accede to	I shall accede *to* your wishes.
accompanied by (a person)	She was accompanied *by* her husband.
accompanied with (an object)	It was accompanied *with* a card.
accord with (an idea)	He is in accord *with* my ideas.

---

*All infinitive phrases, such as *to go,* begin with the preposition *to,* but they are not prepositional phrases.

acquit of (a charge)	The man was acquitted *of* the crime.
adept in (*not* at)	She is adept *in* mathematics.
agree on, upon (a plan)	We all agree *on* a new course of action.
agree to (a proposal)	We shall agree *to* your terms.
agree with (a person or idea)	I agree *with* you in this case.
angry at (a condition)	He was angry *at* the long delay.
angry with (a person)	Never be angry *with* a customer.
compare to (to illustrate)	Compared *to* him, I am doing well.
compare with (qualities)	Compare your TV *with* other sets.
comply with	Katherine will comply *with* your request.
concur with (agree with)	He concurs *with* your point of view.
confer on (an honor)	We conferred an honor *on* the mayor.
confer with (to discuss)	I shall confer *with* the manager.
connect with . . . by	My city is connected *with* his by Route 1.
correlate with	The tests are correlated *with* the text.
dates from (*not* back to)	It dates *from* our first year.
defect in (a thing)	I saw the defect *in* the lamp.
defect of (intangible quality)	His defect *of* judgment is obvious.
differ from (opinions)	My ideas differ *from* his.
differ with (a person)	I regret to differ *with* you.
different from (never *different than*)	Your hat is different *from* mine.
disappointed in (a person)	I am disappointed *in* you.
disappointed with (a thing)	She is disappointed *with* her job.
displeased at (a thing)	He was displeased *at* the discourtesy.
displeased with (a person)	I am displeased *with* Betty.
identical with (not *to*)	Her pen is identical *with* mine.
inferior to (not *than*)	This one is inferior *to* yours.

invite to (not *for*)	I invited him *to* dinner.
oblivious of (not *to*)	He was oblivious *of* the fact.
opposite of (not *to*) (When a noun or pronoun follows, omit *of*.)	Good is the opposite *of* bad. My house is opposite yours.
part from (a person)	At last they parted *from* each other.
part with (a thing)	I hate to part *with* my old shoes.
quarter to (not *of* or *till*)	It is a quarter *to* four.
subscribe for (magazine)	I subscribe *for* six magazines.
subscribe to (charity; idea)	Will you subscribe *to* this charity?
talk with (a person)	She talked *with* me.
try to (not *and*)	Please try *to* do better work.
wait for (a person or thing)	I waited *for* her an hour.
wait on (serve a customer)	May I wait *on* you?

Some Prepositions Requiring Attention

Avoiding On. The word *on* should never be used after the following words. (The correct prepositions are shown in italics.)

a clue *to*	to lift *from*
a complaint *of, about*	progress *toward, in*
to convict *of*	reassure *of, about*
developments *in*	a study *of*
dismayed *at, by*	

About. Do not say *at about* when you mean *about*. Do not use *as to* instead of *about*.

He will call me about three o'clock. (not *at about*)
She inquired about your health. (not *as to*)

Between, Among. *Between* refers to two; *among* refers to more than two.*

It is a secret *between* you and me.
The race was *among* five cars.

---

*Since *between* is a preposition, it is followed by the objective case; therefore, "between you and me" is right, and "between you and I" is wrong.

For you to. Avoid the expression *for you to* when you mean *you to*.

> Wrong: I should like *for you to* go.
> Right: I should like *you to* go.

In, Into, In to. (a) *In* denotes location. (b) *Into* denotes a motion from one place to another. (c) *Enter* does not require *into* except in *enter into an agreement*. (d) *In to* is actually two words; the word *in* is usually a part of the verb expressions *come in* or *go in*, and the word *to* is a separate preposition.

> (a) Right: I met him in the hall.
> (b) Right: He fell into the pit.
> (c) Wrong: She entered into the kitchen.
>   Right: She entered the kitchen.
>   Right: The two firms entered into an agreement.
> (d) Right: Let's go in to the meeting.

In back of. *In back of* is colloquially used for *behind*.

> Colloquial: I looked *in back of* the desk.
> Formal: I looked *behind* the desk.

Of. Some careless speakers and writers use *of* instead of *have*. This is a serious error. Example: "I should *have* done it" not "I should *of* done it."

Over with. *Over with* is colloquially used for *over, finished, ended.*

> Colloquial: The play is *over with*.
> Formal: The play is *finished*.

Prior to. *Prior to* is a pretentious way of saying *before*.

Used to (pronounced "uzd"). *Used to* has two meanings: (1) *accustomed to*, (2) *repeatedly*, in referring to a past action. *Observe:* Avoid the localism "used to could"; instead say, "used to be able to."

> He is *used to* cold weather.
> I *used to* go there each week.

Want in, out, off. Colloquially used instead of *to enter, to get in, to get out, to get off*.

> Colloquial: I want off at 96th Street.
> Formal: I want to get off (*or* out) at 96th Street.

Want to. Colloquially used instead of *ought, should*.

> Colloquial: You want to be more careful.
> Formal: You should be more careful.

Progress Quiz 8-A. Select the word that correctly completes each of the following sentences.

1. This chart correlates (*to, with*) your book.
2. Is it (*inside, inside of*) the cabinet?
3. He put his foot (*in, into*) the water.
4. Can you afford to subscribe (*for, to*) another magazine?
5. Is it a secret (*between, among*) the three boys?
6. How long have you been waiting (*for, on*) her to arrive?
7. His sports car is different (*from, than*) mine.
8. I want (*in, to get in*) the front door.
9. It is no longer a secret between you and (*I, me*).
10. I differ (*from, with*) John in regard to this matter.

Sentences Ending with Prepositions. Many persons believe that it is incorrect to end a sentence with a preposition. In modern English usage, however, only the most formal writers try to avoid a preposition at the end of a sentence. Most speakers, even those noted for formality, place a preposition at the end of a sentence if it seems natural to do so. Sir Winston Churchill, a formal speaker and one of the great modern writers, commenting on avoiding a preposition at the end of a sentence, said, "This is the sort of impertinence up with which I will not put." Churchill's answer clearly shows that awkward sentences sometimes result in trying to avoid a preposition at the end of a sentence. Of course, when two prepositions come together at the end of a sentence, the construction *is* awkward; for example, "A preposition is a poor word to end a sentence up with."

Language is often clearer and more direct when a preposition is used at the end of a sentence, especially a question.

> Whom is Mr. Granata looking at?
> What are you sending for?
> Which one is he complaining about?

Idiomatic Verbs. Certain verb idioms require the use of a word that may be considered either an adverb or a preposition. Some authorities say, however, that such expressions are verb phrases. Examples: *get up, look up someone*.

Avoid Superfluous Prepositions. Poor speakers sometimes use prepositions that are not needed. Such superfluous prepositions should be avoided.

> Wrong: Where is he going to?
> Right: Where is he going?
> Wrong: Where is she at?
> Right: Where is she?

Conjunctions

A *conjunction* is a word that joins words, phrases, or clauses. The types of conjunctions are (1) *coordinating,* including correlative conjunctions and conjunctive adverbs, and (2) *subordinating.*

Coordinating Conjunctions. A *coordinating conjunction,* also called *coordinate conjunction,* joins words, phrases, or clauses of equal rank. The most common coordinating conjunctions are *and, but, or,* and *nor.** The correlative conjunction and the conjunctive adverb are types of coordinating conjunctions.

> Words joined: They saw Todd *and* Julio.
> Phrases joined: Look in the drawer *or* on the table.
> Clauses joined: She wanted to sing, *but* no one would listen.

Correlative Conjunctions. When a certain conjunction requires another word to complete its meaning, the two words are referred to as *correlative conjunctions.* Correlatives are *either . . . or; neither . . . nor; not only . . . but also; both . . . and.*

> *Either* you *or* she must be present.
> *Neither* Pat *nor* I can be there.
> He excels *not only* in French *but also* in Spanish.

Conjunctive Adverbs. A *conjunctive adverb* carries the thought from one independent clause to another. Some common conjunctive adverbs are *however, nevertheless, therefore, moreover, consequently, namely, still, then.*

---

*When *but* means *except,* it is a preposition.

Note: When such words are used parenthetically, they are regular adverbs.*

Conj. adverb: I told him to go; however, he refused to listen.
Parenthetical: I told him to go, however, but he remained.

Subordinating Conjunctions. A *subordinating conjunction,* also called *subordinate conjunction,* introduces a subordinate clause and connects it with the main clause. Many subordinating conjunctions can also be used as adverbs. Some of the more common subordinating conjunctions are *when, although, since, if, because, so that, as, in order that, while, unless.*

She seemed embarrassed *because* she was late.
If you are careful, you help prevent accidents.

Parallel Construction

Coordinating conjunctions and correlative conjunctions require that parallel construction be used—that is, that elements of the same grammatical value be joined by the conjunctions.

Wrong: She likes singing and to dance.
Parallel: She likes singing and dancing.
Wrong: He is either late or you are early.
Parallel: Either he is late or you are early.
Wrong: Betty is both speedy and is accurate.
Parallel: Betty is both speedy and accurate.

Using Some Prepositions and Conjunctions Correctly

All of. Use *all of* before a pronoun; use *all the* before a noun.

All of them have arrived.
All the boys have arrived.

---

* A parenthetical expression is one that can be omitted without changing the sense of a sentence. Such expressions are set off by commas. In the middle of a sentence, a semicolon precedes and a comma follows most conjunctive adverbs. If a conjunctive adverb, such as *still* or *then,* contains only one syllable, a comma usually does not follow it.

As if. *As if* is often followed by the subjunctive of the verb.

> He looks as if he *were* ill.

Blame. In formal English avoid *blame it on.*

> Informal: Don't blame it on him.
> Formal: Don't blame him for it.

Deny that. Avoid the expression *deny but that;* instead use *deny that.*

> Wrong: No one can deny but that she will succeed.
> Right: No one can deny that she will succeed.

Different from. Since *from* is a preposition, *different from* is followed by the objective case or the possessive case. "Different than" should always be avoided.

> Wrong: They are twins, but she seems different than he.
> Right: They are twins, but she seems different from him.
> Right: Mine is different from yours.

Due to. The expression *due to* can be used after a form of the verb *to be;* in all other cases use *because of* or *owing to.*

> Right: His absence is due to illness. (after form of *to be*)
> Wrong: Due to rain the game was postponed.
> Right: Because of rain (*or* Owing to rain) the game was postponed.

If. The subordinating conjunction *if* begins a conditional thought. When a clause expresses doubt, formal usage requires *whether.*

> Condition: She will not be present *if* it rains.
> Doubt: I do not know *whether* she will be present.

In regard to. *In regard to* is an American idiom; *as regards* is its British counterpart. Always avoid *in regards to. Regarding* is always correct.

Kind of; Sort of. Omit *a* after these two expressions.

Like, As. *Like* is a preposition, requiring that the objective case follow it. When *as* is a conjunction, the nominative case follows it.

> Does John look like *her?*
> He is not so tall as *she* (is).

Plan. *Plan* is followed by *to*, not *on*.

> Wrong: I plan on seeing him next week.
> Right: I plan to see him next week.

Rarely. Avoid *rarely ever;* instead use *rarely; rarely, if ever; rarely or never; hardly ever.*

Seldom. Avoid *seldom ever* and *seldom or ever;* instead use *seldom* or *seldom, if ever.*

> Wrong: Seldom ever do we spend so much.
> Right: Seldom, if ever, do we spend so much.

The reason is that. Avoid the expression *the reason is because;* instead, use *the reason is that.*

Than. *Than* is usually a conjunction, requiring that the nominative case follow it.

> Evelyn ate more sandwiches than *he* (ate).

Note: Than is occasionally used in an elliptical construction—that is, a construction in which certain words have been omitted.

> For president I would rather have Jill than *him*. (The word *him* is the direct object of the elliptical verb *have,* for the complete idea is: I would rather have Jill *than have him* for president.)

Build Your Word Power

Avoiding Two or More Negatives. Some common negatives are *no, not, never, none, neither.* When two or more negatives are used in expressing a single thought, the language is illogical. Persons who commonly use two or more negatives in a sentence are considered illiterate.

ILLITERATE	CORRECT
I don't want none, neither.	I don't want any, either.
He never has no money.	He doesn't ever have any money.

Each other, One another. *Each other* refers to two; *one another* refers to more than two.

> The two women greeted each other.
> All five members of the family love one another.

Everyone, Every one. *Everyone* means all the people; *every one* refers to each one of a group.

> Everyone is expected to work.
> Every one of the customers was notified.

Hardly, Scarcely, Barely. *Hardly, scarcely,* and *barely* are negatives; therefore, they should not be used with other negatives.

> Wrong: I can't hardly believe that she is guilty.
> Right: I can hardly believe that she is guilty.

Progress Quiz 8-B. Change the following sentences so that each will contain parallel construction.

1. His talk was neither informative, nor did we find it amusing.
2. She says that she has tried skiing and to sail.
3. She is short, with brown eyes, and has a friendly manner.
4. Her song was sad, long, and could not be understood.
5. She repeated that the chicken needed cleaning and to be cooked.
6. Not any of the carpenters nor their apprentices understood the bulletin.
7. This room is twelve feet in length and nine feet wide.
8. You are either behind the times, or I am ahead of the times.

Progress Quiz 8-C. Correct all errors.

1. Beth don't want none, neither.
2. Joe can't hardly believe that his sister has went.
3. The three men looked at each other.
4. I told everyone of the children that there mother would return.
5. Bill looked like he was angry at me.
6. Is your glove different than mine?
7. Our plans were changed due to the bad weather.
8. I don't know if I can do this here job.
9. Is Albert shorter than her?
10. I don't deny but that Jean is competent.

Section 8 - Prepositions and Conjunctions—Words That Connect   **83**

Check Your Knowledge

1. List ten prepositions.
2. List the coordinating conjunctions.
3. Compose one sentence that contains both an adjective phrase and an adverbial phrase.
4. Discuss using prepositions at ends of sentences.
5. The word *but* may be either a preposition or a conjunction. Compose two sentences to show the two uses of this word.

Business Speech

Words borrowed from French that have a final *ge* end with a *zh* sound.

1. barrage (RAZH)
2. camouflage (FLAZH)
3. corsage (SAZH)
4. garage (RAZH)

5. massage (SAZH)
6. prestige (TEEZH)
7. sabotage (TAZH)
8. fuselage (LAZH)

Spelling

Guide: When a word ends with *c,* write *k* before adding a final syllable—for example, *panic, panicking, panicked, panicky.*

Study Spelling List 8. (See page 408.)

Unit Three

CONTROLLING IDEAS BY USING PUNCTUATION

Section

9

USING THE PERIOD, QUESTION MARK, AND EXCLAMATION POINT

In typing, leave two spaces after periods, question marks, and exclamation points that end sentences. Do not leave any space before those punctuation marks. Leave one space after a period that follows an abbreviation in a sentence. If an abbreviation ends a sentence, use only one period.

End-of-Sentence Punctuation

Your Stop Lights. The three punctuation marks used at the ends of sentences—periods, question marks, and exclamation points—are like stop lights. They tell you that you have come to the end of a complete thought —that you should come to a full stop. If you do not come to a stop in such cases, you will bump into the next idea, causing a collision of thoughts—something that no good writer ever allows to happen.

The Kinds of Sentences. Classified according to how their ideas are expressed, sentences are of four types—*declarative, interrogative, imperative,* and *exclamatory.*

Declarative sentences are statements. Place a period at the end of a declarative sentence.

Interrogative sentences are questions. Place a question mark at the end of an interrogative sentence.

Imperative sentences are either commands or requests in the form of "polite commands." Place a period at the end of an imperative sentence.

Exclamatory sentences show strong feeling or surprise. Place an exclamation point at the end of an exclamatory sentence.

Declarative: Betty uses the Dictaphone every day.
Interrogative: Does Betty use the Dictaphone every day?
Imperative: Stop using the Dictaphone.
Exclamatory: What a beautiful new Dictaphone she has!

Avoiding the Comma Fault. Be sure to place a period at the end of a complete statement. The writer who uses a comma instead of a period at the end of a sentence is guilty of the *comma fault.*

> Wrong: Spelling is important, I am improving mine.
> Right: Spelling is important. I am improving mine.
> Right: Spelling is important; I am improving mine.
> Right: Since spelling is important, I am improving mine.

Other Uses of the Period

1. Use a period as a decimal point to show decimal subdivisions, to separate dollars and cents, and to precede cents expressed only in figures.

> 348.904 $350.25 $.09 (used only in columnar work)

2. Use a period after each initial in a person's name.

Caution: Always express a person's name exactly as that person writes it; do not use initials unless the writer uses them.

> K. R. Davies   Dolores E. Perez   E. W. Franklin Company

3. Use a period after each part of an abbreviated expression.

> pp. (pages)   Ed.D. (Doctor of Education)

Expressing Abbreviations. Formerly the use of periods with abbreviations was necessary. Today, however, many common abbreviations, especially when composed entirely of capitals, are written without periods or spaces between the letters.

> TWA (Trans World Airlines)
> FHA (Federal Housing Administration)

Most abbreviations should be avoided in business letters, on envelopes, and in other forms of business writing. The following abbreviations, however, are always used instead of the spelled-out forms:

> Mr. (Mister)   C.O.D., c.o.d., COD (cash on de-
> Mrs. (Mistress) *   livery, collect on delivery)
> Messrs. (Messieurs, the   No. (number) in referring to a
>   plural of Mr.)   numbered item

---

* *Miss* is not an abbreviation; it requires no period.

Spacing Used with Abbreviations. If an abbreviation consists of all small letters (lower case), do not leave a space after any period except the last one. If an abbreviation consists of all capitals, a space may be left after each period; the present tendency, however, is to leave no space except after the last period. If an abbreviation contains both small letters and capitals, do not leave any spaces except after the final period.

> a.m. p.m. (no space between letters)
> U. S. A. U.S.A. (either spaces or no spaces between letters)
> Ph.D. (no space after first period)

Abbreviations of foreign words not accepted in general English usage are printed in italics. Such abbreviations, as well as any others consisting of more than one letter in each part, always require a space between the two parts of the abbreviations: *op. cit.* (in the work cited).

Certain abbreviations sometimes use the virgule (/) instead of a period; n/f (no funds).

In business writing do not abbreviate the names of the months and days of the week. Do not abbreviate *Street, Avenue,* and so on in addresses unless it is necessary to save space in an envelope address.

Always write company names exactly as the company does, abbreviating only when the company abbreviates: Franklin & Co., Inc.; Careers, Incorporated.

Other Uses of the Question Mark and the Exclamation Point

The Question Mark. The question mark is used in the following cases, also:

1. After individual items in a series, each of which may be made into a complete question.

> Are you studying typing? shorthand? accounting?
> What is the capital of Idaho? of Oregon? of New York?
> How much money is needed? How much land? How much effort?

2. After a statement of questionable truth.

> We received the check for $150 (?).

Cautions:

(1) Do not use a question mark to suggest humor or sarcasm.

> Wrong: I have read her courteous (?) letter.

(2) After a request that is actually a "polite command," use a period rather than a question mark.

> Will you please attend to this matter promptly.

(3) Use the period, rather than the question mark, after an *indirect* question.

> I asked him whether he would go.

The Exclamation Point. The exclamation point is used after a single word or a whole expression that shows strong feeling. "Wait! Don't take that road!" (Even though the latter part of this statement is a command, the exclamation point is used to show that strong feeling is intended.)

An interjection standing alone is always followed by the exclamation point. "Oh!" "Behold!" "Alas!" (Interjections comprise the last of the eight parts of speech; however, they have no grammatical values.)

Sentences Ending with Abbreviations. When an abbreviation comes at the end of a declarative or an imperative sentence, the period after the abbreviation ends the sentence. Double periods are never used.

When an abbreviation ends an interrogative or an exclamatory sentence, use the question mark or the exclamation point after the period following the abbreviation.

> Donald will meet you at 4 p.m.
> Will Donald meet you at 4 p.m.?
> Meet Donald at 4 p.m.
> How silly it is to meet at 4 p.m.!

Progress Quiz 9-A. Supply the necessary punctuation and capitalization.

1. what a beautiful autumn day it is
2. travel north three miles if you wish to arrive by 7 pm
3. tom asked her whether she had read the book
4. has dorothy decided to visit yellowstone national park
5. can you be here by 10 am
6. mr johnson was accompanied by miss dawson

Section 9 - Using the Period, Question Mark, and Exclamation Point   **89**

7. she wanted to know when i planned to be in the south
8. kindly send us your check before the first of the month
9. what is the population of iowa of florida of alabama
10. is mrs amy smith working for a phd

Progress Quiz 9-B. Indicate all abbreviations or contractions that should be spelled out.

Dear Mr. Martin:

If you can arrive early on Dec. 5, we shall have a chance to discuss our plans for working with the co. in Ill. This matter will be No. 1 on the agenda for our annual meeting in Jan.

I have written Mrs. Edwards for the 2nd time, but as yet she has not ans'd me. Perhaps if you write her, you will have more luck than I. If you do write, it may be wise to include a stamped, addressed env., for we need her decision by Sat., Dec. 1.

When we meet on Dec. 5, I shall have a no. of new plans to discuss with you.

Sincerely,

Build Your Word Power

Expressing Numbers. Numbers of fewer than three digits should be written in full. Numbers of three or more digits should be written in numerals. The following rules are exceptions to the preceding general rule.

1. Amounts of money should be written in numerals. (In legal documents amounts of money are written in full, and usually included in numerals in parentheses after the spelled-out numbers.)

$25   50 cents $50.25
Two Hundred and Fifty Dollars ($250.00) (*legal form*)

Caution: In a sentence when a single amount does not include cents, do not use a decimal point or two zeros: $25 NOT $25.00

2. Quantities and measurements are usually written in numerals.

10 percent	43 years old
policy No. 34748	9 by 12 feet
96 degrees	160 votes
176 pounds	

3. Hours, minutes, and seconds are expressed in numerals: 9 hours, 45 minutes, 32 seconds. The hour is written in full with *o'clock:* 10:45 a.m. BUT ten o'clock.

4. Page numbers are written in numerals: page 177.

5. Simple fractions are usually written in words: two-thirds BUT 25 2/3.

6. All building numbers except *One* are written in numerals: 137 East Avenue BUT One Madison Avenue.

7. Spell out street names that are numbers through twelve: 155 Twelfth Street BUT 248 13th Avenue, 155 West 42nd Street.

8. Dates: (a) When the day follows the month, use numerals. (b) When the day precedes the month, use numerals with the ending *st, nd, rd,* or *th.* (c) When the day is given without the month, express as in item *b,* or write the number in full: May 24; 24th of May; on the 6th OR on the sixth.*

9. When the first word of a sentence is a number, always write the number in words.

10. When several numbers are used in similar construction, write them all in numerals unless they all contain fewer than three digits: There were 250 women, 20 children, and 9 men.

11. When one number immediately follows another, spell out the smaller number and express the larger in numerals: 150 four-cent stamps.

12. To enumerate each item in a list of words, statements, questions, and so on, use a numeral followed by a period and two spaces.

13. In continuous text, millions and billions may be expressed thus: 150 million; $6.3 billion.

14. Approximations should be written in full: nearly one hundred.

Progress Quiz 9-C. In the following all numbers have been expressed in numerals. Make the necessary corrections.

1. I shall meet him at 3 o'clock on May 28th.
2. She purchased 17 balls of 3-ply yarn at 235 1st Avenue.
3. On the 21 of June he weighed 125 pounds.

---

*The military date style is *30 March 1982.*

4. We counted 8 men, 3 women, and 10 children.
5. Jody gave $50. to the fund, but I could afford to give only $10.00.
6. 30 people requested a refund.
7. Nearly 500 letters reached us on the 15.
8. Colleen lives at 1 Oak Street, and Randy lives at 21 Maple Street.
9. This pen sells for only $.39.
10. More than ½ of the people earned a dividend of 6¼ percent.

Check Your Knowledge

1. Which kinds of sentences are followed by a period?
2. In addition to their use as end-of-sentence punctuation, state one other time when the question mark and the exclamation mark are used.
3. If an abbreviation is the last word in a sentence, is any punctuation needed other than the period following the abbreviation?
4. How are numbers expressed in dates? in addresses?
5. Name three times that numbers must be spelled in full.

Skill Builders

List ten facts that you have learned from your communications course thus far. Make complete statements, punctuate correctly, and spell all words correctly.

Business Speech

Pronounce the *h* in these words: *homage, huge, human, humane, humanity, humble, humid, humidity, humor, humorous.*

Avoid Saying "You know"! Many persons, in conversing, keep interrupting their ideas by saying "You know." This is a bad habit. Note the following; if you leave out "you know" each time it appears, you have a good sentence: "I told him, you know, that I should like to help him, you know, but he didn't believe me, you know, and went away, you know, in a hurry." Don't distract your listeners by using meaningless words!

Spelling

There are many commonly misspelled words for which there are no memory guides. Such words are sometimes called *spelling demons*. Spelling Lists 9 through 12 consist of such words.

Study List 9. (See page 408.)

Study List 9. (See page 408.)

Section

10

USING THE COMMA

In typewritten material one space is usually left after a comma. If a comma follows a word after which you must type closing quotation marks or a parenthesis, do not leave any space after the comma. If a comma is used in a number, do not leave any space after the comma. Never leave a space before a comma.

The Comma Slows You Down. When you see a comma, you tend to slow down. For that reason the comma helps you to express ideas clearly and correctly. If a page did not contain any commas, you would have trouble reading its contents with proper expression. Without expression language is vague and sometimes ambiguous.

Using the Comma Correctly. Before the invention of printing, most punctuation was unknown. As our present system of punctuation evolved, many writers became especially fond of the comma. If you examine some of the writing of the eighteenth and nineteenth centuries, you will notice that many of the sentences are very long and contain many commas. Today we use shorter words and shorter sentences. We use commas only when necessary but should not omit them when they are necessary.

Your state highway department provides "Slow" signs for definite reasons. The comma is a "Slow" sign, and you should know the reasons for its use.

Rules for Using the Comma Correctly (First Part)

Correct writing requires commas in the following cases:

1. To separate words, phrases, and clauses in a series of three or more.*

Words: The clerk needs pens, pencils, paper, and ink.
Phrases: Look under the sofa, over the cabinet, and in the trunk.
Clauses: He knew that she was young, that she was beautiful, and that she was popular.

2. To separate the two clauses of a compound sentence. (The comma is placed before the coordinating conjunctions *and, but, or,* and so on.) If the sentence is very short, the comma is omitted.

Robert saw her leave the house, and I saw her enter the office.
She went but I remained.

Caution: Do not use a comma to separate the two parts of a compound predicate. "She took the basket and walked down the road." "Send the letter to Tom but keep the invoice yourself."

3. To set off the name of a person directly addressed. (In the middle of a sentence, an element is set off by placing a comma before and after it.)

I assure you, Maria, that I shall do my best.

4. To set off an expression in apposition.

Jack, the captain of the team, talked with Mr. Day, the coach.

---

*British usage usually does not require a comma before *and* in a series.

Caution: Do not set off a word in close (restrictive) apposition.

> The philosopher Socrates was a Greek.
> My sister Helen is a rapid thinker.
> *Note:* His wife, Jane, has left.

5. To separate the parts of dates.*

> We first met on Monday, July 10, 1981, in Hartford.

6. To set off a state name after a city name.

> The order from Akron, Ohio, reached us today.

7. To set off explanatory terms in the names of persons or firms.

> *Jr., Sr.; Inc. (Incorporated); Ltd. (Limited).*
> Mr. George Markham, Jr., is the new treasurer.
> She works for Dawson, Inc., of North Carolina.

8. To set off an introductory expression containing a verb form. Such an expression may be an adverbial clause, a participial phrase, an infinitive phrase, or a participle. (Many adverbial clauses coming first in a sentence begin with *after, although, if, when, while.*)

> Having stayed up late, she was tired today. (participial phrase)
> To be sure of his accuracy, check each bill. (infinitive phrase)
> Exhausted, he could not travel any farther. (participle)
> When winter comes to the city, I remain at home. (adverbial clause)

Caution: Prepositional phrases coming first in a sentence are usually not followed by a comma. If the phrase contains five or more words, however, it may be followed by a comma. "In the spring I shall see you."

9. To set off a nonrestrictive participial phrase. (A *nonrestrictive* element is one that is not needed for the complete sense of a sentence.)

> Ms. Brown, having read the report, left the room. (nonrestrictive)
> Every person owning a car is invited to the picnic. (restrictive)

---

*When only the month and year are given, no commas are needed—*May 1982.*

10. To set off nonrestrictive clauses.

Mr. Fiske, who is my neighbor, won the trophy. (nonrestrictive)
Anyone who is honest deserves to succeed. (restrictive)
Please let the book stay where he put it. (restrictive)
I shall see you in Denver, where I hope the weather will be good. (nonrestrictive)

Progress Quiz 10-A. Insert all necessary commas.

1. After he had filed the letters bills and other papers he typed two more letters three memos and several statements.
2. Mr. Foxe the new office manager knows Beatrice McLaine who worked for your uncle.
3. Don't tell anyone my secret even though you may wish to do so.
4. Her brother Paul gave a talk about the Alamo which is located in San Antonio Texas.
5. Meet Robert Quick Jr. on Tuesday April 19 in Albany New York.
6. I told him that any man who wins this prize will be lucky.
7. To gain promotion you must deserve it.
8. Rose Bush who wrote this essay lives in Portland Oregon.
9. If you are willing to go I shall let them know.
10. Ms. Flax has typed ten letters but Mr. Martin has finished only six.

Rules for Using the Comma Correctly (Second Part)

11. To set off parenthetical expressions. (A parenthetical expression is one that interrupts the thought of a sentence and is not necessary for its sense. Some parenthetical words are *however, moreover, nevertheless, therefore, though.* Some parenthetical phrases are *as a result, of course, in addition.* If a parenthetical word immediately follows the subject or a form of the verbs *to be* or *to have*, the comma usually is not needed.)

> I told him, therefore, that I would not go.
> These people, as you know, are not satisfied.
> We therefore hope that you are correct. (commas not needed)
> She has therefore left our company. (commas not needed)

12. To set off *Yes, No,* and mild interjections at the beginning of a sentence.

> No, I don't agree with your ideas this time.
> Oh, how I wish you would stop that noise!

13. To set off *also, too,* and *either* to show emphasis.

> Your uncle, too, will be asked to participate.
> Chris has not seen the car, either.

14. To set off internal phrases beginning with such expressions as *as well as, including, together with, such as.**

> Eve Crowley, as well as her husband Paul, will be here.
> Order some fruit, such as grapes and pears, for the party.
> Your manuscript, including the index, is now typed.

15. To indicate an omitted word.

> She played the piano; he, the violin. (This sentence may also be written: She played the piano, he the violin.)

16. To separate two or more adjectives modifying the same noun. (If the word *and* can be substituted for the comma, the comma is correct; if *and* cannot be substituted, a comma is not needed.)

> She is a helpful, kind, friendly girl.
> He spoke to the young French waiter.

Caution: A comma does not follow an adjective coming immediately before the noun.

> Wrong: He is a tall, husky, lad.
> Right: He is a tall, husky lad.

17. To separate a conjunctive adverb preceded by a semicolon. (Some common conjunctive adverbs are *therefore, however, namely, for example, that is.*)

> He wanted to remain; however, I told him to leave.
> Supply an action sketch: that is, provide a picture with a person in it.

Caution: Many words that are conjunctive adverbs may also be used parenthetically.

> They told me, however, that I could not go. (parenthetical)
> They told me to eat; however, I refused to touch a morsel. (conjunctive adverb)

---

*When *such as* introduces a restrictive expression, do not use any commas: "A man such as he is needed."

18. To separate two contrasting expressions.

Use a sharp pencil, not a dull one.
The more you eat, the more you want.

19. To separate a short question from a preceding statement.

He has already visited you, hasn't he?

20. To indicate thousands in numerals containing four or more digits.

5,000 *   10,000   200,000   1,500,000

Caution: A comma is never used in numbers of insurance policies, buildings, or pages.

21. To prevent misreading.

Long before, she had told me about that brief meeting.
At six, fifteen guests appeared at the door.
Shortly after, he came into the room.

22. After the salutation and complimentary closing of friendly letters. (The comma may also be used after the salutation of business letters when the person's first name is used. The comma is used after the complimentary closing with some styles of business letters.)

Dear Sally,   Dear Fred,   Your friend,   Sincerely yours,

Progress Quiz 10-B. Punctuate these sentences.

1. She told me nevertheless that I was wrong.
2. Yes I think this is your hat Mr. Byrd.
3. I wanted to go; nevertheless I had to stay here and study.
4. He purchased a new blue sweater from the friendly eager salesclerk.
5. The longer you sleep the more tired you become.
6. Read something worthwhile such as a good novel or play.
7. Shortly after the girl brought me her book.
8. Elated she started to sing and dance.
9. Thomas having seen the accident reported it to the police.
10. This new book which has a red cover will be put on display.

---

*Some writers do not use a comma unless there are five or more digits.

Comma Pointers

Here are eight pointers for using the comma correctly:

1. Do not use a comma before *so that*.

> She worked quietly so that she would not disturb the others.

2. Set off an adverbial clause following *that* in the middle of a sentence.

> I told him that, if he is late, I shall not wait for him.

3. Do not use a comma after a single adverb coming first in the sentence. Parenthetical expressions and enumerations coming first, however, are followed by commas.

> Recently we have received several new applications.
> For example, bring along several good books. (parenthetical)
> First, be sure that your material is waterproof. (enumeration)

4. Set off an entire absolute phrase. (An absolute phrase consists of a noun followed by a participial phrase, neither of which has a direct grammatical connection with any other word in the sentence.)

> *The bear having frightened us,* we ran away. (absolute phrase)
> The bear, *having frightened us,* seemed pleased. (participial phrase)

5. A clause introduced by *because* or *since* may be either restrictive or nonrestrictive. Observe these examples:

> (a) I know that he works well because Alice says he does. (Restrictive)
> (b) I know that he works well, because Alice says he does. (Nonrestrictive)
> (c) He has known me since I was five years old. (Restrictive)
> (d) He will be late, since he must stop at the market. (Nonrestrictive)
>
> In (a) the meaning is this: He works well only because Alice says he does.
> In (b) the meaning is this: Alice's word can be trusted; if she says that he works well, he does work well.

6. If the comma is omitted before *and* at the end of a series, the meaning may not be clear. This sentence is not clear: "My suite consists of a living room, kitchen, bathroom with shower and patio." (When a comma is placed before *and,* the meaning is perfectly clear.)

7. When *with* begins a phrase, it is often necessary to set off the phrase with commas.

She ran down the street, with the dog racing after her.
Tom, with his two brothers, is going to Denver.

8. The comma is used to show the logical arrangement of elements in a sentence. Note the following:

Wrong: He is as tall as, if not taller, than I.
Wrong: He is as tall, if not taller, than I.
Right: He is as tall as I, if not taller.
Right: He is as tall as, if not taller than, I am.

Progress Quiz 10-C. Supply all necessary commas.

1. Tom having surprised us we prepared for our next move. 2. The boss said that if I wanted to leave early I must obtain my supervisor's permission. 3. Check your work so that you will be sure it is accurate clear and complete. 4. Since I have not seen him in five years I do not know whether I shall recognize him. 5. Slowly she rose from her seat walked across the room and pointed at Ray. 6. Mrs. Roberts realizing that she was fighting a losing battle finally admitted defeat. 7. The athlete who broke the world's record is one of the persons who live in Los Angeles. 8. This hotel is known for its large rooms with TV baths with showers and friendly service. 9. The price including tax amounts to $10. 10. Ms. Freeman too has been asked to inspect the Western Bank San Francisco.

Build Your Word Power

Both. Do not use *both* with the words *between, alike, at once, equal,* or *equally.* These two sentences are correct:

Both you and I are to blame.
You and I are equally to blame.

Else. Do not use *else* with *but* or *except.*

Wrong: No one else but me was there.
Right: No one but me was there.
Right: I was alone there.
Right: No one else was there.

When *else* follows *everybody, somebody,* and so on in a possessive idea, use *else's.* "Nobody else's paper is ready."

Size. *Size* is a noun; *sized* is an adjective. The noun, however, may be used in forming compound adjectives: "large-size dress" or "large-sized dress." Use *of* after *size* in expressions such as "this size *of* box."

Each. (a) *Each* used as a subject requires a singular predicate and a singular personal pronoun. (b) When *each* comes between a subject and predicate, the predicate and personal pronouns are plural. (c) When *each* follows the predicate, the personal pronoun is singular.

(a) *Each* of the girls *is* to bring *her* books.
(b) The girls *each have their* own books.
(c) The girls are responsible *each* for *her* own books.

Note: Each other and *one another* are singular, even when possessive.

The two boys looked at *each other's* books.
The three boys looked at *one another's* books.

Had better. Had rather. The idiomatic verb *had better* is followed by the present or the present perfect. "He had better go." "He had better have gone." The verb *had rather* requires the same usage. Avoid saying "would better" and "would rather."

No such. Follow *no such* with a noun or an adjective.

Wrong: No such a plant exists.
Wrong: No such of a plant exists.
Right: No such plant exists.

Check Your Knowledge

1. Which elements coming first in a sentence are always followed by a comma?
2. Explain what is meant by the expression *to set off.*
3. What is a nonrestrictive element? How is it punctuated?
4. What is a parenthetical expression? How is it punctuated?
5. When is a comma needed before *and?*

Skill Builders

Rewrite the following letter, supplying all necessary punctuation and capitalization. Correct all errors in punctuation and capitalization.

Dear Jack;

When I saw you in Cleveland last month I forgot to tell you that one of your former bosses Bill Davis is looking for a manager for his new branch in the east. Would your brother, Paul be interested? If you think he might be please have him write Mr. Davis.

I have already checked the maps pamphlets and folders you sent me. I am sure Jack that we can improve them. However if we are to do so we must be ready to spend some additional money. Johnson Printers Inc. which is located in Houston Texas can do a good inexpensive job, for us. After you have given this matter further consideration. Please write me.

As soon as I hear from the Davis company I shall wire you.

Sincerely,

Business Speech

Be sure to accent the correct syllable of the following words. Learn the definitions of all unfamiliar words.

ACCENT FIRST SYLLABLE	ACCENT SECOND SYLLABLE
1. impious (IM-pee-us)	1. municipal (mu-NIS-ipl)
2. infamous (IN-fa-mus)	2. acumen (a-KU-men)
3. impotent (IM-po-tent)	3. plebeian (ple-BEE-'n)
4. champion (CHAM-pee-'n)	4. robust (ro-BUST)
5. influence (IN-flu-ence)	5. remonstrate (re-MON-strate)

Spelling

Study List 10, which consists of words for which there is no memory guide. If you type or write such words ten times each, you will tend to learn them faster! List 10 is on page 408.

USING THE COLON, SEMICOLON, AND DASH

In typing sentences, leave two spaces after the colon and one space after the semicolon. The dash is usually made by typing two hyphens without a space before or after. Printers call this kind of dash an *em dash*. The dash is sometimes expressed by typing one hyphen with a space before it and a space after it. This style, however, is not preferred.

Using the Colon

The colon indicates that more material follows. The material that follows may be an expansion, an explanation, a question, or a restatement. When a series of items follows the colon, each item may be numbered or lettered —for example, (1), (2), and so on, or (a), (b), and so on. Always use both parentheses!

Use the colon in the following cases:

1. After a statement introducing information that is to follow.

> You must meet these four requirements:
> The following items will be on sale:
> Here are your supplies: erasers, envelopes, and stamps.

Caution: The colon is used after a complete thought. Do not use a colon after most verbs or after a preposition. (A colon is used after a verb that introduces a long quotation.)

2. Before a long or formal appositive. A dash may be used instead of the colon in this case.

> I have three tables: one for writing, another for painting, and a third for eating.

3. Before a statement or question that explains a preceding statement.*

It's up to you to decide: Which is the better course to take?
Over the door hung the sign: Don't scare the dog.
He has a new job: he is an advertising copywriter.

4. Before a long quotation.

The speaker cleared her throat and began: (Several paragraphs of
direct quotation follow.)

5. To separate the figures for hours and minutes, as 9:15 a.m. Some timetables use the period.

6. After the salutation with some styles of business letters.

Dear Mr. Carston: Gentlemen:

Caution: Never use the semicolon (;) after a salutation.

7. To separate the two parts of identification initials at the end of a business letter. (The first initials are the dictator's; the second initials are the secretary's.) The virgule (/) may be used in place of the colon.

JKL:ert *or* JKL/ert

Using the Semicolon

The semicolon is sometimes called a *heavy comma,* since it usually indicates a stronger break than that required by the comma.

The semicolon is used in the following cases:

1. Between the two parts of a compound sentence when the conjunction is not expressed.

You type the letter; I shall type the bill.
John typed the letter; Mary, the bill.†

---

*Capitalize the first word of a question following a colon. Capitalize the first word of a following statement if the statement is an independent thought. If the statement is a close explanation, do not capitalize the first word.

† This sentence may be punctuated differently: "John typed the letter, Mary the bill."

2. Before a conjunctive adverb. (Observe that a comma follows the conjunctive adverb.)

> She was late; consequently, she missed the speech.

Caution: When the clause following the conjunctive adverb is long, it is usually better to use two sentences.

> She was late for the meeting. Therefore, she did not hear the principal speaker when he made several statements about her.

3. Before expressions such as *as, for example, that is,* and *namely* when a complete statement follows them. If what follows is not a complete statement, use the dash.* A comma always follows such expressions.

> This is an automated machine; that is, it possesses a "memory."
> For this job you need one thing—that is, a good memory.

4. Before the coordinating conjunction in a compound or compound-complex sentence when one or more of the clauses are punctuated with commas.

> If she is invited, she will come; but since she has been ill, perhaps you should not invite her.

5. After each complete unit in a series in which a comma or commas are used within each unit of the series.

> She visited Canton, Ohio; Albany, New York; and Bangor, Maine.

Using the Dash

The dash indicates special emphasis or an interruption in thought. The dash is used in the following cases:

1. To indicate a sudden break or change in thought.

> He might have succeeded—but why think of that now?
> The men who worked—and many did—deserve our praise.†

---

* Some writers always use the semicolon before such expressions; however, the modern trend is to use the dash before partial statements. The abbreviation of *for example* is *e.g.;* of *that is, i.e.;* of *namely, viz.* Such abbreviations should be avoided in business writing.

† Some writers use parentheses, rather than dashes, in a sentence of this type. Dashes, however, indicate greater emphasis.

2. After a series coming first in a sentence when the series is later explained.

> Red, yellow, and blue—these are the primary colors.

3. Before an appositive (a) that is the same word as the one with which it is in apposition or (b) that is the word *one*.

> He sent me a special report—the Dowson report.
> Here is a good book—one that you will enjoy.

4. Before and after a compound appositive.

> Three subjects—typing, English, and speech—are required.

5. Before and after an appositive expression containing a comma or commas.

> This machine—Model 212, which is reduced in price—has proved popular with farmers.

6. Before an appositive or appositives at the end of a sentence.

> One element is more necessary than food—water.
> Here are the winners—Tom Bright and Lucy Smart.

7. Before such expressions as *for example, that is,* and *namely* when a complete statement does not follow.

> Discuss an electronic typewriter—for example, the Lanier.

8. To separate an author's name from a quotation from his or her writing.

> "A small leak can sink a great ship."—Franklin

Caution: Use the dash wisely. Many writers tend to overuse it, causing their writing to lack unity and clearness. Some advertising copywriters tend to overuse the dash for special emphasis. If you use the dash wisely, it will be as effective as a speaker's use of a gesture or a pause.

Progress Quiz 11-A. Supply all the necessary punctuation.

1. The three cheerleaders Sue Whitman Tom Hartland and Ken Bunker won merit awards
2. If you can be present I shall be delighted but if you cannot attend I shall understand

3. Ask her to requisition these items typewriter ribbons calendar pads and pencil sharpeners
4. Make up your mind how do you want to travel by plane or train
5. You will need one more ingredient salt
6. This is beautiful furniture furniture anyone would like to have in the home
7. Draw a tropical fruit for example the papaya
8. Gerald has failed in one respect that is he has not been punctual
9. Alice discussed swimming I discussed boating
10. Frank Jentry who is usually slow typed faster than I today

Progress Quiz 11-B. Correct all errors in punctuation.

1. Recommend a lightweight coat; one that I can wear, at the beach.
2. The message on the door read gone to lunch.
3. The cities to be discussed are: New York; Buffalo and Cincinnati
4. You must do one more thing, finish the work in this tray.
5. Technique, speed and accuracy: these are necessary for good typing.
6. Meet me at 8/30 p.m. on January 6; if you possibly can
7. This typewriter, an inexpensive, efficient, attractive, machine, is for sale.
8. You need three changes of clothing; one for street wear, one for formal occasions; and one for hiking.
9. I showed her the suits, coats and dresses, but when she had seen them all she could not decide, which ones she preferred.
10. I told him consequently that he was wrong, but if he heard me he did not say anything.

Build Your Word Power

Note the following examples of correct usage:

WRONG	RIGHT
Can't help but think	Can't help thinking
Doubt but what	Doubt that
As for my part	As for me *or* For my part
Reason is because	Reason is that
Convince someone to	Convince someone that

WRONG	RIGHT
Persuade someone that	Persuade someone to
Each and every	Every
Had ought; hadn't ought	Ought; ought not
In regards to	Regarding, in regard to
On the (an) average of	About, almost
Right along	Directly, at once
Right away	Immediately

Progress Quiz 11-C. Correct all examples of poor usage.

1. The reason for her absence was because she was ill.
2. I convinced him to do the job when I told him that his work is equally as good.
3. In regards to your letter, she couldn't help but think that you were trying to be sarcastic.
4. As for my part, I tried to convince Ruth that she should audition.
5. He takes dictation on an average of an hour each day.
6. If you see him right away, both of you can go right along.
7. She hadn't ought to say them things.
8. I don't doubt but what each and every clerk need a vacation.
9. Do you agree that Timothy had ought to see the play?
10. He don't know how to repair that there engine.

Check Your Knowledge

Answer with True or False.

1. The colon is more commonly used than the comma.

2. The dash indicates emphasis or an interruption.

3. The semicolon can usually replace the dash.

4. The semicolon is often used after the salutation of a letter.

5. In typewritten work leave two spaces after the colon.

Skill Builders

In writing business letters, always be sure to express each thought completely. Rewrite the following letter so that each thought will be complete. Correct the one verb error.

Dear Miss Swensen:

      After I saw Mr. Clayton at the meeting. I told him that you are interested in selling your cottage. Which is located near his present summer home. He seemed interested in this information, he will probably telephone you soon.

      If I may be of further help. Please let me know.

                  Sincerely,

Business Speech

In all the following words *g* is pronounced like *j*. Learn all meanings.

1. generic	3. gesture	5. longitude
2. gesticulate	4. gist	6. turgid

Note: When *gill* refers to a liquid measurement, the *g* sounds like *j*. When *gill* refers to an organ of a fish, the *g* is hard, as in *good*.

Spelling

Study List 11 (page 408), which contains more of the words most frequently misspelled.

Section
12
USING OTHER PUNCTUATION MARKS

Quotation marks, parentheses, ellipses, brackets, and the virgule are the least frequently used punctuation marks. You should, however, know how to apply the rules governing their use.*

Using Quotation Marks

Use quotation marks in the following cases:

1. To enclose a direct quotation. (A *direct* quotation consists of the actual words of a speaker or writer. An *indirect* quotation expresses the thought, rather than the actual words, of a speaker or writer and does not require quotation marks.)

> "Let us plan," he said, "to spend a week in California." (direct)
> He said that we should spend a week in California. (indirect)

Cautions: (1) If a quotation consists of several sentences, use quotation marks before the first sentence and after the last sentence.

> She said, "The morale of the workers is good. We should do whatever we can to keep it that way. Good morale boosts production."

(2) When a quotation consists of more than one paragraph, place quotation marks at the beginning of each paragraph and at the end of the last paragraph.

2. To enclose the titles of magazine articles, short stories, and chapters or sections of published works. (Remember that the titles of books, essays, newspapers, magazines, plays and other complete publications are italicized.† On the typewriter italics are shown by underscoring.)

---

*The apostrophe is not a punctuation mark; rather, it is a spelling device. The hyphen is also a spelling device.

† To display titles, publishers often type them in full capitals, without underscoring.

For her lecture, "Word Processing in Today's Business World," she consulted Brown's *Electronics Today,* Chapter XI.

"Poultry and Success" is an article that appears in the April issue of *Farming Journal.*

Poe's "The Black Cat" appears in *Great Tales.*

3. To enclose unusual terms used in a special way.

This great computer is called a "giant brain."

Note: To indicate quotation marks within a quotation, use single quotation marks. (With the typewriter the single quotation mark is made by striking the apostrophe.)

Bob said, "I have read Chapter II, 'Endorsing Checks.'"

4. To indicate a slang expression.

Maybe you think he is a "bonehead," but I like him.

Hints for Quoting Material. In writing term papers, theses, and so on, it is often necessary to quote from reference works. If your quotation is longer than one sentence, do not use quotation marks; rather, single-space it and indent it at both right and left.

Whenever you quote material you should type a footnote (usually at the bottom of the page) stating the source of the quotation. Before quoting more than one or two sentences, you should obtain written permission from the publisher of the work from which you wish to quote. The writer who quotes the words of others, pretending the material is original, is guilty of *plagiarism*—stealing literary material. Plagiarism is an offense subject to legal action in the courts and to disciplinary action in schools and colleges.

Using Parentheses

Use parentheses in the following cases:

1. To set off explanatory, directional, or supplementary expressions.

This device (see the enclosed brochure) is copyrighted.

2. To set off an expression that interrupts the main thought. (Some writers use dashes for this purpose, since dashes indicate greater emphasis.)

> He will be there (I am sure of it) by eight o'clock.
> He will be there—I am sure of it—by eight o'clock.

3. To enclose letters or numerals that enumerate items run into the text. Use *two* parentheses!

> The class is in three sections: (1) beginners, (2) intermediate, and (3) advanced. Note: (a), (b), and (c) may be used.

4. To enclose an amount in numerals following the same amount in words. This device should be used in legal letters and legal documents only. Observe that each word is capitalized and that two zeros follow the decimal point.

> We shall pay her Two Hundred Dollars ($200.00). (*Legal*)

Using Ellipses

Ellipses, sometimes called *omission marks,* indicate that material has been omitted. They are expressed by three periods with spaces between. If ellipses end a sentence, add a fourth period.

Ellipses are most commonly used to indicate omissions in quoted material.

> "Plough deep . . . and you will have corn to sell and keep."—Franklin

Note: The preceding quotation is a short one. Although ellipses can be used in short quotations, they are more commonly used in long ones.

Using Brackets

Brackets are used in the following cases:

1. To enclose material of an editorial nature—material not part of the author's text.

The law of that state [Louisiana] is based on the Napoleonic Code.

2. To enclose the word *sic* (meaning *thus it is*), which indicates that the preceding error in spelling or grammar is in the work quoted and that it is not the error of the writer who is quoting it.

Speak respectively [*sic*] of your elders.

3. On library index cards, to enclose information that does not appear on the title page of the book represented.

A tale of two cities [by] Charles Dickens [1962]. (Librarians capitalize only the first word of a title and do not underscore the title.)

Using the Virgule

The virgule is commonly called the *diagonal*, the *slash*, or the *oblique*. The virgule is used in the following cases:

1. To separate the parts of the date on certain business forms, such as invoices.

1/8/83 (This means January 8, 1983; however, in many nations it means August 1, 1983.)

2. To separate the parts of split years—for example, 1982/1983. A split year does not extend from January of one year through December of the next; it can begin at any time during a calendar year and run into the following year. Although 1982-1983 should indicate two full calendar years, in the United States we tend to use the hyphen to indicate split years. Many European writers, however, use the virgule to indicate split years.
3. To separate the parts of certain abbreviations—for example, W/B (waybill).
4. To indicate the ends of lines of poetry that are run in.

The world stands out on either side,/No wider than the heart is wide./Above the world is stretched the sky,/No higher than the soul is high./—Millay

The Order of Punctuation Marks

Quotation Marks with Other Marks

(1) Period and Comma — always come inside double or single quotes.*

(2) Question Mark and Exclamation Point — come *inside* quotes if the quoted material is a question or an exclamation, *outside* quotes if the quoted material is not a question or an exclamation.

(3) Colon and Semicolon — come outside the quotation marks.

EXAMPLES

(1) I have read the timely article "How to Make Money."
Your article, "Living and Learning," will be reprinted.
Paul said, "She called her brother a 'blockhead.' "

(2) Joyce asked, "Have the letters been typed?"
Did she say, "All these letters must be typed"?
"Stop!" he shouted, and then said, "Wait for me, please." †

(3) We have seen the article "Wonders of Science"; but since you have not, I shall save it for you.‡

Parentheses and Other Marks

If a punctuation mark applies to the material in parentheses, the mark is placed inside the ending parenthesis. If it does not apply to the material in parentheses, the mark is placed immediately after the ending parenthesis.

When I heard his question (he asked, "Where is Lucy?"), I became frightened.
Her project was finished on Monday (see Schedule 3).

---

*Quotation marks are commonly called *quotes.*

† A comma or period never follows a question mark or an exclamation point.

‡ Sometimes an interrupted quotation ends with a semicolon; if the semicolon is a part of the actual quotation, place it inside the quotes. Since *article* is a restrictive appositive, no comma follows it.

The period following an abbreviation comes before any other punctuation mark. If an abbreviation ends a sentence, do not use two periods.

> I heard him calling you at 8:30 a.m.
> Did he call you at 8:30 a.m.?
> Theresa Billings, Ed.D., who read your letter, is interested.

Spacing Pointers

You have already learned the rules for spacing with most punctuation marks. Here are a few further spacing rules:

1. Do not space before or after a period used as a decimal point— *5.038.*

2. Do not space before or after a hyphen in a word—*well-known man.*

3. Do not space before or after an apostrophe within a word: *didn't, Shirley's.*

4. Do not space after a beginning parenthesis or bracket.

5. Do not space before a closing parenthesis or bracket.

6. Do not space after opening quotes.

7. Do not space before closing quotes.

8. Do not space before or after a dash.

Build Your Word Power

Here are some expressions that should be mastered. The two expressions in each group have the same sound but different spellings and meanings.

all together	Grouped in one place.	Place them all together.
altogether	Entirely, completely.	You are altogether wrong.
all ready	Completely prepared.	We are all ready to go.
already	Previously.	We have already done it.

any one	One of several.	Any one of us can tell you.
anyone	Anybody.	Anyone can tell you.
every day	Each day.	Work hard every day.
everyday	Usual, routine.	It is suitable for everyday use.
may be	Possibly am, is, are.	You may be right.
maybe	Perhaps.	Maybe he will arrive early.
some one	One of several.	Some one of them will win.
someone	Somebody.	Someone called you today.

Note: Alright—All right. All right is the preferred spelling.
Cannot is always spelled as one word.

Progress Quiz 12-A. Supply all the necessary punctuation and capitals.

1. Did Mr Tomlin say John I shall expect your answer by 9:30 a.m.
2. The article on page 18 how to see new york is good I admit but since I am not going to new york it isnt of much interest to me
3. Charles Shih said this Janet has reported on your article investing your money
4. His remarks see the attached sheet are worthy of further attention don't you agree
5. The ruling affects these four nations 1 france 2 italy 3 spain 4 england
6. Barbara inquired who filed Smith Companys correspondence in this drawer
7. The invoice was dated 5 4 82 wasnt it he asked
8. He answered yes i think you are right but then added however i wont back you up
9. The two women Barbara Lutz and Betty Morley will be promoted he said because they are deserving of advancement
10. The weather in the west is excellent in the summer and I know that when you visit that part of the country you will agree with me

Progress Quiz 12-B. Correct all types of errors.

1. Someone of the technicians maybe willing to do the job everyday.
2. It maybe that you have all ready wrote him.
3. They were altogether wrong, as any one of us could see.
4. Is it alright to send them all together in this package?
5. Anyone of you could of done this every day task, but Nancy maybe the best one for it.

Check Your Knowledge

1. Which punctuation marks are always put inside quotes?
2. Where are quotes put when a quotation consists of several paragraphs?
3. What are two uses of brackets?
4. On an invoice what would 10/21/83 mean?
5. What two institutions might pass judgment on a writer guilty of plagiarism?
6. "Hurry to work and don't be late again." Is a comma needed before *and?* Explain.

Business Speech

Learn the pronunciation of these words containing *ch.* Remember that you are responsible for locating and learning the definitions of all unfamiliar words.

ch sounds like *k:*   (1) archaic, (2) archeology, (3) archives, (4) chameleon, (5) chaos, (6) chaotic, (7) charisma, (8) chasm, (9) chord.

ch sounds like *sh:*   (1) chagrined (accent second syllable); (2) chaise longue (SHAYZ LONG); (3) chamois (SHAMMY); (4) chandelier; (5) chef; (6) chartreuse; (7) chevron; (8) chic (SHEEK).

Spelling

Study List 12 (page 408), which consists of ten of the words most commonly misspelled.

Unit Four

KNOWING THE RIGHT WORDS

HOMONYMS AND SIMILAR WORDS

Mark Twain said that the difference between the right word and nearly the right word is like the difference between lightning and the lightning bug. In speaking and writing, make your language powerful by using the correct specific words.

A certain young woman, armed with her college diploma, went job hunting with a high degree of confidence. Her college grades had been good, and she had been a popular student. During her first job interview, she was given a test—one on which she did good work except in the vocabulary section. She did not receive the job.

Successful persons know how to use words. They usually have command of a large vocabulary, too. This does not mean that you should use only "ten-dollar words." Rather, use language that your listeners and readers will understand readily.

By using words correctly and by constantly striving to increase your vocabulary, you take a necessary—and important—step toward a successful business career.

Homonyms—Words That Sound Like Other Words

A *homonym* is a word that sounds like another word or other words but is spelled differently and has a different meaning.*

Here are some homonyms that you should know: *hear, here; their, there; wait, weight; some, sum; loan, lone; know, no; so, sew, sow; weak, week*. If you do not know the meaning of each of those words, consult a reliable dictionary.

---

*A few of the words included as homonyms, such as *for, fore,* and *four,* do not have identical sounds. Since many persons pronounce such words alike, however, they have been presented with the information on homonyms.

Affect, Effect; Principal, Principle. The four words *affect, effect, principal,* and *principle* cause many errors.

Affect is always a verb, meaning *to influence* or *to have an influence on.**

Effect as a verb means *to bring about.* As a noun *effect* means *result.*

Principal as a noun means *head of a school, amount of money,* or the *chief person.* As an adjective *principal* means *chief* or *main.*

Principle is always a noun, meaning *rule.* The rule may be either written or stated, or it may be an accepted moral rule.

EXAMPLES

affect	Will cold weather affect your plans?
effect (verb)	We shall effect a few changes soon.
effect (noun)	This will have a good effect on the employees.
principal (noun)	The principal of the school has a principal of $500.
principal (adj.)	This is the principal street in our city.
principle	Learn this principle of grammar.

Progress Quiz 13-A. Correct any misspelled homonyms.

1. The some of for dollars will not be here in time.
2. Will this paving job effect the principle street?
3. The principle says that he will affect a few changes next weak.
4. What was the affect of the principle's speech?
5. Please accept the lone offered Mrs. Chaikin, the principal.
6. It is against my principles to deal with dishonest people.
7. The principle rule appears on this page.
8. Do you know what the effect will be if the farmer sews the seed to soon?
9. As the principle in this case, she will effect the other persons.
10. He has affected a new schedule, and the students have told there parents about it.

Other Homonyms To Be Learned

allowed. Permitted.
aloud. Loudly. (*Aloud* is preferable to *out loud.*)

---

*As an adjective *affected* means *assumed artificially,* as "an affected man" (one who puts on airs); or *pretended,* as "his affected illness." As a verb *affected* also means *pretended,* as "He affected illness."

altar. Structure for worship.
alter. To change.

ascent. A climbing; way going up.
assent. Agreement; to agree.

aural. Pertaining to the ear or hearing.
oral. Pertaining to the mouth or speech.

bail. Dip water out of; post a bond. (Boats and prisoners are bailed.)
bale. Tie in a bundle. (Paper and hay are baled.)

bare. Without covering; plain.
bear. Animal; to carry; to produce; to endure with patience.

berth. A bunk on a ship or railway; an allotted space.
birth. Act of being born.

born. Brought into existence.
borne. Carried. (Past participle of the verb *bear*.)

brake. Device for stopping motion.
break. To separate into parts.

breach. A broken place; a violation.
breech. Back end of a gun; the rear.

calendar. Tabular yearly schedule.
calender. Machine for pressing materials.

canvas. A heavy cloth.
canvass. To solicit.

capital. Money; city that is a seat of government.
capitol. Chief government building.

chord. Group of musical notes.
cord. A string or rope; tendon or nerve.

core. Innermost part.
corps. Organized group of persons. (Plural is spelled the same but pronounced "korz.")

cite. To quote; to mention.
sight. Sense of seeing; a view; to see.
site. Location.

coarse. Rough in texture.
course. Series of studies; direction of progress.

complement. That which completes; to complete.
compliment. An expression of admiration; to express admiration.

council. An assembly; a governing body.
counsel. Advice; to advise; a lawyer.*

dyeing. Act of coloring with dye.
dying. Act of ceasing to live.

fair. Honest; light-complexioned; average, as *fair* grades; a festival or exhibition of wares, livestock, etc.
fare. Price of transportation; to experience.

faze. To worry. (Usually in the negative.)
phase. Aspect.

for. In consideration of which something is done.
fore. The part that is first.
four. One more than three.

forth. Forward or onward.
fourth. The ordinal of *four*.

foreword. Opening message, similar to preface, in a book.
forward. Onward.

gibe. To jeer at; a sarcastic remark.
jibe (followed by *with*). To match.

its. Possessive of it.
it's. Contraction of *it is*.

lead (pronounced *led*). A metal.
led. Guided; directed.

lessen. To decrease.
lesson. That which is learned.

loath. Reluctant.
loathe. To hate.

marshal. A law officer.
martial. Pertaining to war or military life.

---

*Consul is pronounced "kon's'l." A *consul* is an official representative of a foreign nation.

mean. Contemptible; to intend.
mien. Demeanor; pertaining to one's bearing.

medal. Piece of metal having a design.
meddle. To interfere.

miner. One who works in a mine.
minor. One under the age of majority; less important; type of musical scale.

pain. Distress; ache.
pane. A section of glass.

pair. Two. (Plural is *pairs.*)
pare. To peel; to cut off.

passed. Went by; to have gone by.
past. A former time; pertaining to a former time; by.

peace. Tranquillity.
piece. A fragment or part; to put parts together.

pedal. A foot lever; to use a foot lever.
peddle. Sell from place to place.

peer. To look curiously; one of the same rank.
pier. Landing structure built out into the water.

pore. To read studiously; small opening on the skin surface.
pour. To cause to flow.

presence. Act of being present.
presents. Gifts. (In law *presents* means *facts,* as in *"Know all men by these presents."*)

rain. Condensed vapor.
reign. To rule, as a king; the period of a royal ruler.
rein. To check or stop; the strap of a bridle.

raise. To elevate.
raze. To demolish.

rap. To strike; a knock. (Do not use *rap* to mean *talk!*)
wrap. To cover or envelop; an outer garment.

review. To reexamine; a reexamination.
revue. A medley of songs and dances.

shear. To cut, as a sheep's wool.
sheer. Very thin or transparent; unqualified.

stationary. Fixed in position.
stationery. Writing paper.

stake. Piece of wood, a post; that which is risked or may be gained; financial backing.
steak. A slice of meat or fish.

steal. Take what belongs to another. (*Steal away* is an idiom meaning *go quietly*.)
steel. Commercial form of iron.

to. Toward.
too. Also; more than enough.
two. The second number in counting.

vain. Conceited; futile.
vane. A fixture moved by air or water.
vein. A fissure or cavity in a substance.

who's. Contraction of *who is*.
whose. Possessive of *who*.

waist. Middle part of the body; garment that comes to the waistline.
waste. That which is worthless; to expend needlessly.

waive. To give up, as a right.
wave. To shake to and fro; one of a series of risings and fallings.

your. Possessive of *you*.
you're. Contraction of *you are*.

Progress Quiz 13-B. Correct any incorrectly used or misspelled homonyms.

1. I bought some stationary at the state fare.
2. Can you alter the canvass after dying it?
3. She sited the case concerning Juno Darias, the council from a small foreign nation.
4. He made his assent to the upper birth just as the martial music began.
5. I was loathe to admit that I had been pouring over the book.
6. Her words did not phase me; in fact, my piece of mind was complete.
7. I cannot bare to think of what the affect will be.
8. Tonight the City Counsel will have it's meeting for the coal minors.

9. Last weak he lead them too all the tourist cites.
10. Three pair of tickets were presented to each of the drummers in the two corpses.
11. The old building was raised to make room for the steal company.
12. Witches were burned at the steak in that town, to.
13. These shear stockings were rapped in unbrakable boxes.
14. The prisoner was out on bale for the forth time.
15. She bares her burden well and has born it well for many years.
16. He injured his spinal chord in the hallway of the capital.
17. On advice of counsel he has waived his claim.
18. Will you council me regarding the forward for my book?
19. As in the past, he past my home at three; but she did not go past till five.
20. The martial told us that the principal ruling would not effect us.

Similar Words (First Part)

Some words are used incorrectly because they closely resemble other words in spelling, pronunciation, or meaning. Learn the correct uses of the words in the following list.

accede. To comply with. (I shall accede to your request.)
exceed. To surpass. (He is trying to exceed last month's quota.)

accept. To receive with favor. (She will accept your invitation.)
except. *As preposition:* other than; *as verb:* to exclude. (Everyone except John will be excepted.)

adapt. To adjust. (We shall adapt the machine to our use.)
adopt. To take without change. (They adopted two children.)

adverse. Unfavorable; in opposition. (This adverse trend may ruin him.)
averse. Having dislike for. (I am averse to long speeches.)

advice (noun). Recommendation. (Thank you for your advice.)
advise (verb). To recommend. (She has advised me.) (*Note:* Do not use *advise* when you mean *tell* or *inform*.)

aggravate. To make something worse. (It aggravated his scar.)
annoy. To vex. (Valerie annoyed the teacher by talking too much.)
exasperate. Inflame to anger. (His lies exasperate me.)

allude. To suggest without naming. (Did he allude to any example?)
refer. To name specifically. (He will not refer to Jerry.)

allusion. A hint. (She overlooked my allusion to the matter.)
elusion. Being hard to catch. (The criminal's elusion baffles me.)
illusion. Deception of the senses. (This trick is an illusion of the eye.)
delusion. False belief; hallucination. (He has a delusion of grandeur.)

almost. Nearly. (I am almost ready to go.)
most. A preponderance. (Who has done the most work?)

among. Refers to more than two. (He walked among all the trees.)
between. Refers to two. (There was a race between two cars.)

anecdote. A brief narrative. (This is an amusing anecdote.)
antedate. To date as of a prior time. (Your check was antedated.)
antidote. A remedy against poison. (The antidote saved her life.)

anxious. Worried. (The anxious girl asked me about Tom's safety.)
eager. Enthusiastic; avid. (He is eager to begin the job.)

appraise. To set a value on. (She will appraise our property.)
apprise. Tell; inform. (Apprise us of the changes.)

artful. Devious; crafty. (The burglar devised an artful plan.)
artistic. Possessing qualities of art. (This is an artistic arrangement.)

aught. Anything. (Rarely used.)
naught. Nothing; zero.
ought. Should.

avoid. To keep away from. (Try to avoid the bumps in the road.)
prevent. To keep from happening. (Try to prevent accidents.)

balance. The difference between two sides of an account.
remainder. That which is left over.
rest. Means the same as *remainder*.

basis. Foundation. (There is no basis for his suspicion.)
bases. *Bases* is the plural of both *base* and *basis*.

beside. At the side of. (She is standing beside me.)
besides. Moreover; in addition to. (Besides his car, he owns a yacht.)

censor. Overseer of morals. (The censor deleted part of her letter.)
censure: To find fault with; criticism. (Don't censure him.)

census. Population count. (The census is taken every ten years.)
senses. Sight, smell, taste, hearing, touch.

cohort. A band of people. (The cohort marched a mile.)
colleague. An associate. (My colleague has been promoted.)

contemptible. Despicable. (Such gossip is contemptible.)
contemptuous. Scornful. (His contemptuous smile angered the beggar.)

continual. Occurring at intervals. (Continual summer showers are refreshing.)
continuous. Occurring without stopping. (The continuous rain lasted a week.)

credible. Believable. (Is that statement credible?)
creditable. Praiseworthy. (Your creditable conduct will be rewarded.)
credulous. Believing too easily. (Credulous persons are quickly fooled.)

decent. Modest; pure. (We should read decent books.)
descent. A going downward. (The descent from the top was steep.)
dissent. To disagree. (She will dissent when you speak.)

deference. Politeness. (Her lack of deference was noticed.)
difference. Variation. (There is a difference in this toy.)

deprecate. To disapprove of. (I deprecate such remarks.)
depreciate. To decrease in value; to belittle. (My car has depreciated.)

desert (des′ert): Barren land. (de·sert′): To abandon.
dessert (des·sert′). Last course of a meal.

device (*noun*). A contrivance. (Can you operate this device?)
devise (*verb*). To contrive. (He devised a new method.)

different. Not the same as; unusual. (It is different from yours.)
various. A number of. (He tried various methods.)
    (*Note:* After a number, use *different* instead of *various:* He tried five different methods.)

discover. To find what already exists. (Who discovered this island?)
invent. To devise or create. (Who invented the telephone?)

disinterested. Impartial; unprejudiced. (Judges should be disinterested.)
uninterested. Having no interest. (She is uninterested in this work.)

elicit. To draw out. (We elicited a response.)
illict. Illegal. (He was punished for his illicit act.)

emigrate. To go from one nation to another. (An emigrant *from*).
immigrate. To enter a country to take up residence. (An immigrant *to*).
migrate. To pass from one region to another. (The birds migrate to the South.)

eminent. Distinguished; notable. (She is an eminent speaker.)

imminent. Impending; threatening to occur. (He says that war is imminent.)

Progress Quiz 13-C. Correct each error.

1. your advise
2. balance of my time
3. one of his cohorts
4. if he advises
5. the principal one
6. apprising our property
7. between she and I
8. devising the plans
9. aggravated the woman
10. between three of them
11. aught to do it
12. a new device
13. a fattening desert
14. most everyone
15. an imminent lawyer

Similar Words (Second Part)

envelop (*verb*) (accented on second syllable). To wrap around.

envelope (*noun*). A folded paper container.

fiancé. Betrothed male.

fiancée. Betrothed female.

flair. Aptitude. (She has a flair for writing.)

flare. To become angry; outburst of anger; a blaze of anger; a blaze of fire or light; a spreading outward or a part that spreads, as with a type of skirt or trousers. (*Flair* and *flare* are homonyms.)

flammable. Easily set on fire; combustible.

inflammable. Means the same as *flammable*.

nonflammable. Not capable of being set on fire.

flaunt. To display in a boastful manner. (She flaunted her intelligence.)

flout. To mock. (A speeding driver flouts the law.)

formally. In a formal manner. (I was formally escorted through the plant.)

formerly. Previously. (Formerly he worked in Los Angeles.)

healthful. Giving health. (This city has a healthful climate.)

healthy. Having health. (Here is a healthy worker.)

historic. Contributing to history. (This is a historic event.)

historical. Pertaining to history. (I am reading a historical novel.)

impervious. Impenetrable. (This book is impervious to insects.)

indifferent. Unconcerned; lacking interest. (He has an indifferent attitude.)

vulnerable. Capable of being attacked or wounded. (The enemy is in a vulnerable position.)

imply. To hint at. (She implied that I should cut expenses.)

infer. To draw a conclusion. (I inferred from his remark that he was unhappy.)

incite (in-cite'). To arouse to action. (The women incited a riot.)

insight (in'sight). Keen understanding; intuition. (He possesses great insight.)

interment. Burial. (Interment will be in Pinedale Cemetery.)

internment. Type of imprisonment. (She discussed internment of enemy aliens.)

learn. To gain knowledge. (If you wish to learn, you can learn.)

teach. To impart knowledge. (Please teach me the new dance step.)

leave. To depart. (Leave the house at once.)

let. To permit. (Let him do the job.)

liable. Exposed to danger; obliged by law. (She is liable to be prosecuted.)

likely. Probable. (The game will likely be exciting.)
    (*Note:* In formal usage, *apt* refers to natural ability or tendency. In informal use, however, some persons use *apt* in place of *likely.*)

loose. Unfastened; not snug; to free. (This is a loose garment.)

lose. To suffer loss; to fail to win. (We must not lose this game.)

majority. More than half.

most. A preponderance.
    (*Note:* Except in elections, *most* is preferable to *majority.*)

plurality. More votes than any other candidate but less than half the votes cast.

mania. A craze. (He has a mania for playing cards.)

phobia. A fear. (Do you have a phobia of high places?)

marital. Pertaining to marriage.

martial. Pertaining to war or military life.

masterful. Domineering. (She is a masterful employer.)

masterly. Skillful. (They handled the job in a masterly manner.)

militate. To have an effect on. (His age militated against him.)

mitigate. To relieve; to make less severe. (Your apology mitigated the situation.)

moral. Virtuous; virtue. (Moral people cannot desert their morals.)

morale (mo·ral′). Mood or spirit. (The morale of the workers is good.)

party. Group of persons; one entering an agreement; telephone subscriber.

person. One human being.

perpetrate. To commit evil. (They perpetrated the plot against the king.)

perpetuate. To give enduring existence to. (Her charitable act will perpetuate her name.)

persecute. To afflict or harass. (Tyrants tend to persecute minority groups.)

prosecute. To use legal process. (For his violation he will be prosecuted.)

personal. Pertaining to one person; private.

personnel. A body of employed persons; pertaining to a body of employed persons.

practicable. Feasible; capable of being done. (Turning iron into gold is not practicable.)

practical. Useful. (Franklin had a practical mind.)

precede. To go before (another). (She will precede you in the line.)

proceed. To advance; to go ahead. (We proceeded as far as the bridge.)

precedence (accent the second syllable). Priority. (Glen's request will be given precedence over yours.)

precedents (accent the first syllable). Authoritative examples. (These court cases have established two precedents.)

reality (four syllables). State of being real.

realty (three syllables). Real estate.

seasonable. Occurring in a season. (The weather today is seasonable.)

seasonal. Lasting for a season. (Some jobs are seasonal.)

specie. Coin.

species (singular and plural). Types of plants and animals.

suspect. One thought guilty; to distrust. (I suspect that she is the culprit.)
suspicion (always a noun). A mistrust. (He aroused my suspicion.)

telecast. To broadcast by TV; a broadcast by TV.
televise. To record by TV apparatus and then to broadcast by TV.

therefor (accent second syllable). For it. (Legal language only.)
therefore. For that reason.

Build Your Word Power

Expressing Thoughts, Ideas, and Opinions. English contains exact words that logically express what you wish to say. Study the following list and learn the variations involved.

anticipate. To foresee and prepare for. (Having anticipated the war, they built shelters.)
expect. To look for as due. (I expect a letter from Robert.)
guess. To conjecture; to surmise. (If you guess, you may be wrong.)
imagine. To form a mental image. (Imagine that you are on the moon.)
suppose. To think probable; to presume. (I suppose that she is ill again.)
think. To have an opinion; to reflect. (I think that you are wrong.)
surmise. To guess; a guess. (You surmised wrong; I did not win.)

Note: The preceding definitions are all based on formal usage. Colloquially, some persons use *guess* instead of the more specific word.

Progress Quiz 13-D. Correct any errors in the following expressions.

1. jibe at me
2. that she is loathe to
3. the principle chart
4. insighted a riot
5. He expects you are wrong.
6. a specie of animal
7. She proceeded me.
8. I anticipate a guest.
9. Learn me to sew.
10. the personal department
11. Leave me go.
12. I always loose.
13. mitigated his anger
14. practical shoes
15. persecuting attorney

Check Your Knowledge

1. In an election how does a majority differ from a plurality?
2. Compose sentences to illustrate each use of *principal.*
3. Compose sentences to illustrate all uses of *affect* and *effect.*
4. How is the word *morale* related to the word *personnel?*
5. Which of the following are true regarding the word *antici-pate?* (a) It connotes enthusiasm. (b) It indicates that the speaker or writer is in doubt. (c) It means to foresee a future event and to take action accordingly. (d) It means to deny. (e) It does not mean *expect.*

Skill Builders

Correct all errors in the following letter, which is in the *full-block* style—all lines starting at the left margin.

Dear Ms. Carter;

When I sited our new price I did not advise you that we now per-mitt a discount of 5 percent if bills are paid within 2 wks. This will effect the amount owed on our invoice of June 9th. For this new discount plan became effective a week ago.

When we may be of service at anytime Ms. Carter, please let us no.

Sincerely.

Business Speech

An *Anglicized* word is a word borrowed from a foreign language and given an English pronunciation. Many Latin words have been Anglicized. In such cases the *a* in an accented syllable may be pronounced as long *a* or short *a;* however, long *a* is the first choice. Following is a list of such words; the italicized *a* is the one to be considered.

1. data   3. ultimatum   5. pro rata   7. status

2. fracas   4. strata   6. ignoramus

Note: Habeas corpus and *verbatim* are always pronounced with long *a*.

Spelling

Study List 13 (page 408), which contains words frequently misspelled by office workers. There is no guide to help you learn these spellings.

REMINDER: Are you practicing the correct spelling of each word you misspell?

Section

14

COMPOUND WORDS

There are three types of compound words: (1) those that are hyphenated, (2) those that are written as two or more words, and (3) those that are written as one word.

The hyphen is often used to make a compound expression perfectly clear. Knowing the correct spelling of each compound word, including those requiring a hyphen, will provide you with greater writing skill. Keep in mind that a dictionary can often answer your questions on compound-word hyphenation.

Observe the different meanings expressed by compound words in these two sentences:

> I have just received my first yearbook.
> I have just received my first-year book.

Compound Adjectives

A compound adjective is always hyphenated in the following cases:

(a) When it is made up of a participle and another word: *double-faced, interest-bearing, health-giving, old-fashioned, slow-growing* shrub, *stem-winding* watch. A few words are written solidly, such as *timesaving* and *shamefaced*.

(b) When it contains a preposition and precedes the word(s) modified: *face-to-face* interview, *run-of-the-mill* goods, *up-to-date* goods; BUT goods that *are run of the mill*, bringing *it up to date*.

(c) When the first word modifies the second: *well-known* man, *wide-open* door; BUT He is *well known*, The door is *wide open*.

(d) When it is a fraction: *a three-quarter* turn, a *one-third* reduction, *three-quarters* of the papers, *one-third* of the letters.

(e) When it is a compound number from *twenty-one* through *ninety-nine* and an ordinal from *twenty-first* through *ninety-ninth*.

> *Note:* Hundreds, thousands, and so on are hyphenated when they modify a noun: the *one-hundred-yard* dash (or the *100-yard* dash), BUT *one hundred* pieces of mail.

(f) When a noun followed by an adjective makes up a specific idea: *water-repellent, crease-resistant*.

> *Note:* Words beginning *over* and *under* are written solidly: *overhead, underground*.

Other Compound Adjectives

(a) Do not hyphenate an expression beginning with an adverb ending with *ly*: *highly rated* salesperson, *recently discovered* chemical. (Remember that *friendly* and *worldly* are adjectives and require the hyphen for compounding: a *worldly-wise* adviser.)

(b) Adjectives ending with *like, proof, sick, tight, weight,* and *worthy* are written solidly: *businesslike, dustproof, homesick, airtight, lightweight, seaworthy*. (If two *l*'s precede the suffix *like*, the hyphen is used: *bell-like, shell-like*.)

(c) Do not hyphenate capitalized expressions: two *New Jersey* stores, *New England* town meeting. *Exceptions:* The adjective *Sino-Japanese* is hyphenated, although *Latin American* is not hyphenated. The hyphen is used when two nations are involved: *Russo-Finnish, French-Italian.* Consult a recent dictionary when in doubt.

One-Word Compounds

Some compounds are always written as one word: *airmail, blueprint, bylaws* (but *by-product*), *copartner, interurban, intrastate, lawsuit, nevertheless, oneself, policyholder, roommate, secondhand, standpoint, stockholder, textbook, whereabouts, worthwhile.*

Compounds Having Prefixes

Most prefixes join solidly: *antedate, antitrust, biweekly, biannual, disable, multicolored, nonprofit, nonporous, postwar, preset, prefabricated, semiannual, semicircle, subway, subcommittee.*

> *Note:* When prefixes are joined to capitalized words, the hyphen is always used: *post-Revolutionary, pre-Renaissance, anti-French, pro-English, un-American.*

Most words beginning with *ex* and *self* are hyphenated: *ex-treasurer, self-confident, self-control.*

Using the Hyphen in Noncompounds

To avoid confusion, the hyphen is used in words that would otherwise have a different meaning: *recreation—re-creation* (*re-creation* means to *create again*); *redress* (*to adjust*)—*re-dress* (*to dress again*); *remark—re-mark* (*to mark again*).

The hyphen is sometimes used after a prefix to separate two identical vowels: *de-emphasize, pre-estimate, re-establish, semi-independent.*

> *Note:* The hyphen is used in *co-worker,* for it looks strange when written *coworker.* Many dictionaries now show such words as *re-emphasize* without a hyphen.

Compound Verbs

The two words in a compound verb are separated by the hyphen: to *blue-pencil,* to *cross-examine,* to *deep-freeze. Note: cross-examination,* a *deep-freezer, deep-frozen* food.

Compound expressions in which one of the words is a verb sometimes require the hyphen: *a drive-in,* short *write-up;* OBSERVE: blowout, checkup, smashup.

Compound Nouns

(a) When a title contains a prepositional phrase, hyphens are usually not required: *editor in chief, chief of staff,* BUT *attorney-at-law.* However, "in-law" titles are hyphenated: *brother-in-law, sister-in-law,* and so forth.

(b) Compound nouns are hyphenated when they name the same person or thing under two aspects: *actor-manager, poet-statesman.*

(c) Compound nouns of three or more words that are not titles are hyphenated: *forget-me-not, merry-go-round.*

(d) Some nouns consisting of one letter followed by a noun are hyphenated; others are not: *T-shirt* BUT *X ray.* When they are used as adjectives or verbs, such words are hyphenated.

(e) Coined compound nouns are hyphenated: a *cure-all,* a *has-been,* having the *know-how,* land of *make-believe.*

Elliptical Compounds. When part of a hyphenated compound is omitted, the hyphen must be used: "The first- and second-class mail will be sent now."

Show the Specific Word You Mean. Sometimes an expression can be written as two words or one solid word. In such a case, however, each expression has its own meaning.

The florist has a large *hothouse*.
I can't sleep in a *hot house*.
The reporter must meet a *deadline*.
The telephone has a *dead line*.
A *redcap* carried my bags
She is wearing a *red cap*.

Additional Compound Words

Hyphenated	bull's-eye	runners-up	write-up
	loose-leaf	will-o'-the-wisp	
Two words	all right	inasmuch as	trade name
	ball bearings	insofar as	under way
	bona fide	per annum	vice versa
	en route	per diem	
One word	airmail	headache	paycheck
	bondholder	a giveaway	payday
	cannot	a kickback	payroll
	checkbook	the makeup	percent
	a checkup	microfilm	salesperson
	cooperate	newscast	telecommunications
	coordinate	overnight	weekend
	drugstore	passersby	worthwhile

Progress Quiz 14-A. Indicate all necessary hyphens.

1. This is an out of the way route.
2. Two fifths of the letters are typed.
3. Use an up to date dictionary.
4. Are your records up to date?
5. There was hand to hand combat.
6. This material is crease resistant.
7. I visited twenty four South Dakota farms.
8. He is secretary treasurer of that firm.
9. It was a never to be forgotten event.
10. She is well known as a highly rated advertising executive.

Progress Quiz 14-B. Correct any errors in the spellings of compound words. Also, supply all necessary hyphens.

1. A person with his knowhow should hit the bull's eye every time.
2. Her report on trade-names was a 200 page project.
3. You are not being over-charged for this light-weight luggage.
4. A one half mile trip ought to agree with the policy holder.
5. Your bi-annual report should reemphasize economy.
6. A business-like attitude is always worthwhile.
7. This non-profit organization has purchased a pre-fabricated building.
8. Recollect the papers from the skillless students.
9. A water-proof, crease-resistant fabric will be discussed by the sub-committee.
10. My father-in-law has dry docked the recently purchased boat.

Build Your Word Power

When, Where. Do not use *when* or *where* to define a word. Do not say, "An itinerary is when (or where) you plan a trip." Say instead, "An itinerary is a plan for a trip."

Use *that* instead of *where* in a sentence such as this: "I saw in the paper *that* (not *where*) he is in Europe."

After a noun use *in which* instead of *where:* "This is a class *in which* (not *where*) you will learn many facts."

Avoid using *any place, every place, no place,* and *some place.* The preferred forms are *anywhere, everywhere, nowhere,* and *somewhere.* Never add *s* to such words.

> Wrong: I looked everywheres but couldn't find it any place.
> Right: I looked everywhere but couldn't find it anywhere.

Anyway, Any way. *Anyway* means *in any case* or *anyhow.* *Any way* is the noun *way* modified by *any.* Avoid *anyways. Any time* is always written as two words and is preceded by *at* when used adverbially.

> I told him, *anyway,* that I could not see him.
> If I may help in *any way,* please let me know.
> I cannot give *any time* to the work.
> Please see me *at any time* that is convenient.

Note: Anyhow and *somehow* are always written as one word. Never use *nohow.*

However, Whatever. Avoid *however, whatever, whichever,* and so on when there is no reason to use them. The italicized words are correct in the following sentences:

> *How* did you do it? (not *However*)
> *What* are you looking for? (not *Whatever*)

Equally. The word *equally* should not be followed by *as.*

Wrong: This book is equally as good.
Right: This book is equally good.
Wrong: This book is equally as good as hers.
Right: This book is as good as hers. (*or* equally good with hers.)

Contemplate. The verb *contemplate* takes a direct object. Therefore, do not say *contemplate on.* "I contemplate taking (*not* on taking) a trip."

Not all, Not everyone. Always use logical wording.

Illogical: All females are not blondes.
Logical: Not all females are blondes.
Illogical: Everyone isn't an athlete.
Logical: Not everyone is an athlete.

Check Your Knowledge

1. Show how each of the following word groups is related:
   (a) transparent, opaque
   (b) non-French, pro-Italian

(c) self-control, ex-champion

(d) semiannual, biweekly

(e) semi-independent, re-emphasize

(f) all right, en route

2. In certain cases some compound adjectives are hyphenated, but in other cases they are not. Explain.

3. Tell when numbers are hyphenated.

4. Is a single word ever followed by a hyphen? Explain.

5. Tell whether each of the following is a compound noun, a compound verb, or a compound adjective:

(a) well-known   (d) supersalesperson

(b) one-half   (e) semicircular

(c) stockholder   (f) quick-freeze

Skill Builders

Rewrite the following letter, correcting all errors.

Dear Miss Edwards:

It is good to know you like the newly organized chart we send you on the 25 of June. We shall print the rulings in dark red, but we are using a bright green ink for the headings.

You will be glad to no Miss Edwards that we are planning to give this chart a two page spread in our March bulletin. We shall air-mail you a copy as soon as it is ready.

If we can be of help, in the mean-time, please right us.

Sincerely Yours,

Business Speech

Learn the correct pronunciation of the following words:

1. **coupon.** First syllable sounds like *coo.*

2. **escalator.** Second syllable is pronounced KUH.

3. **get.** Pronounced with short *e* as in *met*. Do not say GIT.

4. **idea.** Do not add an *r* to this word! It contains three syllables.

5. **percolator.** Second syllable is pronounced KUH.

6. **vulnerable.** Pronounce both *l*'s.

Spelling

Study List 14 (page 408), which contains words taken from Federal Civil Service Tests.

REMINDER: Are you reviewing and practicing the words you have misspelled?

Section

15

WORD DIVISION

To give typewritten material eye appeal, keep the right margin as even as possible. To do so, occasionally you will have to divide a word at the end of a line. Since dictionaries show only the syllables in words, not the places at which words should be divided, you should know the rules for word division.*

Most authorities recommend that in typed material a word should not be divided after only two letters or before two letters that would have to be carried over to the next line. In printed or typed material that will be done in narrow columns, however, a division may be made after only two letters in some cases. In no case should only two letters be carried over to the next line.

The word divisions shown on page 143 are based on *Webster's New Collegiate Dictionary*. An asterisk following a divided word indicates that certain other dictionaries divide it differently.

---

*In the examples the virgule (/) is used to indicate all possible places at which words may be divided. If no virgule appears in a word, that word cannot be divided. In typing, always indicate word division by using the hyphen.

Rules for Dividing Words

1. *General Rule:* Never divide one-syllable words: part, friend. Words of two or more syllables are divided between pronounced syllables: ter/mi/na/tion, asso/cia/tion (divided after the *a*, which is a single-vowel syllable). In the middle of a word, usually divide after a single-vowel syllable: formu/late.

   Exceptions to the General Rule:

   (a) When there are two consecutive single-vowel syllables, divide between the vowels: con/tinu/ation. (*U* and *a* are single-vowel syllables.)

   (b) Divide before a single-vowel syllable when it is the first syllable of a root word: dis/obey, dis/unite.

   (c) When a single-vowel syllable is part of the endings *able, ible, acle, ical, ity,* or *ety,* divide before the vowel: charge/able, cyn/-ical, lon/gev/ity, vari/ety.

   Note: In many words the vowel is part of the preceding syllable: prac/ti/cal, pos/si/ble. Some authorities divide *ities* after the first *i.*

2. Divide between pronounced syllables only. The following words cannot be divided, for they have only one pronounced syllable: *planned, scorched, shipped.*

3. Divide between two identical consonants unless both consonants are part of a root word: run/ning, ship/ping BUT *drill/ers, fill/ing.*

4. Never divide a word so that one or two letters stand alone. The following are examples of words that cannot be divided: *aroma, around, higher, intend, slowly, sweetly, under.* (Words typed in narrow columns may be divided after a two-letter prefix, such as *in* and *un.*)

5. Divide hyphenated words after the hyphen only: first-/class, self-/confidence.

6. Never divide after a silent consonant: *subtle.* (The *b* is silent.)

7. Never divide abbreviations, contractions, and numerals: *Y.M.C.A., wouldn't, $10,750.75.*

8. Avoid dividing capitalized words. (In typing narrow columns, you may divide such words.)

9. Avoid dividing personal names. If a full name must be divided, divide before the surname: Thomas R./Robertson, Mrs. Mary A./Carter.

10. Never divide words at the ends of more than two consecutive lines.

11. Never divide the last word of a paragraph or the last word on a page.

12. In dividing words from foreign languages, usually divide before a consonant.

Examples of Words Correctly Divided

abbre/via/tion	per/mis/si/ble	rec/om/mended
accom/mo/da/tion	pos/ses/sion	rec/ord (noun)
acknowl/edg/ment	pre/ferred	record (verb)
asso/cia/tion	pref/er/able	remit/ted
can/celed	proba/bly	sam/pling
can/cel/la/tion	prob/lem	ser/vice *
col/lect/ible	pro/cess *	shel/lac
cor/re/spon/dence *	pro/duce (noun) *	shel/lacked
defi/nitely	pro/duce (verb)	speci/fi/ca/tion
fluo/res/cent	prog/ress (noun)	ste/nog/ra/pher
han/dling	pro/gress (verb)	steno/graphic
impor/tant	proj/ect (noun)	tele/vi/sion
inter/plan/etary	pro/ject (verb)	tran/scribe
irrele/vant	prom/ise	trans/fer/able
knowl/edge	psy/chology	trans/fer/ring
orga/ni/za/tion *	psy/cho/log/ically	tran/sient

Examples of Words That Should *Not* Be Divided

away	into	radios
drilled	shipped	strength
eraser	obey	teacher
ideas	places	thought

Help the Reader. In dividing a word, write as much of it as you possibly can before dividing. When this procedure is followed, it is easier for the reader to identify the word; thus, the reader's train of thought is less likely to be broken.

POOR	GOOD
con/tinuation	continu/ation
reg/ulatory	regula/tory
cor/respondence	correspon/dence

Progress Quiz 15. Show all possible places for dividing the following.

1. filing
2. cannot
3. answer
4. awaken
5. question
6. U.S.A.
7. nearly
8. propelled
9. learner
10. history
11. knowledge

12. material
13. reference
14. traveling
15. humidity
16. logically
17. trafficked
18. installing
19. processes
20. recording
21. despicable
22. effectively

23. serviceable
24. transferable
25. stenography
26. teachers
27. acknowledgment
28. correspondent
29. transcription
30. continuation
31. old-fashioned
32. alleviation
33. chemical

Build Your Word Power

Many persons think that there is something wrong with the word *get*. Although it is true that some persons misuse it, *get* is a handy word to have in your vocabulary. It commonly means *to fetch,* as in "I shall get my hat."

In British usage the past participle of *get* is always *got;* however, in the United States either *got* or *gotten* is correct, the former being preferable.

Idioms with Get. The idiom *to get up* is more common than *to arise. To get ready* is more common than *to prepare.* There are many other *get* idioms in everyday use, such as *to get one's feet wet, to get dinner, to get someone away, to get someone to do something, to get free.* The idiomatic noun *getaway* is in good usage, as in "The boy made a quick getaway."

Colloquialisms with <u>Get</u>. There are many colloquial uses of *get*. Some examples follow: "She will surely *get ahead*." "Don't let him *get ahead of* you." "The criminal will *get* at least ten years." "This problem really *gets* me." (In the last sentence *gets* means *baffles*.)

When to Avoid <u>Get</u>. Do not say, "You have got to do it." Rather, say, "You have to do it" or "You must do it."

A slang use of *get* is shown in this sentence: "The burglar got him in the head," which should be "The burglar hit him in the head." "Do I get to go?" is better expressed "May I go?"

Check Your Knowledge

1. Divide *continuation* before the *a,* but divide *association* after the *a.* Why is the division different in these two words?
2. As a verb, *record* cannot be divided; as a noun, however, *record* can be divided. Explain.
3. Why would it be a poor policy to permit *ly* and other two-letter syllables to stand alone on the next line?
4. Why should you avoid dividing the word *shipped?*
5. Give three formal expressions using *get*. Give two that are not acceptable.

Skill Builders

Rewrite the following letter, correcting all errors. (This letter is set up in *full-block style;* notice that all lines begin at the left margin.)

Dear Mr. Jordan:—

When I invested with you a year ago I had no idea that my principle would earn such a large sum for me. Last week you payed me much more than I expected to receive.

I new that you would provide good service but I did not anticipate that you would handle even the most minute details so satisfactory. Thank you for your splendide service.

Perhaps Mr. Jordan I shall be able to be of assistants to you some time in the future. If so, you have got to let me know.

Yours sincerely,

Business Speech

Learn the only correct pronunciation of the following words.

1. **been.** Pronounced BIN. (The British pronounce it the same as BEAN).
2. **just.** Rhymes with MUST.
3. **law, saw, idea.** Do not add *r* to these words.
4. **rinse, since.** Rhyme with WINCE.
5. **wrestle.** Rhymes with VESSEL.

Spelling

Study the words in List 15 on page 408. These words have appeared in various state merit tests for office jobs.

Unit Five

EXPRESSING IDEAS CORRECTLY

16

USING CLAUSES AND PHRASES

Words grouped in proper relationships form sentences, which express complete thoughts. Sentences grouped logically form paragraphs, which expand our ideas and relieve monotony in writing. A written word is a symbol of an idea; groups of words, usually in the form of clauses and phrases, expand an idea into a complete thought. A writer's style is based, to some extent, on the manner in which clauses and phrases are used.

"She's worth her weight in gold. Since she became my secretary a year ago, Barbara has saved me hundreds of hours because she knows how to write good sentences. Now I dictate only about half the letters I used to; she composes the rest."

Barbara has made the grade because she is a master of communications skills. Her command of written English has assured her a bright career.

Kinds of Sentences

According to the type of idea expressed, sentences may be *declarative, interrogative, imperative,* or *exclamatory.*

According to the number and types of clauses they contain, sentences are classified as *simple, compound, complex,* and *compound-complex.*

Simple Sentences. A *simple sentence* contains one independent clause. A *clause* is a group of words containing a subject and a predicate. An *independent clause* is one that expresses a complete thought. A simple sentence may contain a compound subject (one or more subjects joined by a coordinating conjunction) and a compound predicate (one or more predicates joined by a coordinating conjunction).

Compound Sentences. A *compound sentence* contains two or more independent clauses joined by a coordinating conjunction—that is, two simple sentences joined by *and, but, or,* and so forth. The two independent clauses may also be connected by a conjunctive adverb, such as *however, therefore,* and *nevertheless.*

Complex Sentences. A *complex sentence* contains one independent clause and one or more dependent clauses. A *dependent* clause, although it contains a subject and a predicate, does not make complete sense when it stands alone.

Compound-Complex Sentences. A *compound-complex sentence* contains two or more independent clauses and one or more dependent clauses.

Examples of Kinds of Sentences

Simple: I read the letter. (one independent clause)
Compound: I read the letter, and Mr. Jones approved it. (two independent clauses)
Complex: When I arrived, I read the letter. (one independent and one dependent clause)
Compound-Complex: I read the letter, and Lynda approved it when she returned. (two independent clauses and one dependent)

Kinds of Dependent Clauses

There are three types of dependent clauses—*adjective, adverbial,* and *noun.* Dependent clauses, sometimes called *subordinate* clauses, may be either restrictive or nonrestrictive. A *restrictive* clause is needed for the complete meaning of a sentence, but a *nonrestrictive* clause is not needed for the complete meaning. A nonrestrictive clause is set off with commas, but a restrictive clause is not.

Adjective Clauses. An *adjective clause* modifies a noun or pronoun. Since most adjective clauses begin with a relative pronoun (*who, whose, whom, which, what, that*), they are often called *relative* clauses.

> (a) Anyone *who steals* is a criminal.
> (b) The woman *to whom you spoke* is a computer technician.
> (c) The person *whom you mentioned* is not my friend.
> (d) The house *that I have rented* is new.
> (e) Atlanta, *which is the capital,* is beautiful.
> (f) Paul White, *who spoke today,* comes from Canada.

Sentences *a* through *d* contain restrictive adjective clauses—no commas. Sentences *e* and *f* contain nonrestrictive adjective clauses—commas are needed.

Adverbial Clauses. An *adverbial clause* usually modifies a verb. An adverbial clause coming first in a sentence is followed by a comma. Most adverbial clauses begin with a subordinating conjunction, such as *after, although, as if, even though, when, where, while, unless, until.*

> (a) *When I see him next week,* I shall tell him.
> (b) *If you are ready,* let's get an early start.
> (c) *Although he is poor,* he is always generous.
> (d) The book remained *where I had placed it.*
> (e) I shall see you in Bangor, *where Jane lives.*

Observe the comma at the end of the adverbial clause in sentences *a* through *c*. Sentences *c* and *e* contain nonrestrictive clauses.

If sentence *e* were written without the comma, the meaning would not be clear. It might be mistaken for "I shall meet you where Jane lives in Bangor."

Noun Clauses. A noun clause is used in the same way that a noun is used—as subject, direct object, and so on. Noun clauses begin with a relative pronoun; however, in informal English the relative pronoun is sometimes omitted.

That the earth is round is a fact.*	(subject of *is*)
It is true *that the earth is round.*	(in apposition with *It*)
Give the book to *whoever wants it.*	(object of *to*)
I know *he will be on time.*	(direct object of *know*)

Note: In the last sentence, *that* is not expressed.

---

*In introducing a noun clause, *that* is a subordinating conjunction, not a relative pronoun.

Progress Quiz 16-A. Select each dependent clause and tell whether it is an adjective, an adverbial, or a noun clause. Also, tell the type of each sentence.

1. When I saw the man who had told me about John, he had another surprise.
2. I shall go to Troy; but if you need me, write me in care of Mrs. Adams, who will always know my whereabouts.
3. I realize that she could have made the error; but unless I am mistaken, I am sure that someone else is to blame.
4. During the show Alan talked incessantly, and I could not concentrate.
5. He told me to listen; however, since I was distracted, I could not pay attention.
6. I saw Ms. Peters, the coach, walking in the garden, which seems to be her favorite place on the campus.

Kinds of Phrases

A *phrase* is a group of words having neither subject nor predicate. A simple sentence may contain several phrases of various types; phrases, therefore, never change the grammatical value of a sentence, as clauses do.

There are five types of phrases—*verb, prepositional, infinitive, participial,* and *gerund.*

Verb Phrases. Any group of verbs used as a predicate is a verb phrase: *shall be, has been writing, could have seen, should have sent.*

Prepositional Phrases. A prepositional phrase begins with a preposition and contains a noun or pronoun as object of that preposition. There are two types of prepositional phrases—*adjective* and *adverbial.* An adjective phrase modifies a noun or pronoun. An adverbial phrase modifies a verb.

This book *of poetry* is excellent.	(adjective phrase modifying *book*)
The man *with the beard* is my uncle.	(adjective phrase modifying *man*)
Give the invoice to *Miss Collins*.	(adverbial phrase modifying *give*)
There was a race *between the two cars*.	(adverbial phrase modifying *was*)
In the fall we shall visit you.*	(adverbial phrase modifying *shall visit*)

---

*When a prepositional phrase comes first in a sentence, a comma does not follow it unless needed for absolute clarity. Some authorities say that a comma should follow a prepositional phrase of five or more words.

Infinitive Phrases. An infinitive phrase consists of *to* followed by a verb. Infinitive phrases may be used as nouns, verbs, adjectives, and adverbs.

To sing is my desire.	(subject of *is*)
I wanted *to sing.*	(direct object of *wanted*)
The play is *to be read soon.*	(predicate nominative of *is*)
The play *to be read* is long.	(adjective modifying *play*)
The play is read *to please him.*	(adverb modifying *is read*)
I thought you *to be* her.	(verb after *you*)

Participial Phrases. A participial phrase begins with either a present or a past participle and modifies a noun or pronoun. Participial phrases may be either restrictive or nonrestrictive and are punctuated accordingly. A participial phrase coming first in a sentence is always followed by a comma.

I saw Ruth *strolling in the park.*	(restrictive, modifying *Ruth*)
The girl *wearing the red dress* is my cousin.	(restrictive, modifying *girl*)
Having thought it over, I decided to go.	(nonrestrictive, modifying *I*)
John, *having eaten lunch,* fell asleep.	(nonrestrictive, modifying *John*)

Gerund Phrases. A gerund phrase begins with a gerund noun and is always used as a noun. Gerund phrases are always restrictive; therefore, they are not set off by commas unless out of their natural order.

Eating on the patio is fun.	(subject of *is*)
We enjoyed *swimming in the lake.*	(direct object of *enjoyed*)
After *typing the letter,* he left.	(object of *after*)

Punctuation note: If an element containing a verb form is out of its natural order by coming first in the sentence, place a comma after that element.

Progress Quiz 16-B. Select each phrase and tell its type. Supply all commas.

1. The boss having complained about the errors stormed out of the office.
2. The book of poems by Keats was lying on the library table in the corner.
3. I wanted to take a long hike in the country but Mary did not want to go.
4. If you wish to lose weight you must stop eating so many of those sweets.
5. By showing him how to sail I made a friend for the summer.

Dangling Elements

A *dangling element* is an expression that is not closely connected to the word to which it is related. Dangling elements cause confusion and often make sentences seem ridiculous.

Dangling Participles. Note these examples of dangling participles:

> Wrong: Turning the corner, the bank came into view.
> Right: Turning the corner, I saw the bank come into view.
> Wrong: Driving up the road, several bears were seen.
> Right: Driving up the road, we saw several bears.
> Wrong: Packed for mailing, you must send the book.
> Right: You must send the book when it is packed for mailing.

Dangling Gerunds. Note these examples of dangling gerunds:

> Wrong: By working hard, his skill increased.
> Right: By working hard, he increased his skill.
> Wrong: After baiting the hook, the fish began to bite.
> Right: After baiting the hook, I found the fish began to bite.

Dangling Infinitives. Note these examples of dangling infinitives:

> Wrong: To lose weight, dieting is necessary.
> Right: To lose weight, one must diet.
> Right: If one wishes to lose weight, he or she must diet.

Dangling Clauses. Careless writers sometimes do not place clauses near the words they modify. Note these examples:

> Wrong: There was a monkey in the cage that kept jumping.
> Right: There was a monkey that kept jumping in the cage.
> Wrong: The book is about the war that I borrowed.
> Right: The book that I borrowed is about the war.

One-Word Danglers. When a single word is a dangling element, the meaning of a sentence is not clear. Note these examples:

> Vague: She told me frequently to see my dentist.
> Clear: She frequently told me to see my dentist.
> Clear: She told me to see my dentist frequently.
> Vague: He asked me occasionally to stop in.
> Clear: Occasionally he asked me to stop in.
> Clear: He asked me to stop in occasionally.

Progress Quiz 16-C. Rewrite the following sentences so that there will be no dangling elements.

1. In packing my bag, a suit was forgotten.
2. Before washing my car, soap must be obtained.
3. When entering the room, my hair needed combing.
4. Coming home late, the house seemed dark.
5. I returned after a month's vacation on Monday.
6. He bought a dog from a friend that had shaggy ears.
7. Being made of brick, the woman expected her house to weather the storms.
8. He borrowed an egg from his aunt that was cracked.
9. Licking its paws, the child watched the cat.
10. When scoured with cleanser, you will have brighter kettles.

Progress Quiz 16-D. Supply the correct form of *who.*

1. –– could it have been?
2. –– did she think it to be?
3. –– was he speaking to?
4. Give it to –– wants it.
5. To –– house is he going?
6. It is he –– will get the job.
7. The man –– you saw was Mr. Green.
8. Send it to –– Mary chooses.
9. It is she –– I think will succeed.
10. About –– is Mr. Davis speaking?

Build Your Word Power

Want to. Always use *want to,* not *want that.* For example, say, "He wants me to work late tonight." It is an illiteracy to say, "He wants that I should work late tonight."

Perfect Participle. Careless writers often ignore the perfect participle, which should be used for an action completed before another action. For example, say, "Having graduated from Yale, she entered her father's firm," NOT "Graduating from Yale, she entered her father's firm."

Perspective, Prospective. *Perspective* is a noun that means *how objects look in relation to their distances and positions. Prospective* is an adjective derived from the noun *prospect,* which means *possible customer* or *outlook.*

As, Such as, For example. Note that repetition should be avoided in giving examples.

> Wrong: Play a lively song—as, for example, a march.
> Right: Play a lively song—for example, a march.
> Right: Play a lively song, such as a march.

Check Your Knowledge

1. Name the types of phrases and clauses that may be either restrictive or nonrestrictive.
2. Why do dangling elements sometimes produce humorous sentences?
3. Construct three sentences that illustrate each of the three types of dependent clauses.
4. If an adverbial clause comes first in a sentence, which mark of punctuation follows the clause?
5. Which type of sentence is this? John, Paul, and Fred ate, packed, and started on their long trip.

Skill Builders

Rewrite this letter, correcting all errors. This letter is in *full-block* style, with *open* punctuation—that is, no punctuation marks after the salutation and the complimentary close.

Gentlemen

Thanks for your letter of June 28th in which you advice me that I should invest in stocks. I appreciate you telling me about the stock offered by your friend that is low-priced. Never investing before, I am in need of good advise like your's.

If I plan on buying any of your friends stock I shall let you know.

Yours very truly

Business Speech

Note the correct pronunciation of the following words:

1. **modern.** The second syllable sounds like the word EARN.
2. **pattern.** Pronounced PAT-ERN.
3. **perspiration.** The first syllable is pronounced PURR.
4. **prescription.** The first syllable is pronounced PRI, as in PRETTY.
5. **pretty.** This word rhymes with CITY.

Spelling

Study List 16 (page 408), which consists of words taken from a job-entrance test given by a large company.

Section 17

WRITING EFFECTIVE SENTENCES AND PARAGRAPHS

To become an effective writer, you must know how to use the language, how to analyze what you write, how to correct what you write, and how to learn from your mistakes. To write well, of course, you must master the basic rules of English composition.

To be effective, sentences must meet three requirements—*unity, coherence,* and *emphasis.* A paragraph, which is a group of sentences based on a corethought, must also meet the same requirements.

Unity

If you remember the following pointers, your sentences will possess unity:

  (a) A sentence must express a complete thought. A dependent clause or a phrase is never a complete sentence.
  (b) Two separate thoughts not closely related should be written as two separate sentences.
  (c) Supply all the words needed to help the idea move along smoothly.

Sentences Corrected to Show Unity

(a) Wrong: This is our plan. Which has been approved. (*fragment fault*) *
    Right: This is our plan that has been approved.
(b) Wrong: We have a test service, and our main branch is in Dallas.
                                                   (*loose hook-up*)
    Right: We have a test service. Our main branch is in Dallas.
(b) Wrong: These are the new books, they are ready for sale. (*comma fault*)
    Right: These are the new books. They are ready for sale.
    Right: These are the new books; they are ready for sale.
(c) Wrong: Yours of 3rd rec'd. (*telegraphic fault*)
    Right: Thank you for your letter of June 3.

---

* Some writers begin a sentence with *and* or *but* in order to emphasize the idea that follows. Only skillful writers, however, can use this device effectively. Other writers sometimes express an idea in less than a complete sentence. Here, too, only skillful writers know how to use such a device.

Academy of the Arts

2100 Willow Road
Baltimore. MD 21209

April 28, 19--

Miss Amanda Lynn
The House of Music
904 Acklen Street
Louisville, KY 40208

Dear Miss Lynn:

Thank you for your prompt, helpful reply to my recent letter.
I am indeed grateful to you for the informative pamphlet,
Guitars for Everyone, which you enclosed with your letter.

The Musical Arts Society of my school is planning to have a
guitar concert on the evening of May 10; your pamphlet, therefore, is timely and useful. On the back of our printed program
for the concert, we shall be happy to mention the assistance
that you and your splendid company have given us. As soon as
the program is available, I shall send you a few copies.

In your letter you said that you may be in Baltimore sometime
in May. If you do come to Baltimore, I hope that you will have
time to visit our campus. The first two weeks in May, we plan
to have several interesting exhibits.

Best wishes, Miss Lynn, for your continued personal success.

                         Sincerely,

                         (Ms.) Rosalie J. Tyler

                         Ms. Rosalie J. Tyler, President
                         Musical Arts Society

rjw

Dramatics ᪥ Music ᪥ Painting ᪥ Sculpture ᪥ Crafts

A Letter of Thanks (Modified-Block Style)

Coherence

The word *coherence* means *sticking together*. In writing, coherence means connecting words and thoughts so that proper relationships are shown. Clear writing is always coherent writing.

(a) Place your words in the right order so that there will be no dangling elements or separate words that cloud the exact meaning of the message.

(b) Always maintain parallel construction.

(c) Be sure that each pronoun agrees with its antecedent and refers to the correct antecedent.

(d) Express ideas logically by supplying all the words needed to make complete comparisons.

(e) Maintain the same point of view by keeping person, number, and voice in parallel construction.

Sentences Corrected to Show Coherence

WRONG	RIGHT
(a) She says that the report stresses the laws that pertain to trusts on page 15 in detail.	(a) She says that on page 15 the report stresses in detail the laws that pertain to trusts.
(b) The carpet is 15 feet long and 10 feet in width.	(b) The carpet is 15 feet long and 10 feet *wide*.
(c) After John had talked with Jim, he felt more confident.	(c) John felt more confident after he had talked with Jim. *Or* Jim felt more confident after he had talked with John.
(d) Our winter sales are always much better than in summer.	(d) Our winter sales are always much better than *those* in summer.
(e) I like that store, for you receive courteous treatment there.	(e) I like that store, for *I* receive courteous treatment there.

Parallel Construction. The unskilled writer commonly violates the rule of parallel construction. The rule is simple: Parallel construction requires that similar ideas in a sentence be of the same grammatical value. For example, if you say, "I like singing and to dance," you do not have parallel construction, because *singing* is a gerund and *to dance* is an infinitive. To have parallelism, say, "I like singing and dancing" or "I like to sing and dance."

Note these examples of parallel construction:

Wrong: She is tall, with blue eyes, and has a cheerful manner.
Right: She is tall, blue-eyed, and cheerful.
Wrong: She helps her father by cooking and washing the car.
Right: She helps her father by cooking and by washing the car.
Wrong: Paul is a good clerk, and who is a skillful speaker.
Right: Paul is a good clerk and also a skillful speaker.

Parallel construction is also required after the correlatives *either—or, neither—nor, both—and, not only—but also*. This type of parallelism is sometimes called *correlation*.

Wrong: He is either right or you are wrong.
Right: Either he is right or you are wrong.
Wrong: She is good not only in French but in Spanish.
Right: She is good not only in French but also in Spanish.

Progress Quiz 17-A. Rewrite the following sentences so that they will possess unity and coherence.

1. He has a new secretary, he is a fast typist.
2. Advise when goods ready ship Boise.
3. The train is either late or you are early.
4. Fran pointed out that the manager expects the bulletin on Monday that will be duplicated.
5. This typing is blurred, done without care, and not in the center.
6. Although he does not have much time. He will attend the meeting.
7. It looks like rain, which is why I shall not go.
8. Our firm has a testing bureau, and our main office is in Houston.
9. We underestimated the expense of the trip and how long it would take.
10. Not only am I glad, but also I am grateful.

Emphasis

In business writing there are two types of emphasis—*mechanical* and *structural*. Each type serves a useful purpose, but structural emphasis is more important.

Mechanical Emphasis. Mechanical emphasis is achieved by using (a) full capitals, (b) spacing, (c) underscoring, (d) colored inks, and (e) a variety of other devices that attract attention and emphasize certain words or ideas. This type of emphasis should be used carefully and sparingly. *Remember:* All emphasis is no emphasis!

Structural Emphasis. Good writing contains structural emphasis, which consists of arranging ideas emphatically in sentences and paragraphs. The most emphatic part of a sentence is its ending; the next most emphatic part is its beginning; the least emphatic place is its middle. Separate words, as well as sentences, should have emphatic arrangement, depending on the ideas expressed by the words.

Unemphatic: He was given the award because he is an outstanding citizen who has lived here for many years.
Emphatic: Because he is an outstanding citizen who has lived here for many years, he was given the award.

The Periodic Sentence. A *periodic sentence* places the main idea at the end. A *loose sentence* begins with the main idea and places a subordinate idea at the end. The preceding emphatic example is a periodic sentence, because "he was given the award" is the most important of the three thoughts. Emphatic value is lost if too many consecutive sentences are periodic.

The *climactic sentence* is sometimes appropriate. Perhaps the best-known climactic sentence is this: "I came, I saw, I conquered." In a climactic sentence the elements are arranged in order of time, the last element being the climax.

Logical Order. For emphasis logical order must be used.

Unemphatic: Her life was short and sad.
Emphatic: Her life was sad and short.

Repetition. Carefully planned repetition produces emphasis. Remember, though, that careless repetition is a mark of the poor writer.

Poor: When you make an error, find out why you made the error; then be sure not to make any more errors.
Good: He was terrified. He could not forget those eyes. He could not forget that sneer. He could not forget that snakelike hair.

Active Voice. The active voice is more emphatic than the passive.

Passive: I was given praise by my supervisor.
Active: My supervisor praised me.

Balance and Contrast. Emphasis by *balance* is achieved by comparing— that is, balancing one idea against another. Emphasis by *contrast* is achieved by contrasting ideas so that each is given added force.

Balance: John is a fast typist; Ruth, an accurate bookkeeper.
Contrast: The night is for sleep, but the day is for work.

The use of connective words helps to balance and contrast ideas. Some good connectives include *however, nevertheless, moreover, therefore.* Parenthetical phrases, such as *at any rate, I think, I know,* and *we believe,* also help to produce emphasis. Such words and phrases are more effective if placed within a sentence, rather than at the beginning or the ending.

> Weak: We told her that the rate was too high, however.
> Emphatic: We told her, however, that the rate was too high.
> Emphatic: He realizes, therefore, that I am here.

Subordination. We say that a writer has a certain *style.* When asked to explain the writer's style, however, we usually find it difficult to do. Emphatic devices contribute to an effective style.

Most skillful writers help achieve emphasis by subordination. *Subordination* means that one idea is made independent and that related ideas are subordinated to it. Place the main idea in an independent clause so that it will stand out sharply among the other ideas.

UNEMPHATIC	EMPHATIC
I believe that the president was wrong in appointing a person who is known as a spendthrift.	In appointing a person who is known as a spendthrift, the president, I believe, was wrong.

In the preceding unemphatic sentence, the least important idea—"I believe"—is given emphasis by being made the beginning of the independent clause. In the emphatic sentence, "the president was wrong" is rightly made the independent clause.

Subordination may be achieved by placing a phrase or a clause at the beginning of a sentence.

> When spring arrives, I shall buy a new car.

A pronoun referring to a noun should be placed in a dependent clause, not in an independent clause.

> Poor: When a woman is hungry, she eats.
> Good: When she is hungry, a woman eats.
>   A woman eats when she is hungry.

Conciseness Helps Achieve Emphasis. If a person reading a letter must wade through many meaningless words, the important ideas of the letter may be lost. The main ideas, at least, are not immediately apparent.

Excess verbiage—words that add nothing to the message—should be removed from your writing before you type the final form.

Wordy	*Efficient*
am in receipt of	have received
am in a position to	can, am able to
am of the opinion	believe
at an early date	soon
at the present time	now, at present
by means of	by
depreciate in value	depreciate
due to the fact that	because, since
during the course of	during
enclosed please find	enclosed is (*or* are)
for the purpose of	for
if it is possible for us	if we can
inasmuch as	since
in order to	to
in regard to	about, regarding
in the event that	if
our check in the amount of	our check for
prior to	before
type it up	type it
we must ask you to	please
we wish to thank you	thank you
with reference to	about

Writing Effective Paragraphs

A paragraph may be one sentence or a group of sentences that expand a main thought. Paragraphs of varying lengths relieve monotony on a typed or printed page and thus provide mechanical emphasis. Paragraphs aid structural emphasis, also, for by logically arranging ideas in a series of paragraphs, you create a more effective message. As with sentences, paragraphs should possess unity, coherence, and emphasis.

The Corethought. Most paragraphs contain a central thought—the *core-thought*—which is expressed in a *topic sentence;* the rest of the paragraph develops the corethought. If a paragraph is explanatory, the topic sentence comes first, and all other sentences develop the explanation. A *climactic* paragraph is effective in narrating an event, either actual or hypothetical.

In business writing, the topic sentence, whether coming first or last in a paragraph, must often be expanded by (1) facts, (2) reasons, or (3) concrete examples.

Pointers for Effective Paragraphs

1. Vary the length of paragraphs. Too many paragraphs of the same length cause monotony. Good paragraphing makes reading easier and permits the reader to understand your message faster. In business letters the first and last paragraphs should be short.

2. Avoid overparagraphing. Immature writers tend to make a new paragraph after every one or two sentences. Remember that a paragraph contains a corethought and that a new paragraph is not begun until that corethought has been developed.

3. Use carefully chosen devices to emphasize an important idea. Some good emphatic devices are (a) strategically placing a topic sentence; (b) using repetition in various ways; (c) expressing the idea in a short paragraph; (d) indenting at the right and left margins; and (e) using other mechanical devices, such as underscoring or full capitals.

4. Smoothly lead the reader from one paragraph to the next. By doing so you maintain interest, make a favorable impression, and help induce the reader to take the desired action.

Examples of Paragraphs

NEW-GLO is easy to use. Simply put a small amount of the creamy wax on any soft cloth, lightly rub it over the surface to be cleaned and polished, and then relax. Your job is done.

The topic sentence (italicized) comes first. Explanatory details follow.

Our laboratory reports that SOAPEX saves the following amounts on each average-size wash: Electricity—2 cents. (Because of its double-action cleansing power, SOAPEX washes faster.) Life of fabrics—7 cents. (Because it works faster, there is less wear and tear on even the most soiled clothing.) Soap used—3 cents. (Because of its magic action, you use only half a cupful of SOAPEX). *With SOAPEX you save 12 cents each washday and have the satisfaction of whiter, brighter clothes— with less work.*

The topic sentence (italicized) comes last. Effective emphasis is gained by repeating the name of the product, the word *because,* and the word *saving.*

The individual amounts saved, with the reason for each, might be placed in central positions, with spaces before and after. Such an arrangement is an effective use of mechanical emphasis.

The oncoming car swerved toward him at 80 miles an hour. He slammed on the brake—or tried to. It had given out, however, and he clutched the wheel, awaiting the inevitable.

This is a climactic paragraph. Events appear in the order of their occurrence, culminating in the climax.

Progress Quiz 17-B. Rewrite the following sentences so that they will be more emphatic.

1. He had a short and merry life.
2. Ellen was recommended for a salary increase by her supervisor.
3. The mayor was given a citation because of his efforts in helping clear the slums in the eastern part of the city.
4. The children let out piercing screams after seeing the figure at the window and clutching their hearts.
5. We are sure that the criminal made a mistake in trying to loot the treasurer's office.
6. They told me that I would be considered for the next promotion, however.
7. Due to the fact that the goods will arrive at an early date we must plan to send our check in the amount of $200.

8. Act immediately if you wish to take advantage of this offer.
9. If it is possible for us to help you, let us know before too much time passes.
10. Character is what you really are, and what people think you are is reputation.

Build Your Word Power

Because, Since. To introduce a nonrestrictive dependent clause, avoid using *as;* instead, use either *because* or *since.* In such cases *as* may cause confusion.

B.C., A.D. It is correct to say "the tenth century B.C." However, it is *incorrect* to say "the tenth century A.D." *B.C.* is the abbreviation of *before Christ;* therefore, it is sensible to place *B.C.* after the century. *A.D.,* however, means *in the year of our Lord;* and if *A.D.* is placed after the century, an illogical expression results. The exact year should be used with *A.D.*—for example, *A.D. 1963.*

Both. Do not use *both* with such words as *equal, alike, agree, together.* Do not use *both* with *as well as. Both* is followed by *and,* never by *but.* In the following sentences, *both* is in parentheses, indicating that it should not be used. In the last sentence *together* is the superfluous word.

> They are (both) equally important.
> (Both) students, as well as teachers, are invited.
> It is (both) a slow but interesting motion picture.
> Both appeared (together) in the show.

Persons, People. After a number use *persons,* not *people,* since *people* is not the logical plural of *person. People* refers to a general group of persons. *Peoples* refers to many groups, as in "the peoples of the world."

> Wrong: Three people asked for you.
> Right: Three persons asked for you.
> Right: The meeting is open to all the people.

While. Do not use *while* in making a comparison.

> Wrong: Hers is red, while yours is blue.
> Right: Hers is red and (*or* but) yours is blue.
> Wrong: While I agree, I cannot consent.
> Right: Though I agree, I cannot consent.

A while, Awhile. Formal writers use *a while* when a preposition precedes and *awhile* when no preposition precedes. For formal usage, therefore, write "He stayed for a while" or "He stayed awhile."

Check Your Knowledge

1. What are the differences between mechanical and structural emphasis?
2. List five pointers for writing effective paragraphs.
3. If a letter writer ignores unity and coherence, is the letter courteous? Explain.
4. How is emphasis achieved by conciseness? by contrast? by subordination?
5. Exactly what is meant by parallel construction?

Skill Builders

Rewrite the following paragraphs so that they will be effective.

17-A. Every week we receive many letters from our readers. Those who read *Today's Trends* include many well-known people—those who help make the news themselves. They tell us that they like all the photographs and other illustrations in our magazine and that they always read it the minute it arrives in the mail.

17-B. Our special vacation plans include the "All-Expense Family Plan," which is economically priced to fit the smallest budget. We also offer the "Doubles Plan," which is for couples and includes trips to any section of the United States. For individual persons who wish to join a congenial group, we offer the "Tourist Group Plan." Yes, we have three special vacation plans, each of which is described in the enclosed brochure.

Business Speech

Practice pronouncing these words correctly. There is at least one silent consonant in each word.

1. **Connecticut.** The second *c* is silent.
2. **raspberry.** The *p* is silent and the *s* is pronounced like a *z*.
3. **salmon.** The *l* is silent.
4. **subtle.** The *b* is silent.
5. **corps.** Singular pronounced like *core*; plural pronounced *korz*.

Spelling

Guide: Most prefixes, including *sub* and *super,* are added to words without using the hyphen or leaving a space. Study List 17 on page 408.

REMINDER: On page 7 you will find a "Study Help" that will assist you in becoming a better speller. If necessary, review that information. Many companies require all job applicants to pass a spelling test, so be prepared!

Section

18

INCREASING YOUR WRITING POWER

To build your writing power, use language that is euphonious, positive, and current. To gain certain effects, your language may sometimes contain figures of speech—expressions based on techniques used, to some extent, in poetry and literary prose.

Euphony

Euphony means *pleasant sound.* Euphonious language, therefore, is that which is pleasing to the ear. Even though the people receiving a letter may not read it aloud, their mental "ears" may be displeased by language that is not euphonious.

In poetry a pleasing effect is gained by repeating the same sound. In business writing, however, such repetition should be avoided, for it tends to distract the reader. The repetition of certain sounds, such as *s* and *z*, may be particularly annoying.

Unpleasant: He says the blizzard has caused some hazards. (six *z* sounds)
Euphonious: He reports the blizzard has created some dangers.
Unpleasant: We know you noticed the note with no date. (four *no* sounds)
Euphonious: We know you saw the note without a date.

Positive Language

In business writing we always hope to obtain *positive* results. For that reason positive language should be used and negative language avoided. Single words, sentences, or whole paragraphs may be either positive or negative. The choice of positive words and phrases, therefore, is of prime importance in business writing.

Positive Words. A single word can have a positive or negative effect.

POSITIVE	NEGATIVE
accuracy	carelessness
adjustment	complaint
assurance	fear
confidence	uncertainty
cooperation	refusal
honesty	dishonesty
success	defeat
satisfaction	discontent
trust	suspicion
willingness	hesitation

Negative words may make the reader "see red," and a company that uses them may eventually find itself "in the red."

Certain words have proved effective in developing a positive tone in business letters. Such words are sometimes called *quality* words or *prestige* words. Examples of such words follow:

Some Quality Words

American	genuine	modern	only
citizen	healthful	natural	original
dependable	honor	new	unique
established	liberty	nutritious	youthful

The preceding list of quality words cannot be used in all types of business letters; however, such words have proved especially effective in sales letters and advertising copy.

Taboo Words. Certain negative words, sometimes called *prejudice* words, are taboo among business writers. Some of these words have an unpleasant connotation for certain groups of people. Most of the words, however, tend to "rub everyone the wrong way."

Taboo Expressions

artificial	deadbeat	misled	politician
bureaucrat	fail	misrepresented	radical
capitalist	failure	neglect	unfair
claim	insinuation	negligence	you must
complain	labor racketeer	nonsense	your carelessness
complaint	misinformed	obligated	your ignorance

Positive Sentences. The wording of a sentence may cause a negative impression. If you maintain the "you attitude," however, your sentences will be positive.

NEGATIVE	POSITIVE
This is a strange request.	You have made a discriminating choice.
You probably can't understand it.	You will surely understand it.
Mistakes are bound to happen.	We shall take great care to prevent a similar occurrence.
It will never happen again.	Thank you for giving us an opportunity to improve our service.
Your failure to write leads us to believe you have lost interest.	Since we have not heard from you, we are sure that you have been busy.

Positive Paragraphs. Negative language may mean loss of sales. Every paragraph should be positive.

We regret that we cannot fill your order until at least three weeks have passed. We hope that our failure to do so will not inconvenience you too much.

Thank you for your order for a Northland air conditioner, which you will receive in time to install before hot weather comes. Your unit will reach you by May 15.

Current Language

In the early 1900's many businesses patterned their letters after those written by lawyers, whose letters contained many awkward expressions and circumlocutions. A *circumlocution* is a wordy expression—one that requires many words to say what can be expressed in one or two words. Today's letter writers don't "beat around the bush" by using circumlocutions; they quickly get to the point and don't "talk in circles."

Section 18 - Increasing Your Writing Power   **171**

A half century ago, *hitherto, herewith, whereas,* and other similar words were a part of the letter writer's vocabulary. Today such words have no place in business writing. Another old-time favorite was *beg*. For a time it seemed as though all letter writers were beggars. "We beg to state," "We beg to reply," "We beg to remain," and many other begging expressions were the order of the day. Evidently the "beggars" wore themselves out, because today the business world is free of them.

Worn-out Expressions. Worn-out expressions from the jargon of business are sometimes called *stock phrases* or *rubber-stamp* phrases. Although such expressions are in poor taste, many business writers still use them. Expert writers, however, avoid them.

Worn-out Expressions

according to our records	hoping to hear from you soon
as per	in reply we wish to advise
as stated above	permit us to state
at all times	please be advised that
at an early date	recent date
at hand	thanking you in advance
beg to acknowledge	send you herewith
beg to inform	for the time being
beg to remain	trusting this is satisfactory
contents carefully noted	enclosed please find

Figures of Speech

In certain types of letters, sales letters particularly, the use of figures of speech can add power to your writing. Figures of speech are commonly used by literary authors—writers of both prose and poetry. In business writing, however, figurative language should be used sparingly. Three figures of speech can be used with good results in business writing—the *simile,* the *metaphor,* and *hyperbole.*

A *simile* is a direct comparison, which contains *like* or *as.* "For eyes like stars, use I-GLO daily."

A *metaphor* is an implied comparison. "Our Jet-Stream plane is a magic carpet, ready to carry you to adventure."

Hyperbole is an exaggerated comparison. "With only the weight of a feather, a cashmere coat will protect you from the coldest winds."

Everyone realizes that no coat is as light as a feather; therefore, the statement is not misleading. If you say that a coat will last a lifetime, however, you must be ready to prove your statement!

Build Your Word Power

Redundant Expressions. A *redundant* word or expression is one that is repetitious. Such an expression is sometimes called a *pleonasm*. In the following sentences the italicized redundant expressions should be omitted.

Examples of Redundant Expressions

She advanced *forward* toward the car that was black *in color*.
For the first time *in my life* I ate breakfast at 8 a.m. *in the morning*.
They both went *together* to visit the brilliant *and gifted* author.
Filing *of* cards took three hours *of time*.
If you wish to succeed, *then* you must work hard.
John is the clerk who is fastest and *who is* most accurate.
Is there an *old* adage about *new* beginners?

Trite Expressions. A trite expression is one that has been overworked and no longer possesses originality. A trite expression is sometimes called a *cliché* or a *platitude*. The word *nice,* which has had a variety of meanings, is commonly used to mean *pleasant* or *appealing*. In business writing, however, avoid this trite word.

Progress Quiz 18-A. Rewrite the following sentences so that they contain language that is euphonious, positive, and current.

1. We beg to advise you that you can expect to receive your catalog under separate cover at an early date.
2. She saw the slow stream of smoke sail across the sky.
3. You must realize that to err is human, but we promise not to be so negligent in the future.
4. If you had read the directions on the package, you would have discovered that you had failed to use the right kind of bleach.
5. In your recent letter you complain about our service, and in reply we wish to advise that we are taking action as per your letter.

Progress Quiz 18-B. Remove all unnecessary words from these sentences. Wherever possible, make one word do the work of several.

1. In this day and age, many writers tell of their deeds and doings.

2. She is an expert authority in the field of human relations.

3. He called me up on the telephone to tell me that the consensus of opinion is that the modern office of today can profit as a result of automation.

4. A countless number of times, I have seen her buy expensive and costly jewelry.

5. If you wish to see and talk with me after the end of the game, I shall be happy and glad to discuss the plans for the party that is to be held next week.

Check Your Knowledge

1. Tell whether the following words are positive or negative: *failure, dependable, carelessness, opportunity, neglect.*

2. Why should worn-out expressions be avoided?

3. In a sentence use a simile that would be acceptable in a business letter.

4. Redundant and trite expressions are signs of immature writing. Why?

5. Why is it distracting to hear or read a sentence that is not euphonious?

Skill Builders

18-A. Reword the following sentences so that they will be acceptable. 1. Your failure to include all the facts misled us, and that is why you received our complaint. 2. There is still some uncertainty about the date of the meeting; therefore, we hesitate to commit ourselves at this time. 3. Please find enclosed herewith the samples you requested, which we beg you to examine. 4. We are sorry that we cannot fill your order at once, for we know that you are being inconvenienced as a result. 5. According to our records, we find that you are in error regarding your recent invoice.

18-B. In the following tell whether each italicized expression is good or poor usage. 1. Please *permit us to state* that we are *greatful*. 2. Your motor will *purr like a kitten* when you treat it to Nu-Oil. 3. Your AIRCO heater *makes your living room a tropical paradise*—even when the snow is falling right outside your window. 4. *At an early date* we shall let you know whether you will be *obligated* further. 5. This *natural, nutritious* candy is now packed in a box *more unique than ever before*.

Business Speech

In the following words, the italicized letters are to be sounded carefully. Pronounce each word distinctly several times.

1. be*cause*. The second syllable is pronounced *kawz*.
2. go*l*f. Be sure to sound the *l*.
3. pum*p*kin. Both *p's* must be sounded.
4. morn*ing*. Carefully sound both syllables; pronounced *MORE*-ning.
5. even*ing*. Carefully sound only two syllables; pronounced *EEV*-ning.

Spelling

Study List 18 (page 408), which contains words having double consonants.

AREA
TWO

WRITTEN BUSINESS COMMUNICATIONS

About forty years ago many business letters sounded like writing done a century earlier. The first American business letters were written chiefly by lawyers, who borrowed the unusual language and style of letters written in England, and that antiquated style persisted until schools and colleges began offering courses in business English. Today's business letters, with their conversational tone and the application of psychology, are a big improvement over the letters of bygone days. The business executive of today, therefore, seeks office workers well trained in writing effective letters—the kind that obtain prompt action and cause favorable reaction.

Each year billions of pieces of mail are handled by our nation's post offices. The New York City Post Office alone handles several billion pieces of mail of various classes. The business letter is the most common communication found in this tremendous quantity of mail.

Because of the rapid growth of American business and industry, with the resulting increase in written communications, the United States Postal Service sought a more rapid method of sorting and routing mail. Consequently, the ZIP (Zone Improvement Plan) Code evolved. It is designed to speed mail by cutting down on the steps needed to move an item from sender to addressee. The ZIP Code is typed either one or two horizontal spaces after the state name, which now is preferably abbreviated according to a two-letter system (see page 204).

The total cost of producing a business letter is increasing every year. Therefore, persons who compose them must have excellent English skills, the ability to solve communication problems, and an understanding of human relations. Office workers who type business letters must possess adequate typing skills—speed, accuracy, and the ability to locate and correct their errors.

Letter writing is among the important duties of correspondents, secretaries, clerks, and other office workers, as well as business executives. Today some large companies offer, and sometimes require, on-the-job training courses in business correspondence. Persons who are equipped with letter-writing skills on entering their jobs are fortunate, indeed, because they may be assured of promotion faster than those who lack such skills.

If you can write effective business letters, you may be able to take a quick giant step forward in your business career.

Unit Six

PREPARING TO WRITE BUSINESS LETTERS

THE PARTS AND STYLES OF LETTERS

The construction of a business letter is based on its seven essential parts. These parts must be arranged attractively so that the typed letter resembles a framed picture. Since the eye is the quickest of the senses, a letter must have "eye appeal"; that is, it must be immediately pleasing to the eye and thus make a good impression. Automobile manufacturers know that skillful construction and pleasing design bring top sales of cars. And business executives realize that construction and design are important in business letters.

The Essential Parts of All Business Letters

Most business letters should have seven parts. Each part must appear in its correct order and be written so that it conforms to the letter style used. The letter on page 180 shows the essential letter parts in the proper order. The circled numerals refer to the text topics that explain each part.

(1) Heading. A letter should announce its sender. Business letters, therefore, are typed on *letterheads*—good quality stationery having a heading that shows the sender's name and address, including ZIP Code. Other information may appear: telephone number, trademark, slogan, small illustration, locations of branch offices, and so on. The heading may be printed, lithographed, embossed, or engraved.

When using a letterhead, you must always supply a date line. The line on which the date is typed depends on the length of the letter. The date is typed at least two lines below the last line of the printed heading, and it may begin at the left margin or at the center, depending on the letter style used.

Holland Company, Inc.

12366 Iroquois Avenue, Biloxi, Mississippi 39530   (601) 291-7715

October 19, 19--

Mr. Jerome E. McDonald
1184 Washington Street
Nashville, TN 38128

Dear Mr. McDonald:

This letter is typed in the modified-block style, which is
the style most commonly used for business letters.

In this letter style, the date and signature block begin at
the center. The paragraphs are generally blocked as shown
but may also be indented. The efficient typist sets tab
stops for all necessary indentations.

This sample letter contains mixed punctuation, which is the
most popular kind used in business letters. With this punctuation a colon follows the salutation, and a comma follows the
complimentary closing.

Every letter should include the seven parts shown in this sample. The writer's name should be both handwritten and typewritten. Additional parts, such as an attention line, mailing
notation, or postscript, may also be used whenever they are
needed.

With any letter style, Mr. McDonald, try to address the person
by name at least once, preferably near the end of the letter.

Sincerely yours,

(Mrs.) Annette L. Weldon

Mrs. Annette L. Weldon

rsm

Essential Parts of a Letter

All the essential parts are shown: (1) heading, including date; (2) inside
address; (3) salutation; (4) body; (5) complimentary closing; (6) signature; (7) reference initials.

(2) Inside Address. The person or firm to whom you send a letter is called the *addressee*. The name and the address of the addressee comprise the inside address. Begin typing the inside address at least four spaces under the date line. On short letters leave more space between the date and the inside address. Each line of the inside address is typed at the left margin. ZIP Codes should be used.

The first line of the inside address contains the name of the person or company to whom you are writing. Short social or professional titles (Mr., Ms., Mrs., Miss, Dr.) should be used. A business title such as *Treasurer* can be placed immediately after the name. A long title is placed on the second line to balance the length of the lines.

Note the following inside addresses:

Dr. Nathan Morgan, Director   Martindale's, Inc.
Hartford County Medical Clinic   Ott Building, Suite 210
1151 - 21st Street*   345 West Main Street
Hartford, CT 06104   Seattle, WA 91803

Ms. Laura K. Kammerer   Mrs. Fay White, Secretary
Manager, Personnel Department   The Women's League
ABC Security Systems, Inc.   131 Lake Avenue
214 Chester Circle   St. Paul, MN 55103
Englewood, NJ 07631

Cautions: Avoid using two titles that have the same meaning. For example, write "Dr. Nathan Morgan" or "Nathan Morgan, M.D." but not "Dr. Nathan Morgan, M.D."

Do not abbreviate the names of cities or towns. (In addresses, however, *Saint* is written *St.*) Do use the two-letter state abbreviations with ZIP Codes. See page 204 for a complete list of state abbreviations.

(3) Salutation. The salutation greets the reader. Always type it at the left margin, a double space under the last line of the inside address. In business letters with mixed punctuation the salutation is followed by a colon.

Cautions: Never use a semicolon or a dash after the salutation. Capitalize only the first word and each noun.

---

*Use two spaces, or a hyphen with a space before and after it, to separate a house or building number from a numbered street name.

Observe the following salutations. Each list begins with the most formal and descends to the least formal.

TO A MAN	TO A WOMAN
Sir:	Madam:
My dear Sir:	My dear Madam:
My dear Mr. Goode:	My dear Mrs. Goode:
Dear Mr. Goode:	Dear Mrs. Goode:
My dear Paul:	My dear Mary:
Dear Paul:	Dear Mary:

The following are plural salutations:

Gentlemen: Used in writing to a company, a box number, or any group consisting entirely of men.

Dear Sir and Madam: Used in writing to a firm consisting of a man and a woman.

Dear Mr. and Mrs. Smith: Used in writing to a husband and wife when the first line of the inside address contains their names—Mr. and Mrs. Edward Smith.

Ladies and Gentlemen: Used in writing to an organization consisting of men and women.

Mesdames: Used in writing to an organization or group consisting entirely of women. *Ladies* is a popular substitute for *Mesdames.*

Use the Right Salutation. *Sir* or *Madam* is used in writing to persons in high government positions. It is not used in ordinary business letters. Since business letters should have a conversational tone, the salutation "Dear Mr. (Ms., Mrs., Miss) (last name)" is the one most commonly used.

Cautions: (1) Be sure to use the correct name in the salutation! If the addressee's name is "Mr. Charles Roberts," do not write "Dear Mr. Charles."

(2) In writing to anyone having the title *Dr.,* abbreviate the title in the inside address. In the salutation the title may be expressed *Dr.* or *Doctor.* Other professional titles used in salutations, however, should be spelled in full in both the inside address and the salutation—for example, *Professor.**

(4) Body. The body of the business letter contains the message. Begin typing the body two spaces below the salutation. Use single spacing

---

*For a list of official inside addresses and salutations, consult Reference Section C at the end of the book. (See page 414.)

unless the message is very short (about 50 words). When very short letters are double-spaced, all paragraphs must be indented. Always double-space between paragraphs.

The width of your typed line varies with the length of the body. (Some firms use uniform margins for all letters.)

Letter Placement Chart†

Length of Letter	Actual Words in Body	Line Length			Date Line
		INCHES	PICA‡	ELITE	
Short	Up to 100	4	40	50	20
Average	101 to 200	5	50	60	18 to 15*
Long	201 to 300	6	60	70	13
Two-Page	300+	6	60	70	13

*Exact placement of the date line in average-length letters will depend on how close the number of words in the letter is to the maximum or minimum. The longer the letter, the higher the date line is placed on the page.

Two-Page Letters. If you must write a two-page letter, end the first page about one inch from the bottom of the paper. Type at least two lines of a paragraph. The last word on a page should not be divided.

Begin the second-page heading about one inch from the top. Your second-page heading should include the name of your reader, the page number, and the date. Resume your message three spaces below the last line of the second-page heading. Be sure to bring over to the second page at least two lines of a paragraph. Following are two common second-page headings. The first is always used with the full-block style and may be used with other styles. The second is usually used with the modified-block style.

```
The Institute of Life Insurance
Page 2
September 7, 19--


Mr. Donald C. McQuillen   - 2 -   June 5, 19--
```

†SOURCE: Gertrude S. Altholz, Delores S. Cotton, and Vito C. Metta, _Type Right!_ (Belmont, CA: Pitman Learning, Inc., 1980).

‡Pica type has ten strokes to an inch; elite type has twelve strokes to an inch.

The paper you use for the second page and following pages should match the color, weight, and size of the first page. It does not, however, contain a printed heading. Such paper is called *second sheets*.*

(5) Complimentary Closing. The complimentary closing, which is the friendly ending of your letter, is typed a double space below the last line of the body. The complimentary closing may begin at the left margin or at the center of the paper, depending on the letter style used.

Capitalize only the first word of the complimentary closing. When mixed punctuation is used, a comma follows the complimentary closing.

If you wish to be very formal, as in a letter to a high official or to a very respected person, use *Respectfully yours, Yours respectfully,* or *Respectfully.* Never use *respectively* instead of *respectfully.*

In writing to a firm or group, either of these less formal closings should be used:

> *Very truly yours* or *Yours very truly*
> (*Yours truly* and *Truly yours* are rarely used.)

If you have already established friendly contact with your reader, use

Very sincerely yours,	Yours very sincerely,
Sincerely yours,	Yours sincerely,
Sincerely,	

If you are personally acquainted with your reader or if you are extending an invitation, you may use

Very cordially yours,	Yours very cordially,
Cordially yours,	Yours cordially,
Cordially,	

Note: The formality of your closing should match the formality of the salutation. *Faithfully yours* is common in British usage; in the United States it is sometimes used in writing to government officials.

(6) Signature. The reader identifies the writer from the signature. The signature, therefore, must contain your penwritten name and your type-written name. It may also include your business title, department, or the

---

*The paper on which carbon copies are typed is sometimes called *second sheets,* too, although it should be called *copy paper.*

name of your company. The signature is typed four spaces below the complimentary closing. If the writer has very large handwriting, more room may be left. The penwritten signature appears between the complimentary closing and the typed signature.

The parts of the signature. It is appropriate for you to use only your name in the signature portion if (1) you are writing a personal business letter or (2) you are a correspondent for a very small firm.

Your name should be both typed and signed—typed, so that your reader can clearly read and correctly spell your name; signed, to indicate your approval of the letter and to give it authenticity. Always sign your name clearly and carefully. An unreadable scrawl does not make a good impression.

Your business title or department. You may need to add an identification to your name. This identification can be your business title, the name of your department, or both.

Yours very truly,   Sincerely,

(Mrs.) Kathleen Cramer   *James Curran*

Mrs. Kathleen Cramer   James Curran
Vice-President   Engineering Department

        Very cordially yours,

           Jeff

        Jeffrey L. Pearce, Head
        Marketing Department

The company name. If you type your letter on a printed letterhead, you usually do not need to repeat the company name in the signature. You should type the company name, however, if you use plain paper. Some authorities recommend typing the company name above your pen-written signature if the letter contains more than one page.

Very sincerely yours,

NORTHWEST FLOWER SHOP

Marvin Shafer

Marvin Shafer, Manager

Women's signatures. A woman's typewritten name should include the social title she prefers to use: Mrs., Miss, or Ms. Including this title in the typewritten name will let the reader know how the woman prefers to be addressed in future correspondence. Such titles may also be included, in parentheses, in the handwritten name.

Sincerely,   Sincerely,

(Mrs.) Marcia L. Hunt   *Frances C. Jones*

Mrs. Marcia L. Hunt   Miss Frances C. Jones

Yours very truly,

Arlene Collins

Ms. Arlene Collins, Manager
Accounting Department

In writing for her company, a married woman should use her given name rather than her husband's first name.

(7) Reference Initials. The reference initials, also called *identification initials,* indicate either the dictator and the typist or only the typist. Since nearly all letter writers now type their names as part of the signature, the use of the dictator's initials is not considered necessary.

---

*Only the signatures of company owners or officials should appear above the typewritten company name. The person who signs his or her name above a typed company name is personally responsible for the contents of the letter and may be held liable for what he or she has said.

Reference initials are always typed at the left margin, usually two spaces below the last line of the signature block. Observe the following styles of reference initials. The dictator is *Roberta L. Parks,* and the typist is *Mary Lou Derwin.*

mld   RLP:mld   RLP/mld   RLP:MLD

Sometimes typists in a stenographic pool are assigned a number to use instead of initials. This number may be preceded by the dictator's initials: RLP:17, RLP/17, or RLP-17.

When a business mails all letters under a manager's signature, the reference initials should include both those of the dictator and those of the typist. For example, if Mary Lou Derwin typed a letter dictated by Roberta L. Parks but signed by Peter Gresham, the initials *RLP:mld* would be used.

Auxiliary Parts of Business Letters

Sometimes certain other letter parts are needed; the seven essential parts are not enough. On the following page there is a letter containing all the important auxiliary parts. Examine it carefully so that you will see the placement of each part. The circled letters, *A, B, C,* and so on, refer to the text topics that explain each auxiliary part.

(A) File Reference. Some large companies simplify their filing processes by including a file reference on all outgoing letters. When a file reference is used on an incoming letter, you should refer to it in answering the letter. The file reference is usually typed two spaces below the date line; if the date begins at the center, however, the file reference is placed in another location.

Examples of file references   File: AN-6501
                                     In reply refer to An-6501
                                     Our file number: AN-6501

Example in a reply to a letter   Your file: AN-6501
containing a file reference

UNITED
WINDOW
COVERINGS, INC.

1390 Bellevue Parkway • Green Bay, Wisconsin 54301 • (414) 532-6318
Wholesale Distributors of Custom Shades • Venetian Blinds • Vertical Blinds

June 25, 19--

(A) Our file number: 231-45

(B)(C) SPECIAL DELIVERY (or) PERSONAL

The Carver Products Company
114 Orange Boulevard
Newark, NJ 07113

(D) Attention: Mr. Howard L. Dixon

Gentlemen:

(E) Subject: DAMAGED MATERIALS IN OUR ORDER NO. 1168

It is good to know that you are taking prompt action
in regard to the subject order. As yet, however, we
have not heard from the trucking firm.

Since you do not wish us to deal directly with the
trucking firm, we shall appreciate your cooperation
in getting in touch with it at once so that we may
know how to plan our summer sales.

As you requested, we are enclosing a photostatic
copy of our invoice.

Your help will be deeply appreciated.

Very truly yours,

UNITED WINDOW COVERINGS, INC.

(F) *Mark L. Davidson*

Mark L. Davidson, Manager
Adjustment Department

kmg

(G) Enclosure

(H) P.S. If we are to use the goods as planned, this
matter must be settled by July 3.

(I) cc: Ms. Julia Newcomb, Newark Branch Office

Auxiliary Parts of a Letter

(B) Mailing Notations. If your letter requires a special class of service, such as *special delivery, certified mail,* or *registered mail,* make a notation in the letter and on the envelope. In the letter, such notations are typed either two spaces above the inside address or two spaces below the reference initials or the enclosure notation, if there is one. If any auxiliary parts follow the reference initials or the enclosure notation, the mailing directions are placed above the inside address. On envelopes, mailing notations are typed just below the position of the stamp.

(C) Addressee Notations. Special instructions are sometimes needed for handling a letter when it arrives at its destination. These instructions include *personal, confidential, hold for arrival,* and *please forward.* On the envelope, such notations appear a triple space below the return address or a few lines above the addressee's name. In the letter the notations for *personal* or *confidential* are typed at the left margin, in solid capitals, a double space below the date.

(D) Attention Line. When you write to a firm but wish to direct your message to a specific person in the firm, you can use an attention line. In the letter, the attention line is typed two spaces below the inside address and usually begins at the left margin. Leave two spaces between the attention line and the salutation. On envelopes, the attention line is the second line of the address.

Be sure that the salutation agrees with the first line of the inside address rather than with the attention line. Since most letters having an attention line are written to companies, *Gentlemen* or *Ladies and Gentlemen* may be used as the salutation.

(E) Subject Line. A subject line is used when it is desirable to identify, in a few words, the topic of the letter. A subject line greatly aids a busy reader.

The subject line is usually typed two spaces below the salutation. The line is indented, centered, or typed at the left margin, depending on the letter style used. For emphasis, either type the subject line in full capitals or underscore it.

(F) Signature Parts. The company name in full capitals and the writer's title and department are auxiliary signature parts.

(G) Enclosure Notation. When enclosing an item in the envelope with your letter, type an enclosure notation two spaces under the reference initials. When your letter contains an enclosure note, be sure you enclose the necessary item or items. Careless office workers often forget to send enclosures with letters.

Observe the following enclosure notations, which appear under the reference initials:

rfs	rfs	rfs
Enclosure	Enclosures	Enclosures
		Booklet
		Sample
rfs	rfs	Rate Card
2 Enclosures	Enclosures (3)	

(H) Postscript. A postscript is a message added at the end of a letter. It is used either to stress an important point briefly or to include an afterthought. Reminders are expressed effectively in a postscript. Postscript initials are typed either as P.S. or PS, followed by two spaces, and are typed a double space below the reference initials or the enclosure notation.

(I) Carbon Copy Notation. If you send a copy of your letter to one or more persons other than the addressee, note such copies at the end of your letter. The carbon copy notation should be the final part of your letter. (*Note:* Although many companies prefer to use photocopy machines rather than carbon paper for making copies of letters, the carbon copy notation "cc" is still in use.) Double-space between the notation and the item immediately preceding it. The following forms may be used:

cc: Mr. John Jones	cc Dr. Joan Adamson
<u>or</u> CC:	<u>or</u> CC
c: Patricia Chang	C: Mr. Jerome Sherry
Luke Matthews	Mrs. E. Allis Brown

Blind Carbon Copy. Occasionally you may wish to send a copy of a letter to a person, but you do not wish the receiver of the ribbon copy* to know that you are sending such a copy, which is called a *blind* carbon copy. At the top of the copy, at the left margin, type *BLIND CARBON COPY*, followed by the name of the person to whom you will send it.

---

*The ribbon copy is the original copy of a letter—the one sent to the addressee.

The person to whom this copy is sent will realize that the addressee is not aware that a copy has been sent to anyone. Be sure *not* to type this notation on the ribbon copy.

Punctuating the Parts of Business Letters

Mixed punctuation is the most common style used in business letters. No punctuation marks are placed after ends of lines in the inside address or the parts of the typed signature. A colon follows the salutation, and a comma follows the complimentary closing.

When *open* punctuation is used, no punctuation marks appear after any of the lines of the inside address, the salutation, the complimentary closing, or any lines of the signature. Open punctuation is popular in large companies, because in a year typists can save hundreds of thousands of typing strokes, thus boosting production rates.

Many years ago a comma was required after each line of the inside address except the last, which was followed by a period. A comma followed each line in the typed signature except the last, which was followed by a period. A colon followed the salutation and a comma followed the complimentary closing. This style of punctuation, which is no longer popular, is called *closed* punctuation.

Styles of Business Letters

A business letter may be typed in one of several styles, depending on the preference of the company sending it.

Modified-Block Style. The *modified-block* style, sometimes called *semi-block* style, is the most popular. It is illustrated on page 192. Following are the rules for setting up a modified-block letter.

Date: Begin typing it at the horizontal center of the paper.
Inside Address: All lines begin at the left margin.
Body: Paragraphs may begin at the left margin, or they may be indented five spaces. Always indent paragraphs in double-spaced letters.

PORTLAND TRUST COMPANY
916 Fessenden Street
Portland, OR 97203

June 25, 19--

Mr. William L. Walker
29801 Douglas Circle
Detroit, MI 48206

Dear Mr. Walker:

During the past three years, we have employed about forty-five college graduates who concur with you in feeling that banking will be a rewarding career. But the very presence of these ambitious, well-qualified people, Mr. Walker, makes it rather difficult for us to offer starting jobs in our Loan Department.

We feel that the adjustment and collection section of our Installment Loan Department is the very best place to teach young people the loaning function. Because we have several employees who are preparing for promotion to the consumer-finance section, I cannot be at all encouraging about hiring you directly for a position in our installment loan area.

If you wish to call on us when you arrive in Portland, it will be helpful to both of us if you have already completed the form that I have enclosed. I am sorry that I can't write you a more encouraging letter, but I believe you will agree that a firm must follow its policy of internal promotion to these highly desirable jobs in the installment loan field.

Thank you, Mr. Walker, for writing to Portland Trust.

Very truly yours,

Catherine A. Barnes
Miss Catherine A. Barnes
Vice-President

sa

Enclosure

Full-Block Style, with Open Punctuation

2183 Jefferson Avenue
Chicago, IL 60607
September 29, 19--

Mrs. Jeanette Atkinson, President
Chicago Personnel and Management Association
8305 Robinwood Lane
Chicago, IL 60605

Dear Jeanette:

The Program Committee of the Chicago Personnel and Management Association believes that the paramount need of the Association is to revitalize the monthly meetings to afford professional benefits to the membership.

The committee suggests that a specific goal be selected that will be in line with the interests and efforts of the organization. An outstanding objective would be the development of a Chicago Personnel and Management Association Speakers' Bureau, which would have the following features:

1. Members would prepare speeches on appropriate topics regarding personnel and management. The speeches would be polished to suit "after-dinner situations" and to be adaptable to nonprofessional audiences. Usually the speeches would be supported by carefully designed visual aids and handouts.

2. The members would present the speeches as part of the regular program sequence of the Association. The membership critique would be valuable in improving and tailoring the speeches.

3. A loose-leaf brochure would be prepared for each of the speakers. As speeches are completed, we would increase the number of speakers available through the bureau.

We shall appreciate your reaction to these suggestions before our next meeting on October 20.

Sincerely yours,

Leo
Leo M. Wilson
Program Coordinator

lmw

Modified-Block Style, with Mixed Punctuation, Paragraph Indentation, and Numbered Insert

Complimentary Closing and Signature Parts: Begin typing at the horizontal center of the paper.

Auxiliary Parts: The attention line begins at the left margin. The subject line begins at the left margin, or it is indented, centered, or typed on the same line as the salutation.

Full-Block Style. The *full-block* style is easy to set up because every line begins at the left margin. Full-block style is illustrated on pages 188 and 192. Letters in this style should not be double spaced. The full-block letter has become increasingly popular with large companies, because typists do not have to set and use tab stops for indenting. Production rates are therefore boosted considerably.

Simplified Letter Style. The Administrative Management Society (AMS) advocates the use of its "Simplified Letter," which is illustrated on page 194. The AMS simplified style is full-block, but the salutation and complimentary closing are omitted. Instead of the salutation, there is always a subject line (without the word *Subject*) in full capitals. Typists using this style are advised not to divide words at ends of lines. If possible, the addressee should be mentioned by name in the first sentence. If paragraphs are numbered in this style, the figures are at the left margin. The dictator's name and title are typed in solid capitals.

Uniform Letter Style. In their efforts to save time and boost production, some firms have adopted the uniform letter style. With this style the first line of the inside address always begins on the same line, regardless of the length of a letter. The same margins are always used. With the uniform style, letters are not centered; many of them are nearer the top of the page than they would be with other letter styles. Government offices sometimes use this style.

If it mails letters in window envelopes, a company may use the uniform style. By folding the letter properly, you can insert it into the envelope so that the inside address shows through the "window" in the envelope. It is not necessary, therefore, to address envelopes.

Other Letter Styles. The *hanging indented* style, sometimes called the *inverted* style, is occasionally used when emphasis is to be placed on the first word or words in each paragraph. A letter in the hanging indented style may be either full-block or modified-block. The first line of each paragraph, however, begins at the left margin, with each following line indented five spaces.

SOUTHLAND INVESTMENTS, INC.

780 Wilshire Boulevard
Los Angeles, CA 90005

April 7, 19--

Mr. Frank L. Roberts, Manager
Fidelity Insurance Company
101 Sorrento Avenue
San Francisco, CA 94121

LEASE BONDS ON BEHALF OF VERNON MACKEY

Thank you, Mr. Roberts, for your letter of March 30 regarding the lease bonds on behalf of Vernon Mackey. We are writing the Adam Russell Agency to let it know of your problem.

We find on checking our files that we have charged two different premiums for the same type of bond. Here are the facts:

1. Bond 48944 was executed on November 11, 1980, for $2,000 at the rate of $10 per $1,000. Thus, $20 was charged for the bond. This is the correct premium for this type of bond.

2. Bond 61632 was executed on February 17, 1981, for $1,000. A premium of $20 was charged for this bond. This, of course, represents a $10 premium overcharge.

3. Bond 61632 was subsequently changed from $1,000 to $2,000, and an additional $20 premium was charged, making a total premium of $40 charged for execution of the bond.

We are correcting our records to show a premium of only $20 on bond 61632, and would appreciate it if you would see that your company's records are changed.

It is interesting to note that when Mr. Russell wrote us on March 23 to request that we increase the bond to $2,000, he also asked that we change the notation of premium at the bottom of the bond from $20 to $40. He was probably under the assumption that the premium rate on these bonds is $20 per $1,000. We unthinkingly complied with his request.

Marshall Lane

MARSHALL LANE, MANAGER

nht

AMS Simplified Letter Style

The *official* style is a variation of the modified-block. In this style, the inside address is typed as the last part of the letter, at the left margin. The official style can be used in writing to important government officials or other persons in important positions. It is interesting to note that this same style may be used in writing personal letters to friends.

Study all the model letters on the preceding pages so that you will understand how to set up letters attractively.

Business Stationery

"The company has good taste and a modern outlook." "That company is still living in the horse-and-buggy era." Readers quickly form such opinions when they see a firm's stationery.

The Letterhead. The paper on which the first page of a firm's business letter is typed is called a *letterhead*. It should be made of good-quality bond paper and should contain a heading that is printed, lithographed, embossed, or engraved. The rag content in paper determines its quality: the higher the rag content, the better the paper. Many firms use either 16-pound or 20-pound paper.*

The letterhead, which sets the scene for the message in a letter, should reflect the good taste of the sender. The heading should be simple, balanced, and distinctive. Firms that use the full-block letter style should design headings having more printed information at the right than the left.

The printed letterhead is the least expensive, the engraved the most expensive. On the embossed letterhead the words in the heading are raised somewhat, as on one that is engraved. Embossing, however, is less expensive than engraving. Lithographed letterheads are used when color is desired in the heading.

If bright colors, large designs, or too many words are used in the heading, the reader may become distracted and not receive the full impact of the typewritten message. The heading should not occupy more than 2½ inches. Nothing should be printed, no matter how lightly, on that part of the paper on which the message will be typed.

Besides the firm's name and address, a good letterhead may include the telephone number, the locations of branch offices, a trademark, or a

---

*Poundage is based on the weight of a ream (500 sheets, 17 inches by 22 inches); for example, if a ream weighs 20 pounds, the paper is called *20-pound* paper.

slogan in small print. A trademark or a slogan sometimes appears at the bottom of the paper. If a firm sells several products, it should not list them on its letterhead.

Most business correspondence is typed on *standard* (8½ by 11 inch) letterhead stationery. However, there are four other sizes of stationery that may be used. *Half-size* stationery is 5½ by 8½ inches and is sometimes used, for miscellaneous, nonrecurring correspondence. *Executive-size* stationery, sometimes called *monarch-size*, is 7¼ by 10½ inches. This letterhead is often used by top-ranking executives. *Government-size* stationery is 8 by 10½ inches and is used only by certain departments of the federal government. *Metric-size* stationery (21 cm by 29.7 cm) is used by most foreign countries for business letters. Although most letterheads are white, a few firms use paper tinted a light color.

Shell Oil Company

One Shell Plaza
P.O. Box 2463
Houston, Texas 77001

Levi Strauss & Co   Two Embarcadero Center San Francisco, California 94106 Phone 415 544-6000

QUALITY NEVER GOES OUT OF STYLE

PURCHASE, N.Y. 10577

Copies. At least one copy is made of all the letters an office mails. This copy is filed for reference if needed. Although many companies prefer to make copies on photocopy machines, it may sometimes be necessary to make several carbon copies of a letter. As many as eight usable copies can be made with carbon paper if an electric typewriter is used. Some kind of tissue is best for making carbon copies. *Onionskin* paper, sometimes called *manifold* paper, is often used. As a general rule, the greater the number of carbon copies you desire, the thinner your carbon paper and copy paper should be.

Envelopes. The envelope should be of the same weight, quality, and color as the letterhead. The return address should appear in the upper left corner. ZIP Code should be included.

Two sizes of envelopes are commonly used. The small (No. 6) envelope is 6½ by 3⅝ inches and is often used for one-page letters that do not have enclosures. The large (No. 10) envelope, also called *legal-size,* is 9½ by 4⅛ inches and may be used either for one-page letters having enclosures or for two-page letters. The large envelope has become increasingly popular. Today, most large firms use it for all letters, and many individuals use it for their personal business letters.

On small envelopes begin typing the receiver's address on the twelfth line from the top, five spaces left of the center of the envelope. On large envelopes the address begins fourteen or fifteen lines from the top, five spaces left of center. In arranging the address information on the envelope, the address to which the mail is to be delivered, whether a street address or a post office box number, must be shown on the next to the last line. The city, state, and ZIP Code must appear on the last line of the address. Nothing should be typed below the city, state, and ZIP Code. All lines of the address should be single spaced. When typing a foreign address, the name of the country should be in capital letters on the line below the name of the city. Mail addressed to Canada should have the names of the city and province on the next to the last line and the country and Canadian Postal Code on the last line of the address.

Examine the following illustrations so that you will know where to place special notations on envelopes. (Note that all envelopes are single spaced.)

Envelopes with Special Notations

ATLAS CONTAINERS, INC.
481 Dalton Avenue
Omaha, Nebraska 68106

PERSONAL

Mrs. Alice C. Williams, Manager
United Products Corporation
1308 Fielding Street
Chicago, IL 60613

Addressee Notation

ABC Security Systems, Inc.
535 Apollo Way
Reno, Nevada 89503

The Williamson Associates, Inc.
Attention: Mr. Donald R. Blaine
Midwest Arts Building
114 East Main Street, Suite 302
Milwaukee, WI 53204

Attention Line

AMERICAN EMPLOYMENT CONSULTANTS
411 South State Street
Chicago, Illinois 60619

CERTIFIED

Ms. Jeanine Molinelli
8719 Chestnut Street
St. Louis, MO 63103

THE PEOPLE'S BANK OF AKRON
People's Bank Building
12 East Exchange Boulevard
Akron, Ohio 44308

Ms. Rosalie E. Gray
Olympic Hotel
603 Cartier Boulevard
Ottawa, Ontario
CANADA K1A 0B1

Ms. Mary L. Scott
19785 Santa Lucia Drive
San Jose, CA 95102

PLEASE FORWARD

Mr. Thomas H. Goode
48 Harper Avenue, Apartment 6-G
Los Angeles, CA 90006

The model envelopes on page 198 and above are set up in accordance with the revised postal regulations for addressing envelopes. Eventually all machine-written addresses will be sorted automatically by an Optical Character Reader (OCR), which sorts by ZIP Code. Note that two-letter abbreviations, instead of spelled-out words, should be used for state names. The list of these official abbreviations is on page 204.

Special Envelopes. Special envelopes are available for various purposes. The *window* envelope contains a transparent "window" through which the inside address can be seen. Letters typed in the *uniform* style, as well as bills, invoices, statements, and the like, are often mailed in window envelopes. When you use such envelopes, be extremely careful to fold letters or other items so that the inside address will show through the window.

PORTLAND TRUST COMPANY
916 Fessenden Street
Portland, OR 97203

Window Envelope

The *business reply* envelope is important to the letter writer who wants a prompt answer. Since the business reply envelope is already addressed and usually stamped, such an envelope makes it easy for the prospective customer to act. The stamp is printed on the envelope in accordance with a special permit from the United States Postal Service. If the envelope is not returned to the sender, there is no postage charge. If it is returned, the original sender pays the regular postage rate, plus a small fee for using this special service. *Business reply cards* are used in the same manner.

Business Reply Envelope

Folding and Inserting Letters. *For a small envelope:* (1) Fold the lower edge of the letterhead to one-quarter inch of the top edge. (2) Fold the right edge approximately one-third of the width of the paper. (3) Fold the left side slightly less than one-third of the width of the paper. (4) Insert the paper into the envelope so that the open flap of the letterhead is at the top of the envelope.

For a large envelope: (1) Fold the lower edge of the letterhead one-third. (2) Fold the top of the letterhead to one-quarter inch from the bottom fold. (3) Insert the paper into the envelope with the open flap of the letterhead at the top.

For a window envelope: (1) Fold the bottom up one-third. (2) Fold the top *back* one-third. (3) Insert the letter so that the address can be seen through the window.

Folding Letter for a Small Envelope

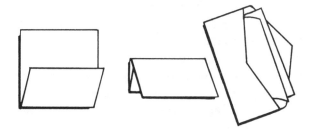

Folding Letter for a Large Envelope

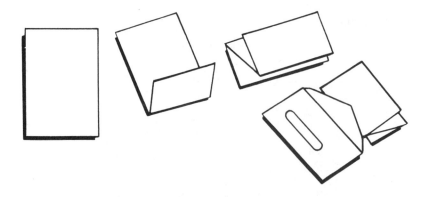

Folding Letter for a Window Envelope

Pointers for Setting Up Letters Attractively

The appearance of your letter makes the first impression. If it does not make a good first impression, your letter may never be read! Remember these points in setting up letters:

1. Use good-quality bond paper. The better the quality of your paper, the less your corrections will show.

2. When you decide on a letter style that looks good on your company letterhead, use the style consistently. You will then become very efficient at typing letters, and your company will save time and money.

3. Plan your arrangement carefully. Use the letter placement chart on page 183. With experience, you will be able to set up your letters "by judgment" only.

4. Your completed letter should look like a framed picture. The more even you keep the right margin, the more you will achieve a framed-picture effect.

5. Clean type and careful corrections help produce an attractive letter. Dirt smudges are unpardonable!

6. The envelope is important, too, since it is seen before the letter is opened and read. Type the envelope address correctly. Check the spelling of the addressee's name. Verify the building number, the street name, and the ZIP Code.

Check Your Knowledge

1. In proper order, name the parts that all business letters must contain. Also, name the auxiliary parts.

2. In what ways do certain letter styles indicate that we are moving from traditional to functional styles?

3. In what ways do open and mixed punctuation differ?

4. Discuss: How to address envelopes.

5. Indicate any corrections needed: Respectively Yours.

Skill Builders

19-A. Following are the official abbreviations that are to be used instead of state names. Each abbreviation consists of two capital letters—no periods. Memorize all the abbreviations and be ready for a quiz on them in class.

State Abbreviations for Use With ZIP Codes

Alabama	AL	Montana	MT
Alaska	AK	Nebraska	NE
Arizona	AZ	Nevada	NV
Arkansas	AR	New Hampshire	NH
California	CA	New Jersey	NJ
Colorado	CO	New Mexico	NM
Connecticut	CT	New York	NY
Delaware	DE	North Carolina	NC
District of Columbia	DC	North Dakota	ND
Florida	FL	Ohio	OH
Georgia	GA	Oklahoma	OK
Hawaii	HI	Oregon	OR
Idaho	ID	Pennsylvania	PA
Illinois	IL	Puerto Rico	PR
Indiana	IN	Rhode Island	RI
Iowa	IA	South Carolina	SC
Kansas	KS	South Dakota	SD
Kentucky	KY	Tennessee	TN
Louisiana	LA	Texas	TX
Maine	ME	Utah	UT
Maryland	MD	Vermont	VT
Massachusetts	MA	Virginia	VA
Michigan	MI	Washington	WA
Minnesota	MN	West Virginia	WV
Mississippi	MS	Wisconsin	WI
Missouri	MO	Wyoming	WY

19-B. Write a letter canceling your acceptance as speaker at the next meeting of the school Business Club. Convey by your tone that you are extremely sorry that you must now decline after accepting. An unexpected meeting has been called for the same date as the speaking appointment, and you are required to attend. (Use modified-block style.)

19-C. George Kennedy, a freshman, has submitted a written proposal to the student council in which he advocates not having a faculty sponsor for the council. "The student council should be only for students," Kennedy asserts. The council has voted down the proposal, since the members feel the need for an experienced person's advice. As a member of the council, you are instructed to write Kennedy and inform him of the decision. Using your school address, type an envelope, properly fold the letter, and insert it.

19-D. Design an appropriate letterhead for your school *or* for a business in your community.

Business Speech

Learn the correct pronunciation of the following city names:

1. Albuquerque. The last part of the word rhymes with *turkey*.
2. Boise. Rhymes with *noisy*. 4. Gloucester. (GLOSSTER)
3. Des Moines. (D'MOIN') 5. Houston. (HYOOST'N)

Spelling

Learn the spellings of the names of the ten cities in List 19. (See page 409.) Since the names of cities and states appear in all addresses, you should know the correct spellings of such words.

REMINDER: Are you practicing the correct spelling of each word you misspell? Some persons keep a list of correct spellings of all the words they have misspelled. Such a list is useful in reviewing for tests and examinations.

Section
20

ELIMINATING SEX-STEREOTYPED LANGUAGE

Roles played by men and women are changing. Years ago, most women were homemakers; they did not earn wages, enter professions, or hold executive positions in business. This is no longer true today.

Today, women are working in the business world in ever-increasing numbers. Women are entering such traditionally male-dominated fields as skilled labor, engineering, and business management. Also, with less stereotyping in the working world, larger numbers of men are performing in what were once traditionally female-dominated fields, such as nursing, homemaking, and secretarial work.

The carryover of male domination in business and the professions still exists in the English language. To avoid discriminating against either of the sexes, care must be used in choosing words and in eliminating words that could be interpreted by your reader as showing bias. The following are examples of terms that were coined in an era when the great majority of workers in business and the professions were male.

common man	manpower
countryman	mastermind
craftsman	salesman
draftsman	sportsmanship
fellow man	statesman
man-hours	workmanship

It is a good policy to avoid all possible bias in your communications. You never know how your audience may react to a careless use of language. In business, this can be translated into dollars and cents. If you take the attitude that everyone in your audience is a potential customer, you will take care not to offend them.

Guidelines for Eliminating
Sex-Biased Language

Eliminating sex bias from your communications is not difficult. A heightened awareness of terms that might convey bias to a reader is all that is required. The following guidelines should help you avoid bias and stereotyping in your business language.

Avoid Job-Title Stereotypes. Do not use job titles that could single out a person as male or female. Instead, use an alternate term.

AVOID	USE
chairman	coordinator
	chairperson
	moderator
	presiding officer
	chair
businessman	business person
	business executive
newsman	reporter
councilman	council member
policeman/policewoman	police officer
fireman	fire fighter
foreman	supervisor
six-man commission	six-member commission
cleaning lady	house or office cleaner
maid	housekeeper
housewife	homemaker
steward/stewardess	flight attendant

Note: When a sex-free term is not in common use, continue to use the current term, even when it is not literally accurate.

Patricia Sullivan is a telephone company *lineman*.

Avoid Job-Title Qualifiers. Do not qualify job titles to show gender.

AVOID	USE
woman lawyer	lawyer
male nurse	nurse
female truck driver	truck driver
male model	model
woman doctor	doctor

Avoid Condescending Terms. With a little thought, you can select words and terms that do not condescend to or demean either of the sexes. Adults should be referred to as women or men, never as girls or boys. Children may be referred to as girls or boys, but whenever there is any doubt, *young woman* or *young man* is the better choice.

AVOID	USE
girl Friday	assistant
career girl	professional (or name the profession)
man and wife	husband and wife
ladies	women (unless used with *gentlemen*)
spinster	unmarried woman
the little woman	wife

Avoid the Generic Use of Masculine and Feminine Pronouns. Do not use the pronouns *he* and *his* or *she* and *her* when you are referring to people in general. Use the plural forms of pronouns when appropriate. If a sentence must remain in the singular form, rewrite it to replace the masculine or feminine pronoun with *one, you,* or (sparingly) *he or she*. In some cases, you may alternate the use of gender-specific terms such as pronouns.

AVOID	USE
Have each employee return his forms as soon as he is finished.	Employees should return their forms as soon as they are finished.
He who applies himself to the task will be successful.	Those who apply themselves to the task will be successful.
Any nurse who wants to go to the convention should bring her registration fee tomorrow.	Nurses who want to go to the convention should bring their registration fees tomorrow.
If the applicant is not satisfied with his performance on the first test, he may retake it.	You may retake the test if you are not satisfied with your first performance.
	The applicant who is not satisfied with his or her performance on the first test may retake it.
Allow each council member to participate in a discussion. Has he had the opportunity to speak? Could he possibly feel left out?	Allow each council member to participate in a discussion. Has she had the opportunity to speak? Could he possibly feel left out?

Reword to Eliminate Unnecessary Sex References. In many cases there are "neutral" words or terms that can be substituted for those that allude to gender or sex. Careful selection of these neutral terms will allow your business language to appeal to a larger number of readers and will help you avoid offending either females or males with whom you correspond.

AVOID	USE
As a co-ed at Yale University, she received many academic awards.	As a student at Yale University, she received many academic awards.
The common man is not aware of the extent of the crisis.	The average person is not aware of the extent of the crisis.
This man-made fiber will outlast every natural fiber on the market.	This synthetic (manufactured, artificial) fiber will outlast every natural fiber on the market.
How much manpower will you need to complete the job?	How many personnel will you need to complete the job?
The working man relies on a steady salary and decent benefits.	The typical worker relies on a steady salary and decent benefits.
This is a man-sized job.	This is an enormous job.

Avoiding Obsolete Concepts

Women now make up a large percentage of the work force. Nearly half of all married women work in paid jobs. In addition, it is no longer uncommon for men to do household chores such as caring for children, cleaning, and cooking. Be sure your writing does not place women and men in stereotyped roles that reveal your own obsolete concepts.

1. Don't imply that the only wage earner in a family is male.

EXAMPLE	ALTERNATIVE
The average worker with a wife and two children has lost 10 percent of his income to inflation.	An average family of four has lost 10 percent of its income to inflation.

2. Don't imply that important jobs are held only by men.

EXAMPLE	ALTERNATIVE
There is widespread agreement in the capitol that the governor has found the best man for the post.	There is widespread agreement in the capitol that the governor has found the best person for the post.

3. Don't assume that homemaking activities are done only by women.

EXAMPLE	ALTERNATIVE
The housewife shopping for an easy-care floor cleaner should buy Nu-Glo.	The consumer shopping for an easy-care floor cleaner should buy Nu-Glo.

4. Don't imply that the responsibility for child care rests only with women.

EXAMPLE	ALTERNATIVE
Mothers should buy only those toys that have a safety clearance tag.	Parents should buy only those toys that have a safety clearance tag.

5. Don't allow your wording to patronize (condescend to) people of one gender. Women and men should be treated with the same degree of respect, dignity, and seriousness. Create a balance in your communications so that both men and women are dealt with as complete human beings. Do not describe men by one set of standards and women by another.

EXAMPLE	ALTERNATIVE
Carl Stewart is a shrewd attorney and his wife, Barbara, is a striking blond.	The Stewarts are an interesting couple. Carl is a shrewd attorney and Barbara is an accomplished pianist.

Tips for Eliminating Sex Bias in Business Communications

The following tips will help you prepare thoughtful, courteous, and sexually balanced business communications.

1. Test your statements to see if they are patronizing or offensive to women by writing *he* in place of *she,* and by rereading the statements to see if they are still valid.
2. Test your statements to see if they are patronizing or offensive to men by writing *she* in place of *he,* and by rereading the statements to see if they are still valid.
3. In all your business dealings, be sure to treat men and women as equally capable and industrious. Do not qualify the endeavors or accomplishments of either men or women by their gender or marital status.
4. If you find that your communications occasionally include some outdated titles or obsolete concepts, refer to the guidelines given in this section and reword your material. Eventually, you will automatically follow these guidelines in your business communications.

Check Your Knowledge

1. List five terms that reflect the era when the great majority of people in business and the professions were male.
2. List five job titles that single out a person as male or female. Next to each title write the current alternative.
3. Give two methods of eliminating unnecessary sex references and one example of each.
4. Which obsolete concepts are implied by the following sentences:
   (a) Every housewife is finding it possible to live on her husband's wages only by careful shopping.
   (b) Pam Murphy is a patient, kind woman; her husband Jim is a very handsome man.
5. List at least five sex-biased terms that you have heard or read in your daily communications and that you find offensive.

Skill Builders

20-A. Rewrite the following sentences to eliminate any sex stereotyping and obsolete concepts.

1. Five extremely competent stewardesses served all the passengers.
2. My girl will see that the room is arranged for the meeting.
3. Many executives become so involved in their work that they neglect their wives and children.
4. Joyce Rosensteil will be chairman of the Finance Committee and William Craig will be chairman of the Administrative Committee.
5. Everyone who wishes to enroll in the seminar on collective bargaining should bring his tuition fee tomorrow.
6. All foremen should report their manpower estimates to management.
7. Today's housewives shop in stores where they get the best bargains.
8. Because lunch was delayed, the ladies discussed last night's meeting.
9. Every department manager must submit his monthly production schedule to the Marketing Department.
10. Mary Jo Aaron, a five-feet-five-inch brunette lady truck driver, received her company's safety award for March.

20-B. Read a magazine or newspaper article and copy from it at least three sentences in which you find obsolete concepts or sex stereotyping. Then rewrite each sentence to correct or eliminate these problems.

Business Speech

1. Arctic. Pronounced ARKTIK.
2. Illinois. The *s* is silent.
3. longevity. The *g* sounds like *j*.
4. longitude. The *g* sounds like *j*.
5. mineralogy. Pronounced min-uh-ROL-uh-jee.
6. genealogy. Pronounced jee-nee-OL-uh-jee.

Spelling

Learn the spellings of the names of the ten cities in List 20. (See page 409.)

Section

21

THE TONE OF THE BUSINESS LETTER

The person who makes good impressions becomes popular. To be effective, a business letter, also, must make a good impression. If the message of your letter has the proper *tone,* you help build goodwill for your company. Since the success of any company depends on goodwill, remember that what you say is important and that *how* you say it is equally important.

A pleasant tone of voice, properly used, is a personal quality that helps to make a good impression on listeners. Your voice tone also helps to convey your exact meaning. A persuasive tone, skillfully directed, can prompt a listener to do what you wish.

Business letters, too, can cause the reader to react in the manner you desire. A letter having the right tone is sure to receive greater attention than one with an improper tone. In business letters, then, *tone* consists of wording your message so that it will produce favorable action. A person may say, "That's a really good letter"; but if that person puts it aside and does not immediately perform the action you wish, your tone may be at fault. If your letter is read and acted on promptly, however, your tone has done the job.

The right tone is achieved by (1) giving your letters a personal touch and (2) using the "you" attitude.

Giving Letters a Personal Touch

When you speak, you can smile, and the listener can see your smile. Regardless of your choice of words, the listener recognizes that you wish to be pleasant in conveying your message. When you speak, you can change your voice to radiate the best tone. You can use gestures to help create the effect you desire. You can also watch your listener and change your approach if you see any unfavorable reactions.

A person reading a letter cannot see your smile, hear your voice, or observe your gestures. The message is complete when it leaves your hands; you can't change your approach if the reader reacts unfavorably.

The only way that your reader can judge the tone of your letter is by the manner in which you have used words to express your ideas. Your letter must be written carefully, therefore, so that your words give a personal touch.

To develop a personal touch, (1) visualize your reader; (2) write *to,* not at, your reader; and (3) observe the rules of good human relations.

Visualize Your Reader. Don't think of your reader as merely a name; try to picture a person. Then base your letter on this mental image. Vary your writing style to suit the different types of persons to whom you write.

Here is an invitation to a picnic as it was written to some young school children:

```
Hey kids!  You won't want to miss the great
picnic to be held at City Park on Saturday,
August 16, from 1 to 5 p.m.  There'11 be
races!  And swimming!  And softball!  And
games!  You'll eat all the ice cream you can
hold!  Bring the whole gang.  Admission, $1
a person.
```

Here is the invitation to the same picnic as it was written to the parents of the school children:

```
We're going to have a wonderful picnic at
City Park on Saturday, August 16, from 1 to
5 p.m.  The park is clean and spacious and
has over a hundred tall shade trees.  You
can choose from a number of activities--
races, swimming, softball--or you can just
plain snooze!  Wholesome ice cream will be
served.  Enjoy a relaxing afternoon with
the whole family.  Admission, $1 a person.
```

Write to Your Reader. The best letter writers use a personal approach, which gives their message a conversational tone. Their letters sound as though the writer were actually *talking* to the reader. Good correspondents put personality into what they write, with the result that their letters have originality. They choose the best and most natural words, as they do in conversing.

Here is a piano tuner's reply to a woman's letter of inquiry:

```
In response to your letter I wish to state
that piano-tuning appointments in your city
will be filled on September 15. Please
advise on the enclosed card if this date is
satisfactory.
```

It's stuffy, isn't it? Think how much more favorably the woman would have reacted to the piano tuner's letter if it had been written this way:

```
Thank you for your recent letter. I shall
be happy, indeed, to tune your piano.

Will September 15 be all right? If so,
please sign and return the enclosed card.
No postage is necessary.
```

Observe the Rules of Good Human Relations. The things you do to get along well with your friends should also be done when you write letters. Undoubtedly you are friendly, sincere, cheerful, courteous, pleasant, straightforward, confident, and truthful. Unless you make definite efforts, however, these fine traits may not reveal themselves in your letters. Many unfavorable impressions are caused by carelessness. If you do not select and arrange your words with care, you may appear to be blunt, demanding, unfriendly, antagonistic, condescending, sarcastic, dogmatic, or irritating.

Here are some basic rules of good human relations:

(1) Request; do not command.

Poor: You must enclose the invoice with returned goods.
Better: Please enclose the invoice with returned goods.

(2) Be courteous; say "thank you" and "please" whenever you can.

Poor: Your letter of July 18 was received today.
Better: Thank you for your letter of July 18.

(3) Be pleasant and courteous; don't be blunt.

Poor: Your order was not clear.
Better: Before filling your order, we shall need more information.

(4) Be considerate; do not appear to be demanding.

Poor: I must have your answer within three days.
Better: I shall appreciate having your answer within three days.

(5) Be friendly; don't be antagonistic.

Poor: Why don't you be reasonable and stop opposing us?
Better: We hope that you will consider our viewpoint.

(6) Avoid insinuations (indirect suggestions) that might cause hurt feelings.

Poor: We don't see how you could have misunderstood our request.
Better: We are happy to give you additional information about our request.

(7) Don't be curt (rudely brief or abrupt).

Poor: (This sentence was the entire letter!) Page 32 of the enclosed catalog answers all the questions you asked about the Ace bicycle.
Better: Thank you for your inquiry about the Ace bicycle. To help you, we are enclosing our catalog and believe that most of your questions are answered on page 32. If you need additional information, please write us again.

(8) Be humble, not arrogant.

Poor: I am sending you a report that tells why school spirit is so low at Central School. Unlike some others I have read, my report gets right to the point and deals with the important causes. You will find it very helpful to follow the suggestions included in my report.
Better: I am sending you a report in which I attempt to tell why school spirit is so low at Central School. I hope you will find the report helpful. I shall appreciate any consideration you give it.

On the other hand, it is just as important not to appear meek or lowly:

Poor: I am sending you a report in which I make a feeble attempt to tell why school spirit is so low at Central School. It probably misses the important points, and I apologize for asking you to take time to read it. Please forgive the way the report is organized.

(9) Be polite, not sarcastic. (Courtesy is always in order!)

Poor: I just received the baseball mitt I ordered over ten months ago. Thanks for the fast service! I'm sending it right back. I hope I don't have to wait another ten months to get my money back!
Better: Thank you for sending the baseball mitt that I ordered some time ago. Unfortunately it arrived too late for me to use; therefore, I am returning it. Please refund my money.

(10) Be earnest and confident but not dogmatic. Don't make statements insisting you are right when you have no proof.

> Poor: (Sentence from a letter written to a large number of persons not known personally by the writer.) I am certain you have poor study habits.
> Better: Do you know how to get the most out of study?

(11) Be straightforward; don't create a negative impression.

> Poor: In response to your request, I don't have any information about how to raise money for your school's trip. Furthermore, I don't think it's possible for you to raise as much as you say you need. The only person in our organization who handles problems of this kind is Mrs. Lynn Butler of our Public Relations Department.
> Better: We are pleased to receive your letter requesting information about raising money for your school's trip. Although it seems you are taking on a difficult project, Mr. Dale, enthusiasm and effort can often work wonders. I am handing your letter to Mrs. Lynn Butler, of our Public Relations Department, who regularly handles problems like yours. You will, I am sure, be hearing from her soon.

Using the "You" Attitude in Your Letters

Whom do you care about most? Psychologists say that people are chiefly interested in themselves. Knowing this fact about people is one of the important secrets of writing effective letters. It tells us we should write our letters with the "you" attitude.

What Is the "You" Attitude? The "you" attitude is considering the other person first. Facts are explained, questions are asked, and ideas are explained from the reader's point of view. You persuade your reader to do what you want. You do so, however, by demonstrating the advantages of your proposal.

John Allen placed this advertisement in the classified section of the newspaper:

> Boy's bicycle for sale. I need to sell it to raise money for my vacation. Please purchase it before Friday, June 30, as my vacation starts July 1.

No one offered to buy the bicycle. After John and his business teacher had discussed the "you" attitude, John rewrote the message thus:

> Boy's bicycle for sale. With this blazing red racer bike, you'll go like the wind. It's priced so low you can afford to buy it NOW.

Within three days the bicycle was sold. Why? In the first advertisement John showed only what he would gain. The second advertisement showed the reader what fun the bike would provide.

The Value of the "You" Attitude. The "you" attitude is the most effective way to get people to do things. Dale Carnegie, author of *How to Win Friends and Influence People,* said that the only way on earth to influence other people is to talk about what they want and show them how to get it. He also said that, if there is any one secret of success, it lies in the ability to get the point of view of others and see things from their angles as well as from your own.*

A stationery firm required that the seller submit two invoices for each shipment of goods it purchased. Some of the companies selling goods to the stationery firm persistently sent only one invoice. To persuade these suppliers to change from one to two invoices, the stationery firm wrote the following letter:

> We know you are eager to receive prompt pay-
> ments of invoices you submit to us. And you
> can be sure that we are equally eager to pay
> our bills promptly.
>
> To help us to pay you promptly, we request
> that you, and all other suppliers, present
> two copies of each invoice, rather than one.
> We keep one invoice copy and return the
> other to you with our check. This can be of
> further benefit to you, too, since you can
> easily apply our payment to the proper invoice.
>
> We greatly appreciate your cooperation, and we
> are sure you will appreciate our prompt pay-
> ments and the greater ease of record keeping.

Notice how the stationery firm persuaded its readers by stressing outcomes favorable to them rather than to itself.

The "You" Attitude Must Be Sincere. The "you" attitude can be truly effective only if it stems from deep sincerity. Readers can usually sense dishonesty, deceit, and flattery. The two-faced writer soon loses face—and customers!

---

*Adapted from *How to Win Friends and Influence People,* copyright, 1936, by Dale Carnegie. By permission of Simon and Schuster, Inc.

Changing Times, the Kiplinger magazine, received a letter from a subscriber who had been receiving two copies of the magazine instead of one. Observe how sincerely the "you" attitude is used in the magazine's reply:

```
Thank you for letting us know that you
received duplicate issues of your Changing
Times subscription.

We've combined your recent renewal with
your current subscription.  When payment is
received, your account will be paid through
June.

Please accept the extra copies with our
compliments.  They didn't affect your sub-
scription records.

It's been a pleasure to serve you.
```

How to Use the "You" Attitude. As you might suspect, the word *you* is often used in letters having the "you" attitude. When *you* appears often, it is usually accepted as an indication that you are writing with the reader's interests in mind.

Some exceptions, however, must be noted. For example, a letter writer might use *you* many times when stern commands or even unkind words are included. Obviously, the "you" attitude can be misused.

The "you" attitude can sometimes be helped by using *I* or *we*. If these words indicate that the writer or the company feels a special concern or is putting forth extra effort, it will be clear that the customer's interests come first.

Ask yourself, "What can my reader gain from receiving my facts, answering my questions, hearing my viewpoints, or being persuaded to take the action I suggest?" The answers to this question can be used as a basis for writing letters with the "you" attitude—letters that result in favorable action.

If beginning letter writers pretend that they are writing to themselves, they may achieve greater success in developing the "you" attitude.

A Positive Tone Produces Positive Results. You may think that you have the "you" attitude; but by using a few negative words or expressions, you can ruin the tone of your letter. Today we know much about the psychology of words. We know that some words produce desirable results and that certain words produce only bad results. Carefully read Section 18 so that you will understand the importance of positive language.

Be an Expert Writer

At the end of each Unit in Area 2, you will be given pointers on how to become an expert letter writer. These tips are recommended by persons who have succeeded in the field of business writing.

When you write letters, remember the following pointers:

1. Your reader is the center of attention. Your words should revolve around the reader.

2. Show unexpected interest. If you handle all letters in a routine manner, your readers will probably treat you the same way. The "something extra" that you put into your letters may be just what is needed to clinch a sale or to keep a customer happy.

3. Get to the point quickly. When you have made your point, quickly and courteously end the letter.

4. In answering letters, it is often advisable to have your opening sentence include three points: (1) Thank the reader for his or her letter (2) of a certain date (3) about a specific subject. This kind of opening device should not be used in all letters; otherwise, your readers will think that you simply copy "form" sentences.

5. Choose your words carefully. Never use *contact* to mean *get in touch with*. Rather, use a specific word, such as *write* or *telephone*. (*Hear from you* is used by many writers.) The expression *feel free* should be avoided. Instead of *kindly,* use *please.*

> Poor: Kindly feel free to contact me at any time.
> Better: Please do not hesitate to write me at any time.
> Best: Please write me at any time.
> Best: Your letters will always be welcome.
> Best: I shall be glad to hear from you at any time.

6. Your closing sentence should leave the reader with a good feeling. Offer to be of further help; say that you are always ready to be of service; express hope for success in a certain undertaking. Say something that will make the reader feel important.

Check Your Knowledge

1. Does the use of positive language help in achieving the "you" attitude? Explain.

2. Tell whether each of the following helps the tone of a letter: arrogance, knowledge of human relations, commands, antagonism, curtness, consideration. Explain your answers.

3. How can you leave your reader with the feeling that he or she is the center of attention?

4. In answering a letter, your first sentence might include three points. What are they?

5. When you speak, your gestures help to emphasize your words. How can you emphasize your words in writing a letter?

Skill Builders

21-A. A well-known business person in a neighboring city has written you to say that she is willing to speak to your business class. She asks for more details, such as the number of persons in the class, time, place and desired topic. Supply additional information that you consider necessary.
    (a) Prepare the written reply to the woman, assuming that she is a stranger to you.
    (b) Prepare the written reply to the woman again, this time assuming that she has been a close personal friend of your family for years.

21-B. Two months ago you placed a one-year subscription for a magazine. You still have not received any issues. Notify the magazine publisher. Be sure that your letter is tactful and that it avoids smugness or sarcasm.

21-C. Your class is preparing for a newspaper drive. The proceeds will be used to help the class take its annual educational trip. Write a message that can be duplicated and left at nearby homes, indicating that students will come by on the next two Saturdays to collect newspapers. It is hoped that your letter will persuade the residents not only to give newspapers but also to have the papers ready for you when you call for them.

21-D. Write to a friend trying to convince him or her of the value of a course in business English. Instead of stressing the values in an abstract way, keep in mind the interests and capabilities of your friend and show how the course will benefit him or her particularly.

Business Speech

Pronounce the following city names correctly.

1. Poughkeepsie (Puh-KIP-see)
2. San Jose (Ho-ZAY)
3. Sault Sainte Marie (*Sault* is pronounced SOO)
4. Sioux City (SOO)
5. Tucson (TOO-sahn)

Spelling

Learn the spellings of the names of the ten cities in List 21. (See page 409.)

Unit
Seven
EVERYDAY BUSINESS LETTERS

During your lifetime you will write many types of personal business letters. Your ability to write such letters is a good foundation on which to build skill in writing the more complex types of business letters. Today most personal business letters should be typed. (A letter of condolence and a brief note of thanks, neither of which is really a business letter, should always be handwritten.)

No one is isolated from the world of business. Even in your social life, you will find it necessary to write personal letters of a business nature. Your employer may ask you to handle some personal business and compose the letters and other written communications involved.

Invitations

Invitations may be *formal* or *informal*. When you accept or decline an invitation, your wording is formal or informal, depending on the wording of the invitation received.

Formal Invitations. In formal invitations avoid abbreviations except *Mr., Mrs., Ms., Messrs.,* and *Dr.* Spell out numbers that express the hour and the date.

```
              Mr. and Mrs. George L. Dixon

                 request the company of

            Mr. and Mrs. Robert B. Clarendon

                       at dinner

            on Saturday, the twelfth of June

                at seven-thirty o'clock

              635 Wayland Avenue, South

                   Chicago, Illinois
```

In accepting or declining a formal invitation, write in longhand.

> *Mr. and Mrs. Robert B. Clarendon*
> *regret they are unable to accept*
> *Mr. and Mrs. George L. Dixon's*
> *invitation to dinner on Saturday,*
> *the twelfth of June, at seven-*
> *thirty o'clock.*
> *243 Maple Road*
> *June the first*

Informal Invitations. The informal invitation resembles a business letter. It is, however, typed on smaller-sized paper than that used for business letters. The regular letter parts are used: the heading (your address and the date), salutation, body, closing, and signature. Your wording should be conversational, as though you were making the invitation orally. The inside address may be included and may appear in its usual place or at the end of the letter.

When a club or other organization plans to issue a large number of informal invitations, it is permissible to duplicate the letters.

> You are invited to the Business Club's annual spring picnic. It will be held this Saturday from 1 to 4 p.m. at Wooddale Park.
>
> Since our treasury is in such good financial condition, the club is providing all the food! You are asked to bring only your own baseball glove or a game that can be shared.
>
> The Picnic Committee members have outdone themselves in planning a gala affair. One of the many exciting features will be a special pie-eating contest.
>
> All those planning to attend should sign up at the desk that will be in the hall all this week. We hope we'll see YOU there.

Answer all invitations promptly. Informal invitations should be answered by letter unless you are requested to give your answer in a different manner. *R.S.V.P.* indicates that you should answer an invitation. It is the abbreviation of the French sentence *Répondez, s'il vous plaît,* which means *Please answer.*

Reservations

Your employer may ask you to make hotel or theater reservations. You may also wish to make similar reservations for yourself.

Hotel and Motel Reservations. You may telephone or write for hotel or motel reservations. In either case make your request well in advance, telling the number of nights for which the room(s) will be needed and the times of arrival and departure. Generally, a deposit of the first night's charge is required to hold a reservation for arrival after 6 p.m. Request that confirmation of the reservation be sent to you.

```
Please reserve a single room, with shower,
for me for the nights of May 16 through 18.
I shall arrive in the late afternoon on
May 16 and leave the morning of May 19.

Since I shall be doing some paperwork, I
shall appreciate having a quiet room with a
desk.  I should like a room at the $45 rate.

I am enclosing my personal check No. 245 for
the $32 deposit.  Please send me a confirma-
tion of this reservation.
```

Theater Reservations. In requesting theater tickets, designate the number of tickets desired, the date of the performance, and the approximate seating location you desire. Enclose a check or money order for the total amount.

```
Please reserve two seats for the matinee
performance of Julius Caesar on Wednesday,
May 8.  If available, I prefer orchestra
seats in about the tenth row, center.

Enclosed is my personal check No. 255 for
$25.

Yours very truly,
```

Obtaining Speakers

A person who receives a good letter is more likely to accept your invitation to speak to your group. Read the following letter, which contains the important points to mention in seeking a speaker. (If you are asked to speak, immediately write a brief letter in which you accept or decline the invitation.)

You are invited to be a keynote speaker at the state convention of the Future Business Leaders of America. The convention will be held on Saturday, April 19, at the Columbian Hotel in Greendale.

Since you are one of the most prominent business executives in our state, all our members will appreciate hearing some of your helpful ideas on how to succeed in business. The time of the keynote address will be 9:30 a.m. on April 19. We have allotted 30 minutes for the talk, to be followed by a 15-minute period for questions. Your audience will consist of 700 high school business students.

We sincerely hope, Mr. Garth, that you will be able to accept our invitation. You can let me know your answer either by writing me or by calling me at 425-1138.

Congratulations

When a person has succeeded in accomplishing a certain goal, you may wish to send a letter of congratulations. Successful business people often write letters of congratulations, appreciation, and praise to colleagues and customers.

Dear Joan:

Heartiest congratulations for a job well done! I am indeed aware of the thorough planning and hard work that were necessary to get the Lander order. Such achievement shows how valuable you are to Marshall, Inc. It is such effort and accomplishment that

have enabled our firm to become a leader in
our field.

I am confident, Joan, that you will continue
to do great things for us in the days ahead.

                        Sincerely,

Letters of Introduction

The letter of introduction has resulted from social and business courtesy.
In such a letter (1) introduce the bearer, (2) give a reason for the introduction, (3) mention a few facts about the bearer's background, and (4)
thank the reader.

Dear Frank,

If you can take a few moments from your busy
schedule, I am sure that you will enjoy talking with Pamela Robbins, the bearer of this
letter. Since she is an alumna of Rutgers
and has had some TV experience, you two should
have much in common.

You will, I am sure, be interested to know
that Pamela's new play has just been accepted
for production at an off-Broadway theater.
She will be happy to give you all the details.

Any courtesy you show Pamela while she is in
Hollywood will be deeply appreciated.

                        Sincerely,

Friendly Letters

How dull life would be if we never received letters from friends! Remember, though, that friendship is a two-way street and that, if you wish to
receive letters from friends, you must write to them. Usually, however, it
is poor taste to answer a letter immediately. Time your friendly letters
so that you will really have something new to write about in each letter.

Friendly letters are highly conversational in tone. Use all the contractions you wish—even some that you might not use in a business letter,
as *I'll, you'll,* and so on. Make the letter sound sincere; make it sound
as though you are happy to be writing it.

```
                              3025 Bluebonnet Lane
                              Dallas, TX 75209
                              June 12, 19--


Dear Susan,

Imagine my surprise when I received Margaret's letter telling
me about your summer plans! Then, two days later, your letter
arrived and gave further details.

You and Margaret evidently aren't going to have much free time,
but that's the way a vacation ought to be.  While you are in
Cincinnati, however, I hope that you find time to look up
Marianne Wexford, who is one of my dearest friends.  She will
give you and Margaret a big welcome, I know, and you will enjoy
meeting Marianne's brother Bob, who is a tennis champion.

On the blue sheet enclosed, I am providing Marianne's address
and telephone number, as well as a few facts about her family.
I hope that you will have time to make good use of the infor-
mation; if not, though, I shall understand.

In your letter you inquired about Mark Youngman.  He is no
longer living in Cincinnati.  He and his family moved to San
Francisco last September, so you won't have an opportunity to
see him during your trip.

Please be sure to send me a card from Cincinnati to let me
know how you like my native city.

Have a wonderful trip!

                              Cordially,

                              Margie

                              Margie Rittenberg


Enclosure
```

A Personal Letter
(Modified-Block Style, with Mixed Punctuation)

The format of the friendly letter is the same as that for the business letter. If you wish, you can have an inside address. If you have a typewriter, it is permissible to type your letter. (Brief letters of congratulations and all letters of condolence should be handwritten.) Use modified-block or full-block style, with mixed punctuation. A comma follows the salutation.

Check Your Knowledge

1. What are five situations that require writing personal business letters?
2. Why is completeness important in a reservation letter?
3. Are there any personal letters that should always be handwritten? Discuss.
4. In proper order, list all the parts that you must include in a friendly letter.
5. On the job for what purposes might you be asked to make various types of reservations?

Skill Builders

22-A. Write a formal invitation to a party your parents are planning for the cast of the Junior Class play. The affair will be held on Saturday, June 3, and will begin at 8:30 p.m.

Assume that you have received the preceding invitation. Write an acceptance.

22-B. Prepare a reservation request for four women at the Biltmore Hotel, 515 South Olive Street, Los Angeles, CA 90013. All four women wish to share the same room; if this is not possible, two adjoining rooms will be acceptable. Request a room rate of $65 for one room or $40 per room if adjoining rooms are reserved. The women will arrive about 1 p.m. on Friday, June 4, and will leave on June 7.

22-C. You are planning a square dance for Friday, November 23, beginning at 8 p.m. Each person invited is asked to dress western style and to bring a date. Write an informal invitation to John Klein.

22-D. As program chairman for your school's Annual Athletic Banquet, you have been asked to write Mr. Morrill Collins, head coach at West College, requesting him to give the main address. Write the letter, being sure to include pertinent information.

Business Speech

Learn the correct pronunciation of the following mechanical terms:

1. chassis (CHASSY)   3. gauge (rhymes with *cage*)
2. circuit (SIRKIT)   4. solder (SODDER)

Spelling

Learn the spellings of the names of the ten cities in List 22. (See page 409.)

Section

23

LETTERS THAT SEEK OR SUPPLY INFORMATION

Letters that seek information and those that supply information are among the most common business letters. Since they are so common, such letters are sometimes called *routine* letters. This does not mean that they are unimportant; such letters require careful planning if you wish them to bring prompt, favorable replies or cause good reactions.

In most offices everyday letters include inquiries, answers to inquiries, requests, answers to requests, acknowledgments, notices, and announcements.

Inquiries and Requests

An inquiry mailed today may bring you an answer sooner than you think. Business people know the importance of answering inquiries promptly. When each day thousands of inquiries are written about everything from aardvarks to zymurgy, executives fully realize the sales advantages to be gained by giving such letters prompt, careful attention.

Product Inquiries. When you write to a firm inquiring about one of its products, be specific. Ask everything you intend to ask. Never try to tell the firm how to operate its business; for example, don't say that it will be to the firm's advantage to give your inquiry prompt attention. Don't make the common error of forgetting to include your name and address!

Note the brevity of this inquiry.

In the October issue of Office Worker, I saw your advertisement for pens. In the information given, mention is made only of ball-point pens. Do you still manufacture the regular fountain pen, No. 231-B?

I shall appreciate your sending me an illustrated catalog, with prices, of all the pens you now manufacture.

Other Inquiries. A letter in which you request information or action for *your* benefit differs considerably from the product inquiry, since the addressee does not benefit directly by filling your request. Your request will be granted only if the addressee is generous, if some real value is seen in your request, or if the addressee wishes to maintain good public relations. You must persuade the reader, therefore, to react favorably.

State the reason for your request and tell why you have chosen the addressee to receive your letter. You might point out how the reader can personally benefit from granting your request.

Be clear and specific. State exactly what you want. Tell enough in your letter so that the reader won't have to write you for additional details. Be fair in your request. Don't ask for too much information or for unreasonable action. Express appreciation for considering your request. It is courteous either to attach a stamp or to enclose a stamped, addressed envelope for the reply.

Here the request is placed near the end of the letter:

Our business English class is working on a project in which we are studying actual sales letters written by business firms throughout the country. Each student has been asked to select and write to five leading concerns.

I am writing to you, therefore, because I know your firm is one of the leaders in your industry.

Will you please send me copies of two or three sales letters you have used recently? I shall indeed be grateful for them.

The request can be stated at the opening of the letter. Many letter writers, however, feel that it is better to build up to the request.

In the following letter the questions are numbered for convenience and clarity.

As part of the information to be used for a term paper project for my class in business communications, I am gathering data regarding secretarial duties. Will you please provide me with answers to the two questions that follow?

1. How many persons in your company transcribe from a machine?

2. How many persons in your company use shorthand for taking dictation?

Your cooperation in answering the preceding questions will be appreciated.

Answering Inquiries and Requests

A golden opportunity is at hand when a firm receives an inquiry or a request. If the firm is generous and prompt in replying, valuable goodwill can be built. This is true whether the letter is received from a customer on the verge of placing an order or from a person who requests a favor.

Remson Company

114 South Street
Muncie, Indiana 47302
Tel: (219) 216-4000

April 30, 19--

State Bank & Trust Company
816 Oklahoma Boulevard
Indianapolis, IN 46204

Ladies and Gentlemen:

As one of my duties for my company, I am teaching a brief
course in consumer economics. The group meets once a week for
ten weeks and consists of any employees who wish to become
better consumers.

In one of our recent sessions, a few questions were asked that
I hope you will be able to answer for me. The questions follow. (If you wish, simply write your answers on this sheet,
which may be returned to me in the enclosed stamped, addressed
envelope.)

1. In what year did the term <u>full-service bank</u>
    begin to replace the term <u>commercial bank</u>?

2. Are there any states that do not allow savings
    banks to provide checking accounts for their
    depositors?

3. In the past ten years, what have been the
    highest and the lowest interest rates paid on
    certificates of deposit?

If you will answer the preceding questions for me, your bank
will be given a credit notice in the next issue of <u>On the Job</u>,
our new house organ for employees and their families.

Your cooperation will be very much appreciated.

Sincerely,

Teresa W. Martineau

Ms. Teresa W. Martineau
Personnel Assistant

ej

Enclosure

A Letter of Inquiry

Replies to Product Inquiries. Replies to product inquiries should be prompt and courteous. Be sure that you have answered the specific questions asked and that your letter is complete. Often you can offer additional information or enclose printed material to supplement your answer. Sending a catalog or brochure in response to an inquiry is usually not enough. Also, send a letter, even though it may be brief.

Alert letter writers do more than merely answer the question asked. Sensing the interest of the inquirer, they turn their replies into sales promotion letters. Never miss an opportunity to sell!

If you cannot provide an answer at once, you should acknowledge the inquiry and tell the date by which you can supply the answer.

```
Thank you for your inquiry of May 3 about
our stainless steel sinks.  Ms. Alana Davis,
who is in charge of our Toledo branch, is
the person qualified to answer your letter.
I therefore am routing the letter to her,
and you will hear from her soon.

Thank you, Mr. Levison, for your interest
in our products.
```

If the inquirer's letter is not entirely clear, courteously ask for more information.

Replies to Requests Made for the Writer's Benefit. Recognizing the writer as a potential customer is important, even though there is no indication of an immediate sale. Replies to writer-benefit requests are usually briefer than replies to product inquiries; they should, nevertheless, be prompt and courteous. If you can fill the request, do so graciously.

Here is how a certain large company handles requests when it is apparent that a reply is needed quickly:

Davis, Inc.   **Akron, Ohio 44303**

**To give you the promptest possible answer
to your inquiry we are noting our reply on your
letter and are returning it to you.**

**It's always a pleasure to be of help to you,
and we will be glad to serve you at any time.**

Sticker Attached to Letter on Which Reply Is Typed

If you must decline a request, express regret. Briefly explain why you must decline. By emphasizing what you *can* do, you will avoid a negative tone. If you know of a source that can fill the request, refer the reader to it. Offer to be of future help.

> Thank you for your letter of April 23 in which you request permission to hold your convention at our plant on the first Saturday of June. Usually we are happy to have groups such as yours visit our plant for tours or meetings. Our plant is always closed on Saturdays, however, and our insurance regulations forbid opening it to outside groups on days other than workdays. I am very sorry, therefore, that we shall not be able to comply with your request.
>
> If your convention can be rescheduled on a regular workday (Monday through Friday) and if we have not already committed our facilities to another group, we will be happy to hear from you again. In any event, Mr. Day, we wish you the best of luck and appreciate your considering our plant for a convention.

Acknowledgments

When the boss is to be gone for several days, the secretary usually acknowledges incoming letters. Acknowledgments are also used by persons handling the mail of high-level government personnel.

> Dear Miss Warren
>
> Thank you for your letter of May 1. Mr. Clay Merwin will be on vacation until June 10. I know that he will wish to give your letter his special attention as soon as he returns.
>
> If I may be of help in any other way in the meantime, Miss Warren, please let me know.
>
> Sincerely
>
> *Joseph Leonard*
>
> Joseph Leonard
> Secretary to Mr. Merwin

Acknowledgments should be brief and simple. You may express thanks to the writer of the incoming letter and state that it will be brought to the attention of the proper person as soon as possible. If an executive is away from the office, tell when he or she will return.

Acknowledgment letters are written for various other reasons. Whatever the reason, however, courtesy and a spirit of service should be reflected in the tone of the letter.

Notices and Announcements

Business firms often send notices and announcements to tell about changes in business policies, new locations, new products, expansion of the business, changes in top personnel, or similar matters. Such announcements are sent to employees, management, stockholders, suppliers of the firm, present or prospective customers, or the general public.

Notices and announcements may be formal or informal. They are always brief. The formal ones are usually printed on cards or special stationery. Informal notices and other announcements are printed on cards, duplicated by machine, or written in letters.

Appointments

When you appoint someone to a position or a committee, it is courteous to make the appointment by letter. Such a letter is necessary, even though you have previously talked with the person about the appointment that is being made.

```
As President of the Student Council, I hereby
appoint you Chairperson of the Athletic Affairs
Committee for the school year (give dates).
This is an important post, since you and your
committee will be responsible for ruling on all
policy matters that concern athletics at our
school.

Will you please indicate in writing your accept-
ance of this office.
```

Your appointment letter should be brief. Tell the person exactly what the appointment is. You might describe the appointment and explain its importance. Give the beginning date and, if you can, the ending date. Express hope that the person will notify you of his or her acceptance.

Check Your Knowledge

1. The everyday type of business letter is sometimes called a *routine* letter. Why?
2. Explain this statement: Every letter is a sales letter.
3. What are some things you can do to help obtain a prompt reply to an inquiry?
4. Mention three reasons for writing acknowledgment letters.
5. What are the characteristics of a good inquiry letter?

Skill Builders

23-A. Write to the AA Model A Shop, 1238 Carolyn Drive, in a nearby city, inquiring about the availability and price of a carburetor for a Model A Ford.

23-B. You are interested in joining a scuba diving club. You have read about such a club headed by a Wayne Nelson, 479 South Louetta Street, Grand Haven, MI 49417. Write Mr. Nelson a letter inquiring about the organization and operation of a scuba diving club. Include in your letter a request to send you any printed materials he may have at hand about the subject.

23-C. Write to a person who is outstanding in a field in which you are interested in having a career. Ask for a brief description of the qualities essential for success in that field.

23-D. General Manufacturing, Inc., a large firm, receives many requests for booklets that it publishes and distributes free. The booklets all deal with some phase of the free enterprise business system in the United States, with special emphasis on competition among manufacturers.

Write a brief paragraph that can be printed on a card and sent with any of these booklets. The paragraph should thank the reader for being interested in the booklet, indicate the general nature of the booklet, and express hope that the booklet will be useful to the reader. Write only the message—omit the address, salutation, and complimentary close. Use General Manufacturing, Inc., as the signature.

23-E. Susan Anderson writes your hobby supplies firm inquiring about types of toy electric trains available. Write the reply, specifically answering her question. Include a closing paragraph hinting that Ms. Anderson may be a potential customer.

23-F. Tom Crain, first-string end on your school's varsity football team, has been placed on the state's all-star football team. A year ago you moved to another town, and you have just read this news in your hometown newspaper. Write Tom Crain, congratulating him for his achievement.

Business Speech

Learn the correct pronunciation of the following city names:

1. Spokane (Spo-KAN)   3. Wichita (WICH-itaw)
2. Terre Haute (Tare-a HOTE)   4. Wilkes-Barre (WILKS-barra)
   5. Worcester (*Worces* rhymes with *puss.*)

Spelling

Learn the spellings of the ten geographical names in List 23. (See page 409.)

Section

24

LETTERS INVOLVED WITH ORDERING GOODS

Certain large companies began as mail-order houses. Today many of such firms have big mail-order businesses but also have wholesale and retail outlets for their products. Many firms, both large and small, however, still operate solely on a mail-order basis.

Orders for goods and services may be given to a salesperson, or they may be placed by letter, telephone, or telegram. Most orders, however, are sent through the mail.

Order Letters

When you order by letter for yourself or your employer, be sure that you are clear, complete, and correct. Large companies say that great numbers of orders cannot be filled promptly because many order letters do not clearly specify the items wanted, do not give all the facts, or do not give correct information.

Make your letter as brief as possible. Place the order—then stop. A certain young man placed an order for a guitar. He wrote a two-page letter that sounded like his autobiography, because he told about his frustration during the many years that he did not have enough money to buy a guitar. The vendor (seller) is not interested in your life history. Give only the facts needed.

Most large companies use a purchase order, which is a ruled form on which all information can be conveniently filled in. Some firms, however, order by letter only or send a brief letter with a purchase order.

Check your order letter to be sure that you have included the following information:

1. *The order:* date of order, order number (for large firms).

2. *The merchandise:* name; catalog number; size; style; color; quality; quantity; and price (price of each article, total price, discount if any, shipping charges, tax).

11876 Fischer Point Road
Denver, CO 80226
August 3, 19--

Kings Sporting Goods
8104 Mountain Road
Golden, CO 80401

Gentlemen:

In your current catalog, I noticed that your line of camping
and hiking equipment will be on sale until August 31. I would
like to order the following sale items:

1 Model 64 two-person tent, nylon, with zippered door and mosquito netting, green, 6 lbs. (Cat. No. 617-3)	$ 42.99
2 "Mountaineer" model fiber-fill sleeping bags, mummy style, regular size, blue, $79.80 each (Cat. No. 545-2)	159.60
1 pair women's Wilkinson hiking boots, Model 8915-3, size 7M (Cat. No. 368-1)	34.95

Subtotal	$237.54
Sales tax	14.25
Shipping	8.25
Total	$260.04

Please send these items to me by parcel post so that they will
arrive before September 15.

Please charge this order to my revolving charge account,
No. 113-48-0500.

                              Yours very truly,

                              (Ms.) Sally A. Swedberg

                              Ms. Sally A. Swedberg

An Order Letter

3. *Shipping method:* freight, express, parcel post, mail, seller's delivery vehicle; land or air; perhaps "best route."

4. *Where to ship:* buyer's complete name and address; location to which goods should be shipped if to a place other than the buyer's address.

5. *Date of shipment:* date by which you need goods; "rush" or other special instructions.

6. *Payment:* amount and form of payment enclosed (cash, check, money order); C.O.D.; consignment charge.

Following Up Orders. If you receive no response from an order, you may have to write a follow-up letter. If so, be courteous and avoid showing irritation. Clearly identify the order by referring to its date and the description of goods in the original order. If the order is lengthy or complicated, enclose a copy of the original.

```
On April 14 we sent you our Purchase Order
No. 1934-R.  We have not yet received this
order, and we have not heard from you about it.

Please investigate this matter at once to
determine whether or not you have received
our order.  If you have, we shall be grateful
if you will let us know what action is being
taken.  For your convenience we are enclosing
a copy of the original order.

Your cooperation will be appreciated.
```

Acknowledging Orders. Many firms have built customer goodwill by sending acknowledgments of all orders received. Business firms are glad to receive an order from a new customer or a large order from a regular customer. In such cases they often send acknowledgment letters that are personalized to fit the individual situation. In writing to new customers, welcome them, discuss interesting aspects of their orders, offer to serve them well, and express a hope for continued business.*

------

*For routine orders, form letters or cards are often used.

We are extremely happy and proud to welcome you as a new friend and customer.

For some time we have watched with interest the growth of your dairy and have long hoped that we might supply your paper carton needs. We were gratified, therefore, when Jessica McDaniel, our representative in your area, reported your order to us.

We always maintain a full inventory of paper cartons and related products and are ready to fill every need your dairy may have for such items.

In the future, Mr. Johnson, we hope to serve you often. Please call on us at any time.

To acknowledge unusually large orders from regular customers, thank them sincerely and show how they will profit from the merit of your goods. Try to build goodwill and express a hope for continued business.

It was with a great deal of pleasure that we received your order of February 17. We were especially glad to learn that the sizable amount of your order is due to your opening another retail store.

Since you have been a customer of ours for six years, evidently you like our merchandise and service. Your approval makes us happy, and we hope to serve you so well that you will always turn our way whenever you need anything in the frozen food line.

Please call on us at any time. We are always ready to serve you.

Handling Unclear Orders. When you receive an order that is incomplete or unclear, telephone or write the customer before filling the order. When calling or writing the customer about an unclear order, avoid stressing the customer's error. Instead, tactfully ask for clarification of the order or for any missing information. Tell the customer that you wish to do everything possible to fill the order correctly.

Thank you for your order of July 10. Since
we are eager to fill your order to your entire
satisfaction, we shall appreciate your furnish-
ing us with some additional information.

Do you wish short- or long-sleeve shirts? The
stock number for short-sleeve shirts is 31-SS,
for long-sleeve shirts 31-LS. Also, please
indicate the color you wish. These shirts are
available in white, tan, blue, and light green.

As soon as we hear from you, Mr. Latcher, we
shall be happy to process your order.

Refusing Orders. Sometimes a firm must refuse to fill an order. Following are a few common reasons for refusing orders: An item may be out
of stock or discontinued. A customer's credit rating may be poor. An
item may be available only to customers that meet certain business or
professional qualifications. A national manufacturer may sell only
through a local dealer.

In writing a refusal, (a) thank the customer for the order, (b)
explain your reason courteously but briefly, (c) tell the customer either
what the customer can do or what you can do.

Thank you for your recent order for our Aztec
copper tubing. Since the first announcements
of this product last May, our offices have
been filling thousands of orders for it each
week.

At present, unfortunately, this tubing is not
available in your area because we do not have
a branch office to handle orders in Florida.
And we do not process any orders at our manufacturing plant.

By next summer, Mr. Cole, we hope to extend
our selling activities to your region. Your
name has been placed on our top-priority list.
As soon as we are established in your area,
you will be among the first to have an opportunity to order Aztec copper tubing.

Modified Handling of Order. Sometimes the seller is unable to fill the order exactly as it was written. Some items may be out of stock, shipment must be delayed, or only substitute items are available. In such cases the buyer should be given a straightforward and brief explanation of the situation. The seller should also express gratitude for the order and hope for the customer's understanding.

Thank you for your order of September 2. The bolts of both Dacron and silk fabrics are on the way to you and should arrive soon.

The bolt of cotton fabric--print, with black-and-white designs--is temporarily out of stock. We expect, however, that a new supply will reach us soon so that we can ship it to you by September 18. We do have the same fabric and design in navy blue and white and shall be happy to ship it to you immediately.

We truly hope that this situation will in no way cause you any inconvenience. Please let us know how you wish us to complete your order.

It is always a pleasure to serve you.

Letters of Remittance

There are several ways of sending money through the mail: personal check, cashier's check, certified check; bank, postal, or express money order; or bank draft. You should not send cash except for very small amounts. Avoid sending stamps in payment unless you receive instructions to do so. If you are rushed, send the money by telegraph.

No matter how you send money, protect yourself by enclosing it with an accurate letter. In the letter indicate the amount and form of the money and the purpose for which it is intended; for example, "I am enclosing my personal check No. 78 for $250." "This is to pay in full Note No. 246-623, dated August 21."

The post office offers two special services that are useful in sending remittances by mail: (1) *registered* mail, which protects against loss; and (2) *certified* mail, which provides proof of delivery.

Be an Expert Writer

Skillful writers know that good writing is not done automatically. To write effectively, think clearly. Before writing, analyze the problem so that your thinking will be more effective. Put your ideas on paper as they come to you. Analyze, rearrange, and reword until your writing says exactly what you want it to say. Proofread your finished writing and correct all errors in grammar, spelling, punctuation, sentence structure, and word usage. When you become an expert proofreader, you will be able to give your writing a final analysis while you are proofreading.

Analyzing Business Letters. You can learn to write better letters by analyzing those written by other persons. Such analysis will help make you aware of your own weaknesses. By studying good letters, you can help improve your own. In analyzing a letter, follow this procedure:

1. Check the letter carefully to determine whether it has the five necessary qualities: courtesy, clearness, completeness, conciseness, and correctness. Make any changes needed to bring the letter up to the proper standard. Be sure that the letter is correct in all possible ways: accurate information, correct placement, perfect English, no poor erasures.

2. Determine whether the letter shows an understanding of the problem. Poor letter writers often fail to solve the problem satisfactorily or fail to express the solution properly.

3. Read the letter to determine whether the tone is friendly and positive and whether it has the "you" attitude. Reading aloud may help if you are in doubt.

4. Determine whether the letter has a good chance of obtaining prompt, satisfactory action.

Check Your Knowledge

1. How do many order letters cause the seller to write to the customer before filling the order?
2. What specific information about the goods should you include in an order letter?

3. Even though a customer may write a perfect order letter, why does the vendor sometimes find it necessary to write the customer before filling an order?

4. Name five types of remittances.

5. The order letter, although it must be written with care, is classified as an everyday, or routine, letter. Why?

Skill Builders

24-A. Write to Campus Corner Shoppe, 1349 Lincoln Avenue, Kent, OH 44240. Order one women's robe, size 12, #WW-2849, moss green, $19.98; two pairs of men's permanent press slacks, size 32, #MW-0028, brown, $18.97 each; and one pair of women's slippers, size 8M, #WW-2763, white, $14.99. Indicate that you need the goods within two weeks. You are enclosing your personal check No. 433 for the amount of the sale, less 6 percent cash discount and plus 5 percent sales tax.

Use modified-block style and open punctuation. Prepare an envelope.

24-B. Assume that three weeks have gone by since you sent the order indicated in 24-A. Write a letter to the Campus Corner Shoppe, indicating your desire to receive the goods as soon as possible.

Use full-block style and mixed punctuation. Make one carbon copy.

24-C. The Whittaker Music House had a sale of new pianos, offering a 10 percent discount on any piano purchased during February. Joyce and Jerry Thompson looked at an $1,800 piano several times during February but made no decision. Then the music store received a letter from the Thompsons, dated March 28, indicating they had decided to buy the piano at the discount price of $1,620. A check was enclosed for $1,701, the discount price plus tax.

Write Mr. and Mrs. Thompson, 721 Oakleigh Drive, your city, and explain that the sale ended on the last day of February and that the regular price of $1,800 must now be paid. Without using high-pressure techniques, see whether you can save the sale.

Business Speech

Learn the correct pronunciation of the following business terms:

1. irrelevant (ir-REL-evant)   3. identify (i-DEN-tify)
2. authorize (AW-thuh-rize)   4. parliament (silent *i*)
     5. spontaneity (spon-ta-NE-ity)

Spelling

Learn the spellings of the ten state names in List 24. (See page 409.)

REMINDER: By this time you should be well on the way to becoming a good speller. Are you practicing the correct spelling of each word you misspell?

Unit Eight

CREDIT AND ADJUSTMENT LETTERS

WRITING LETTERS ABOUT CREDIT

The word *money* sometimes means cash—paper money and coins. More common, however, in daily business operations are substitutes for money. Such substitutes may be in the form of checks, money orders, or written promises to pay at a later date. In all business transactions either money or a promise to pay money is involved, because money is the *medium of exchange* by which business operates.

A promise to pay later in exchange for a product or service forms the basis of credit. *Credit* comes from the Latin word *credere,* meaning *to believe*. Thus, it is easy to understand that the purchase of goods or services with a promise to pay later is based on trust—a belief in the other person's promise.

The Bases of Credit

The trust we display when we permit someone to use credit is the foundation of modern business. Business people must trust one another. They must trust the persons to whom they sell. Banks and other lending institutions, such as finance companies, must trust the persons to whom they lend money. Without trust many of the items we own—automobiles, furniture, TV sets, even daily newspapers—would have to be purchased for cash. Our being able to obtain such possessions and to pay for them later has improved the American standard of living.

No one lends money without knowing something about the borrower. You will discover this when you try to open a charge account in a large department store. Before opening the account, the credit department of the store will ask you and others for information to determine whether you come up to the standard of the three *C*'s of credit—*character, capacity,* and *capital*.

Character. Character is the borrower's or buyer's reputation for paying debts. You will be asked, therefore, to give names of other firms with which you have used credit. If your payment record is good, you will meet the test of character.*

Capacity. Capacity is your ability to pay. Usually capacity is determined by comparing your income with your current obligations.

Capital. Capital is the backing you have for a loan or credit. Your amount of capital is determined by adding your bank accounts to your other assets and subtracting the total amounts you owe.

After checking the *C*'s, the credit department or new-account department will either open an account or decline your request.

Credit Is an Earned Privilege. The use of credit is a privilege you earn because your standing, based on the three *C*'s, is satisfactory. One point to keep in mind in writing credit letters is that using credit is an *earned privilege;* it is not a privilege given to everyone who requests it.

To almost everyone the use of credit is a cherished possession. When we write to someone about his or her credit, we are writing about something of unusual value and great personal pride. We are writing about the privilege that keeps our standard of living high by enabling us to purchase luxuries, as well as everyday necessities.

Types of Credit

Basically, there are two types of credit. When an individual uses credit, it is known as *consumer* credit. The other type of credit, called *commercial* credit, is that used by businesses. When a business borrows money or purchases raw materials on credit, it is actually borrowing money to make more money. In using credit to obtain materials to make products or to obtain merchandise to sell, a business uses commercial credit. Business people often use the word *debtor* to refer to one who has been extended credit. The lender is frequently called the *creditor*, because the lender has extended credit.

---

* A firm's or person's credit rating can be found in *Dun & Bradstreet's Ratings and Reports,* which is used in large credit departments. Local credit bureaus also supply credit-rating information.

Whether you write to consumers or businesses, the basic approach is the same. Without credit neither the consumer nor the producer can operate adequately. Both the debtor and the creditor must use credit to keep our economy growing.

The Credit Department Works with Other Departments

To keep money losses low, the credit department carefully checks the three C's. When a prospective customer is unable to pay, the use of credit must be refused. We must remember, however, that many prospective customers are borderline credit risks. When we extend credit to them, we take the chance of losing the money. On the other hand, if they do pay, we have increased sales and profit. Many firms take such a risk. They plan that a certain percentage of credit sales will be unpaid. Through their experience and cautious judgment, they know that some borderline risks can be extended credit. They know, too, that the chances they take will still return a profit.

The credit department must consider its relationship to the sales department, which is eager to make sales. An enthusiastic salesperson often attempts to sell to borderline risks. The credit and sales departments, therefore, must work together to determine policies of greatest benefit to the company.

When a customer fails to pay, the collection department enters the picture in an attempt to collect the unpaid amount.

The credit, sales, and collection departments are closely related. The way in which they cooperate has much to do with the success of the business.

Asking for Credit Information

Before extending or refusing credit, you must gather information about the three C's. Information about bank accounts can be requested from local banks. Local credit bureaus maintain records about individual buyers and businesses. Although much of this information can be obtained by telephone, information about paying habits is often requested by letter. Many companies use form letters in which only the name of the applicant for credit need be filled in. Because character is perhaps the most important of the *C*'s, information about it is usually given in the form of short answers to simple questions. The credit department then determines how well the applicant meets the requirements.

> Mr. Charles Brennan has applied for charge-
> account credit with us and has given your firm
> as a reference. Will you please give us the
> information requested below?
>
> Length of time as your customer _____
>
> Highest credit extended _____
>
> Balance now due _____ Balance past due _____
>
> Normal paying habits _____
>
> Your reply will be held in strict confidence.
> We thank you for your help.

Notice how the preceding letter (a) identifies the subject in the first sentence, (b) states the request and specifies the information accurately, (c) assures confidential handling of the information, and (d) ends courteously.* This plan is satisfactory for all credit requests.

Often it is necessary to write to the credit applicant for further information.

> We were pleased to receive your request for
> an open account with us.
>
> As part of our routine credit procedure, we
> ask all applicants to complete the enclosed
> credit application form and return it to us.
>
> As soon as you send us the form, we can com-
> plete processing your application.
>
> In the future, Mrs. Beaumont, we assure you
> of the prompt service and quality products
> that have made Marco a leader in the field
> of home furnishings.

---

*All of us who receive or give credit should be familiar with federal laws governing the rights of credit applicants. If credit is denied, an applicant has the right to request and to receive a full disclosure of the reasons for the denial.

Extending Credit

When it is possible to extend credit privileges, write a cheerful letter that will convince the applicant that yours is a good company to do business with. Because the applicant wants to know what action you have taken, tell the good news in the first sentence, then refer to one of the C's in a complimentary manner, as in the following example:

> An account with full charge privileges has been opened for you. The excellent reports of your references are something of which you can be extremely proud.
>
> Simply use the enclosed charge card whenever you make purchases. Your monthly statements will be mailed on the first Monday of each month and will include all purchases made before the twentieth of the preceding month. No service charges are made when your account is paid in full within fifteen days.
>
> We are pleased to welcome you to Danniker's, Mr. Brennan, and assure you of the very best in service and quality.

Notice that the word *extend* is used in offering credit privileges. Because credit is earned, use *extend* rather than *grant,* which implies either something that is free or something that is a right.

In opening accounts for customers, most manufacturers or wholesalers state the credit terms to prevent collection problems later. For example, terms stated as *2/10, net 30* mean that the customer receives a 2 percent discount if the bill is paid within ten days after the date of the bill; otherwise, the total (net) amount is due within thirty days.

> Your order for Provincial Maple dining sets should reach you within the next week by Western Highway Express, as you requested. The shipment has been charged to your new account, which we are pleased to open on the basis of your excellent business reputation in Eureka.
>
> As shown on the enclosed invoice, by paying within ten days, credit terms of 3/10,

n/30 will enable you to save over $18 on this
purchase alone.

The enclosed brochure includes a display
of maple wall and table accessories to complement the Provincial dining sets. Simply use
the handy order form to obtain fast delivery
of these attractive items.

Extending Limited Credit

A frequent letter-writing problem occurs when you must tell the applicants that their credit is limited. For example, suppose you have analyzed
an applicant for the three C's and find that credit can be extended but
not to exceed $300. The letter should be cheerful, and the sentence
limiting the credit should say, "You may purchase up to $300 in mer-
chandise during any one credit period."

Observe that this sentence says "purchase up to $300," rather than
"you may not purchase more than $300." Both methods communicate
the idea. How much nicer it is to say "up to" or "as much as" rather than
the dismal, negative "not more than"! This technique is helpful in letters
in which you must restrict the reader. Simply tell applicants what they
can do and avoid telling them what they cannot do. Positive language
helps build or maintain goodwill.

PACIFIC MART  Los Angeles
Oceanside
San Diego
Ventura

September 6, 19--

Dear Mrs. Davis:

Welcome to our list of preferred customers! Your charge
account is now open, and at your convenience you may begin
saying "Charge it" at any one of our five stores.

With this letter we are sending your BLUE STAR charge card,
which should be presented to the salesperson each time you
make a credit purchase. You may use your charge card even
at special sales at all our stores. It also provides you
with opportunities for savings at the four seasonal sales
for preferred customers only.

If you have any suggestions regarding our merchandise or
service, please let us know. Our chief aim is to provide,
at attractive prices, the kinds of merchandise you wish,
backed up by prompt, efficient service.

Cordially yours,

Thomas P. Weldon

Thomas P. Weldon, Head
Credit Department

TPW/msl

Enclosure

Mrs. Marilyn T. Davis
1013 Willow Lane
San Diego, CA 92114

Letter Extending Credit
(Official Style: Address at End)

Refusing Credit

Frequently a firm must refuse an applicant's request for credit. When credit must be refused, the applicant has fallen short of the standard for one or more of the three *C*'s. The use of credit is an earned, cherished privilege; use tact, therefore, in refusing it. Say no in such a way that you will retain the applicant as a cash customer.

Here is a good plan for an effective, tactful refusal letter:

1. Open with a statement with which the reader will agree. The simplest opening is one thanking the reader for something.

2. Explain briefly that the application has received your usual investigation.

3. Tell why the applicant cannot be extended credit. Make some complimentary remark, if possible.

4. Refuse. Imply the refusal, if possible, by saying you look forward to the time when the applicant can purchase on credit. By using an optimistic tone, you can encourage cash buying.

5. Sell the applicant the idea of purchasing for cash until the time that purchases may be made on credit.

> Thank you for your order for 200 cartons of
> Moore's bayberry candles and for your request
> for a credit account.
>
> As with all initial requests for credit, your
> application was given a routine credit check.
> Although we received several fine personal
> reports about you, the ratio of your current
> assets to current liabilities is smaller than
> the normal 2:1 we require. Please send us
> future financial statements. We are sure
> that before long you can easily qualify for a
> credit account.
>
> In the meantime you can have your candle orders
> filled and save money, also, by taking advantage
> of our generous discount terms for cash purchases.
>
> Together, Mr. Covington, I am sure that we can
> work out a mutually profitable relationship
> and that soon you will be one of our best credit
> accounts.

Credit Pays Off for Everyone Concerned

Credit is treasured by those who use it. About 99 percent of all credit payments are ultimately received. From 30 to 40 percent are received with no difficulty. This is a good record, considering that about 90 percent of wholesale and 60 percent of retail transactions are on a credit basis.

Since credit is the backbone of modern business, credit letters must be tactful and optimistic. Avoid the harsh language and strong tone sometimes used by those who are unaware of the true meaning of credit. To use and dispense credit wisely is to give it the careful treatment it deserves.

Check Your Knowledge

1. Explain the three qualities a person must have before credit can be extended.

2. Discuss the two types of credit.

3. With which two departments does the credit department closely work? Why are such close relationships necessary?

4. List five pointers for writing a good refusal to a credit applicant.

5. Credit is a cherished privilege. How can you make any credit letter reflect this fact?

Skill Builders

25-A. William and Barbara Harris, 1134 North Second Street, your city, both work and have an above-average income. They have three children and have lived in the community for five years. They are buying their home and have no other large debts. As credit manager of the Hale Department Store, you have checked with the local credit bureau and found the Harrises' record to be excellent. Their application for a charge account is on your desk. Write them a letter to accompany their new Hale credit cards. You want the letter to be more personal than the ordinary form letter that usually accompanies new credit cards.

25-B. Mr. John P. Wilson, 516 West Avenue, your city, is a widower. He earns $16,000 a year as an assembler, has an 11-year-old daughter who attends a private school (tuition $1,500 a year), and has several other charge accounts about town. He lives in a very nice apartment building but has indicated no other income than that received in salary. As credit manager of the Hale Department Store, you check with the local credit bureau and find that Mr. Wilson has several past-due accounts. You believe it would not be wise to open an account for him at this time. Write him a letter refusing credit but try to keep him as a cash customer.

25-C. The Morley Automotive Supply Company, Cleveland, OH 44105, has applied to your firm, Ace Tools, for open-account credit. This means that Morley could order any amount it wished without going through additional credit checks. As credit manager for Ace, you find Morley to be an excellent credit risk. However, $5,000 is the maximum you permit any customer to have on credit at any one time. Write a letter to the firm, opening an account but telling of the credit limit.

25-D. As credit manager of the Hale Department Store, write a letter to Miss Penelope Caron, 2432 Ninth Avenue, your city. Miss Caron is a successful business executive and has an outstanding reputation in the community. Credit references are favorable. Hale's is having a private showing of designer clothing on Tuesday of next week. Let Miss Caron know you are opening an account in her name and send her a special invitation to the private showing.

Business Speech

Pronounce these words carefully. Remember: If you do not know the definitions of any words, consult your dictionary.

1. eczema (EK-zima)   3. helicopter (HELLI-copter)
2. specific (spe-CIF-ic)   4. knead (NEED)
        5. municipal (Accent *second* syllable)

Spelling

Learn the spellings of the ten state names in List 25. (See page 409.)

26

REQUESTING AN ADJUSTMENT

An often used slogan of business is *Caveat emptor* (Let the buyer beware). Today the government protects the consumer in many ways and requires the seller to meet the requirements of the transaction. Even though the seller may be at fault, the customer should always be courteous in requesting an adjustment.

Early in the twentieth century, large chain department stores began to replace small local stores. The mail-order business also began to flourish. Firms such as Sears, Roebuck and Co. and Montgomery Ward & Co. found they could increase sales volume by catering to farmers and inhabitants of small towns. These merchandising giants mailed their catalogs to people throughout the United States.

"Satisfaction or your money back" and "The customer is always right" were mottoes of the mail-order business. As a result, customers with any dissatisfaction at all returned their merchandise, with a request for an adjustment. The adjustment was usually made. Today, however, the policy of easy adjustment has changed. Now the policy is more likely to be "The customer deserves a fair deal." In other words, each complaint * from a customer is judged on its own merits. Some adjustments are made; others are turned down.

Reasons for Claims. The letter requesting an adjustment represents your claim against the seller. It provides information to support your request for satisfaction. Requests for adjustments are most often written to seek satisfaction in the following situations:

1. A product has failed to meet either your expectations or the terms of a guarantee.
2. The price is wrong.
3. You are dissatisfied with service.

---

* A request for adjustment is sometimes called a *complaint*. A more positive word, however, is *claim*.

The Two Types of Adjustment Requests

Since there are two types of adjustment requests, a customer who feels the need for satisfaction must consider the problem carefully before writing.

First, it must be determined whether the problem is covered by a guarantee. If it is, the customer simply writes a *direct* letter requesting an adjustment. Second, if information is needed to persuade the reader that an adjustment should be made, a *persuasive* letter must be written.

The Direct Adjustment Request. Notice how the following letter attempts no persuasion but simply asks for the appropriate adjustment.

> Please send me a new watch strap to replace
> the one enclosed. The second time I wore it,
> the stitching came loose.
>
> Enclosed is the guarantee card to which the
> strap was attached. The date stamped on the
> card is that of one week ago.
>
> Your prompt attention will be appreciated.

This is the plan for a direct adjustment-request letter: (1) Open with a request for the adjustment. (2) Explain briefly what the complaint is. (3) Look forward to satisfaction.

Never get angry enough to write a letter that reveals poor taste, as in the following:

> You certainly misled the public with your adver-
> tising. I bought one of your five-year-guarantee
> pens, and it worked for only six months. Do you
> think we customers won't write in for new pens?
>
> I'll expect my new pen right away. Otherwise,
> I'm reporting you to the Better Business Bureau
> as the fakers you really are.

Reread the first example. The company is surely more likely to respond favorably to the first letter. Remember: anger has no place in a request for adjustment. Courtesy will be returned with courtesy.

The Persuasive Adjustment Request. Sometimes you need an adjustment but doubt that the adjuster will understand your side of the problem.

Then you not only must state your case, but also must sell the adjuster on your proposal. This may happen when you have paid for something but find that the price was reduced shortly after you had made your purchase. In the following example, notice the difference between the direct request made in the letter about pens and this persuasive request.

> Just three weeks ago I purchased a new Perk-fect
> coffee maker from your store. Of course, I am
> delighted with it, because it does everything
> you said it would. It was priced at $29.95.
>
> After having your salesperson, Mr. Jordan, show
> me several other coffee makers, I bought the
> Perk-fect. Mr. Jordan told me that, even though
> the price of the Perk-fect was higher than that
> of other models, it would never be priced at
> less because of the manufacturer's pricing
> policy.
>
> Imagine my surprise to see the Perk-fect listed
> for $19.95 in your newspaper advertisement.
> Because I purchased in good faith, I believe I
> am entitled to a $10 refund. I know you want
> to stand behind your salesperson and your own
> reputation for honesty.
>
> May I expect a check immediately.

Opening the Adjustment Request

The first step in preparing an adjustment request is to identify the subject of your letter.

The direct request opens with your request and also names the product. The persuasive request names the product first and holds the request itself until later. This plan is similar to that of the sales letter, which requests action only after the product has been "sold."

Explaining Your Case

Since the direct request is one you expect to have granted, little explanation is necessary. In the persuasive request, however, you must "sell" your idea.

The direct request must do at least one thing: tell the reader the basis for the request—that is, what is wrong with the product or service.

The persuasive request must tell what is wrong, but it goes beyond a simple explanation. You write about the problem from your point of view. Use the pronoun *I* to describe how disappointed you are. Then, after you have expressed your disappointment, use one of the typical appeals found in sales or collection letters to encourage the reader to take the action you will request.

Appeals such as integrity (honesty), fair play, or desire to stand behind the product or service are effective. Say confidently, "I know you will want to stand behind your reputation for fair play" or "You will surely want to support your advertising, which says 'You can't buy for less.'"

Whether your case requires a direct or a persuasive adjustment letter, include enough information to make the message clear. Incomplete letters lead to further correspondence.

Requesting Appropriate Action

Probably the weakest part of most adjustment letters is the request for action. It can, however, be the strongest part. "Please make an appropriate adjustment" really says little. More effective would be "Please return the $19.98 I paid for the toaster, as shown on the enclosed receipt."

Usually the person seeking the adjustment asks for something definite. You should request a replacement, a refund, a repair job, or only a simple apology. The adjustment should meet the needs of the case. The more specific the request, the more likely it is to be granted.

Put Yourself in the Adjuster's Place

In writing adjustment requests, try to put yourself in the position of the person who will receive your letter. The adjuster, too, is human and responds to appeals just as you do. In fact, you have the upper hand, because you have the opportunity to tell your story completely and clearly without interruptions. And your story must be read. Don't use your advantage, however, to try to get something for nothing. The adjuster can see the weak spots in an unethical request.

Since business is based on mutual trust, use this basis to your advantage. Determine which action is rightfully yours, explain fully, and request the rightful action. Then the adjuster will see things your way.

Check Your Knowledge

1. How do the direct and the persuasive adjustment requests differ?

2. What is the weakest part of most adjustment requests? How can this weakness be overcome?

3. A customer has fallen behind in making payments on an account and writes you complaining that a product purchased has not lived up to its guarantee. How would you reply?

4. When a firm is deciding whether to make an adjustment, is goodwill a factor to be considered? Discuss.

5. What are the typical reasons that customers request adjustments?

Skill Builders

26-A. Just four days ago, you, as owner-manager of A-1 Sporting Goods Store, accepted delivery of one dozen Pro Model tennis rackets. The rackets were purchased by you from Acme Manufacturing, 16718 Cermak Road, Chicago, IL 60616. The first three rackets you sold have now been returned because of broken strings. Apparently the material used was either too old or partially rotted. Write a letter requesting an immediate adjustment. You want a dozen good rackets, and you want a company representative to pick up the defective ones.

26-B. After much shopping for a new stereo, you purchased one for $319 from Westchester Electronics, 4400 South Main Street, your city. The salesperson closed the sale with the statement, "Your shopping problems are over. This Zero Model B set is the finest available, and we sell it at the lowest possible price. We'll never be undersold." Now, only a few days later, you see the same stereo advertised for $279 at the Rule Discount Store. You clip the ad from the paper and write a letter to the manager of Westchester Electronics, requesting a refund for the difference in prices.

26-C. Often mail-order items arrive in faulty condition because of negligence in packaging, careless handling by carriers, or other related mishandling. You have sent your check for $12.98 to Disk Records, 2005 McAllister Street, San Francisco, CA 94118, for a special album entitled *Great Bands of the Past.* The album arrives, but the records are stuck together and slightly warped. You put the records back in the album and wrap it for mailing back to Disk Records. You also write a letter to seal in an envelope attached to the package. You want either your money back or an album in good condition.

26-D. Three months ago you canceled your membership in the Mystery-of-the-Month Book Club, 45 Clark Street, Suite 444, Buffalo, NY 14206. Despite your cancellation, you have received a book in each of the past three months. You have refused delivery of the books and had each of them returned to the sender. Now you receive a bill for $22.50 covering the last three months. The bill is stamped "Past Due." A little indignant, you decide to put a stop to this nonsense by writing a letter to the club. Your letter is simply an objection to this practice.

Business Speech

The syllable *psych* is derived from *psyche,* meaning *the mind. Psych* rhymes with *like;* the *p* is silent. *Pneum* means *air;* the *p* is silent. *Pseudo* means *false;* it rhymes with *judo,* and the *p* is silent. Learn to pronounce the following words. If you do not know the meanings of some words, look them up in a reliable dictionary.

1.	psychic	6.	psychopathic
2.	psychiatry	7.	psychosomatic
3.	psychosis	8.	pneumatic
4.	psychotic	9.	pneumonia
5.	psychological	10.	pseudonym

Spelling

Trade names that are registered with the United States government should be capitalized. Names that are not registered should not be capitalized. (*Note:* A registered trade name should be used as an adjective, not a noun.)

Study List 26 on page 409. Also, learn the spellings of the ten words in the "Business Speech" section on the preceding page.

Section

27

HANDLING ADJUSTMENTS

Though the word *claim* has a negative sound, requests for adjustments are often called *claims*. A claim, it is true, makes a charge against a firm, but business looks on claims with a positive attitude. Claims give a company an opportunity to improve its service, its products, and its public relations. In writing to a customer, however, do not use the word *claim*.

People usually make claims when they feel they have suffered. Product failure and poor service always hurt the customer. They would hurt the firm, also, if it were not for fair, prompt handling of adjustments.

Keeping Goodwill

The employee who realizes that claims can help the firm always thanks the customer for writing a complaint. (The word *complaint,* however, is avoided!) The person replying to a complaint can say, for example, "Thank you for writing us about the difficulty you are having with the XYZ dishwasher. Letters such as yours enable us to improve our product." Even if the adjustment is to be refused, the writer can thank the customer.

A goodwill approach to handling adjustments makes friends for the firm. A negative approach can lose many more customers than merely the one turned away by a poor letter. Poorly treated customers tell their friends about the treatment, and the chain reaction begins. LOST—one reputation and many customers!

Granting an Adjustment

When a customer submits a legitimate claim, a business usually makes the adjustment at once. Notice how this letter grants the adjustment:

> A new Popmaster toaster is on its way to you today. The Northern Electric Company stands behind its guarantee 100 percent.
>
> Your Popmaster failed because of a broken coil that probably was partially weakened during shipping from our factory. After a few heatings, the coil broke completely. Accidents such as this occasionally happen because of the delicate nature of the new superheat coils.
>
> You'll like your new Popmaster. The cushioned feet, available on only our latest models, enable you to use the toaster, even on finely polished surfaces, with no fear of scratches.
>
> When your new toaster arrives, Mrs. Gavin, please return the new guarantee card to be sure of Northern's usual prompt service.

The plan for granting an adjustment is clearly shown in the preceding letter:

1. Open with what the customer wants to hear—that the adjustment has been granted.
2. If details are necessary to convince the customer that the problem is not a common one, give such details. Never imply, however, that the customer was at fault.
3. Close the letter with some additional information about the

product or service. Convince the customer that yours is a good firm with which to do business.

Notice how the plan is applied in another letter:

Thank you for writing about your experience in our store last Monday. Letters such as yours give us the opportunity to examine and improve our customer relations practices.

The young clerk who waited on you was a temporary employee filling in for one of our experienced clerks. Although she showed very poor judgment and a lack of tact, I think you'll approve of the following action: a new training program for our clerks has been started. Through it we hope to educate new employees to offer the type of service to which our valued customers are entitled.

Since we believe--and think you'll agree--that the young woman should be given another chance, she is now in the training class and shows much promise.

Thank you again, Mr. Quipp, for giving us this opportunity to improve our service. On your next visit to the store, I hope you'll stop by the same department to see the improvement you have helped us make.

The preceding letter soothes a delicate situation. It also relies on the customer's sense of fair play. Positive action taken in response to a complaint is usually more effective than a mere apology and a promise that something will never happen again. You can't ever be sure that an incident won't happen again!

Refusing an Adjustment

Refusing an adjustment requires tact and skillful writing. The good adjustment writer knows that the customer will not receive the refusal happily. The same customer, however, will probably return if the refusal is fair and shows that there are two sides to the story.

In the following letter, can you detect the plan for a refusal letter?

Thank you for returning the two Ajax shirts and giving us the opportunity to examine them.

After giving the shirts the usual routine examination, our Quality Control Department reported:

The shirts faded because they had not been laundered in accordance with the instructions, which say, "Hand launder only in lukewarm water with a mild detergent." The shirts show indications of machine laundering and traces of soap.

Because we make adjustments only for defects in materials or construction, we are returning the shirts to you. However, Mr. Salter, you'll find the enclosed instructions for tinting very helpful in returning the shirts to their original color.

We assure you of our help whenever possible and look forward to seeing you at Berkeley's soon.

Based on the preceding letter, the following is the plan for the refusal letter:

1. Open with a statement designed to get some agreement from the customer. (In this case, simply thanking him for returning the shirts was a sentence that got agreement.) The big point is to say nothing to which the reader might say no. A negative reaction might lead to disagreement with the entire letter.
2. Follow the opening with a logical development of the story. (Notice that the letter avoided saying "you" in telling the cause of the trouble.)
3. After explaining the cause of the trouble, make the refusal. Not once did the letter use the words *no, unable, refuse,* or *regret.* Such negative words do much to destroy the politeness of the refusal.)
4. End the letter by talking about something other than your refusal. Don't apologize for your action; after all, the customer was at fault by not following directions. If possible, look forward to something pleasant.

Language to Avoid

Several taboo words should be avoided in writing responses to adjustment letters. For example, at times the word *you* has a negative effect!

In the letter about shirts, the writer could have gotten into an argument with the customer by saying, "You didn't wash the shirts according to the instructions." There is a big difference between saying "You caused the shirts to fade" and "the shirts faded." People don't like to be told about mistakes they have made. To put *you* in a sentence pointing out a mistake is to ask for trouble. Avoid such phrases as the following:

You caused	You forgot
You claim	You neglected
You failed	You overlooked

In the refusal letter avoid negative words. The technique of saying no gracefully through implication is a valued one. For example, compare the following examples:

NEGATIVE	POSITIVE
We cannot ship in lots of less than twelve.	We ship in lots of twelve or more only.
Your order cannot be shipped before June 16.	Your order can be shipped about June 16.
We do not make adjustments when the customer is at fault.	We make adjustments only in the event of defects in materials or construction.
We are unable to do as you ask because you have not filled in the form properly.	We can make the adjustment as soon as the form is returned properly completed.

The lesson is obvious. Emphasize what you, the adjuster, can do. Avoid saying what you cannot do. Ordinarily the customer will get the message. If you think you haven't made your meaning clear, it is better to say no than to attempt the implied-no technique and fail. Each letter that you write adds to the expenses of your firm. Remember that it requires many dollars in sales to return $1 in profit.

Compromising on an Adjustment

Whenever possible, a firm will try to meet the customer halfway rather than refuse a request. For this reason, many adjustment replies seek a compromise. For example, let's assume that the Popmaster toaster incident was the customer's fault. At the same time, though, we know that the toaster can be repaired easily and be as good as new. Notice how the following letter refuses but ends with a suggestion for solution:

Thank you for writing us and returning your Popmaster so that we could determine the cause of the problem.

Our service department examined the toaster and discovered that the coil had burned in two because the timing device had been forced beyond its limit. This caused the pop-up mechanism to operate on only a manual basis. This can happen when dark toast is desired, but the toaster is forced to operate in a shorter time. The instructions say to let the toaster stop according to the timing device, rather than to pop the toast by hand.

Since we make no-charge adjustments only in cases of defects in materials or construction, we are unable to replace the coil at our own expense. However, our service department can repair your toaster for only $5.50 and return it to you as good as new.

Simply return the enclosed card, with your approval to go ahead with the repairs. The toaster, with a new coil, will then be returned to you C.O.D.

Notice that the compromise adjustment (1) begins with a statement with which the reader will agree, (2) follows with an explanation of the details, and (3) ends with the offer to meet the customer halfway. This approach to customer service develops goodwill and protects the firm against loss from adjustments that are granted but that should not be made free.

Adjustments Build Business

In writing adjustment letters, keep two points in mind: First, you want to be fair to the customer. Second, in being fair to the customer, you must also be fair to your firm and to all its other customers.

Avoid words that accuse. Try to say no by implying what you can do rather than what you can't do.

Handle every adjustment so that you will keep the customer's goodwill.

Be an Expert Writer

Consult the Subject Index to find the location of these two topics: *subordination* and *parallel construction*. Read the information about them.

To become expert, good writers constantly refresh themselves on points of English composition.

Tips from Top Writers of Adjustment Letters

1. No matter how angry a complaint may sound, keep your head. If you do, you'll keep the customer and the customer's goodwill.

2. If you remain calm when you receive a fiery complaint from a customer, the customer tends to take a more rational view of the situation and will probably agree with you more readily.

3. The adjustment writer should remember that occasionally both the buyer and the seller are at fault. In such cases the adjustment made should meet the seller's obligation.

4. A company should not assume that it has a perfect adjustment policy. Not all aggrieved customers write concerning their dissatisfaction. Instead, they tell their friends about it! At intervals, therefore, a company should reevaluate its adjustment policy.

5. Established customers are worth more than a dozen prospects. In making an adjustment, try to keep them!

6. Don't answer a complaint until you fully understand what the customer is complaining about. But *do* answer the customer.

7. If an adjustment cannot be made at once, write the customer and say that the matter is being considered. Make no promises, however. Never say that a "thorough investigation" will be made.

8. Never tell customers that they have made complaints or placed claims. They believe that they have stated their rights!

Check Your Knowledge

1. In handling adjustments, what is the most important point to consider?

2. How should you open a letter granting an adjustment? refusing an adjustment?

3. Does the word *you* require careful handling in adjustment letters? Explain.

4. Is the passive voice of verbs ever effective in adjustment letters? Discuss.

5. When is a compromise suggested as a method of settling an adjustment?

Skill Builders

27-A. As adjustment manager of Rose May Swimsuit Manufacturing Company, you receive a request to make good on the guarantee printed on the hangtag accompanying all suits. The guarantee says, "This garment is guaranteed against all defects in materials or construction for one year." The customer, Ms. Donna T. Russell, 323 Oak Grove Lane, Overton, NV 89040, has returned her suit to you for examination. It is badly faded. But it is also a model that was discontinued three years ago. Write Ms. Russell a letter explaining the situation.

27-B. As adjustment manager of Acme Manufacturers, write the letter Acme should send to solve the tennis racket problem described in Skill Builder 26-A. You want to accept full responsibility for the defective rackets. The silk string used on the rackets was indeed partially rotted. Twelve new rackets are being sent today. A company representative will pick up the defective rackets.

27-C. As adjustment manager of Disk Records (see Skill Builder 26-C), you examine the defective records that were returned. Because water had apparently leaked into the package and you can find no reason for this to have happened in your shipping department, you'll later make a claim against the carrier, National Freight Lines. In the meantime, however, write a letter to accompany the new records.

27-D. Mr. Ernesto Gonzales, 345 West Adams Street, Webster, IA 52355, bought a stereo set three weeks ago from your large furniture store 150 miles from his home. It worked well for a few days, but then the volume control failed to function. Mr. Gonzales considered the problem minor—one he could easily solve by himself. After taking the set apart, he found the problem quite complex. So he put the parts back together as best he could and returned the stereo to the store, with a request that it be repaired under the terms of the 90-day guarantee against defective materials and construction. But the guarantee specifically states that repairs are to be made only by the manufacturer's representative and any attempt on the part of the owner to do the work invalidates the guarantee. For $35 the stereo can be repaired, but Mr. Gonzales will have to pay the bill. Write him a letter.

Business Speech

1. facetious (fa-SEE-shus)   3. sacrilege (SAC-ruh-lij)
2. posthumous (POS-chu-mus)   4. sacrilegious (sac-ruh-LIJ-us)
                5. tedious (TEE-di-us)

REMEMBER: You are responsible for learning the meanings of all words in "Business Speech" sections.

Spelling

Study List 27, which contains words that have appeared on many civil service tests. (See page 409.)

Unit Nine

PERSUASIVE LETTERS

Section

28

Advertising and its related sales letters form the foundation on which today's business builds success. For example, a certain large company mails over seventy million pieces of direct-mail advertising a year; this material moves at the rate of nine tons a week! The person who can write good sales letters, therefore, is assured of finding a good job, provided other necessary qualifications are present.

On the job you may never be required to write a sales letter. You should know how to write and analyze sales letters, however, because (1) people who can write good sales letters usually can write effective letters of any other type, and (2) all consumers should be able to analyze sales letters so that they will purchase wisely.

If you become a secretary, your employer may dictate various types of sales letters that you will be required to transcribe. If you become a general clerk, you may be required to perform certain duties in connection with sales letters. If you are an expert letter writer, you may obtain a job as correspondent in which you will be required to write many sales letters.

Planning the Sales Letter

If you asked a good salesperson the three major points to consider in planning a sale, you would be told that you must (1) know your product, (2) know your market, and (3) know your customer. When you possess these three types of knowledge, you must decide which *appeal* to use in trying to persuade the customer to buy.

Know Your Product. No matter what your letter tries to sell, product information is of prime importance. Without adequate product information, you cannot speak authoritatively about your product. If you do not write with authority, your reader will not be persuaded to buy.

Physical information. You should be able to answer questions such as the following about the physical description of the product. What is it made of? What are its dimensions? How much does it weigh? What color is it? Does it have scent or taste? What is its shape? Does it have sound? What style is it? The good writer of sales letters capitalizes on the outstanding physical features of the product.

Use information. Thoroughly understand the use and operation of your product so that you can answer questions such as these: How is the product used? How does it operate? How much power does it have? What is its speed? Be able to point out any unusual use features.

Trade information. Trade information includes data that may change occasionally. Be prepared to answer such questions as these: What is the price of the product? What are the terms of payment? Is it new or is it well established? How many sales have been made? What services accompany its purchase? How capable is the firm manufacturing it?

Know the Market. You may know your product thoroughly; but if you do not know the market in which it is sold, you cannot write an effective sales letter. To be assured that you know the market, be able to answer questions such as these: What other companies manufacture similar products? How does this product compare with those of competitors? What features does it have that competitive products do not have? What services does my company provide that competitors do not provide? Has the product been tested in any way?

Know the Customer. Most large firms learn about potential customers by engaging in market research, either through their own research departments or market specialists outside the firm.

In sending a sales letter to thousands of persons, it is impossible to know everything about each of them. It is possible, however, to obtain information that is common to most members of a group. To know your customer, you should have some general information. You must know the kinds of people who buy and use your product and those who probably can be persuaded to buy it; where they live, how they spend their money, and where and how they buy goods and services; their sex, average income, and average age. It is helpful, also, to know why some persons choose your product and others do not. It is equally helpful to know why some persons buy your competitors' products and others do not.

Mailing Lists. When thousands of names have been considered and the most likely customers selected, a mailing list is compiled. If a list is to be used repeatedly, it may be set up in permanent form on the Addressograph or one of the other types of addressing machines. Data-processing equipment now permits high-speed handling. If the list is to be used only a few times, it is typed. Some firms specialize in compiling and selling mailing lists.

The Right Appeal

When you have become thoroughly familiar with your product, your market, and your customer, decide which appeal to use. The appeal is the basis of your sales "pitch." The psychological appeal used in a sales letter can either make or break it. The appeal is based on the fulfillment of a human want or desire. Certain wants and desires are common to everyone. The most important are

Security: feeling secure from real or imagined physical, emotional, or financial dangers.

Usefulness: deriving satisfaction and success from work, service, or social relationships.

Comfort: having adequate food, clothing, and shelter; having good health.

Affection: having affection for and from those you love.

Ownership: possessing certain necessities and luxuries; collecting certain items.

Approval: belonging to a group; being approved by others.

Recreation: having pleasurable mental and physical activity.

Curiosity: having the satisfaction of finding out. This is a strong human urge; and whatever the basic appeal of a sales letter may be, it often can be strengthened by arousing curiosity. The reader, however, should not be left curious about basic product information!

A good sales letter or advertisement may be based on one or more appeals. A letter from a soup company might be based on the appeal to good health by stressing the nutritional value of soup. The letter might, however, have other appeals, such as the ease and speed of preparing the soup (comfort), the pleasing manner in which children respond to soup (affection), and the general nod of approval that the entire family gives when a good meal starts with soup (approval and usefulness), as well as other appeals.

Description in the Sales Letter

Write so that your reader will see the product. By using *physical* description—size, weight, shape, and the like—the product becomes specific in the reader's mind.

Seeing, however, is not enough. The reader must feel a strong need for the product and the pleasure, satisfaction, and so on that the product can bring. *Emotional* description, therefore, plays up your basic appeal and helps to convince the reader.

Both physical and emotional description are important in sales letters. Since adjectives are the picture-makers of language, they should be used skillfully in providing product information and building appeals. Remember that a house is as cold as its architect's blueprint until it becomes a home—a place where the love, companionship, and happiness of a family are nurtured. Physical description helps create an object in space in the mind's eye of the reader. Emotional description moves the object toward the reader's heart.

The Sales Steps

To close a sale successfully, five steps may be necessary:

1. attract attention
2. arouse interest
3. create desire
4. instill conviction
5. obtain favorable action

Not all selling situations require the first of these steps.

The writer of good sales letters realizes that, even though attention may be attracted by a splendid opening and a potential customer's interest may be aroused sufficiently to make the customer feel a need for the product, the prospect will not buy if not convinced.

A sales letter should contain your brightest, most glowing language. If, within the space of one or two pages, you wish to change the reader's feeling from disinterest to conviction, your language must sparkle. Every word must "hit the nail on the head"! Even though your letter may be reproduced 100,000 times, make it seem as though you are writing personally to each reader.

WE MISSED YOU!

During our Semiannual Sale we were indeed happy to see--and serve--many old friends. More than 85 percent of our regular customers took advantage of the big discounts offered during the sale.

We were sorry, however, that you were not able to visit us. The next invitational sale will be held THE WEEK OF MAY 14, so please mark that date on your calendar. We look forward to seeing you!

> BERNARD'S FURNITURE BAZAAR
> of Philadelphia

KEEP YOUR COOL ... ALL SUMMER LONG

In the middle of the worst heat wave in 25 years, Andrew Jenkins' air conditioner broke down. And because service people were so very busy during that time, Mr. Jenkins had to suffer for a week during the 98-degree temperature.

Don't let that happen to you. When you buy a Cool Comfort air conditioner from us, we shall repair it--no matter what the temperature--or lend you a replacement until we can repair it for you. Now, who can promise more than that?

PENINSULA APPLIANCES
1186 Bay Vista Road, Miami, Florida 33122

Sales Promotion Postcards

Postcards may be effectively used for sales promotion purposes. Cards may be standard size or a little larger. Wording should be brief and, whenever possible, imaginative.

Writing the Sales Letter

A letter containing a complete sales message has three parts: (1) *opening,* to attract the reader's attention and set the scene for the persuasion that is to follow; (2) *advertising,* to arouse interest and to persuade the reader to buy; and (3) *closing,* to induce the reader to take favorable action.

Attention. The opening of a sales letter should be an eye-opener, a jolter, or a shocker. It must launch the rocket! It should be fascinating enough to overcome the natural resistance of the reader and cause her or him to continue reading. The opening should deal with the reader's interests, but it should also relate to the subject of the letter. Never use trite openings, apologies, or remarks that may insult your reader's intelligence. Expert sales writers recommend certain types of openers. Observe the following attention-getting opening sentences:

A vivid question	When shall we vacation on the moon? Would you like to play the piano . . . in four hours?
Vivid phrases	The spectacle of the marching band, the whirl of graceful drum majorettes, the tumultuous roar of the crowd, and the frenzy that greets the team as it marches out to the field . . .
A strong or lively statement	You're royalty in our hotel! We are your humble subjects, waiting eagerly to carry out your every command.
An interesting anecdote	The sun and the wind had an argument about who could more quickly make a man take off his coat. The wind boasted, "Let me show you!" It whistled and roared, but the man merely wrapped his coat tightly around him. Then the sun said, "Let me try." It shone warmly and gently, and in a short time the man removed his coat. Silent and gentle the sun may be, but what does it do to the coat of paint on your car?
A moderate command	Start today to ENJOY your meals more.
A quotation or slogan	"A stitch in time saves nine." You can save $9 without even taking a stitch.
A humorous remark	A friend of mine has a "do-it-yourself" kit that he has never used. He can't quite figure out how to open the carton it came in.
Statements showing similarity or contrast	In grandmother's day only one of every 100 persons ever saw a President. Today, thanks to television, nearly everyone has seen and heard the President in action.

A testimonial	"We moved by Mayflower, too . . . they were right on time!" After homeowners have experienced an efficient Mayflower move, they don't soon forget.
News items or current events	In a recent storm New York City was hit by winds that approached 75 miles an hour and by 30 inches of snow. The temperature dipped to zero. Those living in houses with adequate insulation felt warm and snug.
Human interest	In rural France today, one can still come across farming families scything and binding wheat by hand.
An offer	The enclosed stamps entitle you to enjoy *The American Home* for a whole year as our guest. That's what it amounts to when you accept this offer that brings you a two-year subscription for the price of one.
A reader's problem	In only three months a better-read, more informed, more confident YOU can be the center of attention in any group! Thousands of persons who have taken the Magnet Speed-Reading Course can testify that it helps give you a new and vibrant personality!

Openers to Avoid. Your opener must attract attention—the kind of attention that leads to interest. A poor opener causes the reader to lose interest and throw the letter into the wastebasket.

Avoid such openers as these: "Would you like to own a new car?" (An uninteresting question) "We have some good news for you." (Undramatic) "Since we hope that you are one of our good friends, we are letting you in on a secret." (Immature) "Now that spring is here again, you probably will be thinking about your garden." (Don't say the obvious.) "Let's talk about paint." (How can the reader talk?) "Act today and receive the biggest bargain in history." (Don't tell the reader to act until you have described the product.)

Persuasion. After attracting attention, you must persuade the reader to buy. Persuasion is the heart of the sales letter. Effective persuasion causes the reader to become interested in your product, desire to own it, and feel a real need for your product.

The Power of Suggestion. Every sales letter is built on *suggestion*—a powerful psychological force that can cause a person to react in the manner you wish. The buyer must make the decision to buy rather than feel forced into buying. If you accomplish that with your letter, you have applied one of the secrets of successful selling.

Indirect suggestion is achieved by careful wording—wording that causes a reader to want a product without actually being told that he or she needs it. *Direct* suggestion is best avoided in all parts of the sales letter except the last step—action. Direct suggestion is found in commands; and since most persons do not react favorably to commands, it should not be used until the reader is convinced. At the end of the letter, when the reader is told to act, it is permissible to say "Act at once" or something similar. In trying to attract attention, arouse interest, create desire, or instill conviction, direct suggestion should be avoided, since it may cause the reader to become *countersuggestible*—that is, cause a reaction opposite to that desired.

Convincing the Reader. "The proof of the pudding is in the eating." The reader is convinced more easily when assured that you are telling the truth. Concrete facts, therefore, are helpful in instilling conviction. Often, however, facts are not enough, for the reader may be convinced but not led to action.

The type of appeal or appeals used in the sales letter usually determines whether the reader will be adequately convinced. The beauty, style, and quality of the product may be related to the reader's desire for approval. The efficiency of the product may appeal to the reader's desire for comfort. Whatever the appeal, however, the letter should *dramatize* what the product will do for the reader. If a product is priced higher than most competitive products, the letter must dramatize its best points and emphasize the values the reader will receive from owning it.

Persuasion may need supplementary convincers. Booklets, samples, catalogs, and other items enclosed in the letter often help instill conviction. Testimonials from satisfied users may be mentioned in the letter or included as separate enclosures. When an enclosure is sent with a sales letter, the enclosure should be mentioned in the letter in such a way that the reader will wish to examine it.

Action. In the closing part of your sales letter, clearly and concisely tell the reader what to do, when to do it, and how to do it. Do you want an immediate order? Do you wish the reader to write for further information or visit your store? Let your reader clearly understand the action you desire. Do not present a choice of actions. Specify only one action; otherwise, confusion may result. A confused reader does not become a buyer.

Observe the following action closings:

```
Order your subscription today at this special
money-saving price.  There's no need to send
payment now; we'll gladly bill you later.
Mail the enclosed order card today!
```

```
Why not drop in at any of our six stores the
next time you do your grocery shopping?  Remem-
ber, every Thursday is BARGAIN day.
```

Special inducements are often used to cause the reader to take the desired action. Following are a few action inducements: (1) offering to send goods without prepayment; (2) offering a gift for an immediate reply; (3) offering goods on a trial basis for a certain time; (4) offering a money-back guarantee; (5) indicating that the supply is limited; (6) indicating that the price will be increased after a certain date; (7) setting a time limit for ordering; (8) offering a reward for ordering by a certain date.

Make It Easy for the Reader to Act. A reader may be on the verge of acting favorably and still not act. If you make it easy for the reader to act, you have taken the final precaution in safeguarding a sale.

Order blanks and reply cards and envelopes are commonly used to induce prompt action. Business reply cards and business reply envelopes are especially effective, since the reader does not have to write an address or affix any postage. The company to which they are returned pays the postage for all such items.

Massachusetts Sporting Goods Dealers' Association

9000 Brayton Point Road • Fall River, Massachusetts • (617) 961-5080

April 10, 19--

Dear Friend

A mountain lake, fresh air, and camping out...

Those words sound delightful and represent one of the great
thrills of childhood. Yet without the help of others, many
underprivileged children in our community will never have the
opportunity to enjoy and learn from a summer camp experience.

Hi-Y Camp on Lake Wasatch is used summer after summer by
children of families that can afford it. Now our association,
through the City Department of Recreation, has reserved the
camp for two weeks in August just for the underprivileged.

Mike, Jane, and Billy, shown on the enclosed envelope, live
with their mother, who is their sole support. Wouldn't you
like to see them be part of the 400 children who will each
have an entire week at Hi-Y Camp?

All it takes is a small donation from a few of our caring
citizens. Five dollars will cover all expenses for one day;
and $30 can provide an entire week of learning, recreation,
and fun for a deserving child.

You can help provide the experience of perhaps a lifetime
for a youngster. Won't you use the envelope now to help
bring joy to someone? As chairperson of the fund-raising
committee, I'll really appreciate your aid.

Sincerely

Suzanne Cartwright

Mrs. Suzanne Cartwright

sbk

Enclosure

P.S. Your contribution made out to Hi-Y Camp Fund is tax
deductible!

Special Type of Sales Letter—Request for Donation

NUTRITION INSTITUTE
Publishers of FOOD FACTS

1230 Revere Road   Boston, MA 02113   (617) 498-3216

Dear Friend:

Sixteen-year-old Lisa, the child of an affluent family, has just spent
two weeks in the hospital. She has been suffering from malnutrition.

Bill, a highly skilled engineer, thought that maybe he needed a tonic.
He asked his doctor to give him something to pep him up. On examination
the doctor discovered that Bill was in the first stages of malnutrition.

> Today many thousands of young Americans are undernourished
> because they ignore the basic rules of nutrition. Lisa, like
> far too many other teenagers, relied on snack foods and carbon-
> ated drinks. Bill, who was considerably overweight, went on a
> self-imposed diet. Neither Lisa nor Bill had had three well-
> balanced meals a day, and they had ignored the importance of
> vitamins, minerals, and protein in the daily diet.

Today more than 100,000 people are preparing more nutritious--yet often
less expensive--meals because they read and use FOOD FACTS each month.
FOOD FACTS contains interesting, practical articles by the most outstanding nutrition authorities in the nation. It also contains an abundance
of simple, nutritious recipes--all of which have been tested in our laboratory kitchens.

Now, at low cost, you can take advantage of the many helps in FOOD FACTS.
If you act promptly, you can receive the next 12 issues for only $5.00--
a big saving of $2.50 off the regular subscription rate.

> To take advantage of our special offer, simply sign your name
> on the enclosed postage-free card and return it to us at once.
> No need to send money now. We shall bill you later.

BUT REMEMBER: This low rate is for a limited time only. Return this
card to us today so that you can begin reading, using, and enjoying the
wealth of practical information in every issue of FOOD FACTS.

Cordially yours,

Damon E. Bateman
Executive Vice-President

DEB/tjr

Enclosure

Sales Letter with Two Paragraphs Centered for Emphasis

286

Be an Expert Writer

A piece of writing containing corrections, insertions, and so on is called a *rough draft*.

To show corrections and changes in your writing, use proofreader's marks, since they help you to save time. Proofreader's marks are commonly used to indicate corrections on material that will be sent to a printer, as well as on galley sheets and page proof returned by the printer. Study the proofreader's marks that appear in Reference Section D (page 418). Use such marks in revising your letters and other written work.

Tips from Top Writers of Sales Letters

1. Be especially careful to avoid *I* and *we* as much as possible in sales letters. If you must use these words, use *I* to add a personal touch and *we* in speaking of company policy. (This rule can be applied to all types of letters.)
2. Before writing a sales letter, assume that the reader will say no.
3. Don't try to sell something to the reader; instead, make the reader want to buy it.
4. Every letter is a sales letter. An effective letter of any type can build goodwill; a poor one may mean the loss of a customer.
5. The sales letter you write is important. Giant organizations have been built on a foundation of sales letters—for example, Book-of-the-Month Club.
6. Play up your worthwhile offer. Make the reader see its value. Make the reader want to take advantage of it.
7. A good salesperson can't always write a good sales letter. The sales letter is a literary effort to which are applied the psychological principles of selling.
8. Elmer Wheeler, an amazingly successful salesperson, has said, "Don't sell the steak; sell the sizzle." Physical description is not enough to make the reader want to buy; you must use emotional description, too.
9. Don't be afraid to use a postscript to add emphasis to a certain point. Don't use one as an afterthought.
10. No matter how you say it, your sales letter should contain this message: "This is what *you* are going to get out of it."

Check Your Knowledge

1. When would a sales letter contain only the conviction and action steps?

2. Why should everyone understand the principles of writing a good sales letter?

3. "Persuasion is based on the correct use of suggestion." Explain this statement.

4. Which types of questions should be avoided in opening sales letters?

5. Which type of attention-getting opener appeals to you most? least? Explain your answers.

Skill Builders

28-A. Carefully plan and write a one-page sales letter for one of the following: (a) women's wearing apparel, (b) men's wearing apparel, (c) a household appliance, (d) a TV set, (e) an automotive item, (f) sports equipment, (g) a cosmetic.

28-B. Write two different types of attention-getting openers for a sales letter aiming to sell each of the following: (a) teenagers' magazine, (b) motion-picture camera, (c) automobile, (d) laundry service, (e) paint job for car, (f) use of chartered buses.

28-C. Write a sales letter about a steam iron. Use the following information to best advantage: The unique feature of the product is that it sprinkles on any setting—dry, steam, or wash-and-wear. Even when the iron is unplugged the user needs only to touch a button to get a fine spray. The iron uses regular faucet water; it does not require distilled water or demineralizers. It can be filled quickly and easily. A single dial control makes all settings easy to read. There are no separate controls for steam ironing. It uses less electricity than older steam irons.

28-D. As a correspondent for the Dependable Pen Company, you have been assigned the job of writing a sales letter for its new ball-point pen. Your letter will be sent to high school and college students. *Product facts:* Although the tips seem round, under a microscope thousands of little grippers can be seen. These grippers push through slick spots and permit the pen to write a smooth, unbroken line. Its giant cartridge writes up to five times longer than ordinary ball-point pens. The pen is available with four different points: extra fine, fine, medium, and broad. It comes in a variety of colors and is available in a gift box. Price is only $1.98. You wish to have students purchase the pen at the school store or the nearest dealer.

28-E. Write a sales letter about a compact-sized color TV set, using the following information to best advantage: You are writing to anyone who might want the smaller-sized set, presumably heads of families, college or high school students, and people in small housing units. The unique feature of the set is its console-sized screen inside a compact-sized cabinet. It fits any place a portable TV would fit. Hand construction is used in its manufacture. The TV is completely solid-state. The buyer has a choice of a 25-, 21-, or 19-inch screen. The picture and sound come on instantly when the set is turned on. The cabinet is handsome and comes with either a grained-walnut or a polished-oak finish. The color picture is bright and sharp. A special remote control is also available.

Business Speech

1. alias. (AY-le-us)
2. column. (Don't say *yum*.)
3. epitome. (e-PIT-uh-me)

4. poinsettia. Four syllables. (poin-SET-i-a)
5. questionnaire. (The ending rhymes with *millionaire*.)

Spelling

Guide: When a noun ends with *er,* the adjectival form usually ends with *ery*—for example, *stationer—stationery*. Exception: *adviser—advisory*.
Study List 28. (See page 409.)

Section
29

Credit is based on trust. If one does not pay his or her debts, the trust-worthiness of the debtor is open to question. In this situation the creditor can use persuasive messages effectively to obtain payment.

Collecting As a Part of Normal Business

Businesses expect that a certain number of credit accounts will not be paid. They must, however, try to obtain payment whenever possible. In a large firm, collecting may be a function of a separate department. In other businesses collecting is done by the credit department. A collector knows that success in business is measured by the collection of overdue accounts.

Overdue accounts are sometimes called *delinquent* accounts. The amount of money owed is frequently called a *delinquency* or a *past-due amount*. Since delinquencies are owed by widely scattered businesses and individual users of credit, most collecting is done by mail. At times, of course, a telephone call or telegram is used. The basic collection tool, however, is the collection letter.

Analyzing Delinquent Debtors

Whether delinquent debtors are firms or individual persons, the collection person studies each debtor who must be made to pay. This is always done before a collection letter is written.

The basic *C*'s of credit—character, capacity, and capital—are used in analyzing delinquent debtors. In the following examples, observe that the *C*'s are included in the following analyses of debtors.

Sarah Henry: Past pay record good. Still employed in her original job. Income about $1,500 a month. Owns her own home. Conclusion: *A good-pay debtor.*

Albert Watson: Made his last three payments late. Steady employment. Home-owner. Income above average. Conclusion: *A slow-but-sure debtor.*

Terry Grant: Made two payments on time; then made three payments only after being notified several times. Has steady employment but has changed jobs frequently. Below-average income. Rents. Conclusion: *Poor-pay debtor.*

Other information might be considered, of course, such as the re-ports received from other creditors. A collection person may also want to know how each debtor was evaluated before the loan was extended. It is fairly obvious that the good-pay debtor will pay quickly. The slow-but-sure debtor may need a little prodding. The poor-pay debtor may resist payment until the very last minute or may not pay at all.

Having made the analysis, the collection person begins collection proceedings. In most large companies, a series of basic form letters is compiled. The collector uses one of these form letters or an adaptation of one to fit a particular debtor. Such letters cover the collecting process and are called the *collection series* or the *collection follow-up series.*

The Collection Series

Because of the serious nature of credit and its effect on a business and its customers, collection practices are carefully planned. The goal of these practices is to collect the money without offending the debtor. In fact, collecting the money and still keeping the customer are the objectives.

The collection person believes (1) that everyone wants to pay debts and (2) that a debtor knows what is owed. The collection letter, then, is written with those two points in mind. Not until the situation becomes critical does the letter become a stern demand.

The collection series consists of several letters. Most companies classify these letters as *stages.* In a collection series the stages may be

1. The notice stage.
2. The reminder stage.
3. The inquiry stage.
4. The appeal stage.
5. The urgency stage.
6. The ultimatum stage.

The Notice Stage. In the notice stage the most frequent communication is a copy of the bill, with "Past Due" on it. The collection person assumes that the original bill has been misplaced or overlooked.

Vernor Paint
and Varnish Company *Paints for Home and Industry*

5276 Brevator Street • Albany, New York 12203 • (518) 469-4880

Date

Name
Street Address
City, State, ZIP Code

Dear _____: (or Gentlemen if a company)

On __(date)__ we wrote you requesting that you send
us your check or money order for $_____, which is now
long past due.

Every week credit bureaus, banks, and suppliers ask us
about our payment experience with some of our accounts. And
we like to give a good report of our customers so that they
can continue to enjoy a good credit rating.

Enclosed is a postage-free envelope for rushing to us
your payment for $_____. Please do it today so that
you can maintain your good credit standing and so that we can
continue our pleasant business relations with you.

Sincerely,

VERNOR PAINT AND VARNISH COMPANY

Terence R. Kashman
Terence R. Kashman
Credit Manager

Enclosure

A Collection Form Letter

292

The Reminder Stage. Since the debtor has already received a notice, the collection person sends a short letter indicating the assumption that the debtor will pay quickly. The following form letter illustrates a good reminder technique:

> This brief note is simply to remind you that
> we have not received your November 1 payment.
>
> In sending your check, you may wish to take
> advantage of the special sale items listed
> on the enclosed sheet.

To soften the talk about collecting money, the collector wisely mentions the company or the product and how it can aid the customer. The reminder-stage letter always sounds friendly and indicates that the writer looks forward to more business with the customer.

The Inquiry Stage. Having already sent a notice and a reminder to the customer without receiving a reply, the collection person assumes that something is wrong. Some problem has made it difficult for the debtor to pay. The inquiry letter simply "inquires" about the difficulty and offers help. The tone of the letter is one of helpfulness.

> Since we have not heard from you for some
> time, we assume that a problem has prevented
> you from paying your June 1 balance of $87.09.
> If so, we are confident we can work out payment
> arrangements satisfactory to us both.
>
> Simply use the back of this letter to write
> a note explaining your difficulty and return
> it to us in the enclosed envelope.
>
> If nonpayment has been merely an oversight,
> please send us your check by return mail.

The Appeal Stage. After receiving no answer to an inquiry letter, the collector takes sterner steps. The customer must be *persuaded* to pay. Appeals, therefore, are used just as writers of sales letters use them. Moreover, humans react favorably to certain appeals. Among the appeals found effective in collection letters are those to fair play, pride, and fear of the loss of a valued possession. Observe the appeal used in each of the following letters.

Appeal: Fair play

Over two months ago we shipped you six cases
of Blue Star salmon. We fully expected to
receive your payment on June 1, as agreed to
by you in opening your credit account.

When we shipped the salmon, we performed our
part of the agreement. In waiting so long
for payment, we have been more than fair to
you. Now it's your turn.

Won't you be fair, Mrs. Haley, and send us
your check for $87.09 immediately?

Appeal: Pride

"Always pays on time," "a good credit risk,"
and other favorable statements were received
from your references before we opened your
account. Comments such as those are things
to be proud of; they mark you as an honorable
person.

Now, however, you are risking that fine reputation by letting your account with us become
seriously delinquent. You can still preserve
your fine reputation and continue to purchase
from us on the same favorable terms. But
you'll have to act soon. Send us the $87.09
you owe within the next few days.

Appeal: Loss of credit

Credit is one of our most cherished possessions. We earn it by exhibiting character,
by being able to pay, and by having good
financial qualifications. But it can be
easily lost.

The small amount of $87.09, now over three
months past due, can cost you that hard-
earned credit reputation. Please don't
risk it.

> As you know, all accounts more than three
> months past due must be reported to the Down-
> town Credit Association. You can save us the
> trouble of that report and yourself a poor
> credit rating by sending your check.

The fair-play appeal in the first letter is apparent. So, too, is the appeal to pride in the second letter. In the third letter the appeal to loss of a valued possession accompanies a minor appeal to pride. In all collection letters—from the appeal letter to the conclusion of the collection series—some appeal must be used. A past-due debtor becomes increasingly difficult to persuade as the account grows more and more delinquent.

The Urgency Stage. When the debtor's account reaches the urgency stage, strong action must be taken. The creditor's letters do not carry the goodwill tone, but they do not indicate ill will. The collection job is still to obtain payment and keep the customer's business.

The persuasion in the urgency letter results from the writer's emphasis on *urgency*. It reads, "You must do it now." "We must have your payment immediately."

> Now that several days have passed since we sent
> our last reminder appealing to you to pay the
> long-past-due balance on your account, we can
> only assume that you prefer some alternative
> methods of payment.
>
> Those alternatives are simple for us to list.
> You must (1) sign a 60-day, 12 percent note
> for the balance due; or (2) send in half the
> amount due, with a promise to pay the balance
> due within twenty days.
>
> These choices are the only realistic ones you
> have. Either of these actions will put your
> account back in our "good credit" file. Of
> course, we will accept your payment in full by
> return mail, with no questions asked.
>
> We must have a reply from you immediately.
> Your prompt action is the only thing that will
> keep us from using all available legal means
> to collect the money rightfully due us.

The Ultimatum Stage. The last letter ever written to collect payment is the ultimatum letter. It says to the debtor, "This is your very last chance." In the following letter the ultimatum is stated clearly and marks the end of the collection series. The next step on the part of the creditor is to sue in court, to use a collection agency to obtain payment, or to repossess items that have been involved in the transaction.

The following letter was written by the president of the creditor firm:

> Several weeks have passed since your account became delinquent. Before we use the courts and our legal counsel as means of collection, however, I wanted to have the opportunity to write to you.
>
> You must admit that we have been extremely fair in waiting so long for our money. You now have only one more chance to settle your account. Your payment will even enable you to maintain credit with us. Payment will also stop a bad credit report, already prepared, from leaving our office.
>
> Think it over carefully. Is the $87.09 you owe us worth a poor record and a costly lawsuit--one that will cost you far more than the money you owe?
>
> Take advantage of this opportunity. You have exactly 48 hours in which to make payment-- full payment. At noon on May 5, your account will be turned over to our attorneys for action.

Other Collection Methods

The Four-Step Series. Some firms use a series of four letters in their efforts to collect money owed:

1. *Reminder*—merely a statement that the amount is owed, with request for payment.
2. *Stronger reminder*—a statement that the amount is owed, with request for payment and possibly a few pertinent remarks, such as reminding the customer of a good record in the past.

Note: In steps 1 and 2, sales information may be included. Such information may prompt the reader to pay the account and take advantage of special sales rates available to those in good standing.

3. *Discussion*—an analysis of the entire situation. Appeals may be made to pride, community standing, professional prestige, fear of losing a good credit reputation, and so on. This is the longest letter in the series. It "gets down to brass tacks."
4. *Ultimatum*—a brief letter that lets the debtor know what action will be taken if payment isn't made by a certain date.

Collection Devices. As reminders some firms use eye-catching devices that put the debtor in a good mood. For example, one firm uses a small piece of stationery having a picture of a sad-looking dog in the center of the page. Under the picture is the message, "Dawgone it, we need our money. Won't you please help us by sending the (amount) you owe?"

One collection person devised a supposedly clever plan. A persuasive poem was to be printed on postcards. State laws, however, prohibited the use of postcards for dunning notices.* In many states loan companies are not allowed to use their names on envelopes; they can use the street, city, and state but not the firm name.

Enclosing a business reply envelope with a collection letter helps make it easier for the debtor to act. Many firms use this device.

Be an Expert Writer

Careful writers always use exact words to express ideas. Note the following:

An *error* is a deviation from truth or accuracy. "He made a typing error on the annual report."

A *mistake* is an error that results from carelessness or misunderstanding or from lack of good judgment. "In going to the beach for our vacation, we made a costly mistake."

A *blunder* is a wrong action that results from stupidity or inefficiency. "My bursting into the office unannounced was indeed a blunder."

A *faux pas* (foh pah) is a social blunder. Its literal French meaning is *false step*. "He winced when I mentioned her name, so I knew I had made a faux pas."

---

* Also, dunning notices should not be sent on *postal* cards, which are stamped cards purchased from the post office. *To dun* is to demand payment.

Abbott Hotel and Restaurant Supplies

Offering a complete line of supplies to hotels and restaurants
11445 Venable Avenue, Charleston, West Virginia 25315   (304) 349-7000

July 3, 19--

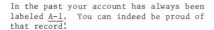

Mrs. Celeste Herderman
125 Bay Ridge Road
Teaneck, NJ 07666

Dear Mrs. Herderman:

> In the past your account has always been
> labeled <u>A-1</u>. You can indeed be proud of
> that record!

During May and June we have not received your regular payments of $25 each. We therefore are wondering whether you
have encountered a difficulty that is preventing you from
paying on time. If so, please let us know. Surely, after
several years of doing business with us, you know that we
are reasonable people.

We are chiefly interested in helping you to maintain the
outstanding credit record you have always enjoyed with us.
Won't you help us to help you by writing or telephoning your
explanation?

> Better still, let us have your check
> bringing your account up to date. We
> want to continue labeling your account
> <u>A-1</u>!

Sincerely,

William L. Macaulay

William L. Macaulay
Head, Charge Records

pjk

Collection Letter, with Device

Tips from Top Credit and Collection Writers

1. Today's credit risk may become tomorrow's most valued customer. Help the customer, therefore, to keep an unmarred record.

2. Poor credit means poor business, and poor credit results from poor paying habits. Remember these two points when you write any type of credit or collection letter.

3. Debts worry most persons. Realizing this, the writers of collection letters always make it possible for delinquents to pay without hurting their ability to continue doing business or using their credit privileges.

4. In credit and collection letters always mention the specific type of charge account. For example, if it is a revolving charge account, say so.*

5. In each collection letter in a series, mention the specific amount owed.

6. If a credit customer is always a prompt payer, send a thank-you note occasionally. The importance of such little goodwill builders cannot be overestimated.

What better time is there than the beginning of a new year to say THANK YOU for your continued patronage and outstanding record of prompt payment.

Please remember that we are always ready to provide you with the finest quality products, backed by courteous, efficient service.

Goodwill Builder Sent to Charge Customers

7. In a credit letter cover all points. Leave no doubt in the reader's mind. Make it easy for the customer to use credit!

8. Credit and collection information belongs in letters. If you discuss such information with the wrong persons, you may find yourself on the losing end of a lawsuit!

---

*A revolving charge account is one that is continuously allowed for a certain amount— for example, $200. As the customer pays, he or she can continue to purchase as long as he or she owes no more than a total of $200.

9. If a customer of long standing fails to make payments promptly, don't be an eager beaver. Allow a little time, and the payment will probably be made. The timing and spacing of collection letters varies and depends on the customer. Stores that sell to persons with low incomes usually begin using pressure as soon as an account is overdue.

10. A telegram may jolt a big debtor into paying. A telephone call may give the personal touch needed to get the money. The telephone collector, however, must be extremely tactful; the voice of the collector must be pleasing, also. Many customers resent being dunned by telephone, and for that reason some firms do not use it for that purpose.

11. Never threaten. The debtor's credit reputation may be at stake, but don't say you're going to ruin that reputation!

12. Most customers respect a firm's credit policy. They realize that, if a firm has a lax policy, its prices will be increased to make up for losses incurred by bad debts (uncollectible debts).

13. You want action to result from your collection letter. Put the customer in an action mood, therefore, by describing what to do and when to do it. Don't become frantic, however. Remember: "You can catch more flies with honey than with vinegar."

Check Your Knowledge

1. What are the three types of debtors?
2. What are the six usual stages, or steps, in a collection series? If a series has only four stages, what are they?
3. In trying to collect money owed, what are some appeals commonly used?
4. List five "Don'ts" to remember in writing collection letters.
5. Is a customer ever called a *good credit risk?* What does the term mean?

Skill Builders

29-A. As credit and collection manager at Eastern Department Store, write the collection letter required for *each* of the following cases:

1. Mr. Roger Brown, 1421 Ninth Street, your city, has average monthly purchases of $50 at Eastern. His past pay record is good, he owns his home, he has held the same good job for twenty years. He owes Eastern $53, how-

ever, and has already been mailed a notice and a reminder. The account is now 45 days past due. Write him an inquiry letter.

2. Mr. Brown has not replied to the inquiry letter. Two weeks have gone by. Write the appeal letter.

3. Mr. Brown has overlooked the appeal letter you wrote. Another two weeks have passed. Write him an urgency letter that asks him to sign a promissory note or, at least, to make partial payment to demonstrate his trustworthiness.

29-B. Janet and Tim King, also Eastern customers, have average monthly purchases of $65. They are slow-but-sure payers. Janet is a customer service representative and Tim sells medical supplies. They have two children and own their home. Their account, however, is two months in arrears, and they owe $127.33. You have already sent a notice and a reminder and have made two telephone calls. During the last call, they promised they would pay within ten days. Two weeks have passed. Since the phone calls have not been effective, you must write an urgency-stage letter.

29-C. As collection manager for *Teen* magazine, a popular periodical for young people, you are faced with the problem of avoiding long-past-due accounts scattered throughout the country. Subscriptions for one year are only $3. Your computer sends a reminder to past-due accounts. Write a discussion letter as part of your four-stage series. Remember that most of your readers are high school and college students. The letter should talk to them.

29-D. Miss Kitty Carson, 2730 Victory Way, Monroe, OH 45050, purchased a small spinet piano from your store, The Music Shoppe, several months ago. She paid $100 as a down payment and signed a contract to pay $50 a month for 18 months to complete her obligation. After making six payments, she missed the next two. She has received two letters about this matter.

(a) Write an appeal letter to Miss Carson. (Remember that this is not the inquiry letter.)

(b) Write the ultimatum letter to Miss Carson. Express your regret at having to write the letter but make it clear that you have no choice other than to collect promptly or take legal action to recover the money.

29-E. The Glendora Transfer Company has consistently violated the credit terms of your company, The Ajax Oil Company. You supply gasoline and oil for all Glendora's trucks. Your terms are 2 percent discount for bills paid within ten days. Glendora consistently waits three or four weeks before sending its check, and each payment shows a 2 percent discount for "prompt" payment. As credit manager of Ajax, you know that such a practice is costing you money and is not fair to customers who pay on time and earn the discount. Write a letter to the Glendora Transfer Company, 1187 Industrial Way,

Glendora, CA 91740, asking it to pay the $127.69 representing the 2 percent discount taken but not earned during the past three months. This will be an appeal letter based on fair play.

Business Speech

The *ea* in words such as *measure, pleasure,* and *treasure* is sounded like the *e* in *met.* To pronounce it like the *a* in *mate* is an affectation.

Speech should be distinct; some words, however, are given more stress than others. Notice how certain words should be pronounced in regular conversation. The apostrophe in the following words indicates that the vowels are slighted and not given their full sound.

an. I have an (*'n*) apple.

and. You and (*'nd*) I.

to. I want you to (*t'*) do it.

Spelling

Study List 29, which contains some of the most commonly misspelled words. (See page 409.)

Unit Ten

EMPLOYMENT LETTERS

Section
30

THE LETTER OF APPLICATION

Some large firms interview only those applicants who have submitted typewritten letters of application and personal data sheets. The letter of application, therefore, may be the most important kind of letter you will ever write. The skill with which you prepare it may mean the difference between success and failure in obtaining the job you wish.

Many persons having excellent qualifications miss job opportunities because they do not know how to write good letters of application. From 80 to 90 percent of all application letters are unacceptable and do not result in interviews for their writers. The purpose of the letter of application is to obtain an interview; without an interview, the applicant does not have a chance of getting the job.

Remember that your letter of application is *you*. It is a *personal sales letter*—one in which you try to sell your qualifications to an employer. To sell yourself most effectively, remember these two points: (1) The "you" attitude is vitally important. (2) Let the employer know what you can do and try to prove that you meet the job's requirements. To satisfy the employer's requirements, you must have *basic employability;* that is, you must possess the right qualifications for the job. If you don't have all the right qualifications for a job, don't apply for it. You won't fool anyone but yourself!

Check Your Basic Employability

WHAT THE JOB REQUIRES	WHAT YOU CAN OFFER
Education required	Your education and skills
Experience required	Your experience, full-time and part-time
Personality requirements	Your personal qualifications

Planning the Letter of Application

Only *you* can write your letter of application. It is unwise, as well as dishonest, to ask someone else to write it for you or to copy a model letter from a book. During your interview the prospective employer or the personnel manager soon knows whether you wrote the letter.

Materials Needed. Type your letter on good-quality bond paper and use a matching envelope. Although plain white paper is recommended, colored stationery has often been used by successful job applicants to get the reader's attention. The type bars or element should be clean, and all errors should be corrected skillfully.

If you are required to write your letter in longhand, type an exact copy and mail it with the handwritten copy.

Although it is not necessary to enclose a stamped, self-addressed envelope for a reply, it is courteous to do so.

Important Pointers. Your information should be specific, straightforward, and smooth-flowing. Make your message interesting. Remember that the person receiving your letter may receive hundreds of others. If you wish it to be read, your letter must get attention and hold interest. It must convince the reader that you are the one for the job, that you deserve careful attention, and that you should be interviewed.

Avoid the following: Don't submit stunt or trick applications. A message such as the following only annoys a prospective employer.

```
Look no further! I am your man! I can fill
the bill and increase your profits. I can be
on the job fifteen minutes after you pick up
your phone and call me at 216-5432.
```

Don't apologize for lack of experience or other qualifications. If you don't qualify, don't apply! Don't appeal to the employer's sympathy by saying how much you need the job; instead, demonstrate how much the job needs you. Don't discuss salary unless you know you are required to do so. Salary is better discussed during an interview.

Preparing to Write Application Letters

Most employers prefer an application consisting of two parts: (1) a letter and (2) a personal data sheet, commonly called a *résumé*. When a personal data sheet accompanies the letter of application, the letter interprets details included in the data sheet.

Types of Application Letters. There are two types of application letters: (1) *solicited,* which is sent to an employer who is seeking someone for a particular job; and (2) *unsolicited,* which is sent to a firm in which a person may wish to work but which has not made any vacancies known. The unsolicited letter is sometimes called a *cold* application. Whether your letter is solicited or unsolicited, you must make the reader feel that you are truly interested in the company and that you can offer qualifications that will benefit it.

Writing to a Firm's Address. If you are writing to a firm but do not know the name of the specific person to whom your letter should be directed, the first line of your address may be either *Personnel Department* or *Employment Department.* The salutation should be *Gentlemen* or *Ladies and Gentlemen.* If you know the name of the person who will read your letter, be sure you spell the person's name correctly. Always be sure, too, that the company name and address are complete and correct in the inside address and on the envelope.

Answering a Blind Advertisement. Many persons obtain jobs by answering advertisements in the "Help Wanted" classified section of newspapers. Such advertisements often do not reveal the name or address of the firm seeking help; instead, a newspaper box number is given.

The Parts of the Application Letter

If possible, limit your letter to one page. If more space is needed, try to keep the total letter within one and a half pages. When a data sheet is used, the letter should seldom be more than one page long. Regardless of the length of your letter, the application must have four basic parts: (1) *point of contact,* (2) *your qualifications,* (3) *references,* (4) *request for interview.*

Point of Contact. In opening your letter, tell how you learned about the job. In an unsolicited letter tell why you wish to work for the company. Always ask to be considered an applicant for the job. Following are some sample openers:

Mr. Vernon Laine, of your Credit Department, has told me about the opening you have for a clerk in your Personnel Department. Please consider me an applicant for this position.

In this morning's _Times_ I read that you have immediate openings for accounting trainees. Because I have the qualifications you require, I would like to be considered for the position.

I would like to talk with you about a job! My experience as editor of my school newspaper, coupled with my strong stenographic skills, has convinced me that I could be valuable to the _Daily_ _News_ in an entry office position.

As a June graduate of East Side High School, I am eager to take a full-time job by July 15. Since your firm has such a splendid reputation in our community, I would like to work for you in your Marketing Department. If you have a need for a conscientious worker, please consider me an applicant.

The preceding openings, all of which establish the point of contact, are somewhat standardized; that is, they are the types used by most job applicants. Some other openings are equally good for establishing the point of contact. An opening that shows originality may cause the reader to warm up to your letter quickly. The third example uses this kind of opening.

Your Qualifications. In discussing your qualifications, be truthful, but don't boast. Don't be long-winded; give all details on the data sheet. The remarks in your letter, however, should help convince the reader that you are the right one for the job.

Your qualifications include (1) education and (2) experience. Be sure to capitalize on any special courses or experiences that particularly fit you for the job. On your data sheet it is wise to include extracurricular activities and hobbies, for such information is often a deciding factor in selecting an employee.

> At Hill High School, I majored in business and took two years of typewriting, one year of short-hand, one year of bookkeeping, and one year of business English. During my senior year I was elected vice-president of the class.

> After graduating from Castlemont High School, I attended the University of the Pacific for two years, where I maintained an A-minus average. I have participated widely in school activities and twice served as class secretary in high school. In college I was secretary of my fra-ternity and chairperson of the committee for the all-school homecoming parade.

> On the enclosed data sheet, you will notice that I have taken two courses in interior decoration and one in home planning. I believe that these courses provide a splendid background for a trainee position in your firm.

> During my third year of high school, my class visited your company. I was deeply impressed with the working conditions, the type of peo-ple you employ, and the efforts you make to give good service to customers. I looked for-ward to the time when I could take a position in a company such as yours. Later I learned that your customer service representatives must have had a course in marketing; therefore, dur-ing my senior year I took courses in marketing and retailing. I am now confident that I can qualify for a position as customer service representative in your firm.

Employers know that excellent personal qualities contribute to job success. Mention significant personal achievements, such as offices held, athletic and academic honors, and extracurricular activities. Be modest but factual. Do not include complimentary opinions of yourself.

```
During my sophomore year I had a leading part
in the annual one-act play.  I was on the golf
team all four years and won first prize in the
district golf tournament during my senior year.
```

```
I was valedictorian of my class of 168 members.
Having a strong interest in public speaking, I
served on the school's debating team and par-
ticipated in seventeen interscholastic debates.
```

Experience. If you are inexperienced and know that a firm definitely demands experience, do not apply for the job. If the firm sometimes takes new workers without experience, play up all your good qualifications, but do not mention your lack of experience.

If you have experience, try to convince the reader that such experience will be valuable.

```
For the past two years I have been employed
as a salesperson by the Pine Department
Store.  During the past year I stood first
in sales among the nine salesclerks.  My
duties included tagging, stocking, and dis-
playing merchandise.  I also painted display
cards, dressed the front show windows, and
worked in the store's credit office.
```

```
For three years I worked part-time during
school terms and full-time during summers.
The work was done in the office of my
father's laundry business, where I wrote let-
ters, filed, and did some of the bookkeeping.
```

References. "The best way to judge a person is to watch him or her perform." A prospective employer places a great deal of faith in reports from past employers, teachers, and professors. For that reason most firms require applicants to provide the names of three or four persons who are familiar with the applicant's capabilities. Such persons are called *references*.

When you wish to use a person's name as reference, obtain permission. Do not use the names of relatives or members of the clergy. If possible, include the name of a person well known to the prospective employer. In your letter mention that references are included on the data sheet. Or, if you prefer, you can mention your strongest reference in the letter and say that additional references are on the data sheet.

> Mr. Thomas B. Overman, Manager, Cambrian Park
> Branch of Bank of America, has permitted me
> to use his name as a reference. On the
> enclosed data sheet, I have listed his address,
> as well as other references.

> On the enclosed data sheet, you will find the
> names of other persons who have consented to
> furnish information about my capabilities.

When you have obtained a position, write a thank-you note to the persons whose names you used as references. Tell them briefly about your new job.

Caution: When a person gives you a letter of recommendation to use as a reference, do not mail it with your letter of application. Instead, make a photocopy to enclose with the application. In this way you will always have the original letter and will be able to make additional copies whenever necessary. By saving original copies you can accumulate a number of valuable records about yourself.

Request for Interview. The last paragraph of your letter should consist of only a few sentences. This is the action section of your personal sales letter—the section in which you request an interview.

> May I have an interview at your convenience?
> I shall be available any afternoon except on
> Fridays. Please write me at the above address
> or call me at 597-1894.

> I shall be pleased to talk with you personally
> at a time convenient to you. If you will write
> me at the above address or call me at 666-7910,
> I shall be available for an interview at any
> time.

```
                                        2189 Blackstone Street
                                        Worcester, MA 01601
                                        October 15, 19--


Mr. John A. Davis, Personnel Director
The Paris Fashion Company
368 Commonwealth Avenue
Boston, MA 02109

Dear Mr. Davis:

In Monday's Daily Tribune I noticed your advertisement for an executive
secretary.  May I please be considered an applicant for the position?

I am a graduate of Hartwell High School and Boston Junior College.  In
high school I took the regular business course and was in a special
advanced-speed class for persons passing a shorthand test at 120 words
a minute.  In junior college I majored in business administration and
took two years of French and one year of fashion merchandising as
electives.

Since receiving my Associate in Science degree three years ago, I have
been secretary to Ms. Nicole K. Topper, treasurer of the Universal Toy
Company in Boston.  My duties have included taking dictation up to 140
words a minute, using the Dictaphone to transcribe long letters, and
supervising the work of several clerks.  I have had the responsibility
of composing many of Ms. Topper's letters and handling confidential
matters for her.  I can type straight copy at 75 words a minute and
transcribe my shorthand at 40 words a minute.

Recently I learned that I have reached the maximum salary for my posi-
tion.  I have decided, therefore, to seek employment with a larger firm--
one engaged in work in which I have a special interest.  Because of my
secretarial experience, as well as my training in French and fashion
merchandising, I am confident that I can do an outstanding job for you.

Ms. Nicole K. Topper has permitted me to use her name as a reference.
On the enclosed date sheet you will find other references and details
regarding my qualifications.

May I have a personal interview at your convenience?  If you wish to
telephone me, my number is 625-4321.

                            Sincerely,

                            (Miss) Helen R. Conover

                            Miss Helen R. Conover


Enclosure
```

Letter of Application

PERSONAL   DATA

<u>PERSONAL DETAILS</u>

Name: Helen R. Conover
Address: 2189 Blackstone Street
           Worcester, MA 01601
Telephone: (617) 625-4321

<u>EDUCATION</u>

Boston Junior College, June, 19--, A.S. degree
Hartwell High School, Worcester, Massachusetts, June, 19--

<u>High School Courses</u>		<u>Junior College Courses</u>	
English and Literature	(3 years)	French	(2 years)
Bookkeeping	(2 years)	Accounting	(1 year)
Shorthand	(2 years)	Advertising	(1 year)
Typewriting	(2 years)	Business Administration	(1 year)
Business English	(1 year)	Business Communications	(1 year)
Business Law	(1 year)	Economics	(1 year)
Business Mathematics	(1 year)	Fashion Merchandising	(1 year)
Economic Geography	(1 year)	Secretarial Training	(1 year)
Office Training	(1 year)	Business Psychology	(1/2 year)
Marketing	(1 year)	Records Management	(1/2 year)

In junior college I was secretary of my class for one year, a member
of the Glee Club for two years, and advertising manager of the yearbook for one year. In high school I was class treasurer for two
years, chairperson of the Career Day committee, and assistant editor
of the school newspaper.

<u>Professional Affiliations</u>: Alpha Pi Epsilon, National Secretarial
Honor Society; and Boston Secretaries Association.

<u>PRACTICAL TRAINING AND EXPERIENCE</u>

Three years with Universal Toy Company as executive secretary to the
treasurer. Two years part-time during junior college as stenographer
at Darwell Company.

I am a trained and experienced secretary, correspondent, and typist.
I can take dictation up to 140 words a minute, transcribe my shorthand notes at 40 words a minute, and type straight copy at 75 words
a minute.

<u>Machines Used</u>	<u>Ability to Use</u>
Typewriter	Excellent
Adding machines	Good
Dictaphone (dictating and transcribing)	Excellent
Mimeograph and Multilith machines	Good

<u>REFERENCES</u> (by permission)

Ms. Nicole K. Topper, Treasurer, Universal Toy Company, Boston, MA 02107
Dr. Ruth Gee, Boston Junior College, Boston, MA 02137
Mr. Paul E. Wells, Personnel Manager, Darwell Company, Boston, MA 02108

Personal Data Sheet (Résumé)

The Data Sheet (Résumé)

It is always best to enclose a data sheet with your application letter. Even though you may be required to fill in a company application blank, you should prepare a data sheet. On the latter you can arrange material attractively and sometimes include certain information not required on the application blank.

If you send application letters to several firms at the same time, you must type each one individually. Your message should vary somewhat, too, so that it will suit each company. Your data sheet, however, may be duplicated.

Try to have a one-page data sheet. After you have worked several years, however, you may find that you cannot include all pertinent information on one sheet.

Study the model data sheet on the preceding page.

Varied Techniques. To gain attention, some applicants mention experience or education in the opening of the letter.

> Today I learned that your company wishes to hire a credit-collections clerk. Since I have taken every available credit course at Eastern College, I am looking forward to a career in credit work. I shall appreciate your considering my qualifications for the position.

> In June I shall be graduated from Fairlawn University, with a major in accounting and a minor in social studies. During my college years, I have had several part-time jobs in accounting offices. Because of my training and experience, will you please consider me an applicant for a position with your company?

> I should like to sell accident and health insurance for your company. At present I am employed as a job analyst for the Atlantic Corporation but for some time have been aware of a growing desire to enter a sales career.

Many authorities recommend that, immediately after the opening paragraph (point of contact), the applicant state his or her understanding of the requirements for the job. This may be good technique for those seeking their first jobs. Following is such a paragraph:

> It is my understanding that you want a person who can take dictation at 100 words a minute and type at 55 words a minute. That person must also be able to compose routine letters, maintain a master file, and perform certain clerical duties.

Tips from Employers and Personnel Executives

1. As the employer reads an application letter, he or she is thinking: (1) "What does this person want?" (2) "What is offered that would make me want to hire such an individual?" (3) "Who can vouch for this person?" (4) "What am I supposed to do now?" If the application is properly written, these questions are automatically answered for the reader.

2. Reputation is an important aspect of employability. You may have developed expert skills; but if you haven't proved to others that you know how to use them, such skills won't mean much to an employer.

3. No matter how good you are, if your application letter doesn't stand the test, you won't get an interview. One smudge or coffee stain can cause your letter to be hurled into the wastebasket!

4. Watch what you say! One misspelled word, one grammatical error, one slang expression, one wrong punctuation mark—these can very well mean that the reader will become a nonreader.

5. You are a living human being. Prove it to the reader by the manner in which you express yourself.

6. Use a positive tone and up-to-date language. Avoid repetition and language that falls flat.

7. You may mail your application letter, unfolded, in a large envelope; or if you prefer, you may send it in a large-size business envelope. Do not, however, use a small-size business envelope.

8. Exert every effort to find the name of the person to whom you should write for a position. A letter that begins "Dear Mr. Jones" puts the personnel manager in a better mood than one that coldly begins "Dear Sir or Madam" or "Gentlemen."

9. Your application letter should bear the mark of your personality. It should indirectly say, "Here I am and here is what I can do for your firm. Wouldn't you like to meet me?"

10. Remember that actions speak louder than words! Don't waste time saying, "I am ambitious and want to get ahead." If you say, "During my college years I held enough part-time jobs to pay my tuition," you prove that you are ambitious and determined.

11. If you have been active in church work, clubs, or civic enterprises, include the facts on your data sheet. Personnel people are looking for active, versatile workers.

12. Your letter and data sheet must be neat and attractive. If they aren't, they ask the reader, "How would you like to hire a sloppy, careless worker?"

Check Your Knowledge

1. Name five ways in which you might obtain information about available jobs.

2. One important executive has said, "When I see a grammatical error in an application letter, it makes me wonder what value the writer has received from going to school." Is this person's attitude justified? Discuss.

3. Education and experience are two important general qualifications. What other qualifications are important?

4. Discuss various methods of establishing the point of contact in an application letter.

5. Discuss (a) understanding the requirements, (b) using the résumé, (c) making the reader want your services.

Skill Builders

30-A. Write an unsolicited application letter for a part-time job for which you are sure you have the correct qualifications. You will work after school and Saturdays. Prepare a data sheet.

30-B. Assume that you have graduated and are job-hunting. Consult your local newspaper and reply to a "Help Wanted" advertisement for which you have the right job qualifications. If you cannot find an advertisement to suit you, assume that the paper contains one. Prepare a résumé to accompany your letter.

30-C. Your uncle, Thomas L. Ricey, has told you that there is a possibility that Dayton Company will hire three new workers—a secretary, an administrative assistant, and a general clerk. Assume that you have graduated and have been working in the office of Martin's Department Store for sixteen months. Apply for one of the jobs at Dayton Company, 118 Points East Way, Dayton, OH 45439. Prepare a data sheet to accompany your letter.

Business Speech

Careful speakers give long *u* its full sound. In the following words, say the long *u* sound, which is the sound in *cue*. Practice pronouncing these words until you have mastered the sound.

1. new	4. student	7. renew	10. consume
2. knew	5. duty	8. overdue	11. presume
3. due	6. stupid	9. assume	12. resume

Note: The long *u* sound usually does not follow *l* or *r*. *Blue* rhymes with *shoe; ruse* rhymes with *shoes.*

Spelling

<u>Guides:</u> When the letter *c* you spy, place the *e* before the *i* when the sound involved is that of long *e*, as in *receipt, deceive,* and *receive.* (There are no exceptions to this rule!) Use *ei* when the sound is long *a*, as in *neighbor* and *weigh.* After many consonants, the order is *ie,* but there are some exceptions.

Study List 30 on page 409.

OTHER EMPLOYMENT LETTERS

After writing a letter of application, you may have to write related letters. Such letters should prove that you are courteous, capable, and determined. Sometimes an applicant is given a job because he or she has written one of such follow-up letters. A company president has said, "We like to hire people who don't just sit back and hope for the best; we appreciate it when an applicant follows up."

Thanking the Interviewer

After an interview you should write a short letter to the person who interviewed you. One personnel director reports that the firm reviewed several hundred application letters in its search for 40 workers. In each case the person hired had sent a thank-you note after the interview. Even if you know at the end of the interview that you have not received the job, you should send a short thank-you letter to the interviewer.

> Thank you for the courtesy shown me during my interview yesterday afternoon. What you told me about your firm's history and progress, as well as the opportunities for advancement, makes me feel confident that Jackson Company offers the ideal job for a beginning clerk.
>
> When you have made a decision about the position, Mr. Carter, I shall appreciate your letting me know. I hope that I shall be the fortunate selection.

Following Up the Written Application

Within a week or two after you have submitted an application letter, it is wise to send a follow-up letter. Most employers welcome follow-up letters, since they feel that such letters show sincere interest and determination on the part of the applicant.

Employment follow-up letters are usually about a half-page; they should never be longer than one page. They serve several purposes: to request information about your status, express appreciation for acknowledging your application, provide new information about yourself, and so on.

> On May 27 I submitted my letter of application for employment as a design drafter. Since I am eager to obtain such a position with your firm, I am writing to inquire whether you have made a decision. I also wish to let you know that I am still available.
>
> Thank you for considering my application.

> Thank you for your letter of June 4 telling me that you have received my letter of application and résumé.
>
> My training and part-time experience have been in the accounting field; and now that I am ready to take a full-time position, I hope soon to begin my career in accounting. I am therefore interested in joining your firm as an accountant trainee.
>
> Your consideration of my application is appreciated.

> On June 15 I applied for the position of personnel clerk in your company. I hope that my qualifications prove suitable.
>
> Since writing you, I have obtained the permission of Mr. William Beckett to use his name as a reference. Mr. Beckett is my typing instructor at Columbus Senior High School.
>
> I appreciate your consideration of my application.

Usually one follow-up letter is sufficient. If you send a second one, however, it should be brief and refer to the original application letter, not the first follow-up.

Accepting or Declining a Position

When you are offered a position, reply promptly. If you accept, state your acceptance, identify the position, and indicate the time you will report to work.

> Thank you for your letter of July 1 in which you offer me the position of clerk-typist. I am happy, indeed, to accept the position.
>
> As you request, I shall report to the Personnel Department at 8 a.m. on Monday, July 10.

In declining a position, be courteous; don't ever say that you have obtained a better position.*

> It is with regret that I must decline your offer of the position of receptionist. Since I have decided to enter State College this fall, I shall not be available for a full-time position.
>
> Thank you for your confidence in my ability.

Reference Letters

Reference letters are commonly called *letters of recommendation*. A reference letter includes information about an applicant's personality, dependability, skills, and so on.

Assume that you apply for a position at the XYZ Company. In your application you list three references. The XYZ Company will write or telephone one or all three references, asking for information about you. The statements will be sent directly to the XYZ Company. Such information is considered confidential by both the giver and the receiver.

---

* When you accept a position, you should notify all other firms that may be considering you for a job. Tell them that you have accepted a position and thank them for considering your application.

> Thank you for your letter of March 5 in which
> you request employment information regarding
> Miss Julie Drossell, who has applied for a
> position with you.
>
> Miss Drossell was employed by our firm from
> May 1979 to June 1981. She was a supervisor
> in our Order Department.
>
> During her employment with us, Miss Drossell
> earned the confidence and respect of all who
> worked with her. Her friendly, cooperative
> personality and her desire to undertake
> responsible duties made her one of our most
> valuable workers.
>
> We were sorry that Miss Drossell left us, and
> we would gladly rehire her.

When they wish information about applicants, some firms send special forms to the persons named as references. Such forms contain questions to be answered and requests for opinions.

The General Reference Letter. *A general reference letter* is one that is given to a person who will use it in trying to find a position. Such a letter does not have an inside address. *To Whom It May Concern* is used instead of the regular salutation. (See "References" in Section 30, page 309.)

Letter of Resignation

Most large firms require a letter of resignation when a worker terminates employment. Sometimes the employee is required to fill in a special resignation form, which is simple and quickly completed. A letter of resignation should be brief and to the point.

> This is my resignation as engineering
> aide, to become effective April 30. I have
> accepted a position as documentation coordi-
> nator in another company.
>
> My employment at Garver Brothers has
> been enjoyable, indeed, and I shall truly
> regret leaving the firm.

Be an Expert Writer

Each time you see a new handbook on writing or English usage, examine it. Try to pick up some new pointers and refresh yourself on a few grammatical principles that you may have allowed to become rusty.

Indicate any changes that should be made in the following sentences. (Expert writers do not make the types of errors that appear in these sentences, all of which were taken from a company test for the job of correspondence supervisor.)

1. When applying for a job put your best qualifications forward.
2. The employee was exhonorated from the charge of theft.
3. He was appointed as Chairman of the committee.
4. The interviewer reassured me on one important point.
5. Despite the fact that she is young, she has reached her goal.
6. He discussed developments on Middle East Problems.
7. We have a suffiicent number of applicants.
8. The building at the intersection of Main and Hayes was entirely destroyed.
9. I shall call you on the matter of complaints on salespeople.
10. My past experience included secretarial work.

Check Your Knowledge

1. Although you fail to obtain the position you desire, you should write a thank-you letter to the interviewer. Why?
2. In declining a job, why should you avoid saying that you have obtained a better one?
3. When is *To Whom It May Concern* used as a salutation in a reference letter? Should the original copy of such a letter be mailed with your application letter? Discuss.
4. What are the psychological advantages of following up your letter of application?
5. What information should be included in a resignation letter?

31-A. Two weeks ago you sent an application letter to McLain Grain Co., 215 West Lake Street, your city, applying for the position of receptionist-typist. You have received no reply. Write a letter seeking information about the vacancy and the status of your application.

31-B. On April 23, you received the following letter from Mr. H. Maxwell Street, Personnel Director of Eagle Paper Co., 996 Bayview Boulevard, your city. Write a letter accepting the position.

> The Eagle Paper Co. is happy to offer you the job of records clerk for which you recently made application. The beginning salary will be $200 a week.
>
> If you wish to accept this position, please write us at once. We should like you to begin work on Monday, May 5, at 9 a.m. Please report to Miss Patricia Harrington in our Personnel Department.

31-C. Refer to the letter from Eagle Paper Co. in problem 31-B. Write a letter declining the position.

31-D. You have been interviewed by Mrs. Alice Mermitt, Assistant Manager of Dale's Department Store, 1296 Chestnut Street, your city. Write a letter thanking her for interviewing you for the position of keypunch operator.

31-E. Assume that for the past year you have been working for Dalley's Food Products. Now your family is moving to Denver, where you must find a job. You have applied at Market Products, Inc., and have given Mr. Oliver Dalley as a reference. Write the letter of recommendation that Mr. Dalley will send to Market Products, Inc., 14328 Newport Avenue, Denver, CO 80229.

31-F. You are resigning your position as Department Head, Word Processing, at Fillmore Savings and Loan, 1167 Brotherhood Way, Salt Lake City, UT 84316, to accept a similar position with an import-export firm. Write a letter of resignation to Mr. Gordon James, Personnel Manager.

Business Speech

Wh is pronounced *hw*; the *h* sound should be distinctly pronounced.

1. what (HWAT)   3. when (HWEN)   5. whether (HWETHER)
2. wheel (HWEEL)   4. where (HWAIR)   6. which (HWICH)

> *Note:* The *w* is not sounded in *who, whose,* and *whom* (HOO, HOOZ, HOOM).

Spelling

Study List 31, which contains more words with *ei* and *ie*. (See page 410.)

Unit
Eleven
PREPARING BUSINESS REPORTS

Section

32

OUTLINING BUSINESS REPORTS

By appealing to the reader's emotions, the business letter tries to obtain prompt action or cause a favorable reaction. The business report, however, is intended to be a direct, logical report of facts and related information about a business problem or situation.

No one can manage a typical business successfully without information on which to base decisions. In a one-person store, for example, the owner may simply count the items in inventory to decide what to buy. The president of a large corporation must make some of the decisions that the one-person owner-manager makes, but he or she cannot know every detail of the business. The corporation president therefore relies on reports.

The Need for Reports

The report is a message to management. It travels from an employee to a supervisor, from a supervisor to an executive, or from the executive to the stockholders or board of directors. On the basis of the information included in the report, a decision may be made. Perhaps several reports are needed before a decision is made. Nevertheless, *the report is a basic management tool used in decision making.* Therefore, the report must be as objective—as factual and honest—as possible. A manager's reputation and the success of a business depend on information that comes in the form of reports.

The Report Problem

Why does management make decisions? It does so because it is faced with a problem that requires an answer of "Yes," "No," or "Perhaps." *The basis for a report is a problem.*

To solve a problem, four steps are required:

1. Recognize and define the problem.
2. Formulate a plan.

3. Carry out the plan (collect and organize the information).

4. Arrive at an answer or conclusion.

Let's examine a business problem that might require a report to management.

A company has always manually made out its payroll checks for about 200 employees. That is, the company had its payroll department compute hours times pay, deduct the typical withholdings, and arrive at a net amount for the paycheck. Because of complicated pay rates and a growing number of deductions or withholdings, the cost of preparing the payroll has increased considerably. What should the company do? Should it continue to do as it has done, or should it change to a computerized system? This is a problem that might be handed to you on the job. If you attack the problem properly and arrive at a logical conclusion, you may be promoted to a better position. If you fail, you may never advance.

Outlining the Report

Thinking the problem through the four steps in the report process, you should come up with a plan something like this.

I. *Definition of the problem*
   The purpose of this study will be to determine whether manual payroll operation or computer payroll operation is less costly to the company.

II. *The plan of attack*
   A. Determine the costs of operation at present.
   B. Determine the costs of installing an electronic system.

III. *Carrying out the plan and organizing the material*
   A. Consult payroll records to determine labor costs; survey equipment records to determine costs of equipment and supplies; analyze the present method to determine whether it is efficient.
   B. Consult computer-equipment manufacturers and sales representatives to obtain estimates of the cost of doing the work by computer.
   C. Compare the two sets of data obtained in steps A and B.

IV. *Arriving at the conclusion*
  A. Attempt to arrive at a dollars-and-cents difference in cost of operation.
  B. Conclude that the method costing less is better for the company.

Notice that the report process requires a considerable amount of information. By the time you assemble all the information, you may be overwhelmed by its abundance. Your next step, then, is to reduce the data to understandable form.

The information can be reduced by putting much of it in table form or in the form of pictures. Because your manager won't want to read estimates and details from several equipment manufacturers, you'll have to condense the information. You should do the same with the information on your own costs of preparing the payroll. Once you have done this, you will find it easy to make comparisons.

Your only remaining step will be to arrive at your conclusion or answer. As a report writer, though, your big task still remains—putting the entire process down on paper.

Planning to Write the Report

Make an outline before writing the report. Based on the four steps in the report process, the outline serves as a guide for writing. To outline data effectively, you must understand the nature of an outline. The report outline follows the steps in the report process.

With Roman numerals and capital letters, this is how an outline looks:

I.
II.
  A.
  B.
III.
  A.
  B.
  C.
IV.
  A.
  B.

Note: If further subdivisions are needed use *1, 2, 3,* and so on, as in the following example:

I.
  A.
    1.
    2.
      a.
      b.

The Roman numeral headings will become actual headings in the report. Look at the *A*'s and *B*'s in the outline. Notice that each Roman numeral has at least an A and a B subdivision or none at all. For example, Section II (The Plan of Attack), shows both *A* and *B* subdivisions. You should always have at least two subdivisions, because something can be divided into only two or more parts. Section I cannot be divided into two or more parts; therefore, it was written without letter subdivisions.

Completing the Organization of a Report

Once the outline is prepared, the report writer must build the other parts of the report around the basic outline. A complete report includes three major parts:

1. introductory material
2. the body of the report
3. addenda

Here is the outline of a report:

    I.   Introductory parts
        A.   Letter of transmittal *
        B.   Title page
        C.   Contents page
        D.   Summary
   II.   Body of the report
        A.   Definition of the problem
        B.   Method of problem
        C.   Findings
        D.   Conclusions
  III.   Addenda
        A.   Bibliography
        B.   Appendix
        C.   Index

The introductory materials and addenda are included to make the report completely understandable.

---

* The letter of transmittal is addressed to the person who authorized the report. It includes the scope and limitations of the report, the methods used, special problems met, and unusual features of the findings. The closing is *Respectfully submitted*.

Check Your Knowledge

1. To solve a problem, what four steps are necessary?
2. In outlining a report, what are the four major divisions?
3. What are the three major parts of a completed report?
4. What types of information appear in the addenda section of a report?
5. Why are business reports necessary?

Skill Builders

32-A. Visit your school library or public library to determine how the decimal system used in marking library books is related to outlining. Prepare to tell the class.

32-B. Prepare an outline of the cars produced by the "Big Three"— General Motors, Ford, and Chrysler. After using the companies as Roman numerals, you might divide your outline with such headings as Economy Cars, Low-Priced Standards, Medium-Priced Standards, and High-Priced Cars. *Or* your outline might emphasize horsepower or sports cars versus family cars. Make an outline based on your interests.

32-C. Outline an article from the editorial page of a newspaper.

32-D. Obtain an annual report of a large corporation. Prepare an outline of the report.

Business Speech

Consult your dictionary to learn the pronunciation and definition of each of the following words:

1. heinous
2. righteous
3. surveillance
4. xylophone
5. linear

Spelling

Study List 32, which contains more words with *ei* and *ie*. Learn the spellings of the endings *cient* and *ciency*. (See page 410.)

Section

33

WRITING IN REPORT STYLE

Objectivity is an absolute requirement in a formal business report. That is, the writer must seem completely detached from it. The writer must remain objective and stay in the background, letting the facts speak for themselves. Objectivity in report writing can be achieved by following a few simple rules.

Objective Style in Reports

Memorandums are a simple form of report. In the memorandum the first-person pronouns *I* and *we* are used. In many formal reports, however, first-person pronouns are undesirable because they produce a subjective tone. Objective tone in a report contributes to the idea of logical development.

Observe the following sentences:

FIRST-PERSON STYLE	FORMAL-REPORT STYLE
I interviewed four teachers.	Four teachers were interviewed.
We found product A to be better than product B.	Product A was found to be better than product B.
I compared three samples of metal.	Three samples of metal were compared.

In some reports either style is acceptable. In such cases use the style preferred in your company.

Using Active Sentences

Reporting usually involves writing about some kind of action. Such writing, therefore, should be active. For example, notice that the following sentence can be changed from passive to active simply by recasting.

> Passive: The superiority of alloy A was shown in the analysis.
> Active: The analysis showed the superiority of alloy A.

In the passive example the subject, *superiority,* did nothing; it "was shown." In the active example, the subject *analysis* did something; it "showed." Here are two more examples:

Passive: In the electronics industry about seven office employees are needed for each engineer.
Active: The electronics industry needs about seven office employees for each engineer.

Of course, you can't write all active sentences. In some cases you wouldn't want to do so. To avoid *I* or *we,* the passive is sometimes used. A happy balance between active and passive writing helps to produce good reports.

Headings Assist the Reader

Outlines do more than give the writer a guide for making the report. Each heading in the outline can become a heading in the report itself. The reader can use the report headings as guideposts, just as the automobile driver uses highway signs. The example on the following page is the first part of the body of a report.

Types of Headings

Notice that the headings used in the following report tell the reader what is going to be discussed. In the example two kinds of headings are used: *No. 1* heading and *No. 2* heading. The word *Introduction* is a No. 1 heading. The introductory section contains three No. 2 subheadings, each underlined and placed flush (even) with the left margin.*

---

* Headings and subheadings are popularly referred to as "heads" and "subheads."

A STUDY OF MERIT RATING AND ITS APPLICATION TO
GREAT NORTHERN SAVINGS AND LOAN ASSOCIATION

Much interest has been developed lately in refined methods of employee evaluation as one step in proper wage administration.

INTRODUCTION

Purpose of This Report

The purpose of this report is to present findings about the place of merit rating in business and particularly in the savings and loan business. Of special importance in the study was the attempt to determine whether merit rating would be a desirable addition to the procedures at Great Northern Savings and Loan Association.

Method and Sources of Information Used

To obtain data for the study, the following sources and methods were used:

1. A questionnaire survey was made of twenty representative savings and loan associations.

2. Authoritative references in the fields of merit rating, personnel administration, and salary administration were consulted.

Organization of the Remainder of the Report

This introductory section of the report has presented the purpose of the study and the methods and sources used to obtain data. In the following section, techniques for using merit rating and its advantages and disadvantages are discussed. Then the report includes the results of the survey of other associations. The report concludes with a recommendation for Great Northern Savings and Loan Association.

First Page of a Business Report

In an outline of the report the headings would appear like this:

A STUDY OF MERIT RATING AND ITS APPLICATION TO
GREAT NORTHERN SAVINGS AND LOAN ASSOCIATION

I. Introduction

    A. Purpose of This Report

    B. Method and Sources of Information Used

    C. Organization of the Remainder of the Report

II. Uses of Merit Rating

    A. Advantages

    B. Disadvantages

We could continue with the outline through the remainder of the report. It is easy to see from the outline, however, just what is included in the report. The *Table of Contents* or *Contents* page presents the outline of the report, just as the contents of this book are shown in the "Contents."

Here is the way the outline would look on a contents page:

CONTENTS

	Page
Introduction	1
Purpose of This Report	1
Methods and Sources of Information	1
Organization of the Remainder of the Report	1
Uses of Merit Rating	2
Advantages	2
Disadvantages	3

All that is done to convert an outline to a contents page is to remove the Roman numerals and capital letters and add page numbers. By indenting the No. 2 headings a few spaces, you show the organization of the complete report.

Simple, Clear Wording Assists the Reader

Reports sometimes contain several pages. As with all other writing, be extremely careful to make your report clear.

Two errors commonly bother readers of reports—improper or indefinite use of pronouns and the wrong tense of verbs.

Whenever you use a pronoun, such as *which, that, those, its,* or *who,* be sure it refers to the proper word. If you question the accuracy, repeat the noun to which the pronoun refers.

Use the past tense of verbs to tell the reader what you *did.* You *surveyed* (past tense) twenty other business firms. But your report *presents* (present tense) the findings. Use the present tense in telling the reader what your report shows. If necessary, tell the reader that the report *will indicate* (future tense) some desirable changes to be made.

The problems of pronoun usage and verb tense will cause you little trouble if you write naturally and remember the preceding suggestions.

Use Visual Aids to Assist the Reader

"A picture is worth ten thousand words" is true in report writing. Look at the charts and graphs in this section. Each represents ideas that might take hundreds or thousands of words to describe—and even then the ideas might not be clear.

Tabulations Assist the Reader

Often you will find that you have several points to stress. For example, if you say, "Four things are important at this point," how will you list the four points? You might begin by saying, "First, all employees should . . ."; and after that long sentence write another saying, "Second, all employees should. . . ." With this procedure you may forget to mention what is third, or you may lose the reader. By indenting ("setting in") and numbering the items, you can tabulate the problem as follows:

Four things are important at this point. All employees should

1. Report for work ten minutes before starting time.
2. Check out with their supervisors before leaving for lunch.
3. Check in with the supervisors after lunch.
4. Sign their names and indicate the time they leave for the day.

Distribution of the Income
Dollar of YXZ Company

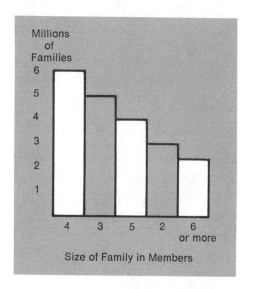

1. A PIE GRAPH. Pie graphs are used to show how 100 percent of something is divided.

2. A BAR GRAPH. Bar graphs are used to show comparison of totals.

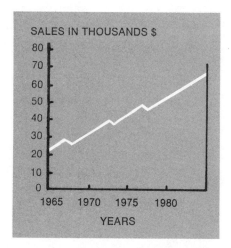

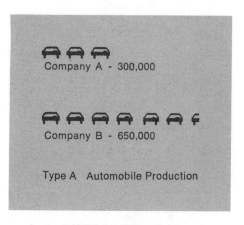

3. A LINE GRAPH. Line graphs are used to show changes over time periods.

4. A PICTOGRAM. Pictograms are used to make picture comparisons of numeric data.

Examples of Visual Aids in Reports

Checking Your Report

When you have finished writing a report, check it carefully to see that each heading is listed in the contents. Then read the report aloud to yourself. This is the best way to check your work for incorrect statements, faulty grammar, and expressions that are not clear. If your report "sounds" good, it probably is good. If parts sound awkward or misleading, you can correct them as you read the report.

Progress Quiz 33. Rewrite the following sentences so they will be acceptable for formal reports.

1. I believe that three coaches are needed to prepare the football team.
2. We can prove the second point.
3. I took three test samples from mixture B.
4. The superiority of test A was shown in the analysis.
5. This report will present the findings of the three committees, which are preliminary.

Check Your Knowledge

1. In report writing, when should active verbs be used? avoided?
2. How do headings assist the reader?
3. In reports what are the values of visual aids?
4. How should you check your finished report?
5. What is a letter of transmittal?

Skill Builders

33-A. Prepare a report to determine whether the school newspaper should include advertisements. Make the study by interviewing students for their opinions. Determine whether the amount of money that can be collected from advertising would help pay for the paper.

33-B. Prepare appropriate charts or graphs to best present each of the following sets of data:

a. To make the school budget understandable to students, you have the task of presenting to them the following information:

Income:

Student Fees	$ 765.00
Athletic Receipts	3,840.00
Food Sales	1,450.00
Other Income	945.00
Total Income	$7,000.00

Expenses:

Student Wages	$2,200.00
Athletic Expenses . . .	3,150.00
Food Costs	850.00
Other Expenses . . .	800.00
Total Expenses	$7,000.00

b. For every dollar collected as student fees, 50 cents is contributed to the yearbook, 25 cents to the school athletic program, 15 cents to the band, and 10 cents to the school newspaper.

c. Sales for a company for five years were reported as follows:

1st year	$125,000
2nd year	250,000
3rd year	500,000
4th year	750,000
5th year	900,000

33-C. Assume you are going to write a report on the career plans of members of the senior class. Prepare a one-page description of how you might gather information for the report. Then prepare a short outline of a final report.

Spelling

Guide: When a one-syllable word ends with silent *e*, drop the *e* before adding a suffix beginning with a vowel: *owe—owing*. If the suffix begins with a consonant, however, keep the *e: care—careless*. Exceptions: *true—truly, whole—wholly; mile—mileage.*

Study List 33 on page 410.

Unit Twelve

OTHER WRITTEN COMMUNICATIONS

Section
34

MEMORANDUMS AND TELEGRAMS

Business is interested in both accuracy and speed. For written messages going from one part of the office to another or to a branch office, the *memorandum* is an effective form of brief written communication. For rapid long-distance messages, telegraphic services are commonly used.

In memorandums and telegrams the good writer uses only enough words to convey the message. The devices and methods used in writing sales letters and other persuasive letters are seldom used in memorandums and telegrams.

Writing Memorandums

The memorandum moves back and forth quickly in business.* It is used to carry information from one office to another, between the office and the plant, and from the home office to a branch office. It moves from a clerk to an executive and from an executive to a clerk. It is the primary means of internal communication in business. The memorandum, therefore, must be economical, clear, and prompt. To meet these requirements, business has adopted these basic requirements for the memorandum: (1) Use as few words as possible. (2) Use a subject line to identify the topic. (3) Use a uniform heading to show the addressee's name, the writer's name, the date, and the subject.

Notice that the following memorandum uses simple, direct sentences to transmit its message:

---

* The memorandum is often called *interoffice memorandum*. Popularly it is referred to as a "memo."

```
DATE:      May 1, 19--

TO:        Arnold Stengel, President

FROM:      Karen Powell, General Manager

SUBJECT:   EMPLOYEE TURNOVER DURING APRIL

During April our employee turnover rate was 3.5 percent.  We
began the month with 2,004 employees.  On April 30 we had
2,007 employees.  Seventy terminated their employment during
the month and were replaced.  We also created three new posi-
tions, and employees were hired to fill those posts.  The 3.5
percent figure compares favorably with our normal April turn-
over of 4.2 percent.
```

The "To," "From," "Date," and "Subject" headings enable the reader to locate quickly information that might otherwise be difficult to find. If printed headings are used, they assure management that certain data will always be in the same place. Uniformity is important in routine messages. Uniformity makes filing and finding easier, too.

Economy of words and clearness might be enhanced if the preceding message were written as follows:

```
                        MEMORANDUM

SUBJECT   Employee Turnover during April      DATE  May 1, 19--

TO        Arnold Stengel, President

FROM      Karen Powell, General Manager


Here is our employee turnover record for the month of April:

          Employees on April 1          2,004
          Terminations            70
          Replacements hired      70
          New positions filled     3
          Employees on April 30         2,007

The turnover rate of 3.5 percent for this April compares
favorably with our normal April turnover rate of 4.2 percent.

                          KP

msl
```

A Type of Interoffice Memorandum (Inductive)

Which memorandum do you think is better? Some business executives would prefer the first because it puts the most important information at the beginning. Other executives would prefer the second because it puts the information in easy-to-read table form and ends with the comparative conclusion.

Direct and Indirect Organization. The two preceding memorandums clearly indicate two frequently used sequences of written organization. The first memorandum is written in *deductive* or *direct* sequence. Since *deductive* means *direct,* a deductively organized memorandum or report begins with a direct statement of the important idea. It begins with the conclusion—the turnover rate for the month. Then it upholds the conclusion by reporting the supporting data.

The second memorandum—the *inductive* or *indirect* type—begins by reporting the details or supporting data. Then the important idea or conclusion follows. The sequence is indirect because it places the conclusion at the end.

The following lists show the differences between direct and indirect types of organization:

Direct	*Indirect*
1. Conclusion	1. Details
2. Details	2. Conclusion

Preparing Telegrams

Although the telephone is the fastest means of normal business communication, the telegram is the fastest way of transmitting written messages. The telegram, like the memorandum, uses as few words as possible and ignores some of the tactful aspects of the business letter. Uniformity is insured, since the telegraph company provides uniform blanks on which the message must be prepared.

Telegrams are used for messages transmitted within the United States and to neighboring countries. When a message is to be sent overseas, the cablegram is used and may be sent through the telegraph company. Telegrams and cablegrams may be telephoned to the telegraph office and charged to your telephone bill.

The language of telegraphic messages may be

1. *plain* (regular words)
2. *code* (words having special meanings)
3. *cipher* (groups of five letters each, such as TMQWZ, that do not spell words)

Classes of Telegraphic Messages. Western Union offices list the current rates for the various classes of telegrams. Based on the length of the message to be sent and the urgency with which it must be delivered, you can determine which of the following classes of service to use.

The *telegram,* sometimes called *fast telegram,* has a flat rate for interstate messages of 15 or fewer words. This type of message receives the fastest telegraphic service.

The *overnight telegram,* often referred to as a *night letter,* has a flat rate for interstate messages of 50 or fewer words. The message is delivered at the start of the next business day. The cost for a night letter is less than for a regular telegram.

The *mailgram* is the least expensive telegraphic message. Delivery is made by the postal service during regular mail delivery on the next day. A flat rate is charged for interstate messages of 50 or fewer words sent by mailgram.

International messages. The *cablegram* is transmitted by means of a cable laid across the ocean floor. The cablegram is used for transmitting messages between continents. The *radiogram* is a message sent by wireless and is used in communicating with ships and aircraft. (See page 344 for further information.)

When you wish to send a telegraphic message of any kind, consult your local Western Union office for rates and special regulations.

Using Telegraph Services. To use telegraph services effectively, consider the following:

1. Carefully check on the telegram blank the class of service desired.
2. Supply complete addresses. No charge is made for the address. Your name, also transmitted free, must be included at the end of the telegram.
3. Leave your own address with the telegraph office so that possible errors or misinterpretation can be cleared by you before the message is sent.

4. Type the message or write it carefully. If you telephone the message to the telegraph company, the operator will read your message back for verification. You can save time and money and increase accuracy by writing the message before you telephone. Keep this copy for your files.

5. Retain a copy of all messages for your own files. In firms where telegrams are used frequently, the telegraph company provides a service by which you can transmit messages in picture form directly to the telegraph office. You can then retain the original for your files.

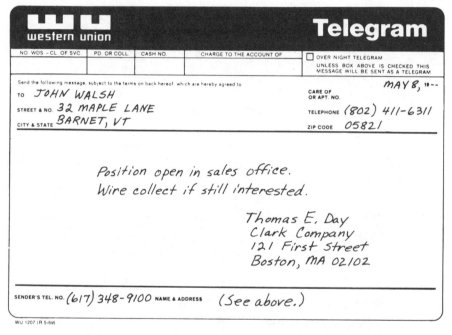

Telegram forms should be filled in clearly, using either hand-lettering or typing.

Other Telegraphic Services. You may send money by telegram. Details of this procedure can be obtained from any telegraph office.

Frequently when financial matters are involved, you wish to be certain that the message was transmitted perfectly. In such cases you can request that the message be repeated back from the receiving office. Although an extra charge is made for this service, it is well worth the cost when either money or a sensitive issue is involved.

Overseas messages (cablegrams) may be sent as *full-rate messages* or *international letter telegrams*. (The latter is also called the *overnight cablegram*.) Full-rate messages may be written in any language using the Roman alphabet (which we use), or the message may be in code. The *international letter telegram* is a less expensive, overnight service. It must be in *plain* language, not code.

Sometimes a telegraphic message is much less expensive but just as effective as a long-distance telephone call.

Using Telegram Language. Because message rates are based on the number of words used, telegram writers have developed the technique of condensing messages. Here are a few examples of telegram language:

EVERYDAY LANGUAGE	TELEGRAM LANGUAGE
In order to	To
Materials you requested	Requested materials
Answer at our expense	Answer collect
A letter is in the mail	Letter follows
Please answer promptly	Wire reply

Simply by analyzing your own writing, you can effect many word economies that are often overlooked. Both the memorandum and the telegram require careful, concise use of words.

Counting Words in Telegrams. Following are the most important rules for counting words in telegrams:

1. The address and one signature are free.
2. Common punctuation marks, as well as the hyphen and apostrophe, are neither counted nor charged for.
3. Numerals are counted as one word for each five characters. In groups of numerals decimal points, commas, and hyphens are neither counted nor charged for.
4. The following symbols are counted as one character each: &, $, #, %, /, ', and " (feet and inches). The following symbols cannot be transmitted by telegraph: @, ¢, and °. The words *at, cents,* and *degree* must be used instead of these symbols.
5. Dictionary words from European and Latin languages, as well as English ones, are counted as one word each, regardless of length. Words that are not dictionary words are counted as one word for each five letters.

6. Compound geographic names, such as *New York* and *United States,* are counted as one word.

7. Abbreviations of single words are counted as full words.

8. Abbreviations of common phrases, such as *a.m.* and *C.O.D.,* are counted as one word if written without space between letters.

9. Each initial is counted as a separate word. However, a word having a foreign prefix, as *LaFrance,* is counted as one word if no space is left after the prefix.

Time Differences. Except for Alaska and Hawaii, there are four time zones in the United States. In making a long-distance telephone call or sending a telegram, you must consider the time zones. Note the following examples of time differences:

STANDARD TIME ZONE	THE HOUR
Pacific	1 p.m.
Mountain	2 p.m.
Central	3 p.m.
Eastern	4 p.m.

Notice that there is a three-hour difference between the coasts. From the Canadian border to the Mexican border, however, the time is the same within a given zone. When Daylight Saving Time is in effect, the time is always one hour later.

LOS ANGELES   NEW YORK

Check Your Knowledge

1. How does an inductive memorandum differ from a deductive memorandum?
2. Which is the fastest type of telegraphic service? slowest?
3. For what reasons does a firm use memorandums?
4. On leaving for the day, your boss tells you to send a fast telegram to a distant city. You find that you can't reduce the message to fewer than twenty words. What do you do?
5. Does a firm ever file copies of its telegrams? memorandums? Discuss.

Skill Builders

34-A. As transportation manager of the American Aircraft Company, you have the task of preparing an easy-to-understand memorandum for all employee bulletin boards. A new bus service between the airport plant and your production plant (located five miles apart) will be put in service on June 1. Buses will be available to all employees traveling between plants. They will load and unload at the main gates of each plant. Two buses will operate; one will leave the airport plant at 8:30 a.m., and the other will leave the production plant at the same time. They will operate on a twenty-minute schedule; that is, a bus will leave each main gate every twenty minutes during the morning beginning at 8:30 a.m. No buses will operate between noon and 1:00 p.m. The afternoon schedule will begin at 1:00 p.m., and the last bus will leave each station at 4:20 p.m. Prepare the memorandum so it will be understood by all employees.

34-B. As treasurer of your student-body association, you are required to write a memorandum each Monday morning reporting the attendance, ticket sales, and refreshment-stand sales for your school's home basketball games. The memorandum is to be addressed to the Student Council, with a carbon copy to the faculty adviser, Mr. J. Cash. Last Friday night your team played a game with Central Academy in your gymnasium. Attendance was 1,283.

Of the total, 950 were members of your student body who were admitted free; 205 were students from Central Collegiate who paid $2.00 each; the rest were adults who were admitted for $3.00 each. Refreshment-stand sales were $776. Both the attendance and the refreshment-stand sales were the best of the season. Prepare a direct memorandum.

34-C. Prepare the memorandum in problem 34-B but use the indirect type of organization.

34-D. Write the copy for a telegram to be sent at the minimum full-rate charge—fifteen words or fewer. The telegram should be addressed to Moore Uniforms, 987 Dutton Drive, Cincinnati, OH 45211. You want to order thirty letter sweaters, Model E, in orange with one black sleeve stripe. The sweaters should be shipped collect by air express to your school. Sign your name as business manager of the school.

34-E. Prepare the message in 34-D as an overnight telegram.

Business Speech

In pronouncing the names of the days of the week—*Sunday, Monday, Tuesday,* and so on—the ending *day* is pronounced as if the *a* were not present. Therefore, *Sunday* should be pronounced SUNDY. Practice pronouncing the names of the days of the week.

Cautions: Pronounce a long *u* in Tuesday. Wednesday has only two syllables; the first *d* is silent.

either, neither. The first choice is EE-ther and NEE-ther; however, if most persons in your locality say EYE-ther and NYE-ther, you should use the same pronunciations. If you live in an area in which persons give these words the first-choice pronunciations, you may be thought affected if you pronounce them with long *i.*

envelope. In the opening syllable the first choice is EN; the second choice, influenced by French, is AHN.

Spelling

Guide: Note the spelling of *cupfuls, spoonfuls,* and so on, which are the usual spellings. *Three cups full* indicates that there are three full cups at the same time.

Study List 34, which contains words commonly misspelled. (See page 410.)

Section 35

BUSINESS JOURNALISM AND NEWS RELEASES

With our emphasis on free enterprise, freedom of speech, and freedom of the press, many business people find it advantageous to make announcements in newspapers and to write articles for magazines. When they write such material, business people help to promote the American way of life to build good public relations for their firms. Sometimes such writing is geared to social or civic issues.

The following are among the most frequently used outlets for business writing: (a) local and national newspapers, (b) business magazines, (c) trade journals, (d) house organs, (e) professional publications.

Everyone is familiar with newspaper articles and their nature. *The Wall Street Journal* and *The New York Times* provide good examples. Magazines, such as *Business Week, Newsweek,* and *Changing Times,* publish articles of national interest. *Printers' Ink* and *American Management* are only two examples of a vast number of trade journals that represent the sales, advertising, and office-management fields. House organs are papers or magazines that large companies publish for employees and stockholders. An example of a professional publication is the *Business Education Forum,* a magazine containing articles helpful to business educators.

Some magazines of a general nature include special sections devoted to business.

Characteristics of Good Business Journalism

Good business journalism covers new and timely developments. It must be honest in presentation and provide either newsworthy items for newspapers and house organs or contributions to knowledge for magazines.

The entire field of business writing for publication is called *business journalism*.

Writing News Releases

For many years newspaper reporters and editors have followed the pattern of writing articles built on three parts: (1) the *lead,* (2) the *details,* and (3) the *summary.*

The lead, or beginning of a news article, carries the *who, what, when, where,* and *why* of the news item. For example, the lead of an article reporting the opening of a new branch of a bank might read:

```
     To serve customers in the new Sunnyside
residential and business area, the First
National Bank announces the opening of its
Sunnyside Branch on June 1.  Located at the
corner of First and Pine Streets, the attrac-
tive new building includes facilities for
drive-in banking, as well as free parking for
over two hundred cars.
```

Following the lead, the article might describe other facilities, include the name of the new manager, and mention something about the history of the organization. This information, which expands on the topics mentioned in the lead, makes up the detail section of the article.

Following the details, the article might end with a summary statement, such as "All residents of the area are invited to an all-day open house on June 1."

Notice that the news release shown on the following page uses an attention-getting headline. This technique attracts attention and encourages the reader to read the remainder of the article.

In preparing news releases, your writing must be straightforward and "newsy." Use only those adjectives that are absolutely necessary to convey your exact meaning. Persons who write news releases for social events often tend to say too much; their writing, therefore, does not get into print. Social editors want facts, not opinions or dressed-up versions of events. Say "The meeting was held at Franklin Hall," not "The meeting was held at Franklin Hall, which was brightly decorated with red roses and white crepe paper."

News releases for social affairs should be short. News releases pertaining to other matters, however, can be longer.

```
                        N E W S   R E L E A S E

     Contact                                Homewood Industries
                                            1800 Common Avenue
        R. L. Edwards                       Los Angeles, CA 90001
        213/777-7777
                                            FOR IMMEDIATE RELEASE


                HOMEWOOD DECLARES STOCK AND CASH DIVIDEND


     Los Angeles, California, June 4, 19-- . . . The Board of Directors of

     Homewood Industries has authorized a six-for-five stock split in the form

     of a 20 percent stock dividend in the corporation's no par value common

     stock, according to R. L. Edwards, President and Chief Executive Officer

     of the company.  The dividend will be payable on June 29, 19--, to share-

     holders of record as of the close of business on June 11, 19--,  Fractional

     shares will be paid in cash based on the June 11 closing price of the cor-

     poration's common stock on the American Stock Exchange.


     Homewood Industries is a major designer and producer of high-speed disper-

     sion equipment, colloid mills, and pressure milling systems for the chemical

     processing industry.  Homewood also manufactures refrigerated air dryers

     for compressed air systems.
```

A Business News Release

Other Forms of Business Journalism

As with news releases, other forms of business journalism, such as magazine articles and manuscripts for other publications, follow an established plan. The opening statements attempt to create interest and identify the subject matter. The supporting facts or ideas are then presented. The article concludes with a summary paragraph, which brings the major points together in a concise conclusion.

Formats for Business Journalism

All types of manuscripts follow a fairly definite plan for typewritten layout.

To enable editors to make changes and indicate instructions to the printer, articles should be double-spaced. Footnotes should be single-spaced, as should quotations that are centered in paragraph form. An additional line should be skipped before a new subheading. Paragraphs should be indented five spaces.

The first page of all manuscripts should have a top margin of at least two inches. All other pages should have top, bottom, and side margins of at least one inch. If your typewritten manuscript is to be bound, however, leave a left margin of one and a half inches. The extra half inch is for the binding.

For articles the page number is usually in the upper right corner. It should be preceded by the author's name. For example, *Jones—2* or *Jones—Page 2* is the identification for page 2 of an article written by Jones. On long manuscripts the author's name is not included with the page number, which is expressed by typing only the figure, without the word *page*.

Selecting Newsworthy Subjects

Like all other writers, business journalists must know what to write about, as well as the correct way to write.

Local newspapers, national newspapers, magazines, house organs, professional journals, and a host of other news and information media provide outlets for almost any kind of news. The journalist should select the right outlet for news releases and articles.

Newspapers are interested in promotions of personnel, in speeches given or to be given, new plant facilities for the community, and new products that will increase employment. House organs or company magazines use similar subjects, but they also include information about births and about weddings, as well as personality profiles of employees and other items of interest only to the company's staff.

In the magazine and journal field, reports of new developments in a company or industry are valued. Items of importance to others in the same industry are particularly worthwhile. Trade and professional publications seek reports of discoveries from research.

Because of the great variety of newsworthy items and the various outlets available, writing the news release or article is only half the job. Careful selection of the outlet can assure the writer of having the material published and of obtaining the best publicity.

Be an Expert Writer

Expert writers recommend the following:

In a manuscript avoid using *above, above-mentioned,* and *below.* Instead use *preceding* and *following.*

The word *case* is a specific word; *instance* is a general word. "In every instance, there has been a case of mishandling."

Avoid using the word *deal* as a noun. Although it may be used colloquially, the best business writers use *transaction* or another word.

A *client* uses the services of lawyers and advertising agencies; a list of clients is the *clientele.* Most other persons providing goods and services have *customers.* A *prospect* may be either a potential customer or client.

Say "great deal" instead of "good deal." The most concise forms, however, are *most* or *many.*

Man, men, woman, and *women* are preferable to *gentleman, gentlemen, lady,* and *ladies.* (Etiquette books often use the latter words.)

Do not say "Our Mrs. Jones" in referring to a member of your firm. Simply say "Mrs. Jones."

On is preferable to *upon* unless you really mean *upon.* Say "depend on."

In writing an article in which you must refer to yourself, don't be afraid of saying "I." Don't refer to yourself as "the writer."

Avoid saying "not too" and "not very." Say "This is not important" instead of "This is not too important."

Tips from Top Business Writers

1. In typing material that will go to the printer, underscore only those words that you wish to appear in italics.

2. Be prepared to defend what you have written. Keep a carbon copy of all written items, including telegrams and memorandums.

3. Good writers avoid circumlocutions—talking in circles. The dog that goes around in circles chasing its tail never seems gratified when it finally succeeds. Avoid circumlocutions, such as "What I mean is" and "If you will permit me." If you get to the point quickly, your point will be sharper!

4. Be wise but economical. In sending an article to a publisher always enclose a stamped, addressed envelope. In sending a news release to a newspaper, however, do not include one.

5. Divide words correctly at ends of lines. Wrong word division indicates a writer who doesn't know the rules of the game.

6. Be sure you know which type of business report you are writing. The *periodic* report usually shows the condition of a business at the end of a certain period. The *progress* report indicates accomplishment in sales, construction, and so on. The *examination* report involves the most planning because it requires careful investigation and makes a recommendation.

Check Your Knowledge

1. Why is conciseness important in writing news releases?

2. Are newspapers required to publish all the news releases they receive?

3. What are the three parts of a news release?

4. Why do some business people try to have their articles printed in magazines?

5. What is the value of having an article published in a trade journal?

Skill Builders

35-A. Select a news article from your local newspaper and rewrite the article in improved form. Attach the newspaper clipping to your revised form.

35-B. Assume that you are to prepare a magazine article about your school. Prepare an outline for the article. Include some specific items you think will be of interest to readers.

35-C. Assume that you are editor of your school newspaper. The paper includes stories about school plans, school activities, and student activities. Interview one of your classmates and prepare an article about that student and his or her activities. Use no more than 200 words. The article will appear in your newspaper in a column called "Know Your Classmates."

35-D. Assume that you are about to open your own business. You have acquired enough money to purchase two electric typewriters, a fine duplicating machine, and other necessary appliances to open a secretarial service. You will be open for business the 20th of next month. Select an address for your company. It will be called "Deluxe Secretarial Service." You will do high-quality typing, expert duplicating, and prompt mailing for customers. For the business person without regular secretarial help, you will take dictation by telephone or send someone to take dictation. Your hours will be 8 a.m. to 6 p.m. every day except Sunday. Prepare a newspaper release to be inserted in the local paper.

Business Speech

1. **advertisement.** Accent *third* syllable; long *i* in third syllable.
2. **irreparable.** Accent *second* syllable. (ir-REP-ar-able)
3. **maintenance.** Accent *first* syllable.
4. **maraschino.** (mara-SKEE-no)

Spelling

The ending *wear* pertains to items of apparel. The ending *ware* pertains to all other items.

Study List 35 on page 410.

Unit Thirteen

YOUR RESPONSIBILITIES AS A BUSINESS WRITER

Section

36

YOUR LEGAL AND ETHICAL RESPONSIBILITIES

To avoid serious legal problems, business writers, including those who write letters, should be familiar with certain principles of business law. Business writers who do not understand their legal responsibilities may involve their companies in costly lawsuits. If in doubt about a legal point, the business writer should consult the company's legal department.

Your Legal Responsibility

Often an employee acts as the employer's legal agent. This means that the employee can enter into contracts involving the employer. When this situation occurs, the employer is known as the *principal,* a legal term used to define one for whom someone else can act. The employee is known as the *agent,* one empowered to act for another. A person having the legal right to sign another person's name is said to have *power of attorney*.

When the boss is absent, a secretary or other office worker sometimes may be required to sign the boss's name to letters or other papers. Such a signature is followed by the actual signer's initials.

Very truly yours,

Ellen J. Bertrand B.A.C.

Ms. Ellen J. Bertrand
Manager

Remember that, although you are not acting as agent, you may get your boss into "hot water" by signing an incorrect or incomplete letter.

Contracts. Without becoming technical about the law, let's examine some of the ways in which the agent-principal relationship occurs. When it is specifically stated that an employee is acting for an employer, the employee becomes an agent. The agent can make purchases on behalf of the employer. The agent can also make and accept offers that require the employer to perform certain actions. The agent can say things in a letter that might later be attributed to the employer.

For example, a secretary might order office equipment or supplies with the employer's permission. If the equipment or supplies later seem to have been too expensive, the employer is nevertheless bound by the agent's act. The secretary who writes and signs letters for an employer may bind that employer to a contract.

Many situations arise in which an employee can act for an employer. It is important for you, as an employee, to remember that you must be acting with the employer's permission, and you must use good judgment. If you order more expensive equipment than the employer specified, you may be held responsible!

Remember, a contract is an *agreement,* and it may be either *oral* or *written.* If you are given the responsibility of being an agent, be sure you do not bind your employer to any type of agreement that may be detrimental to the company.

In carrying out your job duties, exercise discretion and good judgment. Your responsibility is to know the situations in which you can act for your employer.

Libel. One of the most serious types of legal responsibilities concerns *libel,* which may result from careless written remarks about someone.* If a person's reputation is damaged by such remarks, that person can bring a lawsuit against the one making libelous statements. Libelous statements sometimes appear in credit letters and collection letters.

In all your letters, carefully weigh your remarks to or about another person. Usually a letter will not go beyond the one to whom it is addressed. If a letter containing damaging remarks should become available to others, however, a libel suit may result.

Privileged Communications

In credit-information letters and letters of recommendation, the writer can make derogatory statements about a person, provided the statements are true and are necessary in maintaining business relations. For example, if you wish to open a charge account at a store, you will be asked to give a credit reference. The store will write to the name you have provided. That person or firm has the privilege of saying that you are a poor payer if the information is true. Also, when you give a person's name as reference in a letter of application, that person has the privilege of saying that you may not be as good as you think you are, provided, of course, that the statements are true.

---

* Slander is the act of making spoken statements that are damaging to a person's reputation.

Since credit-information letters and letters of recommendation may contain true statements that work against the person being investigated, such letters are called *privileged communications*. The writers of such letters are said to have *qualified* privilege, because they must give facts, not opinions.

So that confidential information will not appear in writing, some firms obtain credit and recommendation information by using the telephone.

Privileged information should *never* be mailed on cards!

Your Ethical Responsibilities

One dictionary defines *ethics* as *the principles of right conduct*. Ethical responsibilities, then, are those matters of right conduct with which you must be concerned as an employee and a citizen.

What are some of the ethical responsibilities that apply to a person's work? In general, they are the same responsibilities of right conduct we assume in our everyday lives. Honesty, courtesy, trustworthiness, charity, and consideration are a few. Because so many persons believe that business is different from everyday living, special attention must be given to the role of these characteristics.

The ethical standards of a person in business should be as high as those of a homemaker, teacher, clergy member, doctor, or lawyer.

To apply ethics to your business life, simply continue to live and act in a way that conforms to the standards of good citizenship. Attempt to treat all customers fairly. To give one customer an unfair advantage over another would be an unethical act. In your adjustment policy, for example, you should be able to say that all customer claims are given a fair review. In your collection procedures, you expect all customers having the same characteristics to pay by certain dates.

Business is not a world apart from the everyday world. The business office is a part of our society. Within business, arrangements are made to accommodate customers in different ways. For example, is it ethical to give a large-volume customer a 5 percent discount on purchases and another customer who buys less only a 2 percent discount? Of course, because the large-volume buyer makes it easy for the seller to ship the product at volume shipping rates. Also, the seller doesn't have to do any more paperwork to keep the large account than to keep the small account. The seller has simply adjusted the price by using discounts to make the profit margin the same in both cases.

Ownership of Written Material

As soon as a letter is placed in a mailbox, it becomes the property of the U.S. government and remains so until delivered to the addressee. Even though the government owns a letter, the Postal Service cannot open the envelope. After delivery of a letter, however, the ownership of the letter is divided. The writer owns the message of the letter; the receiver cannot quote it in print without permission from the writer or the writer's representative. The receiver can use the information in conducting business, however, unless a law or ethics prohibits such use. As a physical item, a letter belongs to the receiver; that is, the writer cannot demand that the letter be returned.

Articles and other published material are the property of the person who holds the copyright. If a writer holds a copyright on unpublished material and later permits someone to publish it, the publisher owns the rights to use the material as outlined in the contract signed by writer and publisher. Before quoting from any published material, writers must obtain permission from the publisher. Publishers of music usually require that permission be obtained even when only one or two lines of song lyrics are quoted.

New literary material may be copyrighted for a period of time consisting of the life of the author plus fifty years. At the end of that period, however, the material goes into *public domain*. That is, anyone can use it without obtaining permission. Since reports, documents, statutes, and the like published by governmental bodies are not copyrighted, they are usually in public domain.

Remember that ignorance of a law is no excuse for violating it! If you think that a legal point is involved in your writing, consult your firm's legal department. If your firm does not have a legal staff, discuss the matter with your supervisor.

Check Your Knowledge

1. As soon as you drop a letter in the mailbox, you remember that you forgot to include some important information. You wait for the mail truck and demand that the truck driver return your letter. Are you within your legal right?

2. (a) What are two types of privileged communications? (b) How far does the privilege extend? (c) Is slander privileged?

3. Cite a case in which a certain action is legal but unethical.

4. "Do right and fear no one" is a good maxim. Someone has changed it to "Do not write and fear no one." Why do you think the latter advice may contain some good sense?

5. When is a piece of writing in public domain?

Skill Builders

Read the following letter carefully; then rewrite it acceptably.

Dear Ms. Chang:

I'm pleased to answer your request for credit information about Sylvester Shadrock and to tell you how little I respect him.

He is lazy, seldom pays his debts on time, and has charged things to other people's accounts.

We don't want to do business with him and neither should you.

Sincerely,

Business Speech

English has borrowed many words from French. In such words *eau* and *eaux* are sounded *oh; oi* is sounded *wah; é* is sounded *ay.*

1. tableau (TAB-loh)
2. Bordeaux (Bor-DOH)
3. coiffure (kwah-FURE)
4. attaché (atta-SHAY)
5. naïveté (nah-eevuh-TAY)*
6. Marseilles (Mar-SAY)†

---

* Two dots over a vowel indicate that the vowel should be pronounced as a separate syllable. The two dots form a diacritical mark called a *diaeresis.* This mark was used in English, also, but has fallen into disuse. The same mark in German is called an *umlaut* (OOM-lowt) but serves a different purpose.

† The French spelling is *Marseille.*

French Accent Marks. Three accent marks are used over vowels in French: *acute* (´), *grave* (`), and *circumflex* (^). Such accents usually show how the vowel should be pronounced. Following are a few examples:

é: sounds similar to the *a* in *day* but pitched higher and pronounced faster. (café)

è: sounds similar to the *e* in *let* but pitched higher. (crèche)

ê: sounds similar to the *e* in *let* but held longer. (fête)

Italian uses the grave accent to show the stressed syllable in certain words. Spanish uses the acute accent to show the stressed syllable in certain words.

Spelling

Study List 36, which contains words that have appeared on tests that private companies have given job applicants. (See page 410.)

37

YOUR RESPONSIBILITY
TO YOUR EMPLOYER

To communicate effectively on the job, you need a sense of responsibility toward your company, your supervisor, and your work. Without the right attitude, you will find that skills alone are not enough to assure your success.

Contrary to popular opinion, a firm's primary objective is not concerned with making money. Of course, a business that loses money cannot operate long. It goes out of business much more quickly, though, if its main purpose is anything other than to provide service. SERVICE—what a simple word, but what a tremendous message it carries!

Has it ever occurred to you that your school system, your government, and your church are conducted like a business? They receive money and they spend it. They have people conducting the typical business services of accounting, managing, selling, and doing office work. They don't operate at a profit but stay in business because they provide service. If the service is faulty, a new management is selected.

When your letters fail to develop goodwill, build business, and carry a favorable picture of you and your firm, you fail. On the job if *you* don't provide the service expected of you, out you go!

Your Firm Is Judged by What You Write

A woman received this letter from a company from which she had been buying for several years:

Dear Mrs. Jones:

How much patience do you think we have? Your last bill with us is long past due.

If we don't receive your payment in the next few days, we'll be forced to turn your account over to a collection agency.

Yours truly,

It was an obvious form letter, usually sent to those whose accounts were more than three months past due. Mrs. Jones's account, though, was only a week overdue. Apparently someone in the office had pulled the wrong letter from the files, but Mrs. Jones didn't know this. She told her friends about the poor treatment she had received. Her friends told their friends. Soon the company had a poor reputation that almost put it out of business. Some employee didn't have the company's objective in mind!

A written report can create bad effects, too. Remember that your writing may be the only thing management knows about you. If your interoffice memorandum or report shows poor taste or lack of knowledge, management will assume that *you* have those characteristics.

Correct English usage, good tone, and attractive layout combine to make communications reflect ability and good taste.

Digesting Material

Some employers expect their secretaries or other workers to read certain materials for them and select the important facts. Condensing material so that only the important points remain is called *digesting, abstracting,* or *abridging.* Busy employers sometimes require secretaries to read trade journals and write condensations of pertinent articles.

An executive secretary or supervisor may attend a meeting or a convention for the employer and take notes of all the important points discussed. Afterwards the employee is expected to present a written report of the meetings attended.

A concise writer will have no difficulty in digesting material. A good listener will be able to give a satisfactory report of a meeting. The employee who digests material for the employer must have a keen sense of responsibility for reporting accurately. The employer trusts such a worker's judgment.

The Employer-Employee Relationship

When you take a job, you are expected to bring more to it than simply the ability to do the work.

Assume that you are the employer or executive who hires a new private secretary. What would you expect? You, like all executives, would expect a person who could take shorthand or use a transcribing machine, type at least reasonably well, transcribe letters accurately and quickly, and meet people well. Is that all? Of course not! You would expect the secretary to be loyal and to respect you and your position. As a loyal employee, your secretary could be expected to handle your confidential information without any fear on your part that it would not remain confidential.

One of the unusual things about the employer-employee relationship is the way an ideal relationship develops. The boss expects certain things from the employee. The employer, moreover, must be convinced through performance that the employee has ability. The employer has a right to expect the employee to begin the job with respect for the company and for the job.

You can expect the employer to have an understanding of employee problems. You can expect the kind of person to whom you can be loyal. Your employer, however, does not have to prove his or her value to you!

In summary, then, the employer expects the following from the employee:

1. Ability to perform the work of the job.
2. Ability to work effectively with others.
3. Unquestionable loyalty to the firm and boss.
4. Ability to handle confidential matters.

A Job Is What You Make It

There is magic in words if you know the formulas for using them well. A bright future awaits the person who has mastered English and can use it well in communicating. When you obtain a job, make the most of your English skills. Make the most of your total job, too, for a job is what you make it. To obtain success in your work, you must earn it.

Check Your Knowledge

1. If your job requires you to write letters, memorandums, and so on, how can what you write help or hurt your employer?

2. Why should a person in a writing job know which things to do first?

3. Is a person who is an excellent writer certain to succeed on the job?

4. Might a person who is late getting to work be considered disloyal? Explain.

5. What do you consider your weakest job qualification? What can you do to strengthen that qualification?

Skill Builders

Read a two-page magazine article. Write a condensation of the article, leaving out unimportant material and stressing the important information.

Business Speech

The *e* in the prefix *ante* (meaning *before*) and the *i* in the prefix *anti* (meaning *against*) sound like the short *i* in *did*. Practice pronouncing the following words:

ante: antedate, antecedent, antechamber, anteroom.

anti: antibiotic, antidote, antifreeze, antisocial, antitrust.

Spelling

Guides: (1) Only two words end with *yze—analyze* and *paralyze*. (2) Add *ize* to full words: *civil—civilize, critic—criticize*. (3) The ending *ise* is usually used for words that are not made from full words: *advertise, despise*. (There are exceptions to rules 2 and 3.)

Study List 37 on page 410.

AREA
THREE

SPOKEN
BUSINESS
COMMUNICATIONS

Speaking is the fastest, most direct method of communication. Words skillfully spoken can either humble or exalt the listener; they can cause crowds to become cheering throngs or frenzied mobs. Spoken words are the magic produced by our most effective musical instrument—the human voice. Written words often have a delayed reaction because the reader has time to analyze them. The listener, however, tends to draw quick conclusions.

Since spoken words usually have a fast impact, the mind and the ear must be trained to listen correctly. As a communications skill, listening is as important as reading, writing, speaking, and observing. An unskilled listener makes errors in following instructions, analyzing ideas, and forming opinions. A skilled listener knows that *observing* a speaker's gestures and facial expressions is also an important part of listening.

Daily life is dominated by spoken communications. The greater your skill in speaking and listening, the greater your chances are of finding success on the job and of becoming a popular person in social life. Outstanding salespeople, secretaries, and other business workers owe much of their success to good speech.

Many persons who are good speakers today did not always have outstanding speaking skill. They realized, however, that speech can be improved by the right kind of practice. They therefore set up a practice program and stuck with it until they reached their goals.

To be considered a good speaker or even a good conversationalist, a person need not be a silver-tongued orator. A pleasant voice properly used, speech that is clear and correct, and a sincere attitude toward the listener —these are the bases of successful speaking. Many experienced speakers say there is no magic formula for impressing an audience or an individual listener. That is probably true; but a speaker who is *confident* and *relaxed* has taken the first two steps needed to impress any listener.

Learn to make words—both spoken and written—work for your welfare. Become the master of words; if you do, you will have at your command the power to open doors through which you will pass to exciting experiences and rewarding work.

Unit
Fourteen
SPEAKING AND LISTENING

YOUR VOICE AND SPEECH

"That last applicant had the right educational background, but as soon as she began to speak, I knew she did not belong in this company." Those words were spoken by an employment interviewer in a large firm. No matter what their good qualities may be, many persons are rejected for jobs because of poor speech. Good speech and a pleasant voice form one of the most valuable assets a person can have in business and social life.

As soon as you begin to speak, you reveal one of the most important aspects of your personality—your speech. All persons, even those who have speech impediments, can improve their speech if they have the desire to do so and are willing to practice.

Expert salespeople know this: The speaker who, with a minimum of effort, can induce others quickly to behave in a desired manner is a good speaker.

Good speech, controlled by a definite purpose in the speaker's mind, is easily heard and understood. Such speech is interesting and holds attention. Future business workers should strive to improve their speaking ability so that, when they go job hunting, they will be equipped with one of the most valuable business skills.

To improve your voice and speech, you should understand and develop skill in the three important aspects of speech—*phonation, articulation,* and *pronunciation.*

Phonation

Phonation involves the production and variation of the speaker's voice tone. Phonation aids the speaker to (1) project the voice and (2) express thoughts and feelings by varying the voice tone.

Voice Attributes. Your voice has four attributes:

Pitch:	how high or how low the vocal tones are.
Intensity:	how loud the vocal tones are.
Duration:	how long the vocal tones are held.
Quality:	how individual the vocal tones are.

The quality of your voice is one of your most personal, individual traits. A friend who recognizes your voice over the telephone can do so because the quality of your voice reveals your identity. Voice quality changes when you are angry, sad, frightened, or emotionally upset in other ways.

THE GOOD VOICE	THE POOR VOICE
a. Has medium or low pitch.	a. Is too high, too low, or monotonous.
b. Is easily heard.	b. Is too loud or too soft.
c. Holds tones adequately and produces smooth sound.	c. Does not hold sounds long enough and produces jerky, distracting speech.
d. Is clear and resonant.	d. Shows that mouth, nasal, and throat cavities do not function as aids to resonance.
e. Is flexible and indicates changes in thought and feeling.	e. Lacks flexibility and does not convey the full meanings of the speaker's thoughts.

How to Improve Your Voice. To improve the voice, speech experts recommend the following:

a. *Breathe properly*. To speak effectively, you should have control of your breathing. You should (1) hold sounds and speak for a reasonable time on a normal intake of air; (2) breathe quietly as often as necessary, without distracting your listeners; (3) maintain a reserve supply of breath.

When you are nervous, you do not breathe properly. The more nervous you become, the less control you have of your voice. Speakers who lose control of their breath gasp like fish out of water and annoy their listeners.

b. *Be completely relaxed*. Your body and your vocal mechanism must be completely relaxed. Emotional control, knowledge of your subject, the ability to adjust quickly to the speaking situation, preparation for the talk, and your experience—all contribute to your confidence. Self-confidence is one of the most important characteristics of any speaker.

c. *Listen to your voice*. Make a recording of your voice on record or tape. After hearing your voice, you are better able to analyze it and to take steps to remedy its weak points. Learn to be critical of your voice. Strive to improve its pitch, intensity, duration, and quality.

d. *Use your normal pitch*. A confident and relaxed speaker tends to use normal pitch. Unrelaxed speakers often use a high pitch that is artificial and distracting. Many otherwise calm people seem to lose much of their natural confidence when they talk, for they begin on a high pitch and progress to a scream.

e. *Develop resonance*. Good speakers, even when they whisper, can be heard in all parts of an assembly hall. The larynx, which is the "voice box," regulates the amount of air entering or leaving the lungs. The person who "swallows words" tries to force his or her voice from the larynx and forgets that good speech is a result of cooperation among various bodily mechanisms. Most of all, however, the throaty speaker and the nasal speaker do not "speak from the diaphragm." The diaphragm is the frontal area just below the ribs. If you stand up straight, breathe properly, and automatically force the air up from your diaphragm, the speech sounds emitted from your voice box will be resonant. Remember, however, that resonance does not mean loudness! Resonance produces enriching vibrations that give your voice a pleasing tone—one that can be heard easily by all your listeners.

When too much air is emitted through the nostrils, speech has an unpleasant, nasal sound.

f. *Develop flexibility*. Good speech is musical. Words and phrases are similar to notes in the musical scale: they go up or down the speech scale to convey the thoughts and feelings of the speaker.

The flexible voice has rhythm, which captivates and holds an audience. Different words and phrases should receive varying emphasis. By giving proper emphasis to the right words and phrases, you aid rhythm and convey the exact meanings to your listeners.

In giving a talk or speaking with a group of persons, use the same kind of voice expression that you use in talking with your family. Don't "put on an act." Your listeners soon know that you are not being natural. A few persons always speak in a monotone; that is, they produce very little variation in the sounds of their voices. Such persons should practice correct vocal expression under the direction of an expert speech teacher.

Read the following sentences, strongly emphasizing the italicized word in each sentence. Notice how each sentence takes a different meaning when you emphasize a different word.

I am glad you are here. (Perhaps no one else is glad, but I am.)
I *am* glad you are here. (Other opinion to the contrary, I am glad.)
I am *glad* you are here. (Truly, I am glad.)

I am glad *you* are here.   (Glad that *you,* especially, are here.)
I am glad you *are* here.   (Maybe you are not glad, but I am.)
I am glad you are *here.*   (*Here*—not somewhere else.)

Articulation

Articulation pertains to the manner in which a speaker produces and joins speech sounds. The good speaker enunciates vowels clearly and gives consonants their proper sounds, without overemphasizing them. The articulate speaker produces smooth, fluent, and pleasant speech.

Inadequate articulation can be a result of: (1) organic defects or disorders of the teeth, tongue, lips, palates, and facial muscles; (2) lack of education, as shown in such pronunciations as "dis" instead of *this,* "wid" instead of *with,* "Wotchya" instead of "What are you," and so on; (3) general carelessness, which may produce sounds that are not properly enunciated, rapid speech that slurs over important sounds, as well as many other poor habits.

How to Improve Your Articulation. The following points will help improve articulation:

a. *Be an alert speaker.* Don't be a lazy speaker; make your tongue, lips, teeth, and so on do the jobs they should to produce proper sounds. The lower jaw should be loose; a tense jaw interferes with proper articulation.

b. *Know the speech sounds.* Each vowel has several sounds, and some of the consonants have more than one sound. You should learn the various sounds of all the vowels and consonants and know which sound to use in any word. When in doubt, consult a reliable dictionary.

The Vowels. The vowels *a, e, i, o, u* and the common diphthongs *oi* and *ow* are voiced speech sounds that result from an adjustment of the mouth, throat, and nose.* There is little interference with the outgoing air when vowels are uttered. For example, the mouth is always open, the lips never come together, the tip of the tongue never presses against the teeth or the hard palate (the roof of the mouth). The vocal chords, however, do vibrate.

---

* At ends of words *y* is a vowel. In the middle of words, *y* is usually a diphthong or a vowel.

The Consonants. Each consonant must be given its correct sound, since consonants are responsible, to a great degree, for the distinctness of speech. Consonants are formed by an interference with or a stoppage of the outgoing breath.

Consonants may be voiced or voiceless, as follows:

VOICED	VOICELESS
b, d, h, j, l, m, n, r,	*f, k, p, q, s, t,* and soft *c;*†
v, w, y, z, and hard *g;* *	*ch, sh, wh;*
th as in *this;*	*th* as in *thin.*
ng (voice and nasalized).	

Voiced consonants produce vibrations in the vocal cords, but voiceless consonants do not.

Dialect. When persons in a certain section of a nation enunciate sounds in ways that are different from those that are most commonly used, such persons are said to have a *dialect.*‡ Although dialect pertains to all types of speech sounds, as well as to grammar and word usage, minor dialects often are those in which only vowel sounds differ from those generally used. For example, speech experts can tell the sections of the United States in which people reside when they hear them pronounce *Mary, marry,* and *merry.* The vowel sounds used in these words help identify speakers' areas of residence.

Note the differences in pronouncing the word *park* in certain sections of the United States:

In parts of New England: *a* midway between *a* in *pat* and *a* in *rah; r* omitted.
In parts of the South: *a* as in *father; r* omitted.
In parts of New York City: *a* nearly like *a* in *all; r* omitted.
In parts of the Midwest: *a* like *a* in *father; r* strongly sounded.

In certain parts of the United States, minor dialects have evolved as a result of foreign influence. When many immigrants have settled in a certain section, they have influenced the English of that section. Human beings cannot live and work together without having an effect on one another—even on one another's speech!

---

* Hard *g* sounds like *g* in *get;* soft *g* sounds like *g* in *gem.*
† Hard *c* sounds like *k;* soft *c* sounds like *s.*
‡ Everyone actually speaks with a dialect.

Be a Careful Speaker. To speak carefully, remember the following: (1) Don't slur sounds by running syllables or words together—for example, saying "wanna" or "didjoo" instead of *want to* or *did you*. (2) Don't omit consonants—for example, saying "reconize" instead of *recognize*. (3) Don't voice a voiceless consonant—for example, saying "ledder" instead of *letter*. (4) Don't pronounce a voiced consonant as if it were unvoiced—for example, pronouncing the *s* in *because* with an *s* instead of a *z* sound. (5) Don't add extra sounds—for example, pronouncing *mail* so that it is "may-ul" or *idea* so that it is "idear." (6) Don't nasalize vowels—for example, saying *at* through the nose.

Habits That Should Be Corrected. It would be a monotonous nation if everyone spoke the same. Certain types of accents and dialect tendencies add individuality to a language. If all Southerners gave up their drawl, for example, our nation would lose a certain charm that is part of its cultural heritage.

According to most speech authorities, however, some speech tendencies and dialects should be avoided. The following list gives examples of such pronunciations:

DON'T SAY	INSTEAD OF	DON'T SAY	INSTEAD OF
boid	bird	căoo	cow *
goil	girl	năoo	now
erl *or* all	oil	toime	time

The Letter r. In some parts of the United States, the letter *r* often is not sounded at ends of words and sometimes is not sounded in the middle of words. The late William Lyon Phelps, an eminent author and lecturer, once said that the sound of *r* is rich and should not be slighted. Speech authorities tell us, nevertheless, that in cultured speech the *r* should be either omitted or slighted in the *er* combination.

Pronunciation

You may have perfect articulation but still mispronounce many words. The correct pronunciation of a word is that used by most of the careful

---

* To pronounce *ow* correctly, keep the mouth nearly in the same position as when you pronounce the *a* in *father*. The correct sound of *ow* is *ah-oo* said fairly rapidly.

speakers in the United States. In the dictionary there are two pronunciations given for many words. Sometimes the second one is the pronunciation prevalent in England. Often the second pronunciation is one that is gaining favor in the language and is included as a second choice. The accepted pronunciation of a word may change. Such changes in pronunciation, however, do not happen quickly.

We live in an age when speed is the order of the day. Our rapid pace of life and work has had an effect on our language, and we tend to speak rapidly, often shifting the accent of a word from the first to the second syllable. At one time nearly everyone accented these words on the first syllable: *despicable, exquisite, hospitable, formidable.* Today, however, many speakers accent these words on the second syllable.

Progress Quiz 38-A. Carefully pronounce each of the following:

1. because	6. saw	11. which
2. what did you	7. iota	12. these
3. What do you want?	8. world	13. fail
4. government	9. never	14. kept
5. somehow	10. want to go	15. crowd

British Pronunciation. Notice the differences in the pronunciation of certain words:

	Americans say	*British say*
again	a-GEN	a-GANE
been	bin	bean
isolate	i-solate (long *i*)	is-olate (short *i*)
laboratory	LAB-er-atory	la-BOR-atory
leisure	LEE-zher	LEZH-er
secretary	SEC-re-tary	SEC-re-tree
schedule	SKED-ule	SHED-ule
issue	ISH-yoo	ISS-yoo
immediately	im-MED-iately	im-ME-jitly
specialty	SPE-cial-ty	spe-ci-AL-i-ty

Many persons of the American theater pronounce words in the British manner. When other Americans use such pronunciations, however, they may be accused of having affected speech.

Progress Quiz 38-B. Read the following sentences, giving them the proper intonation.

(Curiosity)   Do you think he will sing?

(Anger)   I told you to stop working.

(Sadness)   What a pity that she cannot be here.

(Fear)   No, I won't do it.

Check Your Knowledge

1. How does phonation differ from articulation?
2. How do voiced consonants differ from voiceless consonants?
3. Why should a speaker be completely relaxed?
4. When does your voice quality automatically change?
5. Name a public speaker or a TV performer who you think has good speech. State the reasons for your choice.

Skill Builders

Make two recordings of your voice. For the first recording read a page from your textbook. For the second engage in conversation with a friend or a member of your family. Make an analysis of your voice and speech from each recording. If necessary, refer to the information on phonation, articulation, and pronunciation that you have just studied. Be critical!

Business Speech

The silent letters are bold capitals in the following words.

1. a**L**mond
2. of**T**en
3. vi**C**tuals (VIT'ls)
4. indi**C**t (in-DITE)
5. mor**T**gage
6. campai**G**n
7. arrai**G**n (ar-RANE)
8. Arkansa**S** (ARK-ansaw)
9. rende**Z**vou**S** (RAHN-d'voo)

Spelling

Study List 38, which contains words ending with *ise* and *ize*. These words have all appeared on tests given by private companies. (Page 410.)

LEARNING HOW TO LISTEN

"It's a pity that Jack didn't receive the promotion he wanted, but he has one big fault: he doesn't know how to listen." That remark was made by a department head in a manufacturing firm. Listening is a skill—one necessary for success in life and work. Develop that skill now and help to pave the road to success.

"He listens with a tin ear." "What I say to her seems to go in one ear and out the other." Such remarks indicate that the persons referred to are poor listeners.

For a long time most persons assumed that listening was a natural trait. This was a strange attitude, for evidence indicates that many persons do not know how to listen—that listening is a skill that must be developed. In Shakespeare's *Julius Caesar,* Marc Antony realizes that persons don't listen readily, for he begins his famous oration by saying, "Friends, Romans, countrymen, lend me your ears."

Observing and listening are closely related; many persons listen no better than they observe. This is shown in the great number of court witnesses who give conflicting testimony. For example, three persons witnessed a robbery involving gunfire. On the witness stand each of the three persons gave a different description of the suspect, and each claimed to have heard a different number of shots.

Listening is a skill. To improve this skill, you must practice.

The Importance of Listening

"A good listener is a good conversationalist." Make the person you converse with feel that you are truly interested and not unresponsive as a stone wall. If the conversation bores you, take the reins into your own hands and lead it off in a different direction. You can do so skillfully, without offending the other person, provided that you know how to converse—and to listen.

The person who tries to monopolize a conversation, whether it is with one or several persons, is considered a conceited bore. Here is a good rule to remember regarding conversations: If you have something worthwhile to say, say it; if you don't have anything to say, *listen.*

Listening on the Job. On the job you must listen carefully to directions. Never trust your memory, for it has a way of letting you down when you need it most. A secretary in a large company caused the loss of an order amounting to several thousand dollars. During the boss's absence the secretary took a telephone call but did not write down all the facts. Later the secretary could not remember what had been said and gave the boss an incomplete report. The boss lost one of the best orders of the year. The secretary was discharged.

Reasons for Listening. We listen (1) to obtain information, (2) to solve problems, (3) to share experiences, and (4) to persuade or dissuade. The good listener analyzes and evaluates.

Listening to Obtain Information

When you don't get all the facts, don't blame the speaker; blame yourself. If you become keenly critical of your listening ability, you will strive to hear what even the poorest speaker says. Following is a list of suggestions for improving your ability to listen for information. Plan *now* to try to strengthen your weak points.

Suggestions for Good Listening

1. Pay close attention; train yourself not to become distracted.
2. Keep quiet.
3. Enlarge your vocabulary.
4. Improve your reading comprehension.
5. Be interested in what you hear.
6. Bring knowledge to what you hear.
7. Be rested when you listen.
8. Discover the *meaning* of what you hear, not merely the words.
9. Evaluate what you hear; don't be fooled by propaganda.
10. Try to like the speaker.
11. Know how to select the main points.
12. Learn to recognize correct English.
13. Be comfortable and relaxed.
14. Obtain experience in various kinds of listening.

It is a psychological fact that attention automatically shifts. This is what happens when we say that our minds "wander." Our ears "wander," too; but by practicing good listening habits we can develop the concentrated attention needed for good listening.

Interviews. Usually an interview is a conversation between two persons, such as one between a reporter and a prominent person or between a prospective employer and a job applicant. Often in an interview one person uses the question technique, and the other provides the answers.

There are three common types of interviews—the interview (1) to seek information, (2) to give information, and (3) to obtain action. The three types sometimes overlap.

If you are the questioner in an interview, word your questions clearly. Listen carefully. Get the facts straight. If you are not sure of a point, ask for further explanation or repetition. Make notes.

When you apply for a job, the interviewer will ask you many questions. Be alert. Listen carefully to the questions and give your answers promptly. Toward the end of the interview, most interviewers ask whether you have any questions. Be prepared to ask some questions about the company and the job for which you are applying. Don't show that you are a poor listener, however, by asking a question that has already been answered by the interviewer. During a job interview the interviewer asks most of the questions, and the manner in which you answer them may work for or against you.

Conferences. A conference exists when a group meets to discuss specific matters and make decisions. The matters to be discussed comprise the *agenda* of the conference.

The members of a conference should listen carefully to everything that is said. If a secretary takes the minutes of the meeting, the persons in attendance may not be required to take notes. If no secretary is present to record what is said and accomplished, each person in attendance should take notes. Most business conferences are informal; that is, they do not follow the principles of parliamentary law—those rules which govern the meetings of clubs, associations, and the like.

Speeches and Lectures. Some speeches contain very little that is informative, although they may be impressive in other ways. Lectures should contain some "gems of wisdom"; but often they, too, contain more opinions than facts. The listener should learn to separate truth from opinion. The "Suggestions for Good Listening" listed earlier in this Section all apply to listening to informative lectures.

The intelligent, appreciative listener puts forth the effort to get the most out of listening. A person attending a lecture, for example, is alert to new attitudes, new ideas, and so on. The person who says, "I hated that lecture; I couldn't understand any of it," is often a person who had determined beforehand not to understand it. Intellectual curiosity is one of the most valuable personal assets. If you are curious, you will keep your mind, eyes, and ears open so that you will be ready to learn.

Progress Quiz 39. Answer with true or false.

1. To the job applicant, the interview is an action-type interview.
2. Observing and listening are closely related.
3. Discover the meaning, not merely the matter, of what a speaker says.
4. Concentrated attention is necessary for effective listening.
5. At all conferences everyone should take notes.

Listening to Solve Problems

On the job when your boss or supervisor gives you directions for completing a certain piece of work, you listen to obtain information; often you listen also to solve a problem. Good thinking is the basis of effective speaking and listening. If you are a logical thinker, you will be able to form opinions and solve problems faster.

To solve a problem, listen to all the information; then follow these steps:

Step 1. Define the problem.

Step 2. Explore and analyze the problem.

Step 3. Evaluate the possible solutions.

Step 4. Conclude the problem.

While you are listening, you may take each of the preceding four steps. After listening, however, repeat each step.

To solve certain types of problems, you may have to do much more than listen. You may have to consult other persons or reference books in your search for facts that will help you analyze and solve a problem.

When important decisions are to be made during a meeting, the leader or a member defines each problem. The members explore and analyze each problem, as well as evaluate possible conclusions. A member "moves" that a certain conclusion be reached. If another member "seconds the motion," the entire group votes. If a majority vote is in favor of the motion, the motion is adopted and the problem is solved. If a majority of the members are not good thinkers and if they have not listened to all the pros and cons, the problem may be concluded incorrectly!

Listening to Share Experiences

You often converse to share experiences—to "compare notes," as sharing experiences is sometimes called. Sharing experiences is helpful in obtaining information and solving problems.

The "Voice of Experience." In reading the autobiography of a successful business person you may learn much that will help you in your own career. If you listen to talks by successful persons, you will also gain many tips for reaching your goals.

For over twenty years, radio was one of the most popular methods of sharing experiences. Commentators, playwrights, actors, and so on communicated their experiences, and the world listened. When television entered the American home after World War II, sharing experiences became more effective, since TV causes people to observe and to read, as well as to listen.

When you watch and listen to a TV program, a play, or a motion picture, you may do so for only one reason: to find pleasure and relaxation. While you watch and listen, however, you share the experiences of many other persons and, as a result, add to your store of information.

Remember that experience of any type is the true foundation of learning. The overconfident person is often self-satisfied and never listens to advice. That person may be the loser, however, if the advice is offered by someone with many years of experience. On the job listen to the experienced workers. Such workers have preceded you over the road; they know the bumps, the dangerous curves, and the shortcuts.

Listening to Persuade or Dissuade

The Positive Approach to Persuasion. To a certain extent most of us are countersuggestible; that is, when we are told not to do something, we are often tempted to do it and vice versa. "If you tell Johnny not to put fishhooks in his ears," says a psychologist, "he may go in search of fishhooks, even though he does not know what they are." None of us likes to be contradicted or censured, although a skillful speaker may contradict and censure and still cause us to agree.

How to Win an Argument. An argument is won by skillful persuasion. An argument is not a quarrel. A quarrel is an angry dispute, but an argument is an exchange of opinions and facts, backed up by sound reasoning. To win an argument, follow these steps.

1. Carefully listen to each difference of opinion, objection, and so on.
2. As soon as your opponent strongly objects to your opinion, restate the objection in your own words. (Expert debaters say that such restatement often causes the objection to sound less convincing to the opponent. In other words, while you are restating the objection, your listener is analyzing what has been said, and the analysis causes the idea to seem less important.)
3. When you raise an objection, back it up with facts. Evidence is the best convincer!
4. Keep your head. As soon as your opponent's voice rises or becomes louder, you know that, by keeping your head, you will take the lead.
5. Listen for misrepresentation of facts. A fact can be proved. If your opponent cannot prove a statement but you can disprove it, you have won a point.

6. When you win a point, do not gloat. If you have respect for your opponent, your opponent more than likely will respect you.
7. If you lose an argument, cheerfully admit it. Your admitting the present loss may be the means of helping you to win a future argument, because you will be considered a good loser and a sporting opponent.

Listening in Buying and Selling

A business grows by persuading persons to use its products or services. Persuaded customers must be kept happy, however, or a business will cease to exist. Some persons may be persuaded to try a product. When they are *convinced* that the product does what the manufacturer says it will do, they continue to buy it—until a more convincing persuader comes along.

Today's business world is a constant persuasion-conviction tug-of-war. Advertising and the use of good sales techniques are the two methods of persuading persons to change brands or to buy a new type of product. The product itself and the service of the company selling it are the two factors that cause a customer to continue or to stop buying.

In the first quarter of the twentieth century, the only spoken persuasion of a business was handled by its sales representatives. All other persuasion to buy was done by advertising in newspapers, magazines, and the like. Today, however, TV and radio are effective means of spoken persuasion. If you wish to buy the best product, you should learn to analyze and evaluate such persuasion. Although the United States government tries to protect consumers from false or misleading advertising, some untrue or doubtful advertising messages will probably be used each year.

Persuasion and Conviction. The rules for winning an argument can help the consumer and the salesperson. Evidence that proves a salesperson's selling point is the best means of persuading a customer to buy. If adequate proof of sales statements is not provided, the customer would be foolish to make the purchase. "An ounce of conviction is worth a pound of persuasion."

The Question Technique. Skillful persuaders often use a question to plant a fruitful seed in the mind of the listener. "Would you like to cut your cleaning time in half?" All homemakers would like to do so, and most of them would say yes to this question, without giving it much thought. Persons who answer yes cross over to the side of the persuader. If the persuader can prove that the product will really cut cleaning time in half, the persuader has a good chance of concluding the sale.

Other Methods of Persuasion

Building Up for a Letdown. It's a rush period in the office in which you work. The office manager calls you into the office and surprises you by praising your work and your fine spirit of cooperation. Then, while you are basking in the glow of those kind words, the office manager says, "We are several days behind in preparing master copies for our statistical reports." Since your job does not include preparing master copies, you wonder what the speech is all about. "Because you are always eager to help," the office manager continues, "I know that you will be glad to type some of the masters for us." Although you are a correspondent, not a typist, what can you say? After all the fine things that have just been said about you, you wouldn't be much of a person if you didn't lend a helping hand!

In the preceding example, the office manager applied an important principle of persuasion: To get people to do things they do not like or wish to do, praise them; then ask them to do the undesirable task. Also, if you must find fault with a person, first find something to praise. Praise boosts the listener's morale so that doing an unpleasant task or accepting criticism will be easier.

Social Persuasion. Indirect persuasion plays an important part in your daily life. You persuade a person to like you and continue to like you. Qualities that comprise a good personality help persuade acquaintances to become your friends. Maintaining the "you" attitude (see Section 2) is the key to successful social persuasion. Being a good listener—one who looks the speaker squarely in the eye—helps foster the "you" attitude.

Check Your Knowledge

1. What are some ways in which you listen to share experiences?
2. Explain this statement: Today persuasion is big business.

3. Mention three ways in which a worker, by poor listening, might cause a decrease in an employer's profits.
4. How can listening help you solve a problem?
5. State a specific incident in which listening proved profitable to you.

Skill Builders

Select one of the following and complete the necessary requirements.

39-A. Listen to a radio newscast. Report the facts to the class.

39-B. Carefully listen to a TV program while watching it. Report to the class your reasons for liking or not liking the program.

39-C. Listen to the TV or radio commercials for three different brands of a product, such as soap. Tell the differences in the sales "pitches." Tell, also, which one of the three products you would buy as a result of listening to the commercials. Explain your decision.

Business Speech

Do not add extra syllables or extra letters to these words.

1. hindrance (2 syllables)
2. statistics (sta-TIS-tiks)
3. realtor (3 syllables)
4. offertory (4 syllables)
5. suffrage (2 syllables)

Spelling

Guides: Use *ance* and *ant* after a *c* that sounds like *k* (*va-cant*). Use *ence* and *ent* after soft *c* or *g* (*negli-gence*). No fully reliable guides exist for the many other words ending with *ance, ant, ence,* or *ent.*

Study List 39 on page 410.

Unit
Fifteen

USING YOUR SPEECH POWER

PLANNING A TALK

The person who can impress others by voice and speech is worth a fortune to an employer. Many an executive has risen to the top on wings of speech because the public-relations value of a good speaker cannot be overestimated. Wanting to become a good speaker is only the first step because, to become a good speaker, a person must have abundant practice.

An audience recognizes and remembers a good speaker. To hold the audience's attention, you must plan your talk with care.

In planning a talk, you should

1. Know your audience.
2. Know your subject.
3. Outline your talk.
4. Be confidently prepared.

Know Your Audience

Before giving a talk, find out as much as you can about the group to whom you are to speak so that you will use the language of the listeners.

During a convention a certain salesperson gave a talk to a group of prospective customers. They felt as though they were being treated like persons of low intelligence; consequently, the salesperson lost a number of potential sales.

A young woman spoke to a group of dress designers to interest them in a new fabric. Instead of telling what the fabric would do to enhance their designs, she gave a long, technical description of the manufacturing process used for the fabric. Her attitude indicated that she was proud of her technical knowledge and that she felt superior to her listeners. The designers, who were interested only in design, left the talk feeling that they had wasted their time. This young woman overlooked two important points: (1) If your listeners are seeking information, give them facts that will help them—facts they will remember and use. (2) Make your listeners feel that you are one of them and that you respect each of them. If you accomplish these two points, you will gain the respect of your listeners.

Know Your Subject

A person who has the reputation of having something important or interesting to say is asked to give a talk. If you have a "captive audience," you must be certain that your talk is interesting. A captive audience consists of persons who are required to listen, such as those who hear after-dinner speakers, school-assembly speakers, and so on. It is true that many members of such audiences are genuinely interested in hearing the speaker, but there are others who would rather be elsewhere. A speaker who can win and hold an audience in such circumstances is a good speaker.

Gathering Information. To know your subject, you may have to spend considerable time gathering information. Consult reliable reference books, discuss your subject with persons who are well informed about it, and read current articles in periodicals. These are important fact-gathering sources. In collecting data, be sure to make adequate notes. If you wish to express a personal opinion, it is permissible to do so. Be sure, however, that your talk is not merely a list of your opinions. To be on the safe side, let your listeners know that a remark is your opinion; otherwise, you may be accused of making false statements.

As soon as you are sure you have obtained adequate material, outline your talk. Do not give the information a chance to grow old before making your outline!

Outline Your Talk

Two kinds of outlines may be used—the *topic* outline and the *sentence* outline. Do not mix the two types. If you begin by making a sentence outline, be consistent and use that type for the entire talk.*

---

* The information about outlining can also be applied to written material.

Examples of the two kinds of outlines follow:

COMMUNICATING BY TELEGRAPHY (*Topic Outline*)

    I. Importance of telegraphic communication
        A. International telegraph
        B. Speed of telegraphic messages

   II. Telegraphic instrument
        A. Manually operated key
            1. Appearance of key
            2. Operation of key
        B. Today's teleprinter
            1. Appearance of teleprinter
            2. Operation of teleprinter

  III. Telegraphic skills
        A. Complex skills needed by key operator
        B. Skills needed by teleprinter operator

COMMUNICATING BY TELEGRAPHY (*Sentence Outline*)

    I. Telegraphy is one of the chief media of communication.
      A. International telegraphic networks link the nations of the world.
      B. The telegraph is important when speed of communication is the first consideration.

   II. There are two types of telegraphic instruments in general use.
      A. In small or outlying districts, the hand-operated key is used.
         1. The key, or "bug," which is similar to a small stapler, is connected to a panel of sockets.
         2. The key produces electrical impulses—short for dots, long for dashes.
      B. Today's teleprinter is used in large, busy communication areas.
         1. The teleprinter is a complex machine having a hand-operated keyboard.
         2. The teleprinter records and prints telegraphic messages.

  III. Different skills are required for operating the two instruments.
      A. The key operator sends, receives, and translates International Morse Code.
      B. The teleprinter operator uses a keyboard similar to that of the typewriter.

When the outline is complete, check it to be certain that you have included all the necessary information. After studying all the facts, you may wish to reduce a sentence outline to a topic outline.

A common practice is to use reference notes during a talk. Many speakers write such notes on 3″ by 5″ cards; it is possible to include more points on such cards when the topic outline is used.

Helping the Listener. When your final outline is made, underscore in color those items that you wish to emphasize. If you wish to permit your listeners to ask questions during your talk, write a large asterisk or other device at the end of the main division (A, B, and so on) at which questions may be asked. Many speakers prefer to wait until the entire talk has been given before permitting listeners to ask questions. Other speakers, however, feel that it relieves the situation for both speaker and listeners if questions are permitted at intervals during an informal talk. If a speaker is an expert in a subject area, questions asked during a talk may serve as guides for the remainder of the talk. Certain questions, for example, may indicate that points not included in the outline should be raised.

Since it is wise to give the listeners what they want, the expert speaker draws on reserve knowledge and mentally adjusts the outline to fit the needs of the listeners.

Be Confidently Prepared

Never memorize a talk. A memorized talk sounds mechanical; an alert audience usually recognizes a memorized talk.*

Consider the Five Qualities of Communications. Take your outline and mentally plan what you will say under each main division and subdivision. As is true of other communications, your talk must be courteous, clear, complete, concise, and correct. After you have mentally outlined everything that you will say, ask yourself these questions:

Courtesy:	Have I shown every consideration to my listeners? Have I used the "you" attitude?
Clearness:	Have I phrased my ideas so that they are perfectly clear? Do any points need further explanation?
Completeness:	Have I included everything? Is the talk too short?
Conciseness:	Can I express certain ideas more succinctly? Have I wasted words? Is the talk too long?
Correctness:	Is my information correct? Do I know how to pronounce all the words? Am I sure of the grammar?

Planning Your First Talks. In planning your first few talks, you may wish to write your entire talk, using your outline as a guide. If you do write the entire talk, do not memorize it. Use the completely written talk

---

* Long, formal addresses are usually written. They are read by the speaker, who must try to read in such a manner that the listeners are not distracted by the reading process. The speaker who reads should give the impression of referring to notes, not of reading. The eyes should be on the audience most of the time.

to help you in your timing. Even the best speakers sometimes have difficulty in timing a talk exactly. Beginners, therefore, should learn how much they can say in a certain time.

If you follow the steps outlined and make use of the suggestions given, you should be confidently prepared for your talks. Many things about public speaking cannot be learned from books; you will have to learn them by experience, which, after all, is the best teacher.

Check Your Knowledge

1. Why are good speakers in demand?
2. Why is it necessary to outline a talk before giving it?
3. Why would this remark be made about a speaker? "She is charmed by the sound of her own voice." Can better planning help such a speaker? Explain.
4. How can you give the listeners what they want?
5. In what ways can a speaker be incorrect?

Skill Builders

Select a subject for a five-minute talk. Outline your talk in topic form. At the end of the outline, include a list of materials to which you referred for information. Save this outline for use at the end of Section 41.

Business Speech

The following list contains words borrowed from French (1-6) and Latin (7-10). Learn the pronunciations and definitions.

1. à la carte
2. apropos (apro-POH)
3. cuisine (kwee-ZEEN)
4. ennui (ahn-WEE)
5. naïve (nah-EEV)
6. table d'hôte (TAHbluh DOAT)
7. bona fide (BOH-nuh-fide)
8. ex officio (o-FISH-eo)
9. verbatim (ver-BAY-tim)
10. via (long *i:* VI-uh)

Spelling

Study List 40, which contains words ending with *ant, ence,* and *ent.* (See page 410.)

GIVING A TALK

"The person who can effectively organize thoughts and express ideas while standing up is the person who will be promoted to this job." Three persons were in line for the job mentioned by the vice-president who made this statement. None of them met the test. The job was given to a new person—one who had demonstrated speaking ability while working in another firm.

Even though your job may not include giving talks, you should strive to be an effective speaker because (1) good speakers develop poise and adjust to new situations readily, and (2) the ability to make people listen is a social asset that will help you make friends.

A certain man was elected president of an important professional association. He refused to accept the office. "I'm scared stiff when I have to get up in front of a group; I become tongue-tied," he explained. Some of his friends, however, made this man see the light. They told him that all his life he had been talking with people, so why be afraid of getting up in front of those who had elected him—those who had confidence in him? The man took steps to develop the right techniques and today is a good speaker and jokes about the time when he lacked the self-confidence needed to give a good talk.

A speaker must consider what will happen *before, during,* and *after* the talk.

Before the Talk

Outlining what you will say is the most important activity before any talk. Following are other matters that may need attention before you give your talk.

a. *Preparing needed materials.* If you plan to distribute duplicated or printed materials, be sure they are ready in time and available when needed. If the audience is expected to refer to such materials during your talk, the items should be distributed before you begin speaking. If the audience is not expected to refer to such materials, do not distribute them until after your talk; otherwise, persons who should be listening may be reading!

b. *Obtain needed equipment.* Before the scheduled time of the talk, be sure that any needed demonstrating devices, such as a chalkboard or a projector, will be available and ready for use.

c. *Talk with those responsible for the meeting.* If you do not know who is in charge of the meeting, find out. That person can help—for example, by introducing you to others at the meeting.

d. *If possible, familiarize yourself with the room in which you will speak.* If it is a large room, remember that you must project your voice so everyone will hear. If a microphone is provided, test it to be sure it is operating correctly. Adjust it to suit your height. In using a microphone, be careful not to speak too loudly. You should stand a comfortable distance away from the "mike."

e. *Check your grooming.* Be conservatively dressed. Do not wear flashy or jangling jewelry. Nothing should distract from the speaker's message. After you begin talking, forget your grooming; don't adjust collar, hair, sleeves, and so on.

f. *Accept your introduction.* When a person is in charge, that person will introduce you; and if any complimentary remarks are made about you, it is all right to look pleased. Remember: you are every bit as good as they say you are! On that confident note, as soon as the introduction is over, step forward, thank the introducer, pause slightly, and begin your talk.

During the Talk

If you have made all the necessary preparations, your voice will indicate that you are confidently in control of the situation—unless you allow yourself to be nervous. Don't believe the friend who tells you that the best talks are given by persons who nearly "go to pieces" before beginning to speak. It is only natural that you will be nervous before giving your first few talks, but remember that "nothing succeeds like success." If you talk yourself into being nervous, you will not give a good talk;

you will not be successful. When you are successful, your confidence is bolstered, and you look forward to each new talk.

Your Speaking Techniques. Some speakers try to put the audience in a congenial mood by telling a humorous story. This is a good device as long as the story does not poke fun at a particular group of persons. Remember that your listeners may contain persons of various faiths and ancestries. Some people have a knack for telling humorous stories; others do not. If your stories usually fall flat, don't try telling any to your audience.

Developing Rapport. As soon as possible after beginning your talk, try to develop the rapport necessary for a good talk. *Rapport* exists when listeners "lose themselves" in the speaker's words. Expert speakers, as well as talented actors, have the power to make listeners forget where they are. By glancing around, you can tell whether you have obtained the necessary rapport. If all the listeners are looking at you with a wide-awake, contented, interested expression, you have probably developed rapport.

Using Your Notes. If you frequently refer to your notes, you cannot keep your listeners interested. Consult your notes quickly so your listeners hardly will be aware of what you are doing.

Using Your Eyes. Don't select a point on the rear wall and keep your eyes glued to it. You are speaking to human beings; let them know you realize they are there. Speak to them, not the wall! Vary your glances so that during your talk you have looked at all sections of the room many times. Some listeners become so intent on your words that you will gain satisfaction when you notice them nodding their heads in agreement with what you are saying.

Using Your Voice. A pleasant-sounding, musical voice is a speaker's greatest asset. Use your voice rhythmically; use it to express your feelings; use it to paint word pictures. Speak slowly to emphasize important points. If you notice that many persons are taking notes, be sure you do not speak too rapidly.

Avoid saying "uh," "er," and so on. The minute a word won't come, close your mouth. The speaker who stammers or gurgles is irritating to listeners.

Bodily Movements. "Suit the action to the word and the word to the action." This advice is given to persons studying acting. It means that actions should be natural; if they are not, they may have a negative effect and distract the audience.

Without a controlled body, you cannot have a controlled voice. If gestures are spontaneous and natural, they result from bodily control and thinking that is coordinated with speaking. Each gesture should have a meaning. If you "talk with your hands," using them most of the time, you distract your listeners and detract from your message. A gesture should never be made after the words it is supposed to emphasize, since it may produce a comic effect.

Good posture is necessary not only for resonant speech but also for effective bodily movements. Don't lean over a table, desk, or other furniture as though you are about to faint. Don't walk back and forth. No bodily movement should distract or disturb the listeners.

Types of Gestures. *Emphatic* gestures are used for the purpose of drawing attention to what is being said. *Descriptive* gestures help indicate size, shape, and location. *Emotional* gestures indicate the speaker's feelings. These gestures include raising the eyebrow and shrugging the shoulders. Emotional gestures express feelings that cannot easily be put into words.

Many speakers wonder what to do with their hands. Some persons say, "Forget them." This is not sensible advice, however, for the hands serve useful purposes. This is good advice: "Don't worry about your hands; let them rest until they are needed for a gesture."

Dramatic Effects. Gestures help dramatize the speaker's words. Dramatic effects should be spontaneous and suitable. The speaker who practices gestures before a mirror is certain to produce mechanical or comic effects in speaking.

A speaker can dramatize and emphasize by demonstrating, such as writing on a chalkboard, showing how a machine works, and so on. During such activities, a poor speaker, intent on the demonstration, forgets the listeners and loses the audience. In demonstrating, face the audience as much as possible. Look as though you are happy to be demonstrating! If you write on a chalkboard, try not to speak while you are facing it. If you must speak, do so in a voice louder than that used in facing the audience. Your writing should be legible, large, and heavy enough for everyone to read easily.

The Dramatic Pause. One of the most emphatic devices used by expert speakers is the dramatic pause. This pause should come before the words you wish to emphasize. Read the following sentence, pausing briefly at the dash: "He told me that I was walking into a trap—and he was right." By pausing at the dash, you emphasize the danger and indicate that you became caught in the trap.

The pause should be used sparingly and cautiously. Expert speakers know how to use it. Beginners should listen to experienced speakers to learn how to use the dramatic pause effectively.

Maintain Your Poise. Nearly every speaker has had some "embarrassing moments." A good speaker, however, remains calm and is not embarrassed by interruptions or mishaps.

If a table collapses or a dog invades the room, act as though such incidents were commonplace.

If you make a grammatical error, don't worry. Many of the listeners won't notice it; those who do will probably consider it a slip of the tongue.

If the "mike" suddenly goes dead, don't let your talk go dead. Speak a little more loudly and don't become upset. Remember that many of the world's greatest orators lived centuries before the invention of the microphone.

When listeners laugh because of a mishap, laugh with them—even though you are laughing at yourself.

Your listeners will admire you if you don't let the unexpected throw you off guard. Popular speakers take everything in their stride, not letting anything upset them—or the audience. No matter what happens, keep your poise!

After the Talk

After a long talk, the audience usually responds with applause. The volume of the applause lets you know the degree of your success. If the applause is rapid and loud, you have every right to feel like a star performer—but try to look humble. If the applause is slow and sporadic, you didn't make the grade. Expert speakers say that they have good days and bad days. They also say that they have receptive and unreceptive audiences. Such remarks, however, should not be used as excuses. The speaker who realizes that the audience did not respond enthusiastically should try to find the reason. If any of your friends or relatives were in the audience, ask them for frank statements. Explain that, by giving you their truthful opinions, they can help you do a better job next time.

A few days after you have given your talk, write a thank-you note to the person who invited you to speak. Say that you are grateful for having had the privilege of speaking to the group. Make a sincere, complimentary remark about the group.

The Etiquette of Speaking

When You Are a Speaker. If you cough or sneeze, say, "Pardon me." If you do not hear a question, ask to have it repeated. It is permissible to request questioners to speak so that everyone can hear the questions. No matter how superfluous or silly a question may seem, answer it readily. Remember: the more consideration you show all your listeners, the more popular you will be.

When You Are a Listener. Be polite. Avoid doing anything that may distract the speaker, such as talking, whispering, moving around, rustling papers, or making other disturbing sounds. If you wish to ask a question, speak loudly; everyone wants to hear your question. Even though the speaker may inspire you to close your eyes, keep them open or the speaker may think you are asleep.

When You Invite a Speaker. Tell the speaker when and where the talk is to be delivered. Either suggest a topic for the talk or tell the speaker to choose a topic. If the location is difficult to reach, offer to provide transportation. If this is impossible, give exact directions for reaching the location by car or public transportation.

If a speaker's talk is scheduled to begin at a certain time, be sure that it does. Do not expect a speaker to sit through a long club meeting. If your business meeting begins at 7 p.m. but the speaker will not take the platform till 8 p.m., do not require the speaker to be present at the earlier hour.

Your speaker is a guest and should be treated as such.

Tips from Top Speakers

The following tips will help you become an effective speaker:

1. Avoid a hearty meal before giving a long talk. An overworked digestive system doesn't help a speaker.
2. Like your audience and it will like you.
3. Be enthusiastic. Enthusiasm is contagious; if you have it, your audience catches it.
4. Be sincere. The tone of your voice should say, "I mean it; I believe it."

5. Avoid mentioning yourself too often. Such remarks as "I personally," "Let me tell you," "What I mean is," and similar expressions add nothing informative to your talk.

6. Vary your pace. Variations in musical rhythm cause emotional changes in listeners. Variations in speech rhythm do the same.

7. Don't fidget. Your glasses will stay on without your poking them; your ring doesn't need turning; your sleeves will stay on without a reassuring tug.

8. Act as though you are standing on a cloud, speak with a heavenly voice, and your audience will think you're an angel.

9. Watch the sound of *s*. Be sure you're not hissing at the audience.

10. The sound of *oo,* as in *boot,* is pleasant if not overworked. Pronounce it distinctly. This sound occurs in the word *you,* which should always be pronounced carefully.

11. To act as though you are letting the listeners in on a secret, bend slightly forward, and speak in a softer voice. (This technique is especially effective over the microphone.)

12. Watch the time without letting the audience know you are doing it. Don't talk overtime, or you may not be asked to talk another time.

13. Don't sway forward or backward. You may lull your audience to sleep.

14. Don't clown while speaking. If you want to be a clown, join a circus. (This advice pertains to speakers who jump around and try to make comic gestures and grimaces.)

15. Leave your listeners wanting more. That is, make them feel that you know what you are talking about and that you have a large reserve of knowledge.

Check Your Knowledge

1. Recall some speakers you have heard. Mention their most annoying faults.

2. How can you know your audience in advance?

3. Which speaking pointers are most effective for a salesperson? a secretary?

4. Why is rapport important to both speaker and listener?

5. Is a speaker ever permitted to use dramatic techniques? Discuss.

Skill Builders

41-A. Prepare a list of your weaknesses that must be strengthened before you will be an acceptable speaker. Then prepare a list of your strongest speaking points.

41-B. Listen to a TV newscast. Write a paragraph giving your opinion of the newscasters' performance.

41-C. Give a five-minute talk based on the outline you prepared in Skill Builder 40.

Business Speech

The microphone picks up and amplifies all sounds produced near it. If you are using a microphone, therefore, turn your head away from it when you cough or sneeze. In consulting papers, keep them away from the "mike"; otherwise, the audience will hear a loud crackle.

Spelling

Study List 41, which consists of words often misspelled. (See page 410.)

A certain Englishman visiting the United States said that American business life and social life are dominated by the telephone. A Frenchman wrote this to his sister in Paris: "Nearly every American belongs to some kind of club. These people love to attend meetings, which are conducted by a set of rules called *parliamentary law.*" Since the telephone was invented by an American and the rules for parliamentary procedure were written by an American, perhaps we take special pride in using them!

Using the Telephone

Modern business could not exist without the telephone, which has also become a necessity in most American homes. To meet the increasing demands for service, telephone companies have done an outstanding job of providing attractive instruments and a wide variety of services.

Millions of telephone calls are made by businesses every day. One medium-sized company reports that its monthly telephone bill is over $5,000. This figure indicates the extent to which the telephone is used in transacting daily business.

The effectiveness of a telephone communication can be measured by (1) the speed with which it is placed or received; (2) the manner in which the message is handled (speaking, listening, making notes); and (3) the results obtained.

Placing the Call. Be sure that you have the right number. If you dial it, do so correctly. If you give the number to the operator, as with some long-distance calls, give correct, complete information. Pronounce figures distinctly. *Nine* should rhyme with *lion* so that it won't sound like *five*. For a number such as 589-4000, say "Five, eight, nine," pause, "four thousand." For 647-3300, say "Six, four, seven," pause, "three, three hundred." For other combinations, however, say each number separately. For example, for 235-1388, say "Two, three, five," pause, "one, three, eight, eight." When the person called answers, identify yourself immediately.

Receiving a Call. When the telephone rings, answer it at once. It is discourteous to keep a caller waiting. Identify yourself in the manner prescribed by your company. Some firms recommend the following: "Sales Department, Mary Jones speaking."*

During telephone calls, make notes of important information. Do everything possible to be of help to the caller. The tone of your voice reflects your attitude. It is the only personality factor by which a caller can judge you and your company. Keep the mouthpiece close to the lips. A soft, clear voice is pleasant, makes a good impression, and adds to the effectiveness of a telephone communication. Don't shout!

Personality experts say that a laugh tells much about a person's character. If a laugh is in order, remember that you are laughing in the listener's ear, which might have a worse effect than laughing in the listener's face. Subdue your laughter but don't giggle.

If you must obtain information at some distance from your desk, tell the caller that you will call back in a few moments. Never leave a caller "dangling on the line" while you search for information. A minute is a long time to hold a silent receiver!

The Five C's. The five qualities of good communication should be present in telephone conversations.

Courtesy: Speak so that your voice and attitude reflect courtesy. Try to have a "voice with a smile." End the conversation by thanking the person for calling.

Completeness: Give all the information required. Make necessary notes during the conversation.

Clearness: Speak clearly and present all information clearly.

Conciseness: Say no more than necessary to complete the call courteously.

Correctness: Be sure that your language and information are correct.

Parliamentary Procedure

Nearly everyone has opportunities to participate in organized meetings, such as those held by clubs, civic groups, and professional organizations. Such meetings are governed by the rules of *parliamentary procedure,* often called *parliamentary law*. If you become a member of Future

---

*A woman may identify herself variously—for example, "Mary Jones," "Ms. Jones," "Miss Jones," or "Mrs. Jones." A man may say "John Jones" or "Mr. Jones."

Business Leaders of America (FBLA), the National Secretaries Association (NSA), and so on, you will participate in many meetings governed by parliamentary procedure.

The various matters to be discussed and decided during a meeting are called the *items of business*. A list of such items is called the *agenda*.

Order of Business. In most meetings the order of business is as follows:

1. The chairperson calls the meeting to order. (The chairperson says, "The meeting will please come to order" or something similar. As the statement is made, the table may be struck with a gavel, which is a small wooden mallet. The gavel is the customary symbol of the chairperson's authority.)

2. The chairperson asks the secretary to read the minutes of the previous meeting, which are then corrected, if necessary, and finally approved by the group.

3. The chairperson calls for reports of standing (permanent) committees, and the group acts on these reports.

4. The chairperson calls for reports of special committees, and the group acts on these reports.

5. The chairperson calls for a completion of any old business—that is, business left unfinished at the last meeting. The group acts on this business.

6. The chairperson calls for the introduction of new business. The group acts on this business or carries it over to the next meeting.

7. The chairperson adjourns the meeting.

Important Parliamentary Rules. So that everyone will be shown consideration and so communications will flow smoothly, certain parliamentary rules should be understood by everyone attending an official meeting.

Obtaining the floor. A member desiring to speak rises and addresses the presiding officer as "Mr. Chairman," "Madam Chair," or "Madam Chairperson," "Mr. President" or "Madam President," or "Mr. Moderator" or "Madam Moderator." The member waits to be recognized by "the chair" before continuing to speak. Recognition comes from the chairperson, who uses name and title, such as "Miss Jones" or "The representative from the Junior Class."

Making a motion. A member who wishes to have a matter discussed by the group offers the proposal in the form of a motion or resolution. (Complicated proposals are previously prepared in writing and handed to the secretary when recognition is received.) In addressing the chair, the member says, "I move that such-and-such action be taken." The expressions "I make a motion to," "I make a motion that," and "I move you to" are incorrect.

Putting a motion. When a motion has been made, the chairperson asks, "Is there a second?" If there is no second, the motion is declared lost for want of a second. A second may be offered by any member, without rising and addressing the chair. When a motion has been seconded, the chairperson says, "It has been moved and seconded that such-and-such action be taken. Is there any discussion?" The matter is then placed before the house.

Discussing a motion. No subject can be discussed until it has been presented as a motion, seconded, and restated by the chair. (Certain motions, however, are undebatable and are voted on without discussion.) In the discussion of a motion, no member should be heard twice if anyone who has not already spoken wishes the floor.

Voting. The *voice (viva-voce)* vote is the most common. After the discussion is concluded, the chairperson says, "If there is no further discussion, all those in favor will say 'Aye' (pronounced like the pronoun *I*). All those opposed will say 'No.'" After the vote has been decided, the chairperson says "The motion is carried" or "The motion is lost."

Any member is privileged to call for a *division* if it seems that the chairperson has misinterpreted the voice vote. In a division the chairperson asks all those in favor either to stand or raise their hands (called *a show of hands*). The chairperson then asks all those opposed to follow the same procedure. The secretary counts the actual number of votes in each case.

In deciding extremely important issues, the ballot (written) is sometimes used. The ballot provides the advantage of secrecy; also, one person is not influenced by another.

Point of order. A member who feels that parliamentary law has been violated can say, "I rise to a point of order." The chairperson answers, "Please state your point." After the member states the point, the chairperson says, "Your point is (or is not) well taken." No vote is required unless another member questions the chairperson's ruling; then the member says, "I appeal from the decision of the chair." The chairperson asks, "Shall the decision of the chair stand? All those in favor, say 'Aye,' those opposed, 'No.'" A point of order is not debatable; it does not need a second. It is presented when another speaker has the floor, and it is made to safeguard the rights and privileges of all members.

Minutes of Meetings; Official Duties. The secretary and other officers of an organization should be aware of the important rules of parliamentary procedure. The preceding rules are the most important. There are many other rules, however, that apply to official meetings and committee meetings. An understanding of correct procedures will assist the secretary in making adequate notes and preparing typewritten minutes of the meeting.

Officers must regularly communicate with one another. Members should be informed regarding important information, such as the change of date for a meeting.

Business Etiquette

The "you" attitude extends to all phases of business life and daily living. If you treat all persons as you wish to be treated, they usually return the favor.

Tact Is Important. Not intending to be discourteous, a person may make a *tactless* remark. "Think before you speak and look before you leap" is good advice to remember in trying to develop *tact*—saying or doing the right thing. The *tactful* person is one who is diplomatic and who uses discretion in dealing with others.

Many persons lose their jobs because they cannot get along with their fellow workers. Tact and a spirit of cooperation would turn the tide in favor of such workers.

Introductions. The established guidelines of etiquette may be followed when introducing one person in business to another.

A younger person is introduced to the older, but a man is generally presented to a woman regardless of the man's age. A woman's name is mentioned first, except in the case of a young girl who is a member of the family. (If you find yourself saying Mr. Smith's name first, simply continue, "May I introduce you to Mrs. Jones?")

A common method of introduction is to say only the two names: "Mrs. Jones, Mr. Smith." (The first name mentioned should sound like a question.)

An introduction that uses "This is," may seem warmer and more personal: "Mrs. Jones, this is Mr. Smith."

The Question Introduction. Questions are permissible as introductions:

"Mrs. Jones, do you know Mr. Smith?"
"Mrs. Jones, you know Mr. Smith, don't you?" (Never "Do you not?")
"Mrs. Jones, have you met Mr. Smith?"
"Mrs. Jones, may I present Mr. Smith?" (Formal)

Other Introductions. Notice these introductions:

"Mrs. Jones, I should like you to meet Mr. Smith."
"Mrs. Jones, I want you to meet Mr. Smith." (If he is a special friend)
"Sally Jones, this is Bob Smith." (For young persons of the same group)

Expressions to Be Avoided. The following expressions should be avoided:

"Mrs. Jones, shake hands with Mr. Smith."
"Mrs. Jones, I want to make you acquainted with Mr. Smith."
"Mrs. Jones, my friend, Mr. Smith." (Avoid *friend* in all introductions.)
"Mrs. Jones, Mr. Smith; Mr. Smith, Mrs. Jones." (Double talk!)

What to Say and Do When Introduced. The reply "How do you do?" is always acceptable. Never say, "Charmed" or "Pleased to meet you." You may say, "I am *very* glad to meet you," emphasizing *very,* if you really mean it. Never use the words *acquaintance* and *acquainted* in introducing a person or replying to an introduction.

Although men have shaken hands with each other for centuries when introduced, women traditionally had the option of extending a hand to a man. The contemporary business custom is for all people to shake hands when introduced.

What to Do When You Haven't Been Introduced. Very often you may find yourself with a person or group with whom you are not acquainted. The best thing to do in this circumstance is to take the initiative and introduce yourself. Simply say, "I am Sally Johnson," and extend your hand. The other person will most likely introduce himself or herself in the same way. You'll be pleasantly surprised at how quickly you will meet others in this manner. Additionally, you will take on an air of confidence in your ability to introduce yourself to others.

In any case, listen carefully to the names of others when you meet them. If possible, try to remember the names by making some association between the name and the person. Clothing, accessories, and hair color are some cues expert rememberers use in making such associations between names and people. And what a good feeling it is to be able to recall another person's name when necessary! People admire others who appear to have excellent memories, and they are flattered when you remember them.

Perhaps the best advice is to become familiar with the forms of introduction and to act naturally and appear at ease.

Check Your Knowledge

1. Why should "Hello" be avoided in answering a business telephone?
2. List the order of business at an organized meeting.
3. In parliamentary procedure what is meant by the floor? the chair?
4. In the minutes of a meeting, what information should a secretary include in regard to a motion?
5. Why is it a good habit to introduce yourself to others?

Skill Builders

42-A. Obtain a copy of a manual of parliamentary law. Find out what is meant by "rising to a question of privilege." Write the explanation in your own words.

42-B. Obtain a book of etiquette. Learn the formalities involved in introducing members of the clergy and state dignitaries. Be prepared to demonstrate such introductions.

Business Speech

Speech punctuation is achieved by raising or lowering the voice, pausing, or stopping. Persons who punctuate their speech read aloud and talk with good expression. When you punctuate your speech, you clearly say what you mean.

Spelling

Study List 42, which consists mainly of words pertaining to speech. (See page 410.)

REFERENCE SECTION

A: Spelling Lists

The following spelling lists are numbered to correlate with the Section numbers of the textbook. At the end of each textbook Section, the "Spelling" feature directs students to study the proper correlated list. The words in the lists are those most commonly misspelled, as well as those that often appear on civil service tests and tests given job applicants by large companies.

List 1

1. overdue
2. oversight
3. underpaid
4. underprivileged
5. businesslike
6. foolproof
7. bell-like
8. Dutch-like
9. waterproof
10. proofreading

List 2

1. changeable
2. chargeable
3. serviceable
4. noticeable
5. manageable
6. salable
7. advisable
8. blamable
9. usable
10. desirable

List 3

1. indispensable
2. reputable
3. disputable
4. demonstrable
5. permissible
6. admissible
7. reversible
8. deductible
9. divisible
10. convertible

List 4

1. compatible
2. forcible
3. regrettable
4. perishable
5. plausible
6. feasible
7. expendable
8. responsible
9. controllable
10. possible

List 5

1. traveler
2. counselor
3. preference
4. reference
5. transferable
6. cancellation
7. excellent
8. regretting
9. forgotten
10. rebelled

List 6

1. supersede
2. exceed
3. proceed
4. succeed
5. precede
6. concede
7. recede
8. secede
9. procedure
10. accede

List 7

1. icy
2. rosy
3. juicy
4. fleecy
5. iciest
6. rosier
7. juiciest
8. shaky
9. smoky
10. fiery

List 8

1. traffic
2. trafficked
3. trafficking
4. picnic
5. picnicked
6. picnicker
7. shellac
8. shellacked
9. shellacking
10. shellacs

List 9

1. eighth
2. eightieth
3. ninth
4. nineteen
5. ninety
6. ninetieth
7. twelfth
8. forty
9. fourth
10. fourteen

List 10

1. omission
2. barrel
3. adjacent
4. privilege
5. auxiliary
6. interrogate
7. develop
8. development
9. jeopardy
10. definitely

List 11

1. prevalent
2. persuasion
3. pursue
4. likelihood
5. livelihood
6. occurrence
7. accommodate
8. recommend
9. criticize
10. criticism

List 12

1. accelerate
2. circuit
3. biscuit
4. acquiesce
5. embarrass
6. harass
7. parallel
8. anonymous
9. unanimous
10. authoritative

List 13

1. adequate
2. conspicuous
3. ambiguous
4. maintenance
5. mucilage
6. questionnaire
7. millionaire
8. righteous
9. strictly
10. posthumous

List 14

1. duplicator
2. eczema
3. ecstasy
4. necessitate
5. poignant
6. supervisor
7. brochure
8. exercise
9. similar
10. technical

List 15

1. corroborate
2. dilemma
3. gauge
4. pertinent
5. spasmodic
6. strategic
7. tragedy
8. vacillate
9. welfare
10. scissors

List 16

1. responsibility
2. plagiarism
3. scarcity
4. facetious
5. conscientious
6. tedious
7. transient
8. hosiery
9. psychology
10. fraudulent

List 17

1. superintendent
2. superfluous
3. subsequent
4. subpoena
5. supermarket
6. supersede
7. superb
8. substantial
9. supervisor
10. suburban

List 18

1. keenness
2. meanness
3. accommodate
4. recommend
5. sheriff
6. tariff
7. trespass
8. embarrass
9. commission
10. committee

List 19

1. Albuquerque
2. Bismarck
3. Chattanooga
4. Cheyenne
5. Cincinnati
6. Cleveland
7. Corpus Christi
8. Decatur
9. Des Moines
10. Dubuque

List 20

1. Duluth
2. El Paso
3. Frankfort
4. Gloucester
5. Harrisburg
6. Houston
7. Indianapolis
8. Lincoln
9. Los Angeles
10. Milwaukee

List 21

1. Minneapolis
2. Montpelier
3. Olympia
4. Paterson
5. Philadelphia
6. Phoenix
7. Poughkeepsie
8. Raleigh
9. Sacramento
10. San Diego

List 22

1. San Francisco
2. Schenectady
3. Seattle
4. Shreveport
5. Sioux City
6. Spokane
7. Syracuse
8. Tallahassee
9. Terre Haute
10. Tucson

List 23

1. Wichita
2. Wilkes-Barre
3. Worcester
4. Hawaii
5. Puerto Rico
6. Philippines
7. Montreal
8. Toronto
9. Ottawa
10. Canadian

List 24

1. Arkansas
2. California
3. Colorado
4. Connecticut
5. Delaware
6. Florida
7. Illinois
8. Louisiana
9. Massachusetts
10. Michigan

List 25

1. Minnesota
2. Mississippi
3. Missouri
4. New Jersey
5. Oklahoma
6. Pennsylvania
7. Rhode Island
8. Tennessee
9. Wisconsin
10. Wyoming

List 26

1. nylon
2. rayon
3. cellophane
4. vinyl
5. Dacron
6. Orlon
7. Kodak
8. diesel
9. Xerox
10. Kleenex

List 27

1. exonerate
2. exhaustion
3. exhibited
4. pamphlet
5. renown
6. innovation
7. inoculate
8. oculist
9. mediocre
10. congestion

List 28

1. millinery
2. dictionary
3. cemetery
4. advisory
5. directory
6. confectionery
7. usury
8. beneficiary
9. itinerary
10. hosiery

List 29

1. battalion
2. columnar
3. advantageous
4. occurrence
5. relevant
6. irrevocable
7. extravagant
8. exaggerate
9. deficit
10. extension

List 30

1. yield
2. brief
3. niece
4. chief
5. achieve
6. heir
7. beige
8. feign
9. weight
10. freight

List 31

1. field
2. lien
3. grievance
4. reprieve
5. counterfeit
6. receipt
7. forfeit
8. deceive
9. leisure
10. weird

List 32

1. believe
2. relieve
3. shield
4. ceiling
5. receivable
6. deceit
7. seize
8. conceit
9. proficient
10. neither

List 33

1. usage
2. forcible
3. sampling
4. careless
5. wholesome
6. inducement
7. owing
8. arguing
9. truly
10. excludable

List 34

1. clientele
2. commitment
3. aforesaid
4. receptacle
5. colleague
6. spoonfuls
7. cupful
8. versatile
9. corroborate
10. psychological

List 35

1. footwear
2. hardware
3. silverware
4. underwear
5. warehouse
6. kitchenware
7. fulfill
8. physician
9. incessant
10. mechanism

List 36

1. playwright
2. copyright
3. copywriter
4. disciplinary
5. acoustics
6. propaganda
7. Portuguese
8. tariff
9. sheriff
10. nickel

List 37

1. pasteurize
2. advertise
3. analyze
4. paralyze
5. analysis
6. paralysis
7. endeavor
8. misdemeanor
9. collateral
10. susceptible

List 38

1. surmise
2. exercise
3. franchise
4. civilized
5. supervise
6. compromise
7. utilize
8. apologize
9. systematize
10. authorize

List 39

1. sympathize
2. visualize
3. emphasize
4. economize
5. relevance
6. attendance
7. remittance
8. acquaintance
9. dependence
10. confidence

List 40

1. prevalence
2. prominence
3. persistence
4. absence
5. audience
6. opponent
7. apparent
8. diligent
9. defendant
10. equivalent

List 41

1. concession
2. derogatory
3. dilatory
4. flammable
5. inflamed
6. inflaming
7. inflammable
8. inflammation
9. inflammatory
10. nonflammable

List 42

1. addenda
2. agenda
3. arbitrate
4. bilingual
5. diction
6. enunciation
7. gavel
8. mediate
9. nasal
10. pronunciation

B. Principal Parts of Irregular Verbs

The * indicates an intransitive verb. The † indicates an auxiliary verb that does not have all the principal parts; such a verb is called a *defective* verb. Although the present participle is a principal part, it is not included in this list, since all present participles end with *ing*.

Present Tense	Past Tense	Past Participle
arise *	arose	arisen
awake	awoke, awaked	awaked, awoke
be *	was	been
bear	bore	borne
become *	became	become
begin	began	begun
bend	bent	bent
bid (offer, as a price)	bid	bid
bid (command)	bade	bidden
bite	bit	bitten
bind	bound	bound
blow	blew	blown
break	broke	broken
bring	brought	brought
broadcast	broadcast	broadcast
build	built	built
burst	burst	burst
buy	bought	bought
can †	could	*(None)*
catch	caught	caught
choose	chose	chosen
come *	came	come
creep *	crept	crept
deal	dealt	dealt
dig	dug	dug

Note: The verb *dive* is regular.

do	did	done
draw	drew	drawn
dream	dreamed, dreamt	dreamed, dreamt
drink	drank	drunk
drive	drove	driven
eat	ate	eaten
fall *	fell	fallen
feel	felt	felt
fight	fought	fought
find	found	found

Present Tense	Past Tense	Past Participle
flee * (run away)	fled	fled
fly	flew	flown
forecast	forecast	forecast
forget	forgot	forgotten
forgive	forgave	forgiven
forsake	forsook	forsaken
freeze	froze	frozen
get	got	got, gotten
give	gave	given
go *	went	gone
grow	grew	grown
hang (suspend)	hung	hung

Note: The verb *hang*, which means *to take away life,* is regular.

have	had	had
hear	heard	heard
hide	hid	hidden
hit	hit	hit
hold	held	held
keep	kept	kept
kneel *	knelt	knelt
know	knew	known
lay (put)	laid	laid
lead	led	led
leave	left	left
lend	lent	lent
lie * (recline)	lay	lain
let	let	let
light (all meanings)	lighted, lit	lighted, lit
lose	lost	lost
may †	might	(None)
mean	meant	meant
meet	met	met
ought †	(None)	(None)
pay	paid	paid
put	put	put
read	read	read
ride	rode	ridden
ring	rang	rung
rise *	rose	risen
run	ran	run
say	said	said
see	saw	seen

Present Tense	Past Tense	Past Participle
seek	sought	sought
sell	sold	sold
set (to place)	set	set
sew	sewed	sewed, sewn
shake	shook	shaken
shine *	shone	shone

Note: The transitive verb *shine* is regular, as in *I shined my shoes.*

show	showed	shown
shrink	shrank	shrunk
sing	sang	sung
sink	sank	sunk
sit *	sat	sat
slay	slew	slain
sleep *	slept	slept
sow (plant)	sowed	sown, sowed
speak	spoke	spoken
spin	spun	spun
split	split	split
spread	spread	spread
spring	sprang	sprung
steal	stole	stolen
string	strung	strung
strive *	strove	striven
swear	swore	sworn
sweep	swept	swept
swim *	swam	swum
swing	swung	swung
take	took	taken
teach	taught	taught
tear	tore	torn
telecast	telecast	telecast

Note: The verb *televise* is regular.

tell	told	told
think	thought	thought
throw	threw	thrown
tread	trod	trodden
type	typed	typed
wake	waked, woke	waked, woken

Note: The verb *waken* is regular.

wear	wore	worn
weave	wove	woven
weep	wept	wept
win	won	won
wind	wound	wound

Present Tense	Past Tense	Past Participle
withdraw	withdrew	withdrawn
withhold	withheld	withheld
wring	wrung	wrung
write	wrote	written

C. Official Addresses and Salutations

Addresses and salutations are listed so that the most formal comes first. The following rule applies to complimentary closings: In writing to the President or members of the clergy or religious orders, use *Respectfully* or *Respectfully yours.* In all other cases, use *Very truly yours* if the salutation is formal; if the salutation is informal, use *Sincerely* or *Sincerely yours.* Correct ZIP Codes should be used.

1. Federal Government Officials

The President

The President
The White House
Washington, DC

The President of the United States
Washington, DC

Mr. President
Dear Mr. President
Note: The President's spouse is addressed like any other citizen.

The Vice-President

The Vice-President
United States Senate
Washington, DC

The Honorable John M. Doe
Vice-President of the United States
Washington, DC

Dear Sir
Mr. Vice-President
Dear Mr. Vice-President

Speaker of the House

The Speaker of the House of Representatives
Washington, DC

The Honorable John H. Doe
Speaker of the House of Representatives
Washington, DC

Dear Sir
Mr. Speaker
Dear Mr. Speaker
Dear Mr. Doe

Chief Justice of the United States

The Chief Justice of the United States
Washington, DC

Mr. Chief Justice

The Honorable John Doe
United States Supreme Court
Washington, DC

Associate Justice of the Supreme Court

The Honorable John Doe
Associate Justice of the Supreme Court
Washington, DC

Mr. Justice
Dear Justice Doe

Mr. Justice Doe
United States Supreme Court
Washington, DC

Member of the Cabinet

The Honorable John *or* Jane Doe
Secretary of State
Washington, DC

Dear Sir *or* Madam
Dear Mr. *or* Madam Secretary

The Secretary of State
Washington, DC

Senator

The Honorable John *or* Jane Doe
United States Senate
Washington, DC

Dear Sir *or* Madam
Dear Senator Doe

Senator John *or* Jane Doe
United States Senate
Washington, DC

Representative

The Honorable John *or* Jane Doe
House of Representatives
Washington, DC

Dear Sir *or* Madam
Dear Representative Doe
Dear Mr., Mrs., Ms., *or* Miss Doe

Representative John *or* Jane Doe
House of Representatives
Washington, DC

Head of a Government Agency

The Honorable John *or* Jane Doe
Commissioner of Reclamation
Department of the Interior
Washington, DC

Dear Mr. *or* Madam Commissioner
Dear Commissioner Doe
Dear Mr., Mrs., Ms., *or* Miss Doe

Commissioner of Reclamation
Department of the Interior
Washington, DC

2. State and Municipal Government Officials

Governor

His *or* Her Excellency
The Governor of Pennsylvania
Harrisburg, PA

The Honorable John *or* Jane Doe
Governor of Pennsylvania
Harrisburg, PA

Dear Sir *or* Madam
Dear Governor
Dear Governor Doe

State Senator

The Honorable John *or* Jane Doe
The State Senate
Albany, NY

Senator John *or* Jane Doe
The State Senate
Albany, NY

Dear Sir *or* Madam
Dear Senator
Dear Senator Doe

State Representative

The Honorable John *or* Jane Doe
The State Assembly
Albany, NY

Representative John *or* Jane Doe
The State Assembly
Albany, NY

Dear Sir *or* Madam
Dear Representative Doe
Dear Mr., Mrs., Ms.,
or Miss Doe

Mayor

The Honorable John *or* Jane Doe
Mayor of the City of Seattle
City Hall
Seattle, WA

The Mayor of the City of Seattle
City Hall
Seattle, WA

Dear Sir *or* Madam
Dear Mr. *or* Madam Mayor
Dear Mayor Doe

3. Members of the Clergy and Religious Orders

Rabbi (Jewish)

Rabbi John *or* Jane Doe
316 Fifth Avenue
Seattle, WA

Reverend Sir *or* Madam
Dear Sir *or* Madam
Dear Rabbi Doe

Cardinal (Roman Catholic)

His Eminence John Cardinal Doe
Archbishop of New York
451 Madison Avenue
New York, NY

Your Eminence

Archbishop and Bishop (Roman Catholic)

The Most Reverend John Doe
Bishop of Ogdensburg
624 Washington Street
Ogdensburg, NY

Your Excellency

Monsignor (Roman Catholic)

The Right (or Very) Reverend John Doe
Sacred Heart College
Albany, NY

Monsignor
Dear Monsignor Doe

Priest (Roman Catholic)

The Reverend John Doe
24 East Avenue
Cincinnati, OH

Dear Reverend Father
Dear Father *
Dear Father Doe

Brother (Roman Catholic)

Brother John, O.F.M.
St. Francis School
Austin, MN

Dear Brother John
Dear Brother

Mother General or Provincial Superior (Roman Catholic)

The Reverend Mother Mary John
St. Joseph's Motherhouse
Dubuque, IA

Dear Reverend Mother

Mother Superior (Roman Catholic)

Mother Mary John
150 Orange Street
Portland, OR

Dear Mother
Note: In some Orders, Mother is the title for all elder members, even though they are not superiors.

Sister (Roman Catholic or Protestant)

Sister Mary John
St. Mary's Home
Des Moines, IA

Dear Sister

---

* *Father* is also used for Greek-Orthodox and Anglican priests.

Bishop (Protestant)

The Right Reverend John *or* Jane Doe   Dear Bishop
Bishop of New York   Dear Bishop Doe
New York, NY

Member of the Clergy (Protestant)

The Reverend John *or* Jane Doe   Dear Sir *or* Madam
135 East 14th Street
Bangor, ME

4. Educators

President of a University or College

President John *or* Jane Doe   Dear Sir *or* Madam
State Junior College   Dear President Doe
Boise, ID

Dr. John *or* Jane Doe   Dear Dr. Doe
President of State Junior College
Boise, ID

Dean of a College

Dean John *or* Jane Doe   Dear Sir *or* Madam
School of Business   Dear Dean Doe
North Texas State University
Denton, TX

Dr. John *or* Jane Doe   Dear Dr. Doe
Dean of the School of Business
North Texas State University
Denton, TX

Professor at a College or University

Professor John *or* Jane Doe   Dear Sir *or* Madam
Wayne State University   Dear Professor Doe
Detroit, MI

Dr. John *or* Jane Doe   Dear Dr. Doe
Professor of Business Administration
Wayne State University
Detroit, MI

D. Proofreader's Marks

To type final correct copy from rough drafts, you first must understand the meaning of each proofreader's mark. After typing a few rough drafts, you will quickly recognize each symbol when you meet it in the margin or in the text of corrected material. The two marks that follow should be learned first:

$\wedge$ (caret) means to insert something that is indicated in the margin.

/ (virgule) means to take out or make the change indicated in the margin.

PROOFREADER'S MARKS (Classified)°

KINDS OF TYPE			WORD ARRANGEMENT		
In Margin	In Text	Means	In Margin	In Text	Means
caps	≡	capitals	ℱ	$\wedge$	paragraph
lc	/	lower case (small letters)	⊃	⌒	close up
ital	___	italics	ℯ	/ or ℓ	take out
bf	∼∼∼	bold face (heavy)	ℯ̄	⊥	take out and close up
PUNCTUATION			#	$\wedge$	more space
			✓	✓	less space
In Margin	In Text	Means	[	[	move to left
⊙	Use the caret in all cases.	period	]	]	move to right
⌢		comma	*tr*	∼	transpose
⌣		apostrophe or single quote	*stet*	· · · · ·	let stand as it was originally
=/		hyphen	*sp or spell*	◯	spell out
/–/ or $\frac{1}{m}$		dash	*run on*	⌒	not a new paragraph; to follow right after the preceding sentence
(/)		parentheses			
;/		semicolon			
:/ or ⊙		colon			
⌣		double quotes			

---

* Reprinted, by permission, from *130 Basic Typing Jobs, Second Edition,* by Ruth I. Anderson and Leonard J. Porter. Published by Prentice-Hall, Inc.

E. Working on Term Papers and Reports

Typing Specifications

Spacing. Always use double spacing. Triple-space between a title and the first line of copy. Triple-space before each subheading and double-space after each. Leave at least one inch for all margins—sides, top, and bottom. If a manuscript is to be bound at the left, leave a little more room at that side. A top margin of two inches should be left on the first page of each chapter or other major part.

Quotations. Quotations of four or more lines are single-spaced and indented five spaces from both left and right margins. (This is called being *set in.*) No quotation marks are used. The titles of books and magazines are underscored so that the printer will set them in italics. Titles of chapters are enclosed in quotation marks. Titles of unpublished materials are usually enclosed in quotation marks.

Footnotes. Before typing the first footnote at the bottom of a page, type a two-inch underscore. Then double-space, indent five spaces, and type the number of the footnote. Single-space all footnotes but leave a double space between them.

The footnote reference usually includes the author's name, the title of the work from which the quotation is taken, the edition number if there is one, the place of publication, the name of the publisher, the date of publication, the volume number if there is one, and the page number or numbers.

If the reference is the same as the preceding footnote, use <u>Ibid.</u> (meaning *in the same place*) followed by the page number. Do not repeat any part of the original reference.

If the footnote refers to a previously mentioned reference, but not to the one immediately preceding, use the name of the author followed by <u>Op. cit.</u> (meaning *work cited*) and the page number. Do not repeat any part of the original reference.

Examples of Footnotes

One-Author Book	[1] Peter Zender, *Selected Writings* (Albany, NY: River Press, 1974), p. 304.
Two-Author Book	[2] Yancey W. Yellman and Evelyn Moore, *Memories of the Corporate Life* (Seattle, WA: Cascade Publishers, 1975), p. 118.
Three-Author Book	[3] Roy I. Jones, Mary Kort, and E. Guy Davis, *English Niceties,* 2d ed. (New York: Hoyt Press, 1975), pp. 7–10.
Magazine Artitcle	[4] Martin L. Day, "Say It Right," *Language Journal* 19, no. 1 (May 1974): 101.
Newspaper Article	[5] *The New York Times,* 6 November 1974, p. 18.

Unpublished Item   [6] Lucille McDonald, "An Analysis of Transcription Errors Made by Office Workers" (M.A. thesis, University of Chicago, 1975), p. 19.

Note: The word *Unpublished* may precede the degree initials.

Bibliography. The bibliography should include the references that the writer used in preparing the manuscript. The entries are arranged alphabetically. The first line of each reference begins at the left margin; all others are indented five spaces (*hanging indention*). Observe that authors' names are inverted and that the form for certain entries differs from the form used for footnotes.

Example of Bibliography

Day, Martin L. "Say It Right." *Language Journal* 19 (May 1974): 101.

Jones, Roy I.; Kort, Mary; and Davis, E. Guy. *English Niceties*. 2d ed. New York: Hoyt Press, 1975.

McDonald, Lucille. "An Analysis of Transcription Errors Made by Office Workers." Master's thesis, University of Chicago, 1975.

The New York Times, November 6, 1974.

Parker, Henrietta W. *Choosing a Career*. Long Beach: Lambert Publishing Company, 1974.

Southland Industries Inc. *Improve Your Business Letters*. Phoenix: Southland Industries Inc., 1975.

Special Requirements for Publication

Periodicals. The publishers of certain magazines, bulletins, and so on specify that manuscripts to be submitted to them be typed in columnar form, one column to a page. In such cases the column width is given—for example, from 38 to 40 typing strokes.

Footnotes. Sometimes certain publishers specify that a footnote should begin a triple space below the line in which a reference is made. In such cases a ruling is placed above and below the footnote. The ruling, which extends from the left to the right margin, is made by typing an underscore.

End-of-Page Indications. Some publishers request that the word *More* be typed at the bottom of each manuscript page except the last. At the end of the last page, # # # should be typed.

Reading and Handling Proof

Types of Proof Sheets. All manuscript material sent to a printer results in at least one set of proof sheets, called *galleys.* Publications having many pages also require a later set of proof sheets, called *page proof.*

Galleys are long sheets each containing about three printed pages. No page numbers appear on galleys. From galleys the publisher prepares a dummy, which is a "paste-up" made from cut galleys. A dummy shows how the finished book will appear page by page. When a dummy has been made, page numbers are assigned. All preliminary pages, sometimes called *front matter*, such as preface and table of contents, are numbered with small Roman numerals. Beginning with the first page of the text, Arabic numerals are used.

From the dummy the printer makes a set of page proof, which shows how the printed book will appear page by page.

Marking Proof. Galleys and page proof are proofread by the printer, the author, and the publisher. In reading proof, use the standard proofreader's symbols and mark all corrections clearly.

Printers charge for making corrections caused by errors on the part of the author or the publisher. When the printer has made an error, therefore, write *P.E. (printer's error)* in the margin so that a charge will not be made for the correction.

Copyheld Proofreading. When manuscript information is complicated, two persons should read proof simultaneously, one reading aloud from the manuscript while the other checks the proof sheets. This is called *copyheld* proofreading. In reading proof aloud, you can accelerate the work by using the following shortened expressions:

INSTEAD OF	SAY	INSTEAD OF	SAY
apostrophe	apos	parenthesis	paren
capital	cap	period	point
comma	com	question mark	query
decimal point	point	quotation marks	quotes
dollars	doll	semicolon	semi
exclamation point	exclam	underscore	score
paragraph	para	zero	oh

Read down columns, not across. Check the vertical and horizontal alignment of all columns.

In reading a sum, follow this example: For $15,090.53 say, "Dol, one, five, com, oh, nine, oh, point, five, three."

State a designation in its proper order. For example, in reading *South,* say, "Cap, South." In reading an underscored word, read the word, then say, "Score." If an underscored word is to appear in italics, however, as is usually the case, say, "Ital," then read the word.

WORD-USAGE INDEX

This index contains abbreviations, words, phrases, and other expressions often looked up by students, speakers, writers, and workers who wish to know the usage, pronunciation, or spelling of such expressions. The list also shows the pages on which to find punctuation to be used with certain expressions. An asterisk (*) indicates that an expression should never be used. If two or more words are separated by a dash, such words are usually homonyms or similar words that present spelling problems. (A subject index that includes all the topics in the textbook begins on page 428.)

key to abbreviations used in this index

*	expression never to be used	*loc.*	localism
ag.	agreement with	*pl.*	plural
av.	when to avoid	*prin.*	principal parts of verb
cap.	when to capitalize	*pro.*	pronunciation
col.	colloquialism	*pu.*	punctuation used with
div.	division at ends of lines	*sl.*	slang
id.	idiom	*sp.*	spelling

A.D., 166
a.m., 88, 345
a, *omitted* 27, 81; *pro.* 66
a while, awhile, 166
abbreviation of, 74
above, above-mentioned, *av.* 352
accede–exceed, 125
accede to, 74
accept–except, 125
accommodate, *div.* 143
accompanied by, with, 74
according to our records,* 172
acquaintance, *av.* 405
acquit, *prin.* 49
acquit of, 75
ad, *av.* 14
adage, old,* 173
adapt–adopt, 125
adept in, 75
adopt–adapt, 125
advance forward,* 173
adverse–averse, 125
advertisement, *pro.* 354
advice–advise, 125
advise–inform, 125, 172
adviser, *sp.* 289
affect–effect, 120
after having, *av.* 51
aggravate–annoy–exasperate, 125
agree on, to, 75
agree with, 75
ain't,* 13
Albuquerque, *pro.* 205

alike, 100, 166
all of the, *av.* 27, 80
all ready–already, 115
all right, *sp.* 116, 137
all the, 80
all the farther,* 69
all the faster,* 69
all together–altogether, 115
allowed–aloud, 120
allude–refer, 125
allusion–elusion–illusion–delusion, 126
almost–most, 126
alone (*placement of*), 69
aloud–allowed, 120
already–all ready, 115
also, *pu.* 97
altar–alter, 121
although, *pu.* 150
altogether–all together, 115
alumna, alumnae (*pl.*), 23
alumnus, alumni (*pl.*), 23
am to (*col.*), 45
among–between, 76, 126
amount, number, 62
an, 66, 302
and, *ag.* 57; *first word in sentence* 157; *pro.* 302; *pu.* 94, 97, 99, 106
anecdote–antedate–antidote 126
angry at, with, 75
annoy–exasperate–aggravate, 125
annul, *prin.* 49

antedate–antidote–anecdote, 126
anticipate, 131
antidote, 126
anxious–eager, 126
any one, anyone, 116
any other, 71
any place, *av.* 138
any time, at any time, 139
any way, anyway, 139
anyone, any one, 116
anyone's, 32
anyways,* 139
appraise–apprise, 126
apt–liable–likely, 129
aren't I (*col.*), 13, 37
arise, *prin.* 411
artful–artistic, 126
as, *av.* 71, 155; *case after* 33, 81; *pu.* 105; *simile, in,* 172
as a result, *pu.* 96
as . . . as, 100
as for me, 107
as for my part,* 107
as if, were *used after,* 81
as–like, 81
as per,* 172
as regards,* 81
as stated above,* 172
as to, *av.* 76
as well as, *ag.* 33, 59, 166; *pu.* 59, 97
ascent–assent, 121
at, *av. after* where, 79
at about,* 76

SUBJECT INDEX

This index contains all the subjects discussed in the textbook. For references to specific abbreviations, words, and short expressions in regard to their correct usage, consult the Word-Usage Index that begins on page 423.

key to abbreviations used in this index

ag.	agreement	env.	envelope
av.	avoiding	exp.	expressing, expression
beg.	beginning	ital.	italicizing
cap.	capitalizing	pro.	pronunciation

Business-promotion item, 280
Business reply card and envelope, 200, 201, 284
Business report, 325–336; language of, 330–331; outlining, 326–327, 333
Business speech, *see* Speaking; *also,* "Business Speech" at end of each Section of book
Business Week, 348
Buyer: facts about, 277; volume, 242
Buying: for employer, 356–357; listening in, 383; *see also* Credit
Bylaws, *see* Constitution and bylaws

c, adding syllable after, 84
C's of credit, 250–251, 290
Cablegram, 342
Capacity (credit), 251
Capital (credit), 251
Capitalization, 19–21, 87, 110; after a colon, 104; in complimentary closing, 21, 184; in outlining, 327–328
Carbon copy, 196, 353; blind, 190–191; notation, 190
Carbon paper, 196
Card, *see* Business-reply card; Postcard
Caret, 419
Carnegie, Dale, 218
Case and use of nouns and pronouns, 32–34
Cash, 245, 250
ce, adding syllable after, 16
cede, ceed, words ending with, 64
Centering, 191, 193; paragraph, 286
Cents, exp., 87, 90
Century, exp., 166
Certified mail, 245
ch, pro., 117
Chairperson, duties of, 402
Changing Times, 219, 348
Character (credit), 251
Characteristics, *see* Qualities
Charge account, *see* Credit
Churchill, Sir Winston, 78
ciency, cient, words ending with, 330
Circle graph, 335
Circumlocution, 171, 353
City names: comma with, 95; pro., 205, 222, 239; spelling, 205, 212, 222, 231
Civil service tests, words in, 141, 146, 274
Claim, *see* Adjustment
Classified advertising, 306
Clause, 148, 149; adjective, 149, 150; adverbial, 149, 150; comma after, 95, 99; dangling, 153; dependent, 149; independent, 149; nonrestric-

Continued
tive, 96, 99; noun, 149–150; relator, 31; restrictive, 31, 96, 99
Clergy, addressing, 416–418
Cliché, 173
Climactic paragraph, 165
Climactic sentence, 161
Clipped words, 14
Closed punctuation, 191
Closing sentence in letter, 52, 220; adjustment, 267, 269, 271; length, 164; sales, 281
Coherence, 159, 160
Cold application, 306
Collection letter, 290–291; libelous statement in, 357; series, 291–296
Collective noun, 19; ag., 58
Colloquialism, 13, 145
Colon, 103–104, 114, 191
Color: adjective of, 66; stationery, on, 195, 196
Columns, proofreading, 422
Comfort, appeal to, 278
Comma, 93–100, 114, 149, 150, 151, 181, 191; after verb form coming first in sentence, 95, 152; inside quotation marks, 114; to set off, 94–95
Comma fault, 87
Commercial credit, 251
Common gender, 26
Common noun, 18
Communication, *see* Business communications
Company official, signature of, 186
Company tests, words in, 156, 321, 361, 376
Company title: cap., 20; exp., 24, 88, 95, 186; placement in letter, 185–186
Comparison: adjective, 65; adverb, 68
Complaint, *see* Adjustment
Complement, infinitive, 32–33
Completeness, 10, 240
Complex sentence, 149
Complimentary closing, 21, 98, 184, 191, 193, 328; omitted, 193
Composition, 149–174
Compound adjective, 134
Compound appositive, 106
Compound-complex sentence, 105, 149
Compound noun, 23, 136
Compound number, 134
Compound predicate, 149; av. comma in, 94
Compound pronoun, *see* Reflexive pronoun
Compound sentence, 94, 104, 105, 149
Compound subject, 32, 149; ag., 57
Compound verb, 136
Compound words, 133–137, 345

Compromise adjustment, 270–271
Conciseness, 10–12, 162–163
Concrete noun, 18
Condensing material, 363
Conditional verb, 39
Condolence letter, 224
Conduct, ethical, 358
Conference, listening at, 380
Confidential matter, 253, 358, 364; av. on card, 358; blind carbon copy, 190–191
Confirmation of reservation, 226
Conflicting testimony, 377
Congratulatory letter, 227
Conjunction, 33, 79–80
Conjunctive adverb, 79–80, 97, 105, 149
Connector, *see* Conjunction *and* Preposition
Consonant: doubling final, 48–49; emphasizing, 64, 374; enunciating, 64, 73, 373; pro. of words with silent, 142, 168, 231, 376
Constitution and bylaws, use of *shall* in, 45
Consumer: credit, 251; protection, 383; rights, 260
Contents page, 328, 333
Contract, 356–357
Contraction, 37, 228
Contrast in writing, 161, 281
Contrasting expressions, 98
Conversation, 5, 92–93, 377
Conversational tone, *see* Tone
Convincing: buyer, 279, 283, 383; opponent, 382; reader, 279, 283
Cooperation, 384, 404
Coordinating conjunction, 79, 105, 149
Copy: of letter, 196, 310; paper for, 184; *see also* Carbon copy
Copyheld proofreading, 422
Copyright, 359
Corethought, 164
Corporation, 325
Correcting errors, 13, 157, 246, 287, 305
Correctness, 12, 240, 246
Correlative conjunction, 79; parallel construction with, 79, 160
Correspondent, 177, 214; sales letter, 276
Cost of communications: business letter, 177; manuscript errors, 422; telegram, 344–345
Countersuggestibility, 283, 382
Counting words in telegram, 344–345
Course, school, cap., 20
Courteous request, *see* Polite command
Courtesy, 8–9, 215–216
Credit, 250–252

429

Continued

proper, 18; uses, 32–34; verbal, 19

Noun clause, 149, 150

Noun marker, 64

Numbered paragraph, 192; in Simplified Letter, 193

Numbers: building, 91; comma in, 93, 98; exp., 26, 90, 91, 134; hyphen in, 134; proofreading, 422; telegrams, in, 344; two, 91

Numerals, *see* Numbers *and* Roman numerals

----

o, pluralizing words ending with, 22

Object: direct, 32–33; indirect, 32–33; of preposition, 32–33, 34; of preposition understood, 32–33; of transitive verb, 32–33

Objection, making, 382

Objective case of noun and pronoun, 32–33

Objective complement, *see* Infinitive, objective case after

Objective style of writing, 330

Oblique, *see* Virgule

Observing, 377; listening related to, 367; reliability of, 377

of, possessive after, 25

Offer, 282

Official, *see* Company official *and* Government official

Official letter style, 195, 256

Old business (meeting), 402

Omission marks, *see* Ellipses

Omitted word, comma to show, 97; *see also* Ellipses

One-syllable words, av. dividing, 143

One-word compound words, 135

One-word dangling element, 153

Onionskin paper, 196

oo, pro., 29

Open punctuation, 191

Opening sentence in letter: adjustment, 261, 262, 267, 269, 271; application, 306–307; av., types to, 52, 282; credit, 254, 256; examples of, 281–282; length of, 164; reply, 220; sales, 281–282

Opinion, not fact, 388

Optical Character Reader, 199

Oral communication, *see* Listening *and* Speaking

Oral proofreading, 422

Order: acknowledging, 242; following up, 242; incomplete, 243; modifying, 245; payment for, 242; refusing, 244; rush, 242; unclear, 243

Order blank, 240

Order letter, 240–248

Outlining: business report, 327–328, 333; talks and speeches, 388–389

over, words beg. with, 7

Overnight cablegram, 344

Overnight telegram, 342

Overseas message, 344

ow, pro., 374

Ownership: appeal to, 278; of written matter, 359

Page: number, 98; proof, 287, 421–422; two of letter, 183; two of manuscript, 351

Painting, title of, 26

Paper, *see* Letterhead *and* Stationery

Paragraph, 163–165, 193; indented, 183, 191, 192, 193; numbered, 192, 193; pointers for, 164–165; quotation marks with, 110

Parallel construction, 80, 159–160

Parentheses, 111–112; amount of money, 112; enumeration, 103; order with other marks, 114

Parenthetical expressions, 80, 96, 97, 99; punctuating, 80

Parliamentary procedure, 380, 400, 401–404

Partial statements, dash used before, 105

Participial phrase, 51, 152; absolute, 99; av., 52; comma with, 95; dangling, 153; introductory, 95; nonrestrictive, 95

Participle: dangling, 153; past, 51, 95; perfect, 51; present, 51

Parts of speech, names of, 18

Passive voice of verb, 42; av., 42; preferred, 330; report, in, 330

Past emphatic of verb, 45

Past participle, comma after, 95

Past perfect progressive of verb, 44–45

Past perfect tense, 44

Past progressive of verb, 44–45

Past tense, 44; in report, 334

Pause during talk: av., 394; dramatic, 395

Payment, *see* Collection letter; Remittance; Terms of payment

Perfect participle, 154

Perfect tenses, 44–45

Period, 86–88, 89, 114, 115; inside quotation marks, 114

Periodic report, 353

Periodic sentence, 161

Periodical: business, 348; manuscript for, 351, 421; title, ital., 26, 110–111; writing for, 350

Permission to quote, obtaining, 111

Person of pronoun, 32, 33

Personal business letter, 224–230; congratulations, 227; env. for, 199; invitation, 224–225; reservation, 226

Personal data sheet, *see* Data sheet

Personal name, *see* Surname

"Personal" on envelope, 198

Personal pronoun, 31

Personal touch in letter, 213–214

Personality, 214, 384; apparent in application, 305, 314; loyalty, 364; speaking, 369; telephoning, 401; *see also* Success

Personnel: dept., 306; manager, 305, 314; workers, tips from, 314–315

Persuasion, 232, 382–385; adjustment, 261–263; advertising, 279, 282–283, 383; argument, 382–383; collection, 294–295; sales letter, 279, 282–283; social, 384; spoken, 382–383

Phelps, William Lyon, 374

Phonation, 369–373

Phrase, 148, 151–152; absolute, 99; adjective, 74, 151; adverbial, 74, 151; dangling, 153; gerund, 152; infinitive, 152; participial, 152; prepositional, 74, 95, 151; verb, 40, 151

Physical description, 276–277, 279

Physician, addressing, 182

Pica type, 183

Pictogram, 335

Pie graph, 335

Pitch of voice, 369, 370, 371

Placement: adjective, 66; adverb, 69; business letter, 179; *see also* Subordination

Plagiarism, 111

Platitude, 173

Play, 3, 382; ital. title of, 26, 110–111

Pleonasm, 173

Plural, forming, 22–23

Poetry: ends of lines, indicating, 113; figure of speech, 172–173

Point: of contact, 306, 313–314; of order, 403; of view, maintaining, 159

Poise, 392, 396

Polite command, 43, 86, 89

Politeness, *see* Courtesy

Poor-pay debtor, 291

Positive degree: adjective, 65; adverb, 68

Positive language, 169–170, 219; in credit letter, 255

Positive tone, 169–170, 219

Possessive case of noun and pronoun, 24–25, 32, 99–100; after *of*, 25; before gerund, 52

post, words beg. with, 135

Post Office, *see* United States Postal Service

Postage stamps as remittance, 245

Postal card, *see* Postcard

Postal permit, 200

436

PUNCTUATION
Quick Reference Table

PERIOD
(See pp. 86-88.)

●

1. At the end of a statement.
   I am going to the store.
2. At the end of a command or request.
   Please make six copies.
3. To show decimal subdivisions.
   348.904

4. To separate dollars and cents and to precede cents expressed in figures.
   $350.25 and *$.09*
5. After each initial in a person's name.
   K. R. Davies
6. After many abbreviations.
   a.m. but *TWA*

QUESTION MARK
(See pp. 88-89.)

?

1. At the end of a question. *How much profit did we make?*
2. After individual items in a series, each of which may be made into a complete question.
   Did you take typing? shorthand?
3. After a statement of questionable truth. *The check was bad(?).*

EXCLAMATION POINT
(See p. 89.)

!

After an exclamatory sentence, single word, or whole expression that shows strong feeling or surprise. *It's an earthquake!*

COMMA
(See pp. 93-98.)

,

1. To separate words, phrases, and clauses in a series of three or more.
   I need pens, pencils, and ink.
2. To separate the two clauses of a compound sentence. *The rains may come, but I will go anyway.*
3. To set off the name of a person directly addressed. *John, come here.*
4. To set off an expression in apposition. *Maria, the manager, will go.*
5. To separate the parts of dates.
   July 10, 1982
6. To set off a state name after a city name. *Akron, Ohio*
7. To set off explanatory terms in names. *Sam Lee, Jr., is here.*
8. To set off an introductory expression containing a verb form. *Exhausted, he could not travel any farther.*
9. To set off a nonrestrictive participial phrase. *Ms. Brown, having read the report, left the room.*
10. To set off nonrestrictive clauses. *Jane, who had scored 98, placed first.*
11. To set off parenthetical expressions. *These people, as you know, are not satisfied.*
12. To set off *Yes, No,* and mild interjections at the beginning of a sentence. *No, I don't agree.*

13. To set off *also, too,* and *either* to show emphasis. *Your uncle, too, will participate.*
14. To set off internal phrases beginning with such expressions as *as well as, including, together with, such as. Your report, including the index, is typed.*
15. To indicate an omitted word. *She played the piano; he, the violin.*
16. To separate two or more adjectives modifying the same noun. *She is a helpful, kind, friendly person.*
17. To separate a conjunctive adverb preceded by a semicolon. *He wanted to remain; however, I told him to leave.*
18. To separate two contrasting expressions. *Use a sharp pencil, not a dull one.*
19. To separate a short question from a preceding statement. *He has already visited you, hasn't he?*
20. In many numbers containing four or more digits. *5,000*
21. To prevent misreading. *At six, fifteen guests appeared.*
22. After the salutation and complimentary closing of friendly letters. *Dear Sally,* and *Sincerely yours,*

COLON
(See pp. 103-104.)

●
●

1. After a statement introducing information that is to follow. *The following items will be on sale:*
2. Before a long or formal appositive. *I have three tables: one for writing, another for painting, and a third for eating.*

3. Before a statement or question that explains a preceding statement. *Over the door hung the sign: Don't scare the dog.*

Continued

| *Continued* | 4. Before a long quotation. *She cleared her throat and began:*
 5. To separate the figures for hours and minutes. *9:15 a.m.* | 6. After the salutation in some business letters. *Gentlemen:*
 7. To separate identification initials at the end of a business letter. *JKL:ert* |

| SEMICOLON
 (See pp. 104-105.)
  | 1. Between the two parts of a compound sentence containing no conjunction. *You type the letter; I shall type the bill.*
 2. Before a conjunctive adverb. *She was late; consequently, she missed the speech.*
 3. Before expressions such as *as, for example, that is,* and *namely* when a complete statement follows them. *That is an automated machine; that is, it possesses a "memory."* | 4. Before the coordinating conjunction in a compound or compound-complex sentence when one or more of the clauses are punctuated with commas. *I saw the plane land; but in a moment, I saw it take off.*
 5. After each complete unit in a series in which a comma or commas are used within each unit of the series. *He visited Canton, Ohio; Albany, New York; and Bangor, Maine.* |

| DASH
 (See pp. 105-106.) | 1. To indicate a sudden break or change in thought. *He might have succeeded —but why think of that now?*
 2. After a series coming first in a sentence when the series is later explained. *Red, yellow, and blue— these are primary colors.*
 3. Before an appositive. *Here is a good book—one you will enjoy.*
 4. Before and after a compound appositive. *Three subjects—typing, English, and speech—are required.* | 5. Before and after an appositive expression containing one or more commas. *This machine—Model 212, which is reduced in price—is very popular.*
 6. Before such expressions as *for example, that is,* and *namely* when a complete statement does not follow. *Discuss an electronic typewriter—for example, the Lanier.*
 7. To separate an author's name from a quotation from his or her writing. *"A small leak can sink a great ship." —Franklin* |

| QUOTATION
 MARKS
 (See pp. 110-111.)
 66 99 | 1. To enclose a direct quotation. *"Let's go," she said.*
 2. To enclose titles of magazine articles, short stories, and chapters. *Her article, "Coastal Inns," was in last month's issue.* | 3. To enclose unusual terms used in a special way. *The computer actually seems to "think."*
 4. To indicate a slang expression. *I think he is a "bonehead."* |

| PARENTHESES
 (See pp. 111-112.)
 ( ) | 1. To set off explanatory, directional, or supplementary expressions. *This device (see the enclosed brochure) is new.*
 2. To set off an expression that interrupts a main thought. *He will be there (I am sure of it) by eight o'clock.* | 3. To enclose letters or numerals that enumerate items run into the text. *There are three sections: (a) orchestra, (b) mezzanine, and (c) balcony.*
 4. To enclose an amount in numerals following the same amount in words. *We shall pay her Two Hundred Dollars ($200.00).* |

| ELLIPSES
 (See p. 112.)
 • • • | To indicate omissions in quoted material. *"Plough deep . . . and you will have corn to sell and keep."—Franklin* |

| BRACKETS
 (See pp. 112-113.)
 [ ] | 1. To enclose material that is not part of an author's text. *The law of that state [Louisiana] is based on the Napoleonic Code.*
 2. To enclose the word *sic. Speak respectively [sic] of your elders.*
 3. On library index cards, to enclose information not given on a book's title page. *A tale of two cities [by] Charles Dickens.* |

| VIRGULE
 (See p. 113.)
  | 1. To separate parts of dates on business forms. *1/8/83*
 2. To separate parts of split years. *1982/1983*
 3. To separate parts of some abbreviations. *W/B* (waybill)
 4. To indicate ends of lines of poetry that are run in. *The world stands out on either side,/No wider than the heart is wide.* |